THE
MAINE
READER

Maine State Seal, 1837

THE
MAINE
READER

edited by

CHARLES *and*
SAMUELLA SHAIN

A Richard Todd Book

HOUGHTON MIFFLIN COMPANY

BOSTON 1991

For information about permission to reproduce selections from
this book, write to Permissions, Houghton Mifflin Company,
2 Park Street, Boston, Massachusetts 02108.

Library of Congress Cataloging-in-Publication Data

The Maine reader / edited by Charles and Samuella Shain.
p.   cm.
ISBN 0-395-57651-2. — ISBN 0-395-57650-4 (pbk.)
1. American literature — Maine.   2. Maine — Literary collections.
3. Maine — History.   I. Shain, Charles E.   II. Shain, Samuella.
PS548.M2M329   1991   91-16070
810.8'032741 — dc20   CIP

Printed in the United States of America

MP 10 9 8 7 6 5 4 3 2 1

Credits begin on page 519.

Acknowledgments

The selections included in *A Maine Reader* represent our best efforts to meet several self-imposed criteria. The entries reprinted here were chosen with the primary goal of illuminating the experience of Maine as seen and felt and recorded by a wide variety of writers who have either visited or lived in this state.

Second, we have selected pieces that meet our standards for literary merit and for lively content. In addition, we have in most cases included material which is fresh, not previously anthologized, and which is accessible to the reader who chooses to pursue the subject or the author at greater length.

We were, of course, limited by space requirements — it would have been impossible to include in one volume everything fine that has been written about Maine — and by a sense of proportion, the need for balance in the collection as a whole.

We have learned much about Maine — its history, its resources, its beauty, its problems — in the process of reading material for this book, and inevitably the contents of the collection reflect personal choices: our interests and enthusiasms, our own feelings about the State of Maine.

A number of people have generously contributed their knowledge and time to this project. For advice and interest beyond the call of friendship we must thank Garth Hite, Scott Elledge, and John Cole as well as our patient family and friends. David Etnier's photography has enhanced the quality of this book. Paul Hazelton made the Abbie Huston Evans material available to us, Abbie Sewall let us see the photographs taken by her great-great-grandmother, Emma Sewall, and Allene and Joel White shared their photographs of E. B. White. For professional assistance, we could not have done without the patience and expertise of John Ladley, the reference librarian at the Hawthorne-Longfellow Library at Bowdoin College, the cheerful assistance of Laura McCourt at the circulation desk, and the blessings of Arthur Monke, librarian. Similarly, Brian Damien and Stephen Podgajny at the Curtis Memorial Library in Brunswick have been most helpful.

We would also like to thank Christopher Crosman, director, and Edith Murphy, curator, at the Farnsworth Art Museum in Rockland, Margaret Wickes of the Colby College Art Museum, the staff of the Pejepscot Historical Society in Brunswick, the late Dorothy Healy, curator of the Maine Women Writers Collection at Westbrook College, Elizabeth Miller, Elizabeth Maule and the late Roger Howell of the Maine Historical Society, Earle Shettleworth of the Maine Historic Preservation Commission, and Nathan Lipfert of the Maine Maritime Museum as well as the staffs of the Library of Congress's Prints and Photos Division, the Maine State Archives, the McArthur Library in Biddeford, the Baker Library at Dartmouth College, the Portland Room at the Portland Public Library, the American Antiquarian Society in Worcester, Massachusetts, and the Peabody Museum in Salem, Massachusetts. We are also grateful to four college Special Collections librarians: Dianne Gutscher and Susan Ravdin at Bowdoin, Dr. Edward Ives at the Northeast Folklore Archives at the University of Maine, and P. A. Lenk at Colby College.

Contents

MAINE ARTISTS

VACATIONLAND

TWENTIETH-CENTURY MAINE, THE MIDDLE YEARS

Introduction

The common ground for all the pieces in this collection is the State of Maine and the recorded human experience of being here for the past four hundred years. Our purpose is simply to satisfy a reader's urge to know Maine better. As we look back over these reports of how Maine was and how it is now, we are impressed by the richness of Maine as a subject for writers. Why has Maine bred or captured so many writers? Kenneth Roberts said fifty years ago that the urge to write was more powerful and persistent in Maine than in any other part of the nation: "Almost everyone I meet in southern Maine is quick to say that he would write a book himself if he had time." Roberts cited for earlier witness a collection of Maine poetry published in 1888: 400 poets, 850 pages. To show that Maine writers did not just publish in bulk or in vain, we cite another impressive statistic. In 1899 *The London Illustrated News* surveyed British book publishing records for the century that was passing and found that the two best sellers in Britain for the last hundred years had been books with strong Maine connections — for poetry, the poems of Henry Wadsworth Longfellow; for fiction, *Uncle Tom's Cabin*. And let the record also show that the longest series in American publishing history is still held by Gilbert Patten of Corinna: his 208 volumes of the epic of Frank Merriwell and his brother, Dick. Today, Stephen King of Bangor is Maine's modern contender for popular literary success. And in southern Maine a new colony of writers is publishing books in numbers that would not surprise Kenneth Roberts.

The story of Maine before recent times was told not so often in poetry and fiction as in personal accounts. The first texts in our collection cover the familiar ground of the exploration and settlement of the coast. Giovanni da Verrazzano's letter to his patron, the king of France, is not as well known as some other pieces of Maine's earliest history. Maine is only a small part of that new world, the east coast of the United States, which Verrazzano was the first European to see and report on. His description of his reception at what was to be Maine will remind his modern readers of scenes from Shakespeare's *Tempest,* with Maine's natives playing the role of Caliban. No explanation has yet been offered as to why the first visitors should have been greeted with such rudeness, but modern wits may be amused.

Captain John Smith is the master commentator on earliest Maine. In his gritty Elizabethan prose he sets down firm opinions on why the future of America lies along this coast — if only the fools in charge in London and Plymouth would listen to him. Christopher Levett's plans for a colony on Casco Bay were thwarted by the absence of backing at home, but Levett's account foreshadows the long, bloody struggle between settlers and natives that becomes Maine's history for its first hundred and fifty years. Levett, a Yorkshire Puritan, acknowledges with an appeal to God's word that the Maine Indians held the natural rights of inheritance to the 6,000 acres in Maine he had just purchased in England for £110 — for weren't we all, as he puts it, "sonnes of Noah"? His admission was only a momentary mental reservation, however: "They are bloudy minded and full of Tracherie. . . . Therefore I would wish no man to trust them, whatever they say or doe, but always to keep a strickt hand over them, and yet to use them kindly, and deal uprightly with them, so shall they [his colonists] please God and keep their reputation among them and be free from danger." During the long years of Maine's slow beginnings, the few personal accounts that remain to us are cries for help from the forlorn settlers and the story of a settler captured by the Indians.

The real beginnings, the first peopling of Maine, began in earnest after the Revolution — as the opinionated president of Yale, Timothy Dwight, explains. There were fewer than 100,000 people in Maine in 1790. When it entered the Union in 1820, the population had risen to 300,000, and thereafter it grew by 80,000 people every ten years until 1850, the climactic year in Maine's first settling. The rate of growth began to fall and had changed to loss by 1870, when 116,000 people born in Maine had moved away.

But those decades before the Civil War were glorious boom times for Maine. Towns were settled, cities grew, new farmlands were cleared, the great pine forests were lumbered, railroads crossed Maine's long distances, and Maine's shipyards built hundreds of beautiful and profitable vessels that sailed the world. This dynamic economy raised people's expectations, and the popular cultures, especially politics and religion, flourished. Newspapers brought the life of the nation to almost every household, bookstores multiplied, theaters and lyceums sold out their houses for Shakespeare and P. T. Barnum, philosophers and quacks. For this new reading public Longfellow wrote his lovely lyrics and our country's first myth-making national poems. A Maine newspaperman founded another branch of our national literature that is still going strong. Seba Smith, of Buckfield, went to Portland from Bowdoin College, founded the state's first daily newspaper in 1828, and began to write for it the "Jack Downing" letters, political satires about Maine. Smith became America's first national political columnist when he sent Jack Downing to Washington to help Andrew Jackson cope with the job of being the country's first populist president. At one point Downing assisted at a public reception where Jackson was obliged to shake hands with an army of admirers:

> I took hold and shook for him once in a while to help him along, but at last he got so tired he had to lay down on a soft bench, covered with a cloth, and shake as well as he could; and when he couldn't shake, he'd nod to 'em as they came along. And at last he got so beat out, he couldn't only wrinkle his forehead and wink. Then I kind of stood behind him, and reached my arm under his, and shook for him for about a half an hour as tight as I could spring.

From Seba Smith to John Gould, Maine has entertained America by producing more than its share of humorists.

The personal accounts written before the Civil War are from John Springer's classic descriptions of Maine's lumber camps and river drives, the memoirs of a Bath ship captain, the Maine journalism of Harriet Beecher Stowe, the account of what sounds like one of the first where-do-we-head-for-next cruises down east, and the diary of a remarkable fifteen-year-old citizen of Bangor. It is in these reports that we first find ourselves in the presence of people like ourselves and begin to sense our own narrow space in Maine's history. During these years three members of Boston's great literary generation, Nathaniel Hawthorne, Henry David Thoreau, and James Russell Lowell, visited Maine, each for his own purpose. Thoreau seeks in the forest wilderness a revelation, that nature and man are part of one creation and that Maine's Indians live closer to that origin than the citizenry of his home town, Concord, Massachusetts. Hawthorne the novelist is putting into his workbook sketches of life in Augusta and Thomaston. This may have been a writer's exercise in self-discipline. One time Hawthorne said that he wished his novels had as much realism as Anthony Trollope's. Lowell's trip to Maine is a lark. He is the first literary tourist writing for the first *New Yorker*.

The story of Maine's part in the Civil War is represented by the battlefield experiences of a major general and a volunteer enlisted man. It is hard for us to believe that any other northern state could find better portrayers of that proud and tragic history.

Ten years after the war that same major general, Joshua Chamberlain, was asked by the state legislature to give an address on the subject "Maine: Her Place in History" at the United States Centennial Exhibition in Philadelphia. His eloquent oration comes down to us in more than a hundred pages; in it Chamberlain finds greater pleasure in making claims for Maine's glorious past — "The brunt of the [French and Indian] wars fell upon Maine, the vast frontier and flying-buttress of New England" — than in predicting for Maine an equally glorious future. For a man of his generation, all the signs about him in 1876 looked bad:

> Our people are not wretchedly poor, but they are moving away. Our lands are not usurped by the few. They are abandoned by the many. But part of the result is the same. If we have not the misery, we have the desolation. It is a great evil and a hurt to have these farms stripped, and these resources which might by earnestness and skill be made to warm and brighten many a home, left as they have been in the cold clutch of nature.

This farmer's son from Brewer decried what he had seen happen during his lifetime: "The fact of the matter is, that in our way of doing business Maine has become an old and exhausted State, before her true wealth has begun to be developed. We have been stripping off what was easiest to take, without mercy and without foresight." Chamberlain used statistical tables to show that not one of the state's primary industries had proved capable of sustaining the promise of its beginnings. The annual product value of the great lumber industry was, in 1876, less than that of the recently developed cotton mills. Shipbuilding was producing fewer dollars than the new shoe factories. The total value of farm products was less than half that of manufacturing products. Emigration, he discovered, was not only "to the new lands of the West, where nature is more prodigal, 8,000 to Wisconsin, 7,000 to Illinois, 6,000 to Minnesota, — but 43,000 to Massachusetts, 11,000 to New Hampshire." Maine, he concluded, was being left behind as a bypassed rural hinterland, trying to become a part of industrial America but even there being outstripped by Massachusetts and New Hampshire, which offered better jobs in new factory towns that Maine could not find the capital to build. Chamberlain's long-term hope lay in a balance between factories and farms for Maine. The state has "driven off the sons from the homesteads to the Babylon of the marts and cities. We must call our youth home again." Light, diversified industry "widely scattered in local centers" was what he hoped for. But Maine must continue to "stand on its land. If it slights or abuses that, its strength is gone."

Chamberlain had prophesied quite accurately the poor future of Maine's economy for the rest of the nineteenth century and well into the twentieth. Maine's population in 1850 was 583,169. In 1900 it was 649,466, a growth of only 11 percent. In 1900 the population was still two-thirds rural. Only by 1950 did it become narrowly urban, by 51 percent. In 1920 Maine still had 50,000 farms.

Industrial expansion came slowly. Only two new industrial resources developed after the Civil War. One was the paper industry, based on the invention in 1860 of the process of making paper from low-grade wood pulp. The other was the growth of the textile industry and those large cotton and woolen mills in the cities at the fall lines of the Saco, Androscoggin, and Kennebec rivers. These mills brought one of the few cultural changes that affected Maine from the outside: the immigration of thousands of French farm families from Quebec and New Brunswick, who soon became the dominant population of the mill cities. This plain-living, closely knit group has only recently given Maine a literary report in English of its separate world. Many in the first generation of Franco-Americans, with a cultural loyalty to their birthplace of which General Chamberlain would have approved, seemed to be only temporary visitors to Maine: they still sent their dead back to their farm villages in Quebec for burial.

Another set of strangers arrived in the 1850s with an impact that grows bigger every year: Maine's first summer visitors to the seacoast and mountains. Though their first generation came well before 1876, General Chamberlain had not foreseen the power they would exert on Maine's future. He cordially welcomed these visitors, "the brave, the noble, the cultured; — those who love nature's simplicity, and are partakers of her sacraments. . . . Homes of wealth arise, and scorn not humbler ones, but give a helping hand to honest and homely toil." These phrases refer presumably to the wealthy first wave of summer people. But Maine's market supply of the commodity that American consumers wanted most proved to be abundant beyond even its forest products and fish from the sea. "Vacationland," as the license plate puts it, has now become one of Maine's leading industries. It has been estimated that by the year 2000, a hundred million people will live within a day's drive of Maine, so the use of land to satisfy recreational and leisure needs will continue to be one of the state's chief concerns.

The coming of the vacationers to Maine has also provided writers from within Maine and elsewhere with much new material — some humorous, some not. Maine's slow entry into modern times has long been part of its attraction. It offered visitors a look at people living at a moderate rate of change between generations and therefore preserving a sense of order and hierarchy that was not always apparent in the cities and suburbs of the rest of the country. Old-time Maine is fortunately still visible in the rural and coastal landscapes and villages. (However, its exploitation along the highways for tourist dollars seems to know no limit.) The beauty and authentic identity of this earlier Maine lies in paintings, photographs, and books. It is represented here by excerpts from the works of three native daughters, Sarah Orne Jewett, Mary Ellen Chase, and Lura Beam. Edwin Arlington Robinson found in Maine's villages appropriate scenes for his tragic view of human life. In a town like Gardiner he must surely have found the model for Eben Flood, but in no poem does he place his characters in a setting called Gardiner, or even Maine. For Robinson, Eben makes the case that stoicism, fortitude, and wry Yankee humor will keep life going anywhere in the universe. And these same human strategies, both as subject matter and in the stance of the poets themselves, keep appearing in the Maine poets who have come after Robinson: Edna St. Vincent Millay, Abbie Huston Evans, and in the next generation, Louis O. Coxe and Philip Booth.

This attachment of Maine's writers to their quiet, earlier Maine has had to suffer, like the rest of Maine's population, the recent arrival of a moment of dramatic growth and change, a moment that we can date almost precisely to the end of the Vietnam War. From 1970 to 1978 Maine's population rose by 10 percent, a rate of growth not seen since before the Civil War. In 1972 a pamphlet appeared that was a counterpart, a hundred years later, of Chamberlain's address in Philadelphia. It was titled *A Maine Manifest* (called by some "A Maine Manifesto") and written by Richard Barringer, a spokesman for the Allagash Group, a research-minded, privately supported body of Maine citizens based in Bath. Its message was that Maine's "traditional way of life" faced threatening changes from outside the state. A new wave of industrialism and population had begun to move up from Boston. After the seventies, the pamphlet predicted, Maine's economy will be seen as inexorably tied to the national economy. As the nation goes, so goes Maine. Unless the state prepares quickly for the pollution, the poverty, and the pressures that this growth will inevitably bring, Maine will lose what it most values, its "distinctive and proud way of life" and its natural environment. The challenge Barringer and the Allagash Group offered was this: growth is inevitable; can Maine's government manage the kind of growth that will be acceptable to its people?

The state, consciously or unconsciously, is still in the process of digesting *A Maine Manifest.* Some of Barringer's proposals for a correction of course are coming into place: the state is now buying more land for public purposes, and a center for Maine Studies has been established at the state university. Others have not been accepted by the political parties. Barringer's greatest influence has probably been the persuasiveness of his conclusion, remarkably like Chamberlain's, that Maine must "stand on its land." The demand for Maine's land, for industrial and recreational purposes, is "the most significant economic occurrence in Maine in over a hundred years." And Maine can now be seen as fortunate to have been left out of the industrial mainstream. The result is fresh air, clean water, and unspoiled land. The rest of America has learned to value what Maine has had the good luck to retain.

It is too early to make the case that Maine's latest generation of writers has also become responsive to the state's newly described cultural and economic dilemmas. But some urge has moved several Maine writers of fiction — perhaps the remaining radicalism of the sixties protesting the rampant consumerism of the eighties? — to set their stories among the "forgotten" people of Maine. Sarah Orne Jewett, in her generation, wrote about rural poverty in one of its aspects: the pathos of the genteel poor. Carolyn Chute, in her radical social novel, *The Beans of Egypt, Maine,* writes in outrage about a complex working-class poverty that will not easily respond to ordinary human compassion and remedy. Perhaps her novel became a national best seller because, for all their uniquely Maine manners and

morals, the Beans represent people living beyond Egypt, Maine —
the hill people of Appalachia or even the homeless in our cities,
victims of the failure of our national social morality. There have
always been poverty and human desolation in Maine.

If Maine's poverty is of its own kind, so are many of its happier
qualities as a place to live and a people to live with. Included in this
collection are pieces that seem to show that the pleasures of Maine
have moved many good writers to set them down as incomparable:
Robert P. Tristram Coffin's pride and pleasure in his heritage, Rockwell Kent's enthusiasm for Monhegan Island, John Cole's delight in a
short sail around Middle Bay, Louis Coxe's love poem to the midwin-
ter sea around Griffiths Head. Maine may or may not become increasingly like the rest of America. Its writers write as if they don't
believe it will. That same conviction — that living in Maine is a
special experience that imposes certain literary obligations on its
citizens — would explain all those Mainers who told Kenneth Roberts that they had a book in them but no time to write it.

EXPLORATION
AND DISCOVERY

Three Early Explorers

GIOVANNI DA VERRAZZANO
1485–1528

The first European to see and describe the Atlantic coast from the Carolinas up to Maine was the Florentine explorer Giovanni da Verrazzano. The year was 1524, his single ship was the *Dauphine*, and his mission, assigned to him by the French king Francis I, was to find the northwest passage that would lead to the riches of Cathay, Marco Polo's name for China. Five years after Columbus's first discoveries in the New World, another Italian named John Caboto (later Cabot), living in Bristol, England, had sailed under the charge of an English king and planted the English flag in what is now Newfoundland and Nova Scotia. Now Verrazzano, a third Italian and an experienced navigator of the Mediterranean and the "ocean seas," wanted to "perfect our cosmography" by searching the shores of the present United States between the Spanish claims to the south and the English to the north. His financial backing came not from the French throne but from a colony of Florentine merchants and bankers who had established the silk industry in Lyons and wanted to shorten the long land and sea route that raw silk had to travel to their factories from the East. Verrazzano failed his backers. Although he thought he had caught sight of the "eastern sea" while he was sailing along the outer banks of North Carolina, he never found the northwest passage. Instead, he and his brother, Gerolamo, brought back to Europe the first crude coastal map that filled the blank between the Carolinas and Nova Scotia.

One of their place names is now part of New England. Verrazzano's first landfall on his six-month voyage was made near Cape Fear in North Carolina. As he sailed north, he was struck by the beauty of

"Monhegan"

the landscapes and the beatific life of the people who greeted him. He called the land Arcadia after that mythical earthly paradise, originally placed by the ancients in central Greece, which was ruled by the great god Pan and was afterward celebrated by generations of Greek and Roman pastoral poets. But Verrazzano's name was to suffer an overseas change. As later cartographers copied his map, they squeezed Arcadia farther to the northeast. By the seventeenth century, "Arcadia" had become "Acadie" and was identified with northeast Maine, New Brunswick, and Nova Scotia.

Because Verrazzano had only one ship, he was wary of venturing too far inland in his search for a passage through the continent. He missed both Chesapeake and Delaware bays, but he did discover New York Harbor by taking a small boat through the Narrows, where the graceful bridge named for him now stands. The crew of the *Dauphine* rested ashore for fifteen days near the present Newport, Rhode Island, then rounded Cape Cod and sailed for the Maine coast. By this time Verrazzano was running short of both time and food, and he attempted only one more landing, near Portland. In Maine, Verrazzano's Arcadian illusions began to fall away. The islands of

Casco Bay were beautiful, and so were the offshore islands like Monhegan. But the natives . . .

> The people were quite different from the others, for while the previous ones had been courteous in manner, these were full of crudity and vices, and were so barbarous that we could never make any communication with them, however many signs we made to them. They were clothed in skins of bear, lynx, sea-wolf, and other animals. As far as we could judge from several visits to their houses, we think they live on game, fish and several fruits which are a species of root which the earth produces itself. They have no pulse [peas and beans] and we saw no sign of cultivation, nor would the land be suitable for producing any fruit or grain on account of its sterility. If we wanted to trade with them for some of their things, they would come to the seashore on some rocks where the breakers were most violent, while we remained in the little boat, and they sent what they wanted to give on a rope, continually shouting to us not to approach the land; they gave us the barter quickly, and would take in exchange only knives, hooks for fishing and sharp metal. We found no courtesy in them, and when we had nothing more to exchange and left them, the men made all signs of scorn and shame that any brute creature would make such as showing their buttocks and laughing.

On Verrazzano's map, Maine is called Terra Onde di Mala Gente, Land of the Bad People.

CAPTAIN JOHN SMITH
1589–1631

Just ninety years later, Captain John Smith sailed into Maine waters, ready to take a more promising view of the land and its people. His book *A Description of New England* begins: "In the moneth of April, 1614, with two Ships from London, of a few Marchants, I chanced to arrive in New-England, a parte of Ameryca, at the Ile of Monahiggan, in 43½ Northerly latitude: our Plot there was to take Whales and make tryall of a Myne of Gold and Copper." Smith and his crew chased whales but never caught one, and they never lifted a shovel — the mines, he admits, were just a come-on for the Marchants — but the ships went home with enough dried fish, cod liver oil and furs, "1100 Bever, 1000 Martins, and neer as many Otters" to make a profitable voyage.

But Captain Smith's visions went beyond the profits of two English ships. His intentions, in which he succeeded, were to map the coast of New England and then write a prospectus for the first permanent English settlement on this side of the ocean, in Maine, which would last forever because it would be done right. Early American history has so firmly attached Smith to Jamestown, Virginia, and the comely Indian princess Pocahontas that his commitment to the earliest days of New England can easily be overlooked. We forget that he gave New England its name and also named its first town, Plimouth. The last title he attained was Admirall of New England. Smith had gone to Virginia as one of the six leaders of the Jamestown expedition in 1606. Eventually, he had to take charge of a feckless group of colonizers who were about to go under. He established martial law and pronounced that "he that will not worke shall not eat." In the end, his rigorous leadership saved the Virginia colony.

Smith was convinced that his new colony in Maine could be self-sustaining, and in his *Description,* he tells us why.

Captain John Smith

From Pennobscot to Sagadahock the Coast is all Mountainous and Iles of huge rocks, but over growen with all sorts of excellent good woodes for building houses, boats, barks or shippes; with an incredible abundance of most sorts of fish, much fowle, and sundry sorts of good fruits for man's use.

And surely by reason of those sandy cliffes and cliffes of rock both which we saw so planted with Gardens and Corne fields, and so well inhabited with goodly, strong and well proportioned people, besides the greatness of the Timber growing on them the greatness of the fish and the moderate temper of the ayr (for of twentie five, not any was sicke, but two that were many yeares diseased before they went, notwithstanding our bad lodging and accidental diet) who can but approove this a most excellent place both for health and fertility? And of all the foure parts of the world that I have yet seen not inhabited, could I have but means to transport a Colonie, I would rather live here than any where: and if it did not maintain it selfe, were wee but once indifferently well fitted, let us starve.

In 1615 Smith found financial backers and thirty prospective colonists; his two ships sailed from Plymouth in June. Had his attempt been luckier — a storm dismasted one ship, and when Smith set out again he was captured by French pirates — he would have founded the first town in New England five years before the Pilgrims landed at Plymouth Rock. He never got to America again, although he tried to join the Pilgrims and later the Boston colony. Perhaps his last satisfaction was knowing that both groups had benefited from his *Description* and his maps.

CHRISTOPHER LEVETT
1586–1631

When *A Description of New England* was published in London in
1616, it was only a question of time before another enterprising spirit
would arrive who would realize Captain John Smith's plans for
founding a permanent settlement on the Maine coast. Nine years
later he appeared, a Yorkshireman of the Puritan persuasion named
Christopher Levett. He was a captain in the navy and, perhaps as an
extension of his naval world, he was also woodward of the royal
forests in Somersetshire, which provided timber for the navy's ships.
(Levett had written the standard guide for measuring timber.) Better
placed socially and therefore politically than John Smith, Levett was
also richer. In May 1623 he bought 6,000 acres on the coast of Maine
for £110 from a royal monopoly, Sir Ferdinando Gorges's Council of
New England. In the fall of that year he arrived on the Isle of Shoals
in a party of several ships — it is hard to tell how many — with a
group of men ready to become colonists after Levett had explored
and chosen a site in his new domain.

The place he chose is now Portland; the natives called it Quack.
The grant from the council said that Levett could make "a choice of,
enter into, seize and take six thousand acres lying together in one
place . . . together with all waters, rivers, marshes, lakes, woods,
quarries, etc, and to have and enjoy all hunting, hawking, fishing,
fowling, waifs, strays, wrecks, felons' goods, Court Leet and Court
Baron" and other terms appropriate to the conveyance of an English
manor, not excluding all ecclesiastical appointments. But if Levett
was tempted to dream of tenant farmers, market squares, and country lanes lined with hedgerows, he soon discovered instead a world
full of Indians, all Sagamores, all with wives and dogs and remarkably quick and subtle minds. On first acquaintance they called him

"cozen Levitt," and to his astonishment their favorite oath was "a pox on his hounds." These phrases were presumably learned from the sailors who came every year in the fishing fleet.

Levett published *A Voyage into New England* four years after his return to England in 1628. He had left behind a "fortified house," on House Island in Casco Bay, and ten men to look after his new possessions. We know little more about the progress of his new settlement, "to be called Yorke," or about any further activities that brought him back to Casco Bay, except that he was present in Salem in 1630 to greet Governor John Winthrop and his large party of colonists when they arrived to found the Massachusetts Bay Colony.

Levett sold one quarter of his grant to two other "adventurers," as financial risk-takers were called in those times, but, like John Smith, he never lost his enthusiasm for settling the coast of Maine. "I must confesse," he wrote, "I have studied no other Art a long time but the Mysteries of New England's trade, and I hope at last I have attained to the understanding of the secrets of it." In 1825 he wrote to Sir John Coke, the secretary of state for Charles I, that instead of attacking the Spanish fleet, England could best provide for its future by fortifying all the fishing places of New England, for the "Scolls of fish there is better than the Myndes [mines] elsewhere." He persisted with a petition to the king that said he could, with four ships and three hundred men and food for twelve months, accomplish these things: take prizes — that is, capture Spanish ships along the way; secure the coast and protect the forty or fifty ships of the English fleet that fished there every spring; provide enough fish and oil to pay all the expense of fishing gear and men for the first year; draw planters to that place, Casco Bay, where the fleet could store their smaller boats over the winter, the future site of Portland being "most principall on the Country and in the mydst of all the fishinge."

His persistence won this much favor from King Charles and his Privy Council: a command was issued to all archbishops, bishops, archdeacons, and deans to have read in all the churches of the realm a royal proclamation to take up a collection for supporting "our beloved subject Capteyne Levett" and his enterprise on Casco Bay. He was to be made governor of New England, to bring the true faith to the ignorant savages and to strengthen the kingdom. Levett, like Smith, believed that, in Levett's words, "within the space of 20 years, there shall be neither beggar, nor any poore people that shall need maytenance from the parishes" in England. They would all migrate to Yorke, Maine, and other such settlements where life would be self-sustaining. King Charles was not popular, however; the collection was one of many of his ineffectual attempts to raise funds. Levett never got the money or the ships. The last we know of him is that he died on a voyage home in 1630 after greeting the founder of a much more successful enterprise in Massachusetts.

A Voyage into New England

The first place I set my foote upon in New England was the Isles of Shoulds [Shoals], being Ilands in the sea, about two Leagues [six miles] from the Mayne. Upon these Ilands, I neither could see one good timber trcc, nor so much ground as to make a garden. The place is found to be a good fishing place for 6 Shippes, but more cannot be there for want of convenient stage-room [space for wharfs], as this yeare's experience hath proved. The Harbour is but indifferent good. Upon these Ilands are no Savages at all.

The next place I came unto was Pannaway [Portsmouth area], where one M. Tomson hath made a Plantation [settlement]; there I stayed about one Moneth in which time I sent for my men from the East: who came over in divers Shipps. At this place I met with the Governour [Robert Gorges], who came thither in a Barke which he had from one M. Weston about 20 dayes before I arrived in the Land. The Governour then told me that I was joyned with him in Commission as a Counseller, which being read I found it was so. And he then, in the presence of three more of the Counsell, administered unto me an oath.

After the meeting of my men, I went a coasting in two boats with all my company. In the time I stayed with M. Tomson, I surveyed as much as possible I could, the wether being unseasonable, and very much snow. In those parts I saw much good Timber. But the ground it seemed to me not to be good, being very rockey and full of trees and brushwood. There is great store of fowle of diverse sorte, whereof I fed very plentifully.

About two English miles further to the East, I found a great River and a good harbour called Pascattaway [Portsmouth Harbor]. But for the ground I can say nothing, but by the relation of the Sagamore or King of that place, who told me there was much good ground up in the river about seven or eight leagues.

About two leagues further to the East is another great river called Aquamenticus. There I think a good plantation may be settled, for there is a good harbour for ships, good ground, and much already cleared, fit for planting of corne [grain] and other fruits, having heretofore ben planted by the Salvages who are all dead. There is good timber, and likely to be good fishing, but as yet there has beene no tryall made that I can heare of.

About 6 leagues further to the East is a harbour called Cape Porpas, the which is indifferent good for 6 shippes, and it is generally thought to be an excellent place for fish, but as yet there hath been no tryall made; but there may be a good plantation seated, for there is good Timber and good ground, but will require some labour and charge [expense].

About foure leagues further East, there is another harbour called Sawco (Betweene this place and Cape Porpas I lost one of my men) before we could recover the harbour a great fog or mist tooke us that we could not see a hundred yards from us. I perceiving the fog to come upon the Sea, called for a Compasse and set the Cape land, by which wee knew how to steare our course, which was no sooner done but wee lost sight of land, and my other boate, and the wind blew fresh against us, so that we were enforced to strike saile and betake us to our Oares which wee used with all the wit and strength we had; but by no meanes could we recover the shore that night, being imbayed and compassed round with breaches [surf], which roared in a most fearfull manner on every side of us; we took counsell in this extremity one of another what to doe to save our lives; at length we resolved that to put to sea againe in the night was no fit course, the storme being great, and the winde blowing right of the shore, and to runne our boate upon the shore amongst the breaches, (which roared in a most fearfull manner) and cast her away and indanger ourselves we were loath to do, seeing no land nor knowing where we were. At length I caused our Killick (which was all the Anker we had) to be cast forth and one continually to hold his hand upon the roode or cable, by which we knew whether our ancker held or no, which being done we commended ourselves to God by prayer, & put on a resolution to be as comfortable as we could, and so fell to our victuals. Thus we spent that night, and the next morning, with much adoe we got into Sawco, where I found my other boate.

There I stayed five nights, the wind being contrary, and the weather very unseasonable, having much raine and snow, and continuall foggse. We built us our Wigwam, or house, in one houres space; it had no frame, but was without form or fashion, onely a few poles set up together, and covered with our boates sailes which kept forth but a little winde, and less raigne and snow. Our greatest comfort we had, next unto that which was spirituall, was this: we had foule enough for killing, wood enough for felling, and good fresh water enough for drinking. But our beds was the wet ground, and our bedding our wet cloaths. Wee had plenty of Craine, Goose, Duckes and Mallards, with other fowle, both boyled and rosted, but our spits and racks were many times in danger of burning before the meate was ready (being but wooden ones.)

After I had stayed there three daies, and no likelyhood of a good winde to carrie us further, I tooke with me six of my men and our Armes, and walked along the shore, to discover [explore] as much by land as I could; after I had travelled about two English miles I met with a river [the Saco] which stayed me that I could goe no further by land that day, but returned to our place of habitation where we rested that night (having our lodging amended), for the day being dry I caused all my company to accompany mee to a marsh ground, where wee gathered every man his burthen of long dry grasse, which being spread in our Wigwam or House, I praised God I rested as contentedly as ever I did in all my life. And then came into my minde an old merry saying, which I have heard of a beggar boy, who said if ever he should attaine to be a King, he would have a breast of mutton with a pudding in it, and lodge every night up to the eares in drye straw; and thus I made my company as merry as I could, with this and some other conceits, making this use of all, that it was much better than wee deserved at Gods hands, if he should deale with us according to our sinnes.

The next morning I caused four of my men to rowe my lesser boate to this river, who with much adoe got in myself, and 3 more going by land; but by reason of the extremitie of the wether we were enforced to stay there that night and were constrained to sleepe upon the river bank, being the best place wee could find, the snowe being very deepe.

The next morning we were enforced to rise betime, for the tyde came up so high that it washed away our fire, and would have served us too if we had not kept watch: So wee went over the river in our boate, where I caused some to stay with her, myself being desirous to discover further by land, I tooke with me foure men and walked along the shore about six English miles further to the East, where I found another river [the Scarborough?] which staied mee. So we returned back to Sawco, where the rest of my company and the other boate lay. That night I was exceeding sicke, by reason of the wet and the cold and much toyling of my body: but thanks be to God I was indifferent well the next morning, and the wind being faire we put to sea, and that day came to Quack.

But before I speak of this place I must say something of Sawco, and the two rivers which I discovered in that bay, which I think never Englishman saw before. Sawco is about one league to the North-east of a cape land. And about one English mile from the maine lieth six Ilands which make an indifferent good harbour. And in the maine there is a Cove or gutt, which is about a cables length in bredth, and two cables length long; there two good Ships may ride, being well mored a head and starne; and within the Coue there is a great Marsh, where at a high water a hundreth sayle of Ships may floate, and be free from all winds, but at low water must ly a ground, but being soft oase [ooze] they can take no hurt. In this place there is a world of fowle, much good timber, and a great quantetie of cleare ground and good, if it be not a little too sandy. There hath beene more fish taken within two leagues of this place this yeare than in any other in the land.

The river next to Sawco eastwards [the Saco], which I discovered by land, and after brought my boat into, is the strangest river that ever my eyes beheld. It flowes at least ten foot of water upright, and yet the ebbe runs so strong that the tyde does not stem it. At three quarters floude my men were scarce able with foure Oares to row ahead. And more then that, at full Sea I dipped my hand in the water, quite without the mouth of the river, in the very main Ocean, and it was as fresh as though it had been taken from the head of a Spring.

This River, as I am told by the Salvages, commeth from a great mountaine called the Christall hill [Mount Washington], being as they say 100 miles in the Country, yet it is to be seen at the sea side, and there is no ship that arives in New England, either to the West so farre as Cape Cod, or to the East so farre as Monhiggen, but they see this Mountaine the first land, if the weather be cleere.

The next river Eastward which I discovered by land, is about six miles from the other. . . . And now in its place I come to Quack, which I have named Yorke. . . . It lieth about two leagues to the East of Cape Elizabeth. It is a Bay or Sound betwixt the Maine and certain Ilands which lyeth in the sea about one English mile and a halfe. There are foure Ilands [Cushing, Peaks, Diamond, and House] which make one good harbour; there is very good fishing, much fowle and the mayne as good ground as any can desire. There is found one good River [Fore River] which the Savages say there is much Salmon and other good fish. In this bay there has been taken this year 4 Sturgions, by fishermen who drive only for Herrings, so that it is likely there may be a good store taken if there were men fit for that purpose. This River I made bold to call by my own name Levetts river, being the first one that discovered it. . . . In the same Bay I found another River [the Presumpscot], up which I went about three miles, and found a great fall, of water much bigger that the fall at London bridge, at low water; further a boate cannot goe, but above the fall the River runs smoothe againe.

Just at this fall of water the Sagamore or King of that place hath a house, where I was one day when there were two Sagamors more, their wives and children, in all about 50 and we were but 7. They bid me welcome and gave me such victualls as they had, and I gave them Tobacco and Aqua vitae.

After I had spent a little time with them I departed & gave them a small shot, and they gave me another. And the great Sagamore of the East country, whom the rest doe acknowledge to be chiefe amongst them, hee gave unto me a Bevers skin, which I thankfully received, and so in great love we parted. On both sides this river there is goodly ground.

From this harbour to Sagadahock, which is about 8 or 9 leagues, is all broken Ilands in the sea, which makes many excellent good Harbours, where a thousand saile of Shipps may ride in safety; the sound going up within the Ilands to the Cape of Sagadahock. In the way betwixt Yorke and Sagadahock lyeth Cascoe [Casco Bay]. . . . And I am perswaded that from Cape Elizabeth to Sagadahock, which is above 30 leagues to follow the Maine, is all exceeding commodious for Plantations: and that there maybe 20 good Townes well seated, to take the benefit both of the sea, and fresh Rivers. . . .

The next place I came to was Capemanwagan [Boothbay and Southport], a place where nine ships fished this yeare. But I like it not for a plantation, . . . there I staid foure nights, in which time there came many Savages with their wives and children, and some of good accompt amongst them as Menawormet a Sagamore, Cogawesco, the Sagamore of Casco and Quack, now called Yorke, Somerset, a Sagamore, one that hath been found very faithfull to the English, and hath saved the lives of many of our Nation, some from starving, others from killing.

They intended to have been gone presently, but hearing of my being there, they desired to see me, which I understood by one of the Masters of the Ships, who likewise told me that they had some store of Beaver coates and skinnes, and was going to Pemaquid to truck [trade] with one Mr. Witheridge, a Master of a ship of Barnstable and desired me to use meanes [so] that [the savages] should not carry them out of the harbour. . . . I sent for the Sagamores, who came, and after some compliments they told me I must be their cozen, and that Captaine Gorges was so (which you may imagine I was not a little proud of, to be adopted cozen to so many great Kings at one instant, but did willingly accept of it) and so passing away a little time very plesantly, they desired to be gone, whereupon I told them that I understood they had some coates and Beavers skins which I desired to truck for but they were unwilling, and I seemed careless of it (as men must do if they desire anything of them.) But at last Somerset swore that there should be none carryed out of the harbour, but his cozen Levett should have all, and then they began to offer me some by way of gift, but I would take none but one paire of Sleeves from Cogawesco, but told them it was not the fashion of English Captaines alwaies to be taking, but sometimes to take and give, and continually to truck was very good. But in fine, we had all but one coate and two skinnes, which they reserved to pay an old debt with. . . .

When they were ready to depart they asked me where I meant to settle my plantation. I told them I had seen many places to the west, and intended to go farther to the east before I could resolve; they sayed there was no good place, and I had heard, that Pemaquid and Cape Mananwagan and Monhiggon were granted to others & the best time for fishing was then at hand, which made me more willing to retire, and the rather because Cogawesco, the Sagamore of Casco and Quacke, told me that if I would sit downe at either of those two places I should be very welcome, and that he and his wife would goe along with me in my boate to see them; which curtesy I had no reason to refuse, because I had set up my resolution before to settle my plantation at Quacke, which I named Yorke, and was glad of this oppertunity, that I had obtained the consent of them who as I conceive hath a naturall right of inheritance, as they are the sonnes of Noah, and therefore do think it fit to carry things very fairely without compulsion (if it be possible) for avoyding of treacherie.

The next day the winde came fair, and I sayled to Quacke or Yorke, with the King, Queene, and Prince, bowe and arrowes, dogge and kettell in my boate, his noble attendance rowing by us in their Cannow. When we came to Yorke the Masters of the Shippes came to bid me welcome, and asked what Savages those were, I told them, and I thanked them, they used them kindly, & gave them meate, drink and tobacco. The woman or reputed Queene, asked if those men were my friends, and I told her they were; and she drank to them, and told them, they were welcome to her Countrey, and so should all my friends be at any time; she dranke also to her husband, and bid him welcome to her countrey too, for you must understand that her father was the Sagamore of this place, and left it to her at his death having no more children.

And thus after many dangers, much labour and great charge, I have obtained a place of habitation in New England, where I have built a house, and fortified it in a reasonable good fashion, strong enough against such enemies as are those Savage people. . . .

And a little before my departure there came these Sagamores to see mee, Sadamoyt, the great Sagamore of the East Countrey, Manawormet, Opparunwit, Skedraguscett, Cogawesco, Somersett, Conway and others. They asked me why I would be gone out of their Country; I was glad to tell them my wife would not come thither except I would fetch her; they bid a pox on her hounds, (a phrase they have learned and doe use when they doe curse) and wished me to beat her. I told them no, for then our God would bee angrie. Then they runne out upon her in evil tearms, and wished me to let her alone and take another. I told them our God would be more angrie for that. Again they bid me beate her, beate her, repeating it often, and very angerly, but I answered no, that was not the English fashion, and besides, she was a good wife and I had children by her and I loved her well, so I satisfied them. Then they told me that I and my wife and children, with all my friends, should be hartily welcome into that Countrey at any time, yea a hundredth thousand times, yea Mouchicke, Mouchicke, which is a word of waight.

And Someresett tould me that his Sonne (who was borne, whilst I was in the Countrey, and whom he would needs have to Name) and mine should be Brothers and that there should be muchicke legamatch, (that is friendship) betwixt them, untill Tanto carried them to his wigwam (that is untill that they died. . . .)

I have had much conference with the Savages about our only true God, and have done my best to bring them to know and acknowledge him, but I feare me all the labour that way will be lost, and no good will be done except it be among the younger sort. I find they have two

Gods, one they hate; and the other they love; the god they love, they call Squanto, and to him they ascribe all their good fortunes. The god they hate they call Tanto, and to him they ascribe all their evill fortunes, as thus, when any is killed, hurt or sicke, or when it is evill wether, then they say Tanto is hoggry, that is angry. When any dyes, they say Tanto carries him to his wigwam, that is his house, and they never see him more. I have asked where Squanto dwells, they say they cannot tell but up on high, and will poynt upwards. And for Tanto, they say farre west, but they know not where. I have asked them if at any time they have seene Squanto or Tanto; they say no, there is none sees them but their Pawwawes, nor they neither but when they dream. Their Pawwawes are their Phisitians and Surgions, and as I verely beleeve they are all Witches, for they foretell of ill wether, and many strange things, every Sagamore has one of them that belongs to his company, and they are altogether directed by them. . . .

I find them generally to be marvellous quicke of apprehension and full of subletie; they will quickly find any man's disposition, and flatter & humour him strangely, if they hope to get anything of him. And yet will they count him a foole if he doe not shew a dislike of it and will say to one another that such a man is Mechecome. They are slow of speech, and if they heare a man speake much they will laugh at him, and say he is a Mechecum, that is a foole. . . . They are very bloudy minded and full of Tracherie amongst themselves, one will kill another for their wives, and he that hath the most wives is the bravest fellow. Therefore I would wish no man to trust them, whatever they say or doe; but always to keep a strickt hand over them, and yet to use them kindly, and deal uprightly with them; so shall they [his colonists] please God and keep their reputation among them and be free from danger. . . .

And to say something of the Countrey: I will not doe therein as some have done, to my knowledge speak more then is true: I will not tell you that you may smell the corne fields before you see the Land; neither must you think that corne doth growe naturally (or on trees), nor will the Deare come when they are called, or stand still and looke on a man, untill he shute him, not knowing a man from a beast, nor the fishe leap into the kettle, nor on the drie Land, nor are they so plentiful that you may dipp them up in baskets, nor take Codd in netts to make [pay for] a voyage which is no truer than that fowles will present themselves to you with spitts through them.

But certainly there is fowle, Deare and Fish enough for the taking if men be diligent; there be also Vines, Plume trees, Chery trees,

Strawberries, Gooseberries and Raspe, Walnutts, chestnut and small nuts, of each great plenty; there is also great store of parsley and divers other wholesome Earbes, both for profit and pleasure, with great store of Saxifrage, Cersa-perilla and Anni-seeds.

And for the ground their is large & goodly Marsh to make meddow, higher land for pasture and corne. There be these severall sorts of earth, which I have seen, as Clay, Sand, Gravill, yea and as blacke fatt earth as ever I saw in England all my life. . . . Now let any husbandman tell me whither there be any feare of having any kind of Corne, having these severall kinds of earth with these helps, the Climat being full as good if not bettere than England.

I dare be bold to say also, there may be Shippes as conveniently built there as in any place of the world where I have been and better cheape. As for Plancke, crooked Timber and all other sorts what so ever can be desired for such purpose the world can not afford better. Masts and Yeards of all sises; there be also trees growing whereof Pitch and Tar is made. . . .

Thus I have related unto you what I have seene and do know may be had in those parts of New England where I have been. . . . Thus have I done with my commendations of the Countrie. I shall now speak the worst I know by it. About the middle of May you shall have little Flies called Musketoes, which are like gnats; they continue I am told until the last of July. These are very troublesome for the time, for they sting exceedingly night and day. But I found by experience that boots or thicke stockings would save the legges, gloves the hands, and tiffeney [muslin] or some such things which will not hinder the sight will save the face, and at night any smoke will secure a man. The reason of the aboundance of these creatures, I take to be the woods which hinders the aire, for I have observed allwaies when the wind did blow but little, we were not much troubled with them. And I verily think that if there were a good number of people planted together, and that the woods were cut downe, the earth were tilled, and the rubbish which lieth on the ground wherein they breed were burnt, and that there were many chimneyes smoaking, such small creatures would doe but little hurt.

Another evill or inconvenience I see there: the snow of winter did lie very long upon the ground. But I understand that all parts of Chrisendome were troubled with a cold winter as well as wee. Yet would I aske any man what hurt snow doeth? The husbandman will say the Corne is better for it. And I hope Catell may be as well fed in the house there as in England, Scotland and other Countries, and he is but an ill husbandman that cannot find employments for his servants within doors for that time. As for Wives and Children, if they be wise they will keep themselves close by a good fire, and for men they will have no occasion to ride to Faires or markets, Sysses or Sessions [law courts]; only Hawkes and Hounds will not then be useful. . . . And by all reason that countrey should be hotter than England, being many degrees farther from the North Pole. And thus according to my poor understanding I have given you the best information I can of the people and Country, commodities and discommodities.

SETTLING MAINE
AND THE
REVOLUTION

Frontier Maine

In a two-volume history of Maine published in 1832, William D. Williamson began with this statement: "Maine is a corner pillar of the American Republic." It was a strong and loyal metaphor, but he was unable to back it up with persuasive institutional evidence, such as cities, commerce, and stable populations. Rather, he had to admit that, until the previous forty or fifty years, "it has been the destiny of successive generations to struggle with wars and difficulties, reiterated and uncommon, and to wade through sufferings, deep and undescribable." Williamson's history is largely, in fact, a detailed account of 150 years of warfare along one of the bloodiest borders in our early history. Instead of the bright future promised for its coastal towns and cities by such early enthusiasts as John Smith and Christopher Levett, Maine saw only thirty-nine townships — many of them only garrison posts — settled in the seventeenth century. In the first half of the eighteenth century only twenty-one more were established. Finally, however, when the French and Indian depredations at last came under the control of increased English firepower, 125 new settlements were begun within twenty-five years. Modern Maine did not begin until about 1750, later than we sometimes think.

Maine's earliest plantations, as they were called, often had to be resettled, some of them three or four times. The Sagadahoc region — the mainland and islands at the mouth of the Kennebec River — was more celebrated than any other part of the coast except York and Falmouth (Portland). It was colonized in 1607, visited by John Smith in 1614, and settled in 1624. The Plymouth colony had a trading house on the Kennebec, and in the first fifty years of settlement, sixty families had come to Sagadahoc.

Then, in 1676 and again in 1688, the whole region was destroyed by Indian attacks. It lay desolate until 1721, when enough families moved back to form a town on Arrowsic Island called Georgetown. This returning population encouraged the proprietors of nearby Pejepscot (Brunswick) to bring in new families with this enticement: "100 acres of good land, and the removal of them and their effects, free of expense to them if they would become settlers . . . promising them also contributions towards supporting a minister of the gospel." So great was the encouragement, says Williamson, that "several towns as Brunswick, Topsham, Georgetown and Cushenoc (Augusta) began to be settled; a great many fine buildings with saw mills were erected; husbandry began to thrive, and great stocks of cattle were raised." The resettlement also brought entrepreneurs like Dr. Noyes of Boston, whose patrons were London fishmongers; he began a sturgeon fishery that flourished for a few years. As Williamson describes it, "In some seasons, twenty vessels were taken into employment, and many thousand kegs were filled, which were esteemed equal to any that ever came from Hamburgh or Norway. Also vast quantities of pine boards, planks, hogsheads, pipe and barrel staves and all sorts of timber, were annually transported from the river, as well to foreign places as to Boston." But the "peace" that allowed Sagadahoc to flourish was soon over. In 1722 "a large body of 400 to 500 St. Francois and Mickmac Indians fell upon Arrowsick Sept. 10, early in the morning, determined to reduce the garrison and destroy the village. . . . The burning of the greater part of Georgetown which had been settled only six years, filled the inhabitants with every discouragement," says the historian. Some of Brunswick was also destroyed.

The perpetual warfare was caused, of course, by the continuing encroachment of the settlers on land that the Indians believed was theirs. Their French allies also wanted to prevent the spread of English settlements, and often the chief agents of this policy were the Jesuit missionaries. The attack on Georgetown had been instigated by Father Rale's Indian mission in Norridgewock. For thirty years the priest had been the Indians' champion against the English and even accompanied them on their raids. In 1724, in retaliation for the attack on Georgetown, the military authorities in Boston mounted a force of two hundred soldiers and a few Mohawks against Rale and took the mission by surprise, killing the priest and forty Indians. Rale's scalp was taken to Boston as a trophy of war; his Abenaki French dictionary was placed in the Harvard library, where it can be consulted today.

In the letter that follows, two leading citizens of Blackpoint beg John Leverett, the governor of Massachusetts, to send military relief to the settlers in the Scarborough region. The sudden Indian uprising against the English from Kittery to as far east as Pemaquid had begun in the Plymouth colony in Massachusetts but had spread rapidly into Maine, whose small population was not prepared for its fierceness. King Philip's War, as it is called for the Narragansett Indian leader, lasted three years. The colonists' losses were estimated at 600 settlers, 1,200 houses, and 8,000 cattle. One of the terms of the peace treaty, dictated by the Indians, was that each settler family was to pay the Indians for its land, year by year, one peck of corn and, "for Major Philips of Saco, who was a great proprietor, a bushel of corn."

A Letter to the Governor of Massachusetts

For the much Honoured
    John Leveret Esquire
    Gov'r. of the Massachusetts
       Boston

Per Mr. Munjoy   Q.D.C.

          Blackpoint the 15th September 1676

Honoured Sir

After all humble submission, these are to acquaint the present posture of affairs with us, upon the 12th current, the enemy after they had fired all the houses on this side Casco bay, moved towards us within a mile of our garrison & broke up a house in the night & within two miles fired two houses, slew one man, took another prisoner, & wounded a third who escaped with another who hid himself in the bushes & lay within two or three rods of them, heard all their discourse who confidently affirmeth them to be 70 or 80 whom he saw, but doubted not of a greater number on the other side of the river where he lay, & also that there be two or three Frenchmen with them, one who leads being a brave [a gaudy dresser] with blue, black & yellow ribbons on his knees, a hat buckled with a silver buckle, brave belt etc, & heard him enquire in French by an Indian Interpreter who spoke very good English of the Captives, whether it were difficult to take Richmond Island and Blackpoint, of the number of our men, & that their design is to carry all before them as they have done along the Eastern shore, which soe alarmed Richmond Island as that it is deserted, & hath put our inhabitants into such a fright that those that have stood by it all this war being in expectation of relief from our army & none appearing, the body of men are removing, though we hope so many will abide, as with the assistance of the 12 county soldiers will leave us in a capacity to defend ourselves until help come in, for we daily look for having dispatched a post to our Major the same day this accident befell. We fear the Army unless they bring bread with them or soon to be sent them will not be in a capacity to manage a pursuit of them, though the enemy, if they keep their station being so nigh the sea & a Capeland giveth opportunity of descent.

Sir we are at the present the frontier garrison, which if not maintained fear little security this side Piscataquay river knowing the travaile of the spirit for the safety of the whole, beg that a little remnant may be preserved, our poor people having lost two crops sink under discouragement, . . . we shall without your Christian compassion be inevitably exposed to the ruine & rage of the heathen, for want of ability to beare our owne charge, but we hope to find favor from those who have taken us under protection as well as government, thus humbling craving pardon for our boldness, we rest.

Your Honours humble servants
Henry Jocelyn
Josh: Scottow.

JOHN GILES
1677–1755

King William's War, the second Indian war fought in Maine, lasted nine years and was deadlier than the first. At its end, only four towns had not been overrun: Kittery, York, Wells, and Appledore, on the Isles of Shoals. This time the French were actively involved. Their commander, Count Frontenac, directed attacks on the Maine coast from Quebec, and in a new military usage, Indians who took captives were encouraged to sell them to the French, who used them as servants as well as holding them for ransom or prisoner exchanges.

John Giles of Pemaquid was one such captive. Taken when he was twelve, he was held for six years by an Indian master, who then sold him to a minor French official; he, in turn, used Giles as a servant for three years before freeing him to return to Boston. There he found two remaining sisters and a brother. Giles soon became an interpreter for the army; his command of all the Indian languages was especially useful. He saw action as a captain and as the builder and commander of Fort George in Brunswick. He also commanded the fort on the St. George River before he retired to Roxbury, Massachusetts, and wrote this narrative.

Memoirs of Odd Adventures, Strange Deliverances, etc.

CHAPTER ONE

CONTAINING THE OCCURENCES OF THE FIRST YEAR

On the second day of August, 1689, in the morning, my honored father, Thomas Gyles, Esq., went with some laborers, my two elder brothers and myself, to one of his farms, which laid upon the river about three miles above Fort Charles, adjoining Pemmaquid falls, there to gather in his English harvest, and we labored securely until noon. After we had dined, our people went to their labor, some in one field to their English hay, the others to another field of English corn. My father, the youngest of my two brothers and myself, tarried near the farmhouse in which we had dined till about one of the clock, at which time we heard the report of several guns at the fort. Upon which my father said he hoped it was the signal of good news, and that the great council had sent back the soldiers, to cover the inhabitants; for on report of the revolution [of 1688 in England] they had deserted. But to our great surprise thirty or forty Indians, at that moment, discharged a volley of shot at us, from behind a rising ground, near our barn. The yelling of the Indians, the whistling of their shot, and the voice of my father, whom I heard cry out, "What now! what now!" so terrified me, (though he seemed to be handling a gun), that I endeavored to make my escape. My brother ran one way and I another, and looking over my shoulder, I saw a stout fellow, painted, pursuing me, with a gun, and a cutlass glittering in his hand which I expected every moment in my brains. I soon fell down, and the Indian seized me by the left hand. He offered me no abuse, but tied my arms, then lifted me up and pointed to the place where the people were at work about the hay, and led me that way. As we went, we crossed where my father was, who looked very pale and bloody, and walked very slowly. When we came to the place, I saw two men shot down on the flats, and one or two knocked on their heads with hatchets, crying out "O Lord," &c. There the Indians brought two captives, one a man, and the other my brother James. . . . This brother was about fourteen years of age. My oldest brother, whose name was Thomas, wonderfully escaped by land to the Barbican, a point of land on the west side of the river, opposite the fort, where several fishing vessels lay. He got on board one of them and sailed that night.

After doing what mischief they could, they sat down and made us sit with them. After some time we arose, and the Indians pointed for us to go eastward. We marched about a quarter of a mile, and then made a halt. Here they brought my father to us. They made proposals to him, by old Moxus, who told him that those were strange Indians who shot him, and that he was sorry for it. My father replied that he was a dying man, and wanted no favor of them, but to pray with his children. This being granted him, he recommended us to the blessing and protection of God Almighty; then gave us the best advice and took his leave for this life, hoping in God that we should meet in a better. He parted with a cheerful voice but looked very pale, by reason of his great loss of blood, which now gushed out of his shoes. The Indians led him aside! — I heard the blows of the hatchet, but neither shriek nor groan! I afterwards heard that he had five or seven shot-holes through his waistcoat or jacket, and that he was covered with some boughs.

The Indians led us, their captives, on the east side of the river, towards the fort, and when we came within a mile and a half of the fort and the town . . . we saw fire and smoke on all sides. Here we made a short stop, . . . and then moved into a thick swamp. There I saw my mother and my two little sisters, and many other captives who were taken from the town. My mother asked me about my father. I told her he was killed, but could say no more for grief. She burst into tears, and the Indians moved me a little further off, and seized me with cords to a tree. . . .

After the Indians had thus laid waste Pemmaquid, they moved us to New Harbor, about two miles east of Pemmaquid, a cove much frequented by fishermen. At this place there were before the war about twelve houses. These the inhabitants deserted as soon as the rumor of war reached the place. When we turned our backs on the town, my heart was ready to break! I saw my mother. She spoke to me, but I could not answer her. That night we tarried at New Harbor, and the next day went in their canoes for Penobscot. . . .

A few days after, we arrived at Penobscot fort where I again saw my mother, my brother and sisters, and many other captives. I think we tarried here eight days. At that time the Jesuit of the place had a great mind to buy me. My Indian master made a visit to the Jesuit, and carried me with him. And here I will note that the Indian who takes a captive is accounted his master and has a perfect right to him, until he gives or sells him to another. I saw the Jesuit show my master pieces of gold, and understood afterward that he was tendering them for my ransom. He gave me a biscuit, which I put into my pocket, and not daring to eat it, buried it under a log, fearing he had put something in it to make me love him. Being very young, and having heard much of the Papists torturing the Protestants, caused me to act thus; and I hated the sight of a Jesuit. When my mother heard the talk of my being sold to a Jesuit, she said to me, "Oh! my dear child, if it were God's will, I had rather follow you to your grave, or never see you more in this world, than you should be sold to a Jesuit; for a Jesuit will ruin you, body and soul!" It pleased God to grant her request, for she never saw me more! Yet she and my two little sisters were, after several years captivity redeemed, but she died ere I returned. My brother who was taken with me, was, after several years captivity, most barbarously tortured to death by the Indians.

My Indian master carried me up Penobscot river to a village called Madawamkee, which stands on a point of land between the main river and a branch which heads to the east of it. At home I had ever seen strangers treated with the utmost civility, and being a stranger, I expected some kind of treatment here; but I soon found myself deceived, for I presently saw a number of squaws, who had got together in a circle, dancing and yelling. An old grim looking one took me by the hand, and, leading me into the ring, some seized me by the hair, and others by my hands and feet, like so many furies; but my master presently laying down a pledge, they released me.

Here a captive among the Indians is exposed to all manner of abuses, and to the extremest tortures, unless their master, or some of their master's relations, lay down a ransom, such as a bag of corn, a blanket, or the like, which redeems them from their cruelty for that dance. The next day we went up that eastern branch of the Penobscot river many leagues; carried over land to a large pond, and from one pond to another, till, in a few days, we went down a river called

Medocktack, which vents itself into St. John's river. But before we came to the mouth of this river, we passed over a long carrying place, to Medocktack fort, which stands on the bank of the St. John river. My master went before and left me with an old Indian, and two or three squaws. The old man often said (which was all the English he could speak), "By and by come to a great town and fort." I now comforted myself in thinking how finely I should be refreshed when I came to this great town. . . .

After some weeks had passed, we left this village and went up the St. John's river about ten miles, to a branch called Medockscenecasis, where there was one wigwam. At our arrival an old squaw saluted me with a yell, taking me by the hair and one hand, but I was so rude as to break her hold and free myself. She gave me a filthy grin, and the Indian set up a laugh, and so it passed over. Here we lived upon fish, wild grapes, roots &c, which was hard living to me.

When the winter came on we went up the river until the ice came down, running thick in the river, when, according to the Indian custom, we laid up our canoes until spring. Then we traveled, sometimes on the ice, and sometimes on the land, till we came to a river that was open, but not fordable, where we made a raft and passed over, bag and baggage. I met with no abuse from them in this winter's hunting, though I was put to great hardships in carrying burdens and for want of food, But they underwent the same difficulty, and would often encourage me, saying in broken English, "By and by great deal moose." Yet they could not answer any question I asked them. And knowing little of their customs and way of life, I thought it tedious to be constantly moving from place to place, though it might be in some respects an advantage; for it ran still in my mind that we were traveling to some settlement; and when my burden was over-heavy, and the Indians left me behind, and the still evening coming on, I fancied that I could see through the bushes and hear the people of some great town; which hope, though some support to me in the day, yet I found not the town at night.

Thus we were hunting three hundred miles from the sea, and knew no man within fifty or sixty miles of us. We were eight or ten in number, and had but two guns, on which we wholly depended for food. If any disaster had happened, we must all have perished. Sometimes we had no manner of sustenance for three or four days; but God wonderfully provides for all creatures. In one of these fasts, God's providence was remarkable. Our two Indian men who had guns, in hunting, started a moose, but there being a shallow crusted snow on the ground, and the moose discovering them, ran with great force into a swamp. The Indians went round the swamp, and finding no track, returned at night to the wigwam and told what had happened. The next morning they followed him on the track, and soon found him, lying on the snow. He had, in crossing the roots of a large tree that had been blown down, broken through the ice made over the water in the hole occasioned by the roots of the tree taking up the ground, and hitched one of his hind legs among the roots so fast that by striving to get it out, he pulled his thigh bone out of its socket by the hip, and thus extraordinarily were we provided for in our great strait. Sometimes they would take a bear, which go into dens in the fall of the year without any sort of food, and lie there four or five months without food, never going out till spring, in which time they neither lose or gain in flesh. If they went into their dens fat, they came out so, and if they went in lean, they came out lean. I have seen some which have come out with four whelps, and both very fat, and then we feasted. An old squaw and a captive, if any present, must stand without the wigwam, shaking their hands and bodies as in a dance, and singing, "Wegage oh nelo woh," which in English is, "Fat is my eating." This is to signify their thankfulness in feasting times. When one supply was spent, we fasted until further success.

The way they preserve meat is by taking the flesh from the bones and drying it in smoke, by which it is kept sound months or years without salt. We moved still further up the country after moose when our store was out, so that by the spring we had gone to the northward of the Lady mountains [near the St. Lawrence River]. When the spring came and the rivers broke up, we moved back to the head of the St. John's river, and there made canoes of moose hides, sewing three or four together and pitching the seams with balsam mixed with charcoal. Then we went down the river to a place called Madawescook [Madawaska]. There an old man lived and kept a sort of trading house, where we tarried several days; then we went further down the river till we came to the greatest falls in these parts, called Cheanekepeag, where we carried a little way over the land, and putting off our canoes, we went down stream still. And as we passed down by the mouths of any large branches, we saw Indians; but when any dance was proposed, I was bought off. At length we arrived at the place where we left our birch canoes in the fall, and putting our baggage into them, went down to the fort.

There we planted corn, and after planting, went afishing, and to look for and dig roots till the corn was fit to weed. After weeding, we took a second tour on the same errand, then returned to hill our corn. After hilling we went some distance from the fort and field, up the river, to take salmon and other fish, which we dried for food, where we continued till corn was filled with milk; some of it we dried then, the other as it ripened. To dry corn when in the milk, they gather it in large kettles and boil it on the ears, till it is pretty hard, then shell it from the cob with clam shells, and dry it on bark in the sun. When it is thoroughly dry, a kernel is no bigger than a pea, and would keep years, and when it is boiled again it swells as large as when on the ear, and tastes incomparably sweeter than other corn. When we had gathered our corn and dried it in the way already described, we put some into Indian barns; that is, into holes in the ground, lined and covered with bark, and then with dirt. The rest we carried up the river upon our next winter's hunting.

Thus God wonderfully favored me, and carried me through the first year of my captivity.

CHAPTER TWO

OF THE ABUSIVE AND BARBAROUS TREATMENT WHICH
SEVERAL CAPTIVES MET WITH FROM THE INDIANS

When any great number of Indians met, or when any captives had been lately taken, or when any captives desert and are retaken, they have a dance, and torture the unhappy people who have fallen into their hands. My unfortunate brother, who was taken with me, after about three years captivity, deserted with another Englishman, who had been taken from Casco Bay, and was retaken by the Indians at New Harbor, and carried back to Penobscot fort. Here they were both tortured at a stake by fire, for some time; then their noses and ears were cut off, and they made to eat them. After this they were burnt to death at the stake, the Indians at the same time declaring they would serve all deserters in the same manner. Thus they divert themselves at their dances.

On the second spring of my captivity, My Indian master and his squaw went to Canada, but sent me down the river with several Indians to the fort to plant corn. The day before we came to the planting ground, we met two young Indians who seemed to be in great haste. After they had passed us, I understood that they were going with an express to Canada, and that there was an English vessel at the mouth of the river. I not being perfect in their language, nor knowing that English vessels traded with them in time of war, supposed a peace was concluded on and that the captives would be released. I was so transported with this fancy, that I slept but little if any that night. Early the next morning we came to the village, where my ecstasy ended; for I had no sooner landed, but three or four Indians dragged me to the great wigwam, where they were yelling and dancing around James Alexander, a Jersey man, who was taken from Falmouth in Casco Bay. This was occasioned by two families of Cape Sable Indians, who, having lost some friends by a number of English fishermen, came some hundreds of miles to revenge themselves on poor captives. They soon came to me and tossed me about till I was almost breathless, and then threw me into the ring to my fellow captive, and taking him out repeated their barbarities on him. Then I was hauled out again by three Indians, who seized me by the hair of the head, and bending me down by the hair, one beat me on the back and shoulders so long that my breath was almost beat out of my body. Then others put a tomahawk into my hands, and ordered me to get up and sing and dance Indian, which I performed with the greatest reluctance, and while in the act seemed determined to purchase my death by killing two or three of those monsters of cruelty, thinking it impossible to survive their bloody treatment; but it was impressed on my mind that it was not in their power to take my life away, so I desisted. . . . Not one of them showed the least compassion, but I saw the tears run down plentifully the cheeks of a Frenchman who sat behind, though it did not relieve the tortures that poor James and I were forced to endure for the most part of this tedious day, for they were continued to the evening, and were the most severe that ever I met with in the whole six years that I was a captive with the Indians.

THOMAS BURNAM
1644–?

The first governor of the Massachusetts Bay Colony, John Winthrop, arrived in Salem in 1630 on the ship *Arbella*. Before leading his flock ashore, he preached a sermon in which he vowed that he and his fellow Puritans would build "a city upon a hill" that would become "a story and a byword through the world." Some sixty years later, a dark shadow fell on Salem which the world now remembers more vividly than Winthrop's shining promise: the witch trials. Stimulated by Cotton Mather, the most learned of all the Puritan divines, the settlers' search for the presence of the Devil in their fellow townsmen culminated in the frenzy of the trials of 1692, when thirty persons were convicted.

One of those hanged was the minister of Wells, Maine, the Reverend George Burroughs. The last person to be formally accused of practicing witchcraft in Maine was Dolly Smith of Arundel, an elderly "singlewoman" who in 1796 was accused of putting a spell on a fellow townsman and his property. An enlightened judge told her accusers that they were ignorant, deluded men.

The following deposition by Thomas Burnam, Junior, dated 22 April 1692 and naming Rachel Senton a witch, is in the files of the Maine Historical Society.

The Accusation of a Witch

The deposition of Thomas Burnam junior aged 48 yeares; who testifieth and saith that some yeares since one sumer one of my cowes was very often milked and som times tow of them in my yard by my house; and thinking to cach the milker I took paines and watched and one with me and thos nights that I watched my cowes were not milked and I arose one night a litele before day and stood in my indian corn near whare my cowes lay and sone I saw a female stand in the midele of the yeard whar the coews ware which by her atire I thought was Rachel Senton which as I thought vanished a way; and a nother night I a rose before day and walked in the street and just one the breaking of day came sudingly to my yearde wheare my cowes lay and that cow that was most comonly milked stood and a parson a milking which presenly glanced from the cow in the likeness of a gray cat and run up the back side of my house scaching upon the shingells a bought fourty foot and so over the top of my house and further saith not.

Except the spring following the same cow was found dead on the Comon, not mired nor cast nor throw poverty or any distress that we know of.

ABNER STOCKING
1752–?

The march of Colonel Benedict Arnold and his thousand men through the Maine wilderness to Quebec in 1775 is the most famous chapter in Maine's Revolutionary War history. What is remembered is not the role the expedition played in the war or what happened after Arnold reached Quebec: it is the march itself. Kenneth Roberts made it the basis of his novel *Arundel;* the line of march is now marked with granite monuments, and a tourist can find notations on his automobile map to help him follow Arnold's Continentals.

In September 1775, Washington advised the Continental Congress that "encouraged by the repeated declarations of the Canadians and Indians, and urged by their requests," he had sent Arnold to penetrate Canada by way of the Kennebec River and, if possible, "to make himself master of Quebec." He added that in all his inquiries concerning the route, the time of year, and the attitude of the Canadians, he found nothing to deter him from his decision. Washington reasoned that Quebec was the American Gibraltar, and whoever controlled it controlled Canada. If a surprise attack was successful, the Canadians might be persuaded to join the colonies' rebellion.

The ambitious Colonel Arnold was Washington's choice to lead the expedition. At the capture of Ticonderoga, he had proved himself an aggressive and resourceful leader of untrained troops, and he had a better knowledge of the military and civilian situation along the St. Lawrence River than anyone else Washington could turn to. Even so, Arnold was being asked to do almost the impossible: to move a sizable military force though a wild country for which there were no adequate maps along a trail that had been in the past used only by Indians, French Jesuits, and, more recently, a lone English engineer. And with the Maine winter as an added impediment, the question was real: Could Arnold and his men make it to Quebec in time?

Arnold's troops included some veterans, hardy backwoodsmen from Virginia and Pennsylvania, but the rest were new recruits, citizen soldiers, undisciplined and certainly unknowing about navigating mountain streams in crude, leaky boats. As a military formation, the march ended in chaos. Almost a hundred miles from the promised first settlements and with all provisions gone, the officers admitted that it was every man for himself, make it if you can.

Our soldier's report comes from twenty-two-year-old Abner Stocking of Chatham, a small town near present Middletown, Connecticut. He was no backwoodsman but an educated villager, patriotic and pious; one of his brothers was a Methodist minister. Stocking's story suggests that his often elevated prose style was formed from his reading of both moral tracts and romantic novels. But he was tough enough both to withstand great physical hardships and to face human horrors. During Arnold's unsuccessful attack on the Quebec fortress, Stocking was captured and spent seven months in prison "affected with scurvy and the flux . . . all of us without comfortable clothing and many of us almost entirely naked." When summer came, the British commander offered to send the prisoners home by ship on their word that they would fight no more. As a result, Stocking was back in Connecticut by September. His journal was published in 1810.

Arnold's March to Quebec: The Journal of Abner Stocking

All things being in readiness for our departure, we set out from Cambridge, near Boston, on the 13th Sept. at sunset, and encamped at Mistic at eight o'clock at night. We were all in high spirits, intending to endure with fortitude all the fatigues and hardships that we might meet with in our march to Quebec.

"Mount Katahdin from Ripogenous Gorge"

September 14th.

This morning we began our march at five o'clock, encamped at Danvers, a place twenty miles distant from Mistick. The weather through the day was very sultry and hot for the season of the year. The country through which we passed appeared barren and but thinly inhabited.

September 16th.

Zealous in our cause and not knowing the hardships and distresses we were to encounter, we as usual began our march very early. At eight o'clock we arrived at Newbury Port where we were to tarry several days and make preparations for our voyage. We were here to go on board vessels which we found lying ready to receive us, and carry us to the mouth of the Kennebeck. The mouth of the Kennebeck is about thirty leagues to the eastward of Newbury.

September 17th.

We are still at Newbury Port and are ordered to appear in a general review. We passed the review with much honor to ourselves. We manifested great zeal and animation in the cause of liberty and went through the manual exercise with much alacrity. The spectators who were very numerous appeared much affected. They probably thought we had many hardships to endure and many of us should never return to our parents and families.

September 18th.

We this day embarked at six o'clock in the afternoon. Our fleet consisted of eleven sail, sloops and schooners. Our whole number of troops was 1100 — eleven companies of musketmen and three companies of riflemen. We hauled off into the road and got ready to weigh anchor in the morning if the wind should be favorable.

September 19th.

This morning we got under weigh with a pleasant breeze, our drums beating, pipes playing and colours flying. Many pretty girls stood upon the shore, I suppose weeping for the departure of their sweethearts.

At eleven o'clock this day we left the entrance of the harbor and bore away for the Kennebeck river. In the latter part of the night there came on a thick fog and our fleet was separated. At break of day we found ourselves in a most dangerous situation, very near a reef of rocks. The rocks indeed appeared on all sides of us, so that we feared we should be dashed to pieces on some of them. We were brought into this deplorable situation by means of liquor being dealt out too freely to our pilots . . . but through the blessings of God we all arrived safe in the Kennebeck river.

September 20th.

This day was very pleasant, and with a gentle breeze we sailed and rowed 30 miles up the Kennebeck river. By the evening tide we floated within 6 miles of Fort Western where we were obliged to leave our sloops and take to our batteaus.

September 21.

This day we arrived at Fort Western where we tarried until the 25th in order to make farther preparation for our voyage up the river and our march through the wilderness. While remaining in this place I was called to witness a scene which to me was awful and very affecting; the more so I presume as it was the first of the kind I had ever beheld. A civil, well behaved and much beloved young man belonging to Captain Williams' company was shot. He lived but about twelve hours and died in great horror and agony of mind at the thought of going into eternity and appearing before his God and judge. He was from the north parish of New London and had a wife and four or five children.

The supposed murderer was James McCormick. The circumstances of his being out all night, and his guilty looks and actions, were pretty convincing proof against him. He was tryed by a Court-Martial and sentenced to be hanged until dead, his gallows erected and all things prepared for his execution. Our Chaplain conversed with him respecting his crime, the awful punishment he was soon to suffer, and the more awful and never ending punishment that would await him in the eternal world if he did not repent and believe in Christ. He would not confess himself guilty of intentionally murdering the young man; but that he intended to have killed his captain, with whom he had the night before a violent quarrel. He was brought to the gallows, a prayer made and the time for his execution almost arrived, when Colonel Arnold thought best to reprieve him and send him to General Washington. I have been informed that he died in gaol before the day of his execution arrived.

September 25th.

Early this morning we embarked on board our batteaus and proceeded on our way. We labored hard through the day and found ourselves at night but about 7 miles from the place of our departure. The current began to be swift. We encamped at night by the edge of a cornfield and fared very sumptuously.

September 29th.

This day we arrived to the second carrying place called Skowhegan falls. Though this was only 60 rods over, it occasioned much delay and great fatigue. We had to ascend a ragged rock near on 100 feet in height and almost perpendicular. Though it seemed as though we could hardly ascend it without any burden, we succeeded in dragging our batteaus and baggage up in it.

September 30th.

After getting over the carrying place we found the water more still. We proceeded 5 miles and at sundown camped in a most delightful wood, where I thought I could have spent some time agreeably in solitude, in contemplating the works of nature. The forest was stripped of its verdure, but still appeared to me beautiful. I thought that though we were in a thick wilderness, uninhabited by human beings, yet we were as much in the immediate presence of our divine protector, as when in a crowded city.

October 2nd.

This day we carried over Norridgewock falls, one mile and a quarter. At night we encamped at a place formerly inhabited by the natives and afterwards by the French and Indians; the former had erected a mass house for their devotions, but had deserted it at the time the New England forces made great slaughter among them in the French war. A few inhabitants are now living there, who rendered us some assistance. The temple of worship contained some curiosities, such as crosses &c. We took up our lodgings here for the night and were much pleased with our accommodations. The place had the appearance of once having been the residence of a considerable number of inhabitants.

October 3rd.

Having had some better refreshment than usual, we pushed on our way with increased resolution. We had now taken leave of the last inhabitants. The remainder of our route would be through a trackless wilderness. We now entered a doleful, barren woods; the timber mostly pine and hemlock — some thick patches of spruce and fir and some groves of sugar maple. One of the riflemen of Captain Hendricks' company this day killed a young moose which weighed about 200 pounds.

October 4th.

This day with much exertion we got forward 8 miles to Tentucket, or Hell-gate falls, which are of an astonishing height and exhibit an awful appearance. At the foot of the falls we found fine fishing for salmon trout. The land carriage here was about 40 rods but very difficult to effect.

October 7th.

This day we reached the head of the Kennebeck river. Here was a carrying place of three and a half miles through a wilderness without any tract to guide us.

October 9, 10 and 11th.

These three days were employed in carrying our batteaus, provisions and baggage over this long and difficult carrying place. Some were employed in cutting and clearing a road, and others in carrying. We had to go through swamps and quagmires — much of the way knee deep in mud and water. We here left behind everything which we did not deem absolutely necessary to our journey. Our pork we took from the barrels and strung it on poles, leaving the barrels behind. In the afternoon of the 11th, we launched our boats into a pool of considerable extent, crossed over it and camped on the west side.

October 12 and 13.

We carried our batteaus and baggage three quarters of a mile to another pond, one mile over — then to a third two miles over. Though the water was now very cold, we caught trout in these ponds in great abundance. Between these ponds we built a block-house, and gave it the name of Fort Meigs, designed for our sick in case they should return this way. We viewed with much anxiety winter approaching — we had some snow squalls during the day.

October 14 and 15th.

These two days we were diligently employed in carrying our batteaus, provisions, &c. to Dead river. Our hardships were greater than on any preceding day — the land carriage was 4 miles; one mile of which was a sunken marsh. Four men were assigned to each batteau — under the weight of their loads they almost every step sunk to their knees in mud and were entangled in the low shrubbery. We arrived at the bank of Dead river at 3 o'clock and proceeding one mile up said river by sunset took up our encampment for the night. On our right and left were excessively high mountains, the summits of which were covered with snow and ice. Could I have ascended to the top of one of these mountains I thought I could have overlooked all creation.

The land between the mountains appeared to be very rich and fertile — wild grass covered the ground, four and five feet in height, and served us a good purpose for covering for the night. . . .

October 24.

This day our afflictions increased, fear was added to sorrow. We found to our astonishment that our journey was much longer than expected; what was more alarming our provisions were growing scant. Some of our men appeared disheartened, but most of them with Col. Arnold stood firm and resolute. . . . At this critical and alarming crisis a counsel was called to consider what was most prudent to be done. They determined to send back immediately the disabled and the sick, with provisions sufficient to carry them to the first inhabitants on the Kennebeck river. They also determined to send a party forward to the nearest settlement in Canada to procure provisions and return to meet the army with all possible expedition. Captain Oliver Hanchet with one subaltern and fifty privates set out with ten days provisions, each man taking 10 pints of flour and 5 pounds of pork. The sick, forty in number, went back. We then pushed forward with all possible speed. We gained nine miles against the stream this day, but suffered from losses, on account of which we felt greatly distressed. Several of our boats were upset by the rapidity of the stream, and much of our provisions, cloathing, ammunition and some money was lost.

October 25th.

This morning we proceeded on our way very early: the weather was somewhat cold, as it had snowed most of the night. . . . To add to our discouragement, we received intelligence that Colonel Enos who was in our rear had returned with three companies and taken large stores of provisions and ammunition. These companies had constantly been in the rear, and of course had experienced much less fatigue than we had. They had their path cut and cleared by us; they only followed, while we led. That they therefore should be the first to turn back excited in us much manly resentment. . . .

October 27th.

This day we crossed a pond, one fourth of a mile over, and soon came to another two miles in width. In this pond we caught plenty of trout. We had now come to the great carrying place, 4 miles and 50 perches over. As we were all greatly fatigued, it was resolved to leave here most of our batteaus, which had already been reduced from 10 to 6 to each company — but I think 6 were carried from this place. We overhauled our ammunition and found most of our powder damaged and unfit for use; all of this description we destroyed on the spot. The last pond we crossed appeared to be the head of Dead river, or rather, as some suppose, the fountain from which Kennebeck river takes its first rise, that and the Dead river being one and the same. . . . We now appear to be on the height of land, to be several hundred feet higher than we were when we were at Fort Western.

October 28th.

We this day passed the height of land. We then divided our provisions which we found did not exceed 4 pounds of flour and forty ounces of pork to a man. We were in a meadow by the side of a small stream, running N.E. into Chaudiere lake. We sent our batteaus down this creek and a little before sunset we had the inexpressible satisfaction to meet a messenger we had sent into Canada to find out the disposition of the inhabitants and know whether we should be well received. He was the bearer of good tidings, he assured us that we should be kindly received and furnished with provisions. He brought some fruit to Col. Arnold, sent to him by a lady, as a token of friendship and fidelity. Our joy on this occasion was too great to be suppressed. The whole valley was made to ring with our exultations. Our worthy Major Meigs was exceedingly elevated, and expressed such zeal and animation in the glorious cause of his country as revived the drooping spirits of all the soldiery. We were now to leave the remainder of our batteaus — what little we had to carry we put into our knapsacks, the whole of the detachment having now orders to march and make the best of their way to Chaudiere river. We returned unto the rising ground and encamped for the night.

October 29th.

Very early this morning we left our encampment on the rising ground and began descending towards an ocean of swamp that lay before us. We soon entered it and found it covered with a low shrubbery of cedar and hackmetack the roots of which were so excessively slippery that we could hardly keep upon our feet. The top of the ground was covered with a soft moss filled with water and ice. After walking a few hours in the swamp we seemed to have lost all sense of feeling in our feet and ankles. As we were constantly slipping, we walked in great fear of breaking our bones or dislocating our joints. But to be disenabled from walking in this situation was sure death. We traveled all day and not being able to get through this dismal swamp, we encamped. I thought we were probably the first human beings that ever took up their residence for a night in this wilderness — not howling wilderness, for I believe no wild animals would inhabit it.

October 30th.

This morning we started in great haste and soon got through the swamp. For the time we had been traveling in it, we judged it to be about 7 miles in width; of its length from east to west I can give no account. On leaving the swamp we had to pass a river two rods over and about three feet in depth. The water was excessively cold. As we had to make our way through thickets and low sunken marshes, our progress was slow. During the fore part of the day we steered E.N.E. but thinking we were bearing too much to the east we changed our course to W.N.W. which soon brought us in sight of a large pond or lake, which we supposed communicated with Chaudiere lake. We encamped about a half mile from the lake. Our march this day we supposed was about 20 miles.

October 31st.

This morning we began our march very early and pushed on with all speed for the head of Chaudiere river; at 11 o'clock we passed it. We here came up with Captain Morgan's company, which had gone before us. We learned to our great sorrow that in attempting to go down the river in their batteaus, which they brought to this place, they were carried down by the rapidity of the stream and dashed on rocks; that they had lost most of their provisions and that a waiter of Captain Morgan was drowned. Their condition was truly deplorable — they had not when we came up with them a mouthful of provisions of any kind, and we were not able to relieve them as hunger stared us in the face. Some of us were entirely destitute and others had but a morsel of bread, and we now supposed ourselves 70 miles from the nearest inhabitants. Some of Captain Morgan's company we were told had perished with the cold.

November 1st.

Our fatigue and anxiety were so great that we were but little refreshed the last night by sleep. We started however very early, hungry and wet. Knowing that our lives depended on our speedy arrival to an inhabited country, we marched very briskly all day and even late in the evening. We then encamped in a fine grove, but in a starving condition. Captain Goodrich's company had the good fortune to kill a large black dog that providentially came to them at that time. [Here Private Stocking is mistaken. It was Captain Goodrich's pet, and he offered it to his starving men.] They feasted on him heartily without either bread or salt. Our hunger was so great that many offered dollars for a single mouthful of bread. Such distress I never before felt or witnessed. I anxiously turned my thoughts back to my native land, to a country flowing with milk and honey. I was surprised that I had so lightly esteemed all the good things which I there once enjoyed. Little, thought I, do we know of the value of the common blessings of Providence, until we are deprived of them. With such reflections I lay myself down on the cold, wet ground, hungry and fatigued.

November 2nd.

When we arose this morning many of the company were so weak that they could hardly stand on their legs. When we attempted to march, they reeled about like drunken men, having now been without provisions five days. As I proceeded I passed many sitting, wholly drowned in sorrow, wishfully placing their eyes on every one who passed by them, hoping for some relief. Such pity-asking countenances I never before beheld. My heart was ready to burst and my eyes to overflow with tears when I witnessed distress which I could not relieve. The circumstances of a young Dutchman and his wife, who followed him through this fatiguing march, particularly excited my sensibility. They appeared to be much interested in each other's welfare and unwilling to be separated, but the husband exhausted with fatigue and hunger fell a victim to the king of terrors. His affectionate wife tarryed by him until he died, while the rest of the company proceeded on their way. Having no implements with which she could bury him she covered him with leaves, and then took his gun and other implements and then left him with a heavy heart. After traveling twenty miles she came up with us.

Just at evening this day, we met with cattle coming up the river, sent us for our relief. This was the most joyful sight our eyes ever beheld. The French people that drove them informed us that Colonel Arnold had arrived at their settlement two days before, with the advance party, and had purchased cattle as soon as possible and sent them on. A cow was immediately killed and cut open in great haste; a small calf being found in her, it was divided up and eaten without further ceremony. I got a little piece of the flesh, which I ate raw with

a little oat meal wet with cold water, and thought I feasted sumptuously.

November 3rd.

This day we proceeded on down the river about 20 miles, wading
several small rivers, some of which were up to our middles. The water
was terrible cold as the ground was covered with snow and ice. At
evening we came in sight of a house which was the first we had seen
in a space of 31 days. Our joy was inexpressible in breaking out of
that dismal wilderness in which we had been so long buried, and once
more beholding a country inhabited by human beings; it was like
being brought from a dungeon to behold the clear light of the sun.
The French people received us with all the kindness we could wish,
they treated our sick with much tenderness, and supplied us with
everything they could for our comfort. They seemed moved with pity
for us and to greatly admire our patriotism and resolution, in encountering such hardships for the good of our country. But they were too
ignorant to put a just estimate on the value of freedom.

November 4th.

Last night we got a plenty of good beef and potatoes, but little bread
could be procured. It snowed most of the night and the weather was
cold. After marching down the river about ten miles, we began to get
such necessaries as we wanted; such as bread, milk, eggs, butter and
most kinds of sauce [vegetables]. To be supplied with these articles,
of which we had been so long deprived was a great luxury. The
kindness and hospitalities of the inhabitants was to us very pleasing.
After having been lately our enemies, at war with us, we did not
expect from them too much friendship. . . .

November 6th.

This day we came up with Colonel Arnold and the advance party at
St. Mary's. At two o'clock we marched off together, and continued
on the road until 12 o'clock at night. The roads were very bad by
means of the great rains and snows that had fallen — we most of the
way waded half leg deep in the mud and water. Though we were very
industrious through the day and half of the night, we marched but 17
miles.

November 7th.

We this day marched down the river about three miles and halted
until night. We now had arrived before the city of Quebec, to take

which by surprise was the great object of our expedition. A Lieutenant with 20 men was sent forward to see if our way was clear. At 2 o'clock at night the advance party reached the St. Lawrence and halted. In the morning we perceived that we were in fair view of Quebec, nothing but the river separating us.

November 8th.

We took up our residences in houses along the south side of the river St. Lawrence, and remained until the 13th, waiting for the sick, the halt and the feeble who had been left behind at different places to come up. By the 13th all had arrived who were to be expected; many we learnt to our great sorrow had perished by the way. When a general muster was made, and all appeared who had survived the perils of the wilderness, a more pitiful and humorous spectacle was exhibited than I had ever before seen.

In our long and tedious march through the wilderness, it was not with us as with the children of Israel, "that our cloathes waxed not old," ours were torn in pieces by the bushes, and hung in strings — few of us had any shoes, but moggasins made of raw skins — many of us without hats — and beards long and visages thin and meager. I thought we much resembled the animals that inhabit New-Spain, called the Ourang-Outang. The French appeared a little surprised at the first sight of us; and had not Colonel Arnold gone forward to apprise them of our approach, they might have fled from their habitations.

TIMOTHY DWIGHT
1752–1817

Timothy Dwight was a major figure in the religious and academic worlds of the late eighteenth and early nineteenth centuries. He was a writer, a Congregational minister, and, from 1795 until his death, president of Yale College. He was a sternly moral man, with strong religious and political convictions, and he had the dual platforms of church and college for expressing his views.

As a young man from Massachusetts, Dwight joined an association of poets known as the Hartford Wits whose purpose was to further the cause of poetry and to develop a literary tradition in New England. His early writings include a lengthy epic poem with a biblical theme (thought by some to be virtually unreadable) and a later, less ambitious poem about the small Connecticut town of Greenfield Hill, where he served as pastor from 1783 to 1795.

Dwight is best known, however, for the letters he wrote on his trips throughout the Northeast during the long college vacations. Published in 1821–1822 as *Travels in New-England and New-York,* these four volumes were designed to tell how "New England appeared, or to my own eye would have appeared eighty or a hundred years before." They discuss the scenic, economic, historical, and cultural aspects of the places Dwight visited, including a overlay of his own strong and often critical opinions. We learn much of the nature of the countryside, its inhabitants, and the author himself.

The sections on Dwight's visits to Maine, excerpted here, present his theories on the settlement of Maine and how the unforgiving land and the less-than-admirable early residents slowed development for many years.

Thoughts on the Settling of Maine

Dear Sir,

Being now about to quit the District of Maine, I will give you such general observations, as I have had an opportunity to make concerning this country. . . .

When a traveller remembers that the first settlements in New England were begun here, and that, with a few short intervals, they have been continued ever since, he naturally wonders why this country should, for so long a time, have been so thinly inhabited, since such numbers now regard it as a desirable residence. The following observations may in some measure explain this subject.

When the first settlers planted themselves in Maine, their object was not husbandry, but commerce and fishery. Fishermen, and casual traders, are never, in the proper sense, Colonists. Neither their views nor their habits qualify them to convert a wilderness into a permanent residence. Men, accustomed to patient labour, of persevering firmness, and superiour even to the real ills of life; men, influenced by some great and commanding motive connected with a settlement on the soil, such as the hope of civil or religious freedom, or the necessity of providing for an increasing family, are the only persons, fitted to subdue forests, encounter frost and hunger, and resolutely survey the prospect of Savage incursions. Traders and fishermen will stay in any place, while they can trade and fish with advantage, but they commence their business with an original intention of retreating as soon as their gain is acquired or the acquisition becomes hopeless. From the first settlers, as they are called, of Maine all that could be rationally expected was that which actually took place. They traded, caught fish, and went home. Such, chiefly, were the visitors of this country for the first fifty years.

All the evils of climate and all the discouragements of soil and

The Reverend Timothy Dwight

surface were in a high degree felt by these people. The winter is sufficiently cold to terrify, at first, any European educated South of the fifty-second degree of North latitude, unless born on the sides of the Alps or Pyrenees, and much more, men accustomed only to the mild winter of England. The soil of the coast is generally cold and lean and the surface by no means inviting. All these facts the settlers, mentioned above, published so generally that until the close of the Revolutionary war Maine was considered as little less than an immense waste, unfit for the habitation of man. To the complete establishment of this character travellers, who visited only the same grounds and the inhabitants who resided on them, jointly contributed. Except in some small tracts, principally in the County of York, scarcely any husbandry was pursued in this extensive country. The few persons devoted to this business were so unskillful as to employ their labour, even here, with much less advantage than the same soil and climate would have furnished to abler hands. The only visible effect of their industry was, therefore, a collection of half-starved crops, growing on grounds wretchedly prepared, and serving only to discourage future attempts of the same nature. So general was the prepossession against the possibility of successful agriculture, that, as I have observed, the people of Standish were astonished to see, (and that several years since the Revolutionary war was finished,) their first crops come to perfection. Until this period almost all the inhabitants were merchants, land-jobbers, sawyers, lumbermen, or fishermen. Both the corn and meat on which they fed were imported from Connecticut and some other States. These facts completely riveted the opinion throughout New-England that the lands in Maine were of little or no value, and that farmers could not here obtain even a subsistence.

A number of the people, however, were real colonists, and came to this country with an intention to cultivate the soil. These persons met with endless perplexities in the numerous interfering and contradictory grants, made in England, of these lands; distracting those who were in possession; and bringing upon them the litigation and distress produced by the claims of other grantees, who had or pretended to have, as good or better titles than themselves. Disputed titles will effectually prevent the regular settlement of any country. Had Maine been originally granted in regular townships by a government sufficiently acquainted with the country and sufficiently attentive to the interests of the grantees to make out consistent patents, and to invest the grantees with the proper powers of internal government, the settlement of the country would undoubtedly have advanced with a more rapid progress. But the government of Great Britain was at that time too ignorant of the country and too careless about the concerns of the adventurers to do either. From this ignorance and unconcern probably arose another serious discouragement. The French, in the neighbourhood of whom Englishmen have hitherto never been able to live peaceably, began early a settlement on the Eastern shores of this District. The French government, originally in the year 1603, granted this tract, together with the rest of New-England, New-York, New-Jersey, and a great part of Pennsylvania, or in other words the whole country between 40° and 46° North latitude, to Monsieur De la Motte who took possession of it in 1604 by planting himself in the District of Maine. In the following years several other scattered settlements were formed as far Westward as [the] Kennebeck river. In 1613, Sir Samuel Argall dispossessed the French and carried the settlers to Virginia. Charles I gave it up to them again. From this time the French, though repeatedly driven off, renewed their settlements, and the inhabitants of both nations experienced the usual distressing vicissitudes attendant on the frequent wars between the English and French, and peculiarly felt by the Colonists of the contending nations bordering on each other. No habitation was for any length of time safe from the flames, and no person from plunder, captivity, or death. In this hazardous situation the people of Maine continued for a long time. You will not wonder that the settlement of the country did not proceed.

In 1675, Philip's war, which affected all the Indians in New-England and embarked most of them in actual hostilities, spread its influence over the Indians of Maine, and produced among its exposed inhabitants the customary horrours. The people were few, scattered, and almost defenceless. Their brethren, in southern New-England, were too distant and too much occupied in their own defence to lend them the assistance which they needed. The Indians of Maine were too numerous to be attacked by these few Colonists with any hope of success, and too well secured in the fastnesses of an immense and unknown wilderness to be pursued with any prospect of advantage. In the subsequent wars, these Indians were so engaged in the interests of the French that they continually took their part against the English. Nor were the inhabitants finally safe from their incursions till the peace of 1763.

Another cause of the slow progress of settlement has been found in the character of the inhabitants. These, heretofore, have been chiefly lumbermen and fishermen. Both these classes are usually employed, during the mild season, in severe toil, and not a small proportion of those, belonging to both, spend the winter in idleness and dissipation. At the same time, very many of them are in great measure destitute of property through life. This is, indeed, less extensively applicable to fishermen, some of whom almost every where and most in towns distinguished for sobriety, acquire at least a comfortable living.

But those who are mere lumbermen are almost necessarily poor. Their course of life seduces them to prodigality, thoughtlessness of future wants, profaneness, irreligion, immoderate drinking, and other ruinous habits. The farmers of New-England have never willingly resided among people of such a character. In the mean time, also, other countries labouring under few of these disadvantages have offered to such as were willing to emigrate the allurements of an inviting climate and a rich soil, where lands might be obtained at prices equally moderate. The stream of colonization, once begun, is naturally continued by the tidings of success, and by the strong ties of attachment which prompt men to follow their neighbours and friends in enterprizes of this nature.

But, not withstanding this uncommon assemblage of disadvantages, the progress of population in this District has become wonderfully rapid. Since the Revolutionary war, the Government of Massachusetts has ordered it to be explored by men of understanding and integrity, and a great part of it to be surveyed and to be divided into regular townships. It has been found that the country contains large quantities of good land, and that it is capable of furnishing a comfortable residence and sufficient rewards to well-directed industry. Not only merchants and fishermen, but substantial farmers have planted themselves in this District, and in great numbers. By these men agriculture is pursued with new industry, skill, and success. Settlements are extensively spread over the interiour; particularly on the borders of the numerous rivers, as well as along the coast. Business of every kind is carried on with an energy which here was never before seen, and with a prosperity which has outrun the most sanguine expectations. In the year 1790 this District contained 96,440 inhabitants. In the year 1800 they were increased to 151,719; and in 1810, to 228,705. Its population is, therefore, ultimately secured, and all those parts of it which are fitted to become a comfortable residence for mankind will, within a moderate period, be probably filled with inhabitants.

GEORGE F. EMERY
1817–1904

The idea of separating the District of Maine from the Commonwealth of Massachusetts first arose shortly after the Revolutionary War. In 1785 the Falmouth, Maine, *Gazette,* which favored separation, printed a notice inviting all those who supported such a move to meet and discuss the prospect. Arguments in favor of separation were based on the differing interests of the two communities, on Maine's distance from the seat of government in Massachusetts, including the courts, and on inequities in trade regulations, taxation, and representation.

The government of Massachusetts was initially opposed to the prospect of independence for Maine. Governor James Bowdoin called it "a design against the Commonwealth of very evil tendency, being calculated for the purpose of effecting the dismemberment of it." For more personal reasons, opposition also surfaced on the part of those Maine men who felt that their commercial interests might be ill served by separation and by some state and county officials who saw their jobs in jeopardy should a new government be formed.

Although these early stirrings of independence came to naught, the pressure was felt by Massachusetts, which responded by passing several laws designed to allay some of the Mainers' discontents. By 1815, Massachusetts' attitude toward separation had changed for political reasons. Many Massachusetts Federalists feared that the growth of the Democratic party in the District of Maine would threaten the Federalist party's control of Massachusetts.

By 1816 the controversy had begun to heat up. On the one side, coastal trade was going to be complicated by customs laws if separation prevailed, support of private education was expected to suffer, and the availability of good men to govern a new state was questioned. On the other, it was claimed that Maine could indeed govern itself — and at no greater expense than as part of Massachusetts, that an independent state would be free of the perceived inequities of Massachusetts rule, and that taxation and education would improve for families in Maine.

The convention held to decide this issue was a contentious one. Voting records were challenged, suppressed, and even destroyed. Finally, in 1819, the previously fragmented support for separation coalesced, and a majority vote at the annual election in favor of separation assured the outcome. Maine assumed statehood on March 15, 1820.

The origin of the state's name has never been satisfactorily explained. Its official use dates from 1622, when a land grant to Sir Ferdinando Gorges referred to the "Province of Maine." This use was reinforced in 1778 by Congress, which named the three eastern counties of Massachusetts (including the Province of Maine) the District of Maine.

Governor Joshua Chamberlain, in 1876, said that the early belief that the state was named in honor of Queen Henrietta Maria's connection with the Province of Maine in France was probably inaccurate. Her ties with the French Maine were disputed, and she did not become the consort of England's Charles I until several years after the use of "Maine" in these parts.

The most likely theory is the differentiation made by early explorers between the islands they met with along the coast and the *main,* or mainland. References to "the Maine" or "Mayne" appear as early as 1603 in the journals of Captain Martin Pring and 1605 in Rosier's account. In any event, the delegation gathered to plan for the new state found itself charged with determining once and for all the name of this great land mass.

These men who assembled in October of 1819 primarily to write a constitution for the new state were like any other committee trying to solve a problem: earnest, but often contentious and occasionally testy. Signs of this first appeared when the men disagreed about whether they should appoint a subcommittee to determine a name for the state while the main body of the convention worked on the problem of writing a constitution. A Mr. Whitman expressed the concern that it appeared to be a great absurdity to form a constitution for a state until a name had been given to it: he would christen the child before it was born. His sentiments prevailed, and soon the

#191

Capital Speculation for Industrious Farmers.

PROPOSALS FOR SETTLING A FINE
Township of Land in Massachusetts.

HAVING recently purchased of the Commonwealth of Massachusetts, whose warrantee I hold, a Tract of Land, containing about thirty thousand acres; I am desirous of having it settled by sober, industrious citizens, on the most liberal and beneficial terms to them.

This tract is lotted out in 100 acre lots. It is situated in nearly the centre of the State of Massachusetts, about 130 miles from Boston, 50 from Portland, the capital of Maine, and about 80 from Portsmouth, the capital of New-Hampshire. The *Saco* River runs near the land; which conducts to one of the best markets for produce, particularly *Lumber*, in New-England. The Land is surrounded by the well settled, prosperous, incorporated towns of Lovell, Waterford, Albany, Bethel, Gilead, and Chatham.

The soil is of the best quality, heavily timbered with the oak, maple, pine, beach, and birch trees. It is intersected by numerous rivulets of the purest water, many of them capable of turning water mills, machinery, &c. The cleared lands will produce, with little labor, the finest *wheat*, rye, oats, barley, and other grains; vegetables of all kinds, particularly potatoes of the best quality; and plenty of hay. No part of America is better calculated for a grazing country. There are now twenty-five families settled on the land.

Pot and Pearl Ashes can be manufactured in great abundance, from the ashes made in clearing up the lands, and at seasons when the business of farming is at a stand. These ashes will be received in payment for the land; and an industrious farmer would be enabled to produce enough of this valuable article to pay for his lands within the periods of credit, which will be given him.

Conditions of sale, from one to three dollars per acre, according to quality; and payment to be made in one, two and three years.

Inquire of RICHARD BACHELDER, on the premises; or of
JOSIAH BACHELDER, Boston.

April, 1818.

From
J H Drummond 2 X Vol 77

Broadside to attract settlers

subcommittee was formed and found itself wrestling with surprising problems of nomenclature and phraseology. Alternatives to "the State of Maine" were presented, argued, and ultimately rejected. Just when it seemed as if all these problems were resolved, a late dissenter came forth with the suggestion of "Ligonia," the name of a 1630 land grant to Gorges, so called for his mother's family, Lygon. This notion was quickly and firmly suppressed, and the State of Maine was so named.

This report of the committee's deliberations comes from a paper based on Perley's debates, written by the Honorable George F. Emery, which was read before the Maine Historical Society in 1890.

Our State Christening

The convention for framing our constitution met at Portland, October 11, 1819. On the second day of its session Preble of Portland, afterward judge, offered a resolution to raise a committee to report a proper style and title for the new state, prefaced by remarks to the effect that the law required this of the convention, while the previous resolutions for a committee to frame the constitution, which might or might not be adopted by the people, did not meet the necessity. . . .

Mr. Preble felt it his duty to further explain his reasons, his object being to expedite business, indicating that a variety of opinions prevailed as to the name, and that the subject could be discussed in convention and decided while the committee on the constitution was at work and thus save time, which, if not to members, was money to their constituents. He also suggested nine as the proper number for the committee, one from each county. . . .

A vote was taken and the resolution for a committee of nine was adopted. In the afternoon the names of all the committees were announced, that on the style and title of the new state being Preble of Portland, Allen of Sanford, Wood of Wiscasset, Cutler of Farmington, Stetson of Hampden, Abbott of Castine, Chandler of Paris, French of St. Albans, and Vance of Calais. On the next day came in the report of "an ordinance" to determine the title as "The Commonwealth of Maine," which was assigned for the next day for consideration.

October 14: Judge Thacher moved postponement of the consideration of the subject until the committee on constitution could be present. Mr. Preble again let the gaze of a vigilant constituency in upon the convention, and urged immediate action, to save time, and carried his point again by adverting to the expenses incurred by the convention, which he affirmed were little less than five thousand dollars per week.

Mr. Moody of Hallowell moved acceptance of the report.

Mr. Parsons of Edgecomb moved to substitute "state" for "commonwealth" on account of saving time and expense in printing.

Mr. Allen of Sanford seconded that motion.

Mr. Wallingford of Wells thought "state" preferable to "commonwealth," the former being the common designation, and there being no provision for admitting commonwealths into the Union.

Mr. Cutler of Farmington explained why the committee adopted "commonwealth," by remarking that custom had made it more congenial to our feelings, and we felt a kind of pride in that designation.

Mr. Preble gave as an additional reason, which had weight with the committee, that mistakes would be likely to occur, in view of the fact of the long use of "commonwealth" in legal papers. He also thought "commonwealth" indicated our civil polity, that it belongs to us as much as to Massachusetts, was a name of the revolution, and the title was more respectable than "state."

Mr. Adams of Gorham hoped the motion to strike out "commonwealth" would not prevail. That title sounded better than "state."

Judge Cony of Augusta favored "commonwealth." He looked with veneration on the men who formed the Massachusetts convention — was not much in favor of "Maine," but was decidedly so of "commonwealth."

Judge Thacher did not think the matter of great importance, but rather preferred "state" on the score of brevity, a consideration which had led to the change of the names of Pepperelborough to Saco, and Pownalborough to Dresden.

Mr. Wallingford replied to Mr. Preble's suggestion as to liability to mistakes by saying we should be as likely to make them in writing "Massachusetts" as "state."

The motion to strike out "commonwealth" prevailed, one hundred and nineteen to one hundred and thirteen. "State" was then inserted in lieu thereof.

Mr. Tucker of Standish moved to strike out "Maine" for the purpose of inserting "Columbus."

Mr. Vance of Calais objected, "Maine is the name by which we are known in this country and in Europe. All our maps, or plans and records have that name, as the designation of the territory. If altered

half a century would be required to make a new name equally familiar. It is suitable to retain Maine, because for many purposes we shall
be the main state of the union."

October 15: the subject was resumed.

Judge Cony was impelled "by a view of consecrating the opening
era of the new community by rendering an act of justice long delayed," to propose as a substitute the name of Columbus. By the
successful usurpation of a mercantile adventurer, a Venetian manu-
facturer of maps and charts, the real discoverer of the new world had
been defrauded of the glory which was his due, of affixing his own
name to the Western continent. "Sir, what idea either great or distinguished can we affix to Maine? I have not been able to trace it to any
satisfactory source; but, Sir, the name of Columbus is associated with
all that is noble, all that persevering fortitude or manly virtue could
bestow or bequeath. The success of his voyage of discovery stamped
immortality on his name. On such a name the mind will always
delight to contemplate and will repose with satisfaction. The eleventh
of October, the day on which this convention commenced its session,
was the anniversary of that on which Columbus first discovered signs
of land, which the dawn of the following morning fully confirmed."
Judge Cony also alluded to the late ordinance of Congress, by which
the new national ships of the line were to be named after the different
states, in the process of which the turn of Maine would come late;
but, already, he said, the finest ship in the navy bore the name of
Columbus, and after the lapse of a few years it would be supposed
she was christened for our state. The question however, he considered, was very much a matter of taste and feeling.

Judge Thacher agreeing with Shakespeare, observed "that as
names of things were but sounds or words, they hardly afforded
grounds or data for much argument *a priori* in favor of one over
another." He felt very little preference on that account. The name of
Columbus was about as grateful to his ear as that of Maine, but he
did not perceive any good reason for the alteration. The territory
now to be made a new state and about to take the rank of a nation
abroad, is already well known in the commercial world by the name
of Maine, which was a good reason with him for adhering to it. The
district of Maine is probably as well known among foreign nations as
the state of Vermont, which has no commercial interest and connections and is rather regarded as a settlement in the wilderness. To give
the new state any other name than that by which its territory and
district have always been known, would tend to introduce some

uncertainty in the opinions of foreigners respecting its geographical position, at least for a time. He doubted whether the name of Columbus was much known in general throughout the Old Continent and, if his name was mentioned in the seaports of the nation under whose flag he made his discoveries, it is doubtful whether many would know much about him or where his discoveries were, and the probability is that application must be made to some antiquarian to get information. Columbus is more known and more frequently spoken of in the United States than any where else. He was not disposed to deprive old Columbus of any honors, but he did not think that it was among them to give a name to the state of Maine. Columbus did not discover this part of the continent, nor did he know as long as he lived that the continent he discovered extended to these latitudes. This country was first discovered by Cabot, Gosnold, and others. Abroad the name of Columbus would be more naturally associated with some part of South America or, perhaps, with the Columbia river far beyond the Mississippi, on the western shores of the continent. He wished not to break up and derange the associations that time and business have well fixed in people's minds. The district of Maine is everywhere known as to its situation, commerce and products, and the state of Maine will naturally take its place in the human mind. The mind has regular laws of association as the material world has its laws of gravity, attraction, etc., and these associations were as liable to be disturbed and broken as the elements were to convulsion and tempests. He expressed the wish that his worthy friend, Dr. Cony, whose age was about the same as his own, might have the pleasure with himself of passing the remainder of their days, in peace and tranquility, under the old name of Maine.

The motion to substitute Columbus for Maine was lost. . . .

This was supposed to have finally closed all controversy on the subject. But it turned out otherwise. Upon the coming in of the report of the committee to draft the constitution, a blank had been left for inserting the name of the state, which Mr. Holmes of Alfred, its chairman, moved to have supplied by filling it with "state of Maine" agreeably to the former vote of the convention.

Mr. Whitman of Portland begged this, his first opportunity, to enter his dissent to the name now suggested, saying though familiar to us it was not so abroad. He then proposed a name derived from a territory once comprehending a considerable part of Maine and therefore not new or arbitrary, one well sounding and respectable to wit, Ligonia.

Judge Bridge observed that the committee on the constitution did not think it within their province to discuss the subject, which had been specially committed to another committee.

Judge Greene thought the gentleman from Portland entirely out of order. A committee charged with the subject had made their report; nearly an entire day had been consumed in the discussion, after members of the committee on the constitution had been notified to be, and a large part of whom had been, present, and if anything had been done by the convention, this question had been settled.

After further remarks by Mr. Holmes in support of his motion, the blank was ordered to be filled with the title and style of "State of Maine," and probably for all time.

THE YEARS BEFORE
THE CIVIL WAR

NATHANIEL HAWTHORNE
1804–1864

In our national literature Nathaniel Hawthorne will always be the supreme novelist of New England, identified with that region as closely as Faulkner, in our time, is identified with the South. We especially associate him with novels and stories that center on the dark, guilt-ridden lives of the Puritans and their descendants. Hawthorne is our first psychological novelist. In his preface to *The House of the Seven Gables,* he describes his literary purpose as a search for "the truth of the human heart."

But there is another Hawthorne, less well known to modern readers. He is Hawthorne the journalist, the essayist, the writer of a winning president's campaign biography and other political sketches. Until late middle age, Hawthorne had to live by his workaday pen. He early became the master of a clear, direct prose that could serve any publishing opportunity that opened to him. Besides his published prose, he always kept a writer's notebook, and it is as a diarist that he wrote his most interesting pages about Maine.

The District of Maine played a large role in Hawthorne's boyhood. It was his second home. Salem was his first. His father, Captain Nathaniel Hawthorne, a globe-traveling ship's captain in the years of Salem's maritime prosperity, died in Surinam, Dutch Guyana, when his son was four years old. Hawthorne's mother and her three young children moved back into her family home in Salem and became dependents. Robert Manning, her prosperous older brother, owned a stage company with lines all over New England and had invested in Maine lands around Sebago Lake. He was the Hawthorne family's financial mainstay, and for three years they lived in a house owned by him in Raymond, Maine, then a raw new town on the edge of a forest wilderness. From his twelfth to his fifteenth year Hawthorne

HALLOWELL, AUGUSTA & BANGOR

MAIL STAGE.

THE Hallowell, Augusta and Bangor *Mail Stage* will leave Hallowell every *Thursday* at 3 o'clock, A. M. Passes through Augusta, Vassalborough, China, Albion, Unity, Joy, Dixmont, Newburg, Hampden, and arrives at Bangor same day at 6 o'clock, P. M.—leave Augusta every *Sunday* and *Tuesday* at 3 o'clock, A. M. and arrive at Bangor same days at 6 o'clock, P. M.

Returning, leave Bangor for Augusta every *Monday* and *Friday* at 3 o'clock, A. M. and arrive at Augusta same days at 6 o'clock, P. M.— Leave Bangor for Augusta and Hallowell every *Wednesday* at 3 o'clock, A. M. and arrive at Hallowell same day at 6 o'clock, P. M.

Stage Books kept at CHICK'S *Maine Coffee House*, Bangor, at HAMLEN'S *Kennebec & Stage Tavern*, Augusta, and at DILLINGHAM'S *Washington Hotel*, Hallowell.

The Proprietors of the above line, inform the public, that they will not be accountable for any Baggage, unless the fare is paid and the same entered on the Way Bill.

BURLEY & ARNOLD.

Bangor, Jan. 30, 1826.

Advertisement for the mail stage

lived in Raymond with his mother and two sisters like, he said later, "a bird in the air." He called them the happiest years of his life.

After Raymond and two years of schooling in Salem he entered Bowdoin College in 1821 with a remarkable group of young men. His class had thirty-eight members; twelve of them attained national recognition before they were middle-aged. We meet two of his up and coming classmates, Horatio Bridge and Jonathan Cilley, in the following journal pages.

In the summer of 1837, twelve years after leaving college, Hawthorne made a month's visit to Maine. His accomplishments during these years did not invite happy comparisons with the attainments of his two fortunate classmates. After graduation he had gone back to his mother's house and committed his days to writing fiction. He had not much to show for his labors: a melodramatic novel of college life, *Fanshawe*, published at his own expense — and so bad, he soon decided, that he made all his friends promise to burn the copies he had given them — and beyond that, more than forty "tales," some published in magazines, that no publisher would take a chance on.

Then, in 1836, his Bowdoin classmate Horatio Bridge, from Augusta, who believed in Hawthorne's talent, offered a Boston publisher $250 to insure him against loss if he would publish Hawthorne's first book, *Twice-Told Tales*. The book was a success. Bridge's money wasn't needed. In July 1837 Hawthorne was coming to Augusta to thank his benefactor.

After his visit with Bridge, Hawthorne moved on to Thomaston to visit Jonathan Cilley, who had just been elected to his first term in Congress. He did not serve long. Seven months after their reunion, which is described here, Cilley was challenged by a Kentucky congressman to a duel with rifles and was killed.

Hawthorne Visits Two Friends in Maine

Wednesday, July 5, 1837 [Augusta]

Here I am settled, since night before last, with Bridge, and living very singularly. He leads a bachelor-life in his paternal mansion, only a small part of which is occupied by a family who do his washing, make the beds, &c. He provides his own breakfast and supper, and occasionally his dinner; though this is oftener, I believe, taken at the hotel or an eating house, or with some of his relatives. I am his guest, and my presence makes no alteration in his way of life. Our fare, thus far, has consisted of bread, butter, and cheese, crackers, herrings, boiled eggs, coffee, milk and claret wine, besides a plentiful variety of liquors, should we desire them. He has another inmate in the person of a queer little Frenchman, who has his breakfast, tea, and lodging here, and finds his dinner elsewhere. Monsieur Schaeffer does not appear to be more than twenty-one years old — a diminutive figure, with eyes askew, and otherwise of ungainly physiognomy; he is ill-dressed also, in a coarse blue coat, thin cotton pantaloons, and unbrushed boots; altogether with as little of French coxcombry as can well be imagined; though with something of the monkey-aspect inseparable from a little Frenchman. He is, nevertheless, an intelligent and well-informed man, apparently of extensive reading in his own language; a philosopher, Bridge tells me, and an infidel. His insignificant personal appearance stands in the way of his success, and prevents him from receiving the respect which is really due his talents and acquirements; wherefore he is bitterly dissatisfied with the country and its inhabitants, and often expresses his feelings to Bridge (who has gained his confidence to a certain degree) in very strong terms.

Then here are three characters, each with something out of the common way, living together somewhat like monks. Bridge, our host, combines more high and admirable qualities, of that sort which make up a gentleman, than any other that I have met with. Polished, yet natural, frank, open and straightforward, yet with a delicate feeling for the sensitiveness of his companions; of excellent temper and warm heart; well-acquainted with the world, with keen faculty of observation which he has had many opportunities of exercising . . . and never varying from a code of honor and principle, which is really nice and rigid in its way. There is a sort of philosophy developing itself in him, which will not improbably cause him to settle down in this, or some other equally singular course of life. He seems almost to have made up his mind not to marry — which I wonder at; for he has strong affections, and is fond of both women and children. . . .

Then here is myself, who am likewise a queer character in my way, and have come here to spend a week or two with my friend of half a life-time; — the longest space, probably, that we are ever destined to spend together; for fate seems to be preparing changes for both of us. My circumstances, at least, cannot long continue as they are and have been; and Bridge, too, stands between high prosperity and utter ruin.

I think I should become strongly attached to our way of life — so independent, and untroubled by the forms and restrictions of society.

"Oaklands"

The house is very pleasantly situated — half a mile distant from where the town begins to be thickly-settled, and on a swell of land, with the road running at a distance of fifty yards, and a grassy tract and a gravel walk between. Beyond the road rolls the Kennebec, here two or three hundred yards wide; putting my head out of the window, I can see it flowing steadily along, straightway between wooded banks; but arriving nearly opposite the house, there is a large and level sand island in the middle of the stream; and just below this island, the current is further interrupted by the works of the Mill Dam, which is perhaps half-finished, yet still in so rude a shape, that it looks as much like the ruins of a Dam destroyed by the spring freshets, as like the foundation of a Dam yet to be. Irishmen and Canadians are at work on it, and the echoes of their hammering and their voices, come across the river and up to the window. Then there is a sound of the wind among the trees round the house; and when that is silent, the calm, full distant voice of the river becomes audible. . . .

I have not seen much of the people; there have been, however, several incidents which amused me, though scarcely worth telling. A passionate tavern-keeper, quick as a flash of gunpowder, a nervous man, and showing in his demeanor, it seems, a consciousness of his infirmity of temper. I was a witness to a scuffle of his with a drunken guest; the tavern-keeper, after they were separated, raved like a madman, and in a tone of voice having a queerly pathetic or lamentable sound mingled with its rage, as if he were lifting up his voice to weep. Then he jumped into a chaise which was standing by, whipped up the horse and drove off rapidly; as if to give his rage vent in this way.

On the morning of the fourth of July, two printer's apprentices, lads nearly grown, dressed in jackets and very tight pantaloons of check — tight as their skins; so that they looked like harlequins or circus clowns, yet appeared to think themselves in perfect propriety — a very calm and quiet assurance of the admiration of the town. A common fellow, a carpenter, who, on the strength of partisanship, asked Bridge's assistance in cutting out great letters from play-bills &c., in order to print Martin Van Buren Forever, on a flag; — but Bridge refused. "Let every man skin his own skunks," says he. Bridge seems to be considerably of a favorite with the lower orders, especially with the Irishmen and the French Canadians, the latter accosting him in the street to ask his assistance as an interpreter, in making their bargains for work. . . .

Sunday, July 9, 1837

With Bridge to pay another visit to the shanties of the Irish and the Canadians. He says they will sell and exchange these small houses among themselves continually. They may be built in three or four days, and are valued at four or five dollars. When the turf, that is piled against the walls of some of them, becomes covered with grass and white, it makes quite a picturesque object. It was about dusk — just candlelighting time — when we visited them. A young Frenchwoman, with a baby in her arms, came to the door of one of them, smiling and looking pretty and happy. Her husband, a dark, black-haired, lively little fellow, caressed the child, laughing and singing to it; and there was a red-headed Irishman, who likewise fondled the little brat. Then we could hear them within the hut, gabbling merrily, and could see them moving about briskly in the candlelight, through the window and open door. The old Irish woman . . . sat in the door of a hut, under the influence of an extra dose of rum — she being an old lady of somewhat dissipated habits. She called to Bridge, and began to talk with him about her resolution not to give up her house; for it is his design to get her out of it. She is a true virago, and although somewhat restrained by respect for him, she evinced a sturdy design to remain here through the winter, or at least for a considerable time longer. He persisting — she took her stand in the doorways of the hut, and stretched out her fist, in a very amazonian attitude — "Nobody," quoth she, "shall drive me out of this house, till my praties [potatoes] are out of the ground." Then she would wheedle and laugh, and blarney, beginning in a rage and ending as if she had been in jest. Meanwhile her husband — or the man who passes for such — stood by, very quiet, occasionally trying to still her; but it is to be presumed that, after our departure, they came to blows; it being a custom with the Irish husbands and wives to settle their disputes by blows; and it is said that the woman often proves the better man. The different families often have bitter battles; and occasionally the Irish fight with the Canadians. The latter, however, are much the most peaceable, never quarreling among themselves, and seldom with their neighbors. They are frugal and thrifty, and often go back to Canada with considerable sums of money. Bridge has gained much influence both with the Irish and the French — with the latter, by dint of speaking to them in their own language. He is the umpire in their disputes, their adviser, and they look up to him as a protector and a patron-friend. I have been struck to see with what careful integrity and wisdom he manages matters among them — having hitherto only known him as a free and wild young man. He appears perfectly to understand their general character; of which he gives no very flattering description. In these huts, less than twenty feet square perhaps, he tells me that upwards of twenty people, male and female, have sometimes been lodged.

Tuesday, July 11, 1837

A ride with Bridge to Hallowell yesterday, where we dined, and afterwards to Gardiner. The most curious object in the latter place was the elegant new mansion of Robert Hallowell Gardiner. It stands on the site of his former dwelling, which was destroyed by fire. The new building was estimated, I believe, to cost about thirty thousand dollars; but twice as much has been expended, and a great deal more will be required to complete it. It is certainly a splendid structure; the material, granite from the vicinity. At the angles, it has small circular towers; the portal is lofty and imposing; relatively to the general style of domestic architecture in our country, it well deserves the name of a castle or a palace. Its situation, too, is fine, far retired from the public road, and obtainable by a winding carriage road, standing amid fertile fields, and with large trees in the vicinity. There is also a beautiful view from the mansion adown the Kennebec. Nevertheless, this new palace, with all the fresh dust of the stone cutting and the freshness of the quarry about it, conveys an impression quite as sad as could be produced by the most venerable ruin in Old England. The projector has undertaken a business beyond his proper means, and unsuited to the situation of our country. Having been deeply engaged in land speculations, his splendid fortune has been put in great hazard, and probably much diminished. He is hard pressed for money; and some doubts are expressed whether he will be able to pay his debts. The work on the new house is at a standstill for want of funds. Should he ever finish it, it will be too splendid a residence for his impaired fortunes; and when his estate shall be divided among his children, this mansion, estimated at its cost, will be more than the share of any one of them, leaving nothing to support the expenses of such a style of living. This subject offers hints of copious reflection, in reference to the indulgence of aristocratic pomp among democratic institutions. The doorway and the lofty windows of the house were closed up with rough boards, with the exception of one or two chambers, which appeared to be furnished, probably for the residence of Mr. Gardiner's son, who must feel somewhat melancholy, amid the abortive efforts of his father's vanity. The old gentleman — nor the young one for that matter — will never enjoy a single thrill of exultation within these spacious halls; on the contrary, it must already have become a humiliating and hateful idea to him; it has rendered him an object of pity to the public; and the edifice is like to be known by the name of Gardiner's Folly, for centuries to come. If it were in the vicinity of a large city, it might be converted into a summer hotel; but standing where it does, I do not exactly see what can be done with it. It will perhaps be sold, for ten thousand dollars or so, to some Boston merchant, to be his pleasure house for a few weeks of the summer, and desolate all the rest of the year. Or possibly an ordinary farmer or country squire may find it within his means to become master of this abortive magnificence; though such persons would prefer a white-painted, green blinded, two story house, close to the dusty highway. Beneath some of the large trees, we saw the remains of circular seats, where the family used to sit before the former house was burned down. There was nobody now in the vicinity of the place, save one man and a yoke of oxen; and what he was about I did not ascertain. Mr. Gardiner at present resides in a small house, little more than a cottage, beside the main road, not far from the gateway which gives access to his palace. . . .

On the road from Hallowell to Augusta, we saw little booths, in two places, erected on the roadside, where boys offered beer, apples &c for sale. Passed an Irish woman with a child in her arms, and a heavy bundle, and afterwards an Irishman, with a lighter bundle, sitting by the roadside. They were husband and wife; and Bridge says that an Irishman and his wife, on their journeys, do not usually walk side by side, but that the man gives the woman the heaviest burthen to carry and himself walks on lightly a-head. A thought comes into my head; — which sort of house excites the most contemptuous feelings in the beholder — such a mansion as Mr. Gardiner's, all circumstances considered, or the board-built and turf-buttressed hovels of those wild Irish, scattered about as if they had sprung up like mushrooms in the dells and gorges, and along the banks of the river. Mushrooms, by the bye, spring up where the roots of an old tree are hidden under the ground.

Wednesday, July 26th, 1837

Dined at Barker's yesterday. Before dinner, sitting with several persons on the stoop of the tavern. There was Bridge — J. A. Chandler, clerk of the court, a dissipated man of middle age or beyond, — two or three stage people — and nearby a negro, whom they call "the doctor," a crafty looking fellow, one of whose occupations is that of a pimp. In the presence of this goodly company, a man of depressed, neglected air, a soft, simple-looking fellow, with an anxious expression, in a laborer's dress, approached and inquired for Mr. Barker. Mine host being gone to Portland, the stranger was directed to the Barkeeper, who stood at the door. The man asked where he should find one Mary Ann Russel — a question which excited general and hardly suppressed mirth; for the said Mary Ann is one of a knot of whores, who were routed on Sunday evening by Barker and a constable. The man was told that the black fellow could give him all the information he wanted. The black fellow asked "Do you want to use her?" Others of the by-standers, or by-sitters, put various questions as to the nature of the man's business with Mary Ann, and the connection between them. One asked, "Is she your daughter?" "Why, a little nearer than that I calkilate," said the poor devil. Here the mirth was increased, it being evident that the prostitute was his wife. The man seemed too simple and obtuse to comprehend much of the ridicule of his situation, or to be rendered very miserable of it. Nevertheless, he made some touching points. "A man generally places some little dependence on his wife," said he, "whether she's good or bad." He meant, probably that he rests some affection on her. He told us that she had behaved well, till committed to jail for striking a child; and I believe that he was absent from home at the time, and had not seen her since. And now he was in search of her, intending, doubtless, to do his best to get her out of her troubles, and then to take her back to his bosom. Some advised him not to look after her; others recommended him to pay "the doctor" aforesaid for guiding him to her haunt; which finally the doctor did, in consideration of a treat; and the fellow went off, having heard little but jibes, and not one word of sympathy. I would have given considerable to witness his meeting with his wife. On the whole there was a moral picturesqueness in the contrasts of this scene — a man moved as deeply as his nature would permit, in the midst of hardened, gibing spectators, heartless toward him. It is worth thinking over and studying out. He seemed rather hurt and pricked by the jests thrown at him, yet bore it patiently, and sometimes almost joined in the laugh. He was cowed by his situation; being of an easy, unenergetic nature.

Friday, July 28th, 1837

Saw my classmate, and formerly intimate associate, Cilley, for the first time since we graduated. He has met with good success in life, and that in spite of circumstance, having struggled upward against bitter opposition, by the force of his own abilities, to be a member of Congress, after having been some time the leader of his party in the state legislature. We met like old friends, and conversed almost as freely as we used to in College days, twelve years ago and more. He is a singular man, shrewd, crafty, insinuating, with wonderful tact, seizing on each man by his manageable point, and using him for his own purposes, often without the man's suspecting that he is made a tool of; and yet, artificial as his character would seem to be, his conversation, at least to myself, was full of natural feeling, the expression of which can hardly be mistaken; and his revelations with regard to himself had really a great deal of frankness. He spoke of his ambition; of the obstacles which he had encountered; of the means by which he had overcome them, imputing great efficacy to his personal intercourse with people, and study of their characters; then of his course as a member of the legislature and speaker, and of his style of speaking and its effects; of the dishonorable things which had been imputed to him, and in what manner he had repelled the charges; in short, he would have seemed to have opened himself very freely as to his public life. Then as to private affairs, he spoke of his marriage, of his wife, his children, and told me with tears in his eyes of the death of a dear little girl, and how it had affected him, and how impossible it had been for him to believe that she was really to die. A man of the most open nature might well have been more reserved to a friend, after twelve years separation, than Cilley was to me. Nevertheless he is really a crafty man, concealing like a murder-secret, anything that is not good for him to have known. He by no means feigns the good feeling that he professes, nor is there anything affected in the frankness of his conversation; and it is this that makes him so very fascinating. There is such a quantity of truth, and kindliness, and warm affections, that a man's heart opens to him in spite of himself; he deceives by truth. And not only is he crafty, but, when occasion demands, bold and fierce as a tiger, determined, and even straightforward and undisguised in his measures — a daring fellow as well as a sly one. . . . His person in some degree accords with his character — thin, and a thin face, sharp features, sallow, a projecting brow, not very high, deep-set eyes; an insinuating smile and look, when he meets you, or is about to address you. I should think he would do away this peculiar expression; for it lets out more of himself than can be detected in any other way, in personal intercourse with him. Upon the whole, I have quite a good liking for him; and mean to go to Thomaston to see him.

Saturday, August 12, 1837

Left Augusta a week ago this morning, for Thomaston. Nothing particular in our ride across the country. Fellow passenger, a Boston dry-goods dealer, travelling to collect bills; at many of the country stores, he would get out and show his unwelcome visage. In the taverns, prints from Scripture, varnished and on rollers; such as the Judgment of Christ — also a queer set of color engravings of the story of the Prodigal Son, the figure being clad in modern costume — or at least not more than a half century back. The father, a grave clerical person with a white wig and a black broadcloth suit. The son with a cocked hat and laced clothes, drinking wine out of glasses, and embracing a whore in fashionable dress &c. At Thomaston, a nice, comfortable boarding-house tavern, without a bar, or any sort of wines or spirits. An old lady from Boston, with her three daughters, one of whom was teaching music and the other two schoolmistresses.

A frank, free, mirthful daughter of the landlady, about twenty-four years old, between whom and myself there immediately sprung up a flirtation, which made us both feel rather solemncholy when we parted on Tuesday morning. She is capable, I know, of strong feelings; and her features expressed something of the kind, when we held out our hands for a parting grasp. Music in the evenings, with a song by a rather pretty, fantastic little devil of a brunette, about eighteen years old, who has married within a year, and spent last summer in a trip to the Springs and elsewhere. Her manner of walking; by jerks, with a quiver as if she were made of calves-feet jelly. I talk with everybody — to Mrs. Trott, good sense — to Mary, good sense with a mixture of fun — to Mrs. Gleason sentiment, romance, and nonsense. — Sunday, walked with Cilley to see General Knox's old mansion — a large rusty-looking edifice of wood with some grandeur in the architecture, standing on the banks of the river, close by the site of an old burial ground, and near where an ancient fort had been erected for defense against the French and the Indians. General Knox formerly owned a square of thirty miles in this part of the country; and he wished to settle it with a tenantry, after the fashion of an English gentleman. He would permit no edifices to be erected within a certain distance of his mansion. His patent covered, of course, the whole present town of Thomaston, together with Waldoboro and divers other flourishing commercial and country villages; and would have been of incalculable value, could it have remained unbroken to the present time. But the General lived in grand style, and received throngs of visitors from foreign parts; and was obliged to part with large tracts of his possessions, till now there is little left but the ruinous mansion, and the ground immediately around it. His tomb stands near the house, a spacious receptacle, an iron door, at the end of a turf-covered mound and surmounted by an obelisk of the Thomaston marble. There are inscriptions to the memory of several of his family; for he had many children, male and female, all of whom are now dead but one daughter, a widow of fifty, recently married to the Hon. John Holmes. There is a stone fence around the monument. On the outside of this are the grave-stones, and large flat tomb-stones of the ancient burial ground; the tomb-stones being of red-freestone, with vacant spaces, formerly inlaid with slate, on which were the inscriptions and perhaps coats of arms. One of these spaces was in the shape of a heart. The people of Thomaston were very wrathful that the General should have laid out his grounds over this old burial-place; and he never dared throw down the grave-stones, though his wife, a haughty English lady, often teazed him to do so. But when the old General was dead, Lady Knox, as they called her, caused them to be prostrated, as they now lie. She was a woman of violent passions, fond of gallants, and so proud an aristocrat, that, as long as she lived, she would never enter any house in Thomaston except her own. When a married daughter was sick, she used to go to her in her carriage to her door, and send up to enquire how she did. The General was personally very popular; but his wife ruled him. The house and its vicinity, and the whole tract covered by Knox's patent, may be taken as an illustration of what must be the result of American schemes of aristocracy. It is not forty years, since this house was built, and Knox was in his glory; but now the house is all in decay, while, within a stones throw of it, is a street of neat, smart, white edifices of one and two stories, occupied chiefly by thriving mechanics. But towns have grown up, where Knox probably meant to have forests and parks. On the banks of the river, where he meant to have only one wharf, for his own West-India vessels and yacht, there are two wharves, with stores and a lime-kiln. Little appertains to the mansion, except the tomb, and the old burial ground, and the old fort. The descendants are all poor; and the inheritance was merely sufficient to make a dissipated and drunken fellow of one of the old General's sons, who survived to middle age. This man's habits were as bad as possible, as long as he had any money; but when quite ruined, he reformed. The daughter, the only survivor of Knox's children (herself childless) is a mild and amiable woman, therein totally differing from her mother. Knox, when he first visited his estate, arriving in a vessel, was visited by a deputation of the squatters, who had resolved to resist him to the death. He received them with great courtesy, made them dine with him aboard their vessel, and sent them back to their constituents in great love and admiration of him. He used to have vessels running to Philadelphia, I think, and bringing him all sorts of delicacies. His way of raising money, was to give a mortgage on his estate, of a hundred thousand dollars at a time, and receive that nominal amount in goods, which he would immediately sell at auction for perhaps thirty thousand. Died by a chicken bone. . . .

The Death of Cilley

Hawthorne, after seeing his Bowdoin classmate Jonathan Cilley twelve years after their graduation, wrote of his puzzlement at trying to understand the sort of person Cilley had become. He had risen swiftly in the Maine Democratic party, becoming Speaker of the House at thirty-three. Now, at thirty-five, he had been elected to Congress. Would he become a national leader in Washington? Hawthorne doubted that he would. Cilley, he wrote, lacked real distinction as a person and there was something about him: his smile was insinuating and insincere. Hawthorne concluded that he was about as honest "as the great run of the world" and as a politician he was well equipped with certain appropriate qualities: he was ambitious and wonderfully self-confident, "as bold and fierce as a tiger," "a daring fellow as well as a sly one."

Cilley's boldness appeared early on the floor of the House. He took a prominent part in a Democratic attack on a group of Southern Whigs, led by Henry A. Wise of Virginia. As a consequence of a comment Cilley made in the debate, he found himself challenged to a duel by Congressman William J. Graves of Kentucky. The insult to Graves that lay behind the challenge was, in Cilley's words, an "absurd pretext." From the floor of the House Cilley had alluded to the low motives and character of a New York pro-Whig newspaper editor named Webb. Webb came to Washington to challenge Cilley, but the congressman ignored him. Graves, egged on by Wise of Virginia, then interpreted the insult to Webb as an insult to himself, for he had carried Webb's challenge to Cilley. Graves and Wise, his second, persisted in asking for "that satisfaction which is recognized among gentlemen" until Cilley felt he had to accept. He named rifles as the weapons. It took three exchanges of fire, at eighty yards, to bring Cilley down. In the intervals between the first shots, Cilley and his second tried to end the matter, but Graves and Wise kept the duel alive. Cilley said to his second, "They thirst for my blood."

The duel became a national sensation. Congress went into mourning for thirty days and gave Cilley a public funeral, but refused to expel the members involved. The affair also became a partisan matter. Henry Clay, the Whig presidential candidate, said that "Mr. Graves was a Kentuckian and that no Kentuckian could back out from a rifle." Andrew Jackson wrote to his successor, President Martin Van Buren, that Congress must do something "to wash out the stain of the murdered blood of Cilley from its walls." Most New Englanders deplored dueling and called Cilley's death murder, but from his pulpit the Reverend Mr. Maltby of Bangor protested honoring Cilley with a public funeral, "a man who died in the act of murder, setting at naught the laws of God and Man." The *Portland Argus* made a pointedly anti-Southern statement under the headline "Murder Most Foul": "A National Government which will not protect the Northern members of Congress in the fearless discharge of their duty is not worth preserving."

What seems apparent now in the hot political climate that surrounded the affair is that the famous duel — the last of its kind to receive national attention — was in large part an expression of the rivalry of two opposed cultures which was one of the paths that led eventually to the Civil War. Cilley had felt the regional nature of his place in history. He said to a friend, "I see into the whole affair. Webb has come here to challenge me because he, and perhaps others, think that, as I am from New England, I am to be bluffed, and Mr. Webb will proclaim himself a brave man, having obtained acknowledgment on my part that he is a gentleman and a man of honor. But they have calculated without their host. Although I know that the sentiment of New England is opposed to duelling, I am sure that my people will be better pleased if I stand the test than disgrace myself by humiliating concessions. Sir, the name I bear will never permit me to cower beneath the frown of mortal man. It is an attempt to browbeat us, and because they think that (and they think that because) I am from the East I will tamely submit."

Congressman Wise was widely attacked, especially in the North, for his seemingly vindictive handling of the duel. Later he defended himself before the House of Representatives in a florid speech that compared the cultures of New England and the South to those of the Puritans and Cavaliers who fought the English Civil War almost two centuries earlier:

> I am ready to be tried. . . . Put me at your bar and I will plead instantly. I am ready to say on the spot, I did on that occasion just what I will do again under similar circumstances. Let Puritans shudder as they may — proclaim that I belong to the class of Cavaliers,

The Honorable Jonathan Cilley

not to the Roundheads! .... You shall not taunt me. ... In the face of an approaching election, I say to my good constituents, ... If you are determined I shall not defend myself when assailed, like a true knight, do not send me to Congress, for I shall just as surely fight, if occasion is given, as you send me; and so I shall ever continue until the holy religion of the cross takes possession of my soul — which may God grant right early.

Mark Twain wrote, after the Civil War, that this taste for chivalric rhetoric on the part of some public Southerners demonstrated how the popularity of Sir Walter Scott's novels of knighthood gave patrician Southerners an image they were prepared to die for. Scott's novels, Twain said, were one of the causes of the war. These same novels must have been widely read in Maine with, presumably, no similar effect.

In Portland, a week after the duel, a printer named Withington was ready with a penny broadside.

Cilley of Maine,

MURDERED BY

GRAVES OF KENTUCKY.

Once more, kind reader, we are called
To take our pen in hand,
An awful tragedy to write,
Of Murder in our land.

The murder'd man, as we are told,
Was one from our own state :—
Cilley, the Representative,
Met with this awful fate!

'Twas from Kentucky we are told,
This bold assassin came,
A Murderer!—to his Grave will go,—
Graves is his real name.

Their Seconds are no better off,—
They are branded with the same ;
They are all Murderers, and we can
Give them no better name.

If Justice could but now take place,
They one and all would be,
Hung on a gallows by the neck—
Not only one but three.

We wish our Government would now
Take Dueling in hand,
And pass a law for to expel
This practice from our land.

This murderous practice has prevailed,
Long in the southern States ;
And many have been called to mourn
Of ancient and modern dates.

Our Northern people all disdain
This cursed practice here.
They call it honor (!) but to us
No honor doth appear.

Instead of honor, we should hold
A Murderer in disgrace.
How can a Murderer ever wish
To see a human face?

The widow's heart he fills with grief,
The orphan's eyes with tears :
Instead of giving them relief,
In their declining years.

Portland, March 3, 1838.

Their father's blood, thus spilt, will cry
For vengeance from the ground,
And God, who, from his throne on high,
Will listen to their sound.

Vengeance is his, he will repay
Despisers of his laws ;
Widows and orphans here may know
He undertakes their cause.

We often hear our people tell
Of heathen lands around,
But paralel with Duelling,
On earth cannot be found.

To see a Monster in cool blood,
Take what he never gave,
And send a fellow creature off
With malice to his grave.

Our 'southern chivalry,' you know,
Will never bear a word ;
But next a challenge you must take—
To meet them with the sword.

And if by chance they have the luck
To bring you to the ground,
They think their honor is redressed,
And then their praise will sound.

But all such honor you will find,
Will end in deep disgrace ;
And all such vagabonds as these
should be hissed (?) from the place.

They call it honor, but we think,
It cannot be denied
By any but a heathen, that
'Tis vanity and pride.

We now shall end this tragedy ;
But bear it in your mind,
We have not had a chance before
To write one of this kind.

We hope our friends will all forgive
The errors we have made,
And give a trifle for to help
The printer in his trade.

WITHINGTON.

Broadside about the death of Cilley

HENRY WADSWORTH LONGFELLOW
1807–1882

Maine gave to the literary world in the middle of the nineteenth century the most popular poet in modern history. As Henry Wadsworth Longfellow approached his last years, his Boston publisher, James T. Fields, described his international popularity in these terms:

> At present his currency in Europe is almost unparalleled. Twenty-four publishing houses in England have issued the whole or part of his works. Many of his poems have been translated into Russian and Hebrew. "Evangeline" has been translated three times into German, and "Hiawatha" has not only gone into nearly all the modern languages, but can now be read in Latin. I have seen translations of all Longfellow's principal works, in prose and poetry, in French, Italian, German, Spanish, Portuguese, Dutch, Swedish, and Danish. The Emperor of Brazil has himself translated and published "Robert of Sicily," one of the poems in *Tales of a Wayside Inn,* in his native tongue, and in China they use a fan which has become immensely popular on account of "A Psalm of Life" being printed on it in the language of the Celestial Empire. Professor Kneeland, who went to the national millennial celebration in Iceland, told me that when he was leaving that far-away land, on the verge almost of the Arctic Circle, the people said to him: "Tell Longfellow that we love him; tell him that we read and rejoice in his poems; tell him that Iceland knows him by heart." Today there is no disputing the fact that Longfellow is more popular than any other living poet.

The stories about Longfellow's celebrity abound. He wrote to James and Annie Fields from his shrinelike house in Cambridge: "A stranger called here and asked if Shakespeare lived in this neighborhood. I told him I knew no such person. Do you?" When his son was severely wounded in the Civil War, he went to a Washington hospital to find him. Arriving at the Washington railroad station, he found a "rough-looking officer" walking on the platform who kept looking at him. At last the man came up to Longfellow and said, "Is this Professor Longfellow? It was I who translated 'Hiawatha' into Russian. I have come to this country to fight for the Union."

Longfellow was America's first professional poet. His poetry not only supported him, it made him wealthy. He was entirely in tune with the common tastes of an extraordinarily wide public and was happy to meet their expectations by writing a various and consistent body of work. "The natural tendency of poetry," he wrote, "is to give us correct moral impressions." The poet himself, he said, was born to serve "a highly specialized function," by which he meant that he must speak from a place apart from the crowd and the real world and so be able to fulfill his tribal mission, to entertain, instruct, and encourage. Longfellow never published a personal love poem, nor — except for *Poems of Slavery,* written at the request of his abolitionist friend Charles Sumner — a poem about a contemporary public issue. His favorite subject matter was a carefully selected piece of the romantic past, from Europe as well as from America.

In his most productive years, between 1845 and 1863, Longfellow wrote "Evangeline," "The Song of Hiawatha," "The Courtship of Miles Standish," and *Tales of a Wayside Inn,* those narrative poems that gave America a new poetic tradition and gave Europe the clear evidence that America had indeed produced a poet. When Longfellow reached his seventy-fifth birthday in 1882, every schoolhouse across the land celebrated it with him. Before he died he was already an immortal in high school English classes. But young Americans then and for decades to come would have been surprised to discover that Longfellow had indeed written their favorite poems from a place apart from their America. In his journal for June 4, 1846, he had written, "In truth it must be spoken and recorded — that this is a dreadful country for a poet to live in. Lethal, deadly influences hang over him, the very 'Deadly Nightshade' of song. Many poets' souls there are here, and many lovers of song; but life in its ways and ends is prosaic in this country to the last degree."

Longfellow's work has not lasted so well as that of other nineteenth-century poets who were less "romantic" than he, that is, those who would not have said that America's worst fault was that it was "prosaic." But if twentieth-century critics have seen him as a minor figure who had no original thoughts, whose "passions" were sentiments merely, who showed no signs that he had ever struggled with difficult moral questions, there was still room left to admire his great gifts for formal verse. Longfellow was an excellent narrative poet. His skill in the long poems can best be enjoyed in his famous descriptive and narrative passages that carry the reader along so simply and clearly that he gives no thought or credit to their art. Since Longfellow was not a clever man, he was not afraid of simplicity, and often used it to great effect. His most memorable public verses, the stanzas that conclude "The Building of the Ship," were written twelve years before the Civil War. During the war a visitor recited them to Lincoln in the White House. The visitor reported that "As he listened to the last lines his eyes filled with tears, and his cheeks were wet. He did not speak for some minutes, but finally said with simplicity: 'It is a wonderful gift to be able to stir men like that.' "

Longfellow's beautiful poem "My Lost Youth," about growing up in Portland during Portland's youth, is his finest legacy to the people of Maine. He was not a nature poet, but the symbolic use of the sea and the seashore that stayed in his poetry must have been remembered from Maine. Though his grandfather and father were Harvard graduates, his family's loyalty to the District of Maine sent him to Bowdoin, the new college in Brunswick, in 1822, where he was in the same class as Nathaniel Hawthorne. His meditative poem on that class's fiftieth reunion, "Morituri Salutamus," is a fine Victorian poem.

My Lost Youth

Often I think of the beautiful town
    That is seated by the sea;
Often in thought go up and down
The pleasant streets of that dear old town,
    And my youth comes back to me.
    And a verse of a Lapland song
    Is haunting my memory still:

"A boy's will is the wind's will,
And the thoughts of youth are long, long thoughts."

I can see the shadowy lines of its trees,
    And catch, in sudden gleams,
The sheen of the far-surrounding seas,
And islands that were the Hesperides
    Of all my boyish dreams.
    And the burden of that old song,
    It murmurs and whispers still:
    "A boy's will is the wind's will,
And the thoughts of youth are long, long thoughts."

I remember the black wharves and the slips,
    And the sea-tides tossing free;
And Spanish sailors with bearded lips,
And the beauty and mystery of the ships,
    And the magic of the sea.
    And the voice of that wayward song,
    Is singing and saying still:
    "A boy's will is the wind's will,
And the thoughts of youth are long, long thoughts."

I remember the bulwarks by the shore,
    And the fort upon the hill;
And the sunrise gun, with its hollow roar,
The drum-beat repeated o'er and o'er,
    And the bugle wild and shrill.
    And the music of that old song
    Throbs in my memory still:
    "A boy's will is the wind's will.
And the thoughts of youth are long, long thoughts."

I remember the sea-fight far away,
    How it thundered o'er the tide!
And the dead captains as they lay
In their graves, o'erlooking the tranquil bay
    Where they in battle died.
    And the sound of that mournful song
    Goes through me with a thrill:

"A boy's will is the wind's will,
And the thoughts of youth are long, long thoughts."

I can see the breezy dome of groves,
   The shadows of Deering's Woods;
And the friendships old and the early loves
Come back with a Sabbath sound, as of doves
   In quiet neighborhoods.
   And the verse of that old sweet song,
   It flutters and murmurs still:
   "A boy's will is the wind's will,
And the thoughts of youth are long, long thoughts."

I remember the gleams and the glooms that dart
   Across the school-boy's brain;
The song and the silence in the heart,
That in part are prophecies, and in part
   Are longings wild and vain.
   And the voice of that fitful song
   Sings on, and is never still:
   "A boy's will is the wind's will,
And the thoughts of youth are long, long thoughts."

There are things of which I may not speak;
   There are dreams that cannot die;
There are thoughts that make the strong heart weak,
And bring a pallor to the cheek,
   And a mist before the eye.
   And the words of that fatal song
   Come over me like a chill:
   "A boy's will is the wind's will,
And the thoughts of youth are long, long thoughts."

Strange to me now are the forms I meet
   When I visit the dear old town;
But the native air is pure and sweet,
And the trees that o'ershadow each well-known street,
   As they balance up and down,
   Are singing the beautiful song,
   Are sighing and whispering still,

"A boy's will is the wind's will,
And the thoughts of youth are long, long thoughts."

And Deering's Woods are fresh and fair,
  And with joy that is almost pain
My heart goes back to wander there,
And among the dreams of the days that were,
  I find my lost youth again.
  And the strange and beautiful song,
  The groves are repeating it still:
"A boy's will is the wind's will,
And the thoughts of youth are long, long thoughts."

A Psalm of Life

Tell me not, in mournful numbers,
  Life is but an empty dream! —
For the soul is dead that slumbers,
  And things are not what they seem.

Life is real! Life is earnest!
  And the grave is not its goal;
Dust thou art, to dust returnest,
  Was not spoken of the soul.

Not enjoyment, and not sorrow,
  Is our destined end or way;
But to act, that each tomorrow
  Find us farther than today.

Art is long, and Time is fleeting,
  And our hearts, though stout and brave,
Still, like muffled drums, are beating
  Funeral marches to the grave.

In the world's broad field of battle,

In the bivouac of Life,
Be not like dumb, driven cattle!
Be a hero in the strife!

Trust no Future, howe'er pleasant!
Let the dead Past bury its dead!
Act, — act in the living present!
Heart within, and God o'erhead!

Lives of great men all remind us
We can make our lives sublime,
And, departing, leave behind us
Footprints on the sands of time;

Footprints, that perhaps another,
Sailing o'er life's solemn main,
A forlorn and shipwrecked brother,
Seeing, shall take heart again.

Let us, then, be up and doing,
With a heart for any fate;
Still achieving, still pursuing,
Learn to labor and to wait.

The Building of the Ship

. . . Then the Master,
With a gesture of command,
Waved his hand;
And at the word,
Loud and sudden there was heard,
All around them and below,
The sound of hammers, blow on blow,
Knocking away the shores and spurs.
And see! she stirs!

She starts, — she moves, — she seems to feel
The thrill of life along her keel,
And, spurning with her foot the ground,
With one exulting, joyous bound,
She leaps into the ocean's arms! . . .

. . . Thou, too, sail on, O Ship of State!
Sail on, O Union, strong and great!
Humanity with all its fears,
With all the hopes of future years,
Is hanging breathless on thy fate!
We know what Master laid thy keel,
What Workman wrought thy ribs of steel,
Who made each mast, and sail, and rope,
What anvils rang, what hammers beat,
In what a forge and what a heat
Were shaped the anchors of thy hope!
Fear not each sudden sound and shock.
'Tis of the wave and not the rock;
'Tis but the flapping of the sail,
And not a rent made by the gale!
In spite of rock and tempest's roar
In spite of false lights on the shore,
Sail on, nor fear to breast the sea!
Our hearts, our hopes, are all with thee,
Our hearts, our hopes, our prayers, our tears,
Our faith triumphant o'er our fears,
Are all with thee, — are all with thee!

BENJAMIN BROWNE FOSTER
1832–1903

Ben Foster's adventures growing up in the 1840s in Bangor and in his nearby home town of Orono invite no comparison with the adventures of Tom Sawyer and Huck Finn. At fifteen he was another kind of ordinary-extraordinary boy. Taught by his mother, he could read at three. After what must have been a childhood of omnivorous reading, Ben began to teach himself to write by turning a poem into its prose equivalent, finding synonyms for the original words. His vocabulary at fifteen was astonishing, and in his journal he loved to exercise it. His reading from Plato to Byron to all the current newspapers and magazines could have only partly satisfied his wonderfully curious mind.

Ben Foster's father kept a general store in Orono. Ben was the second of six children, and Charles, his older brother, was as sensitively self-educated and as ambitious as Ben. (At thirteen Ben collaborated with Charles in contributing a column on politics and society to a rural weekly in Dover, New Hampshire, which never discovered their ages.) Ben attended as a matter of course all the public meetings, lectures, and theatrical events in town. As a social historian, he watched closely changes in Bangor's morals and manners, analyzed his own human nature by the principles of phrenology, and discussed with Charles and anyone else in sight and hearing the immortality of the soul, sex, politics, and all in all had a wonderful time growing up during colorful times for Bangor. As we begin our reading in his diaries, Ben is driving down to Bangor with Charles to begin his apprenticeship as a clerk, "counter jumper," in J. Bright's Provision Stores — Fruits and Groceries.

Ben's diaries continue from 1847 to 1853, though almost a year is missing between 1850 and 1851. His editor notes that there are almost a half-million words in the original; the printed version contains about a third of the total. The diary's last years, when Ben was at Bowdoin College, are very informative about that college's rowdiest student days. Ben graduated with honors and eventually decided on government work in Washington, in the Post Office and War departments. The latter job led to employment with government contractors who furnished supplies to the army in the West, and Ben traveled to Kansas and Nebraska. In time he returned to Maine, studied law in Bangor, and was admitted to the bar in 1858. But during those restless years he continued to write for newspapers, out West, in Baltimore and Washington, sometimes as a correspondent for local papers in Maine, and once as two correspondents, under pseudonyms, for the *Boston Post*.

Ben's generation had a fated rendezvous with the Civil War. Ben volunteered early, was elected an officer of the 11th Maine Volunteers, and had a long and distinguished military career. He was a major at the end of the war and was breveted a colonel after the war "for his efficient and gallant services." He married in 1863 and practiced law, at first in Norfolk, Virginia, and afterward in New York City, where he alternated private practice with service in the office of the United States Attorney for that district.

A Few Days in the Life
of Ben Foster

Monday, July 26, Bangor, Maine
Rose at 5. Dressed, ate a piece of pie, harnessed horse, and Charles and I came to Bangor. Arrived at fifteen minutes of 7. Charles said we had been three quarters of a hour and began descanting on the horse being a fast traveller, going faster than he looked, etc. He soon discovered his mistake though. Rockwell and Company's Circus entered the city this A.M.

Tuesday, July 27

Chilly morning. Hear nothing of the circus. Probably not much. Its pole blew down in the squall yesterday and they were obliged to make a long joice do as well as it could.

Simon Walker and Colbath have compromised the matter between them relative to the latter's wife, it is said, by the payment of $1200 to the injured party. This has thrown quite a damper, a *cold bath,* on the high wrought expectations of some who had anticipated rich disclosures.

The *Gazette* states in regard to Fowler's lectures [on phrenology] that they were well attended and spoken highly of. The general impression seems to be that in his "examinations he has made some capital hits and some decided failures."

Dudley Gordon, my ancient school mate, came into the store this evening. He has grown, if not out of my recollection, almost out of my sight. We shook hands and the following sententious colloquy ensued. "How do you do, Benjamin?" "How do you do, Dudley?" "How's the body?" "Right." "How's the flesh?" "Nice." After this laconic preliminary, we launched out into more extensive and general conversation.

Wednesday, July 28

The Atheneum advertises to reopen Thursday evening under the management of Mrs. W. Pierce! Huzzza! The *Mercury* remarks: "The former manager, Mr. J. C. Breslaw, we are happy to state, has either left town or fallen into the clutches of some of the sheriff's deputies."

Commenced raining this P.M. Finished the cake Mother gave me on leaving. . . . It was, as the young ones say, "real good."

The Constable and the husband settled by the payment of 800 instead of 1200 dollars. Some say $300. *Cheap!*

Thursday, July 29

Passed a very restless night last night. Besides being very cold, I dreamed of talking incessantly to customers, thinking myself in the store, and I awoke several times in the midst of a long harangue. I presume I talked at least half the night. When I first came here, I would occasionally *overhear myself* talking of such matters in my sleep.

The Atheneum is out with flaming red and yellow bills: "Engagement of the Ethiopian Opera Singers or the 'Cow-bell-o-gians of Sturgeon Land,' a Burlesque on the Campanalogians or Swiss Bell

Ringers." The plays announced are, *The Intrigue, The Married Rake,* and *The Rake Outwitted.* Characteristic. . . .

Bought at Lewis's today *Dr. Pond's Life, Works, Opinions and Influences of Plato* and paid 35 cents. . . . It appears Plato was a follower of Socrates and pretended to nothing more, though he interwove many of his phantastic theories with those of Socrates. He wrote nothing professedly by himself; all purport to be the opinions of his model, Socrates. . . .

Aristophanes' system of love was that Jupiter cut down man lengthways, because being originally possessed of two faces, four legs and other members in like ratio, as well as proportionately ambitious and strong, man set about besieging heaven, and, by these means (splitting), the race was not extinguished but doubled and made weaker. Ever since, each half has longed for its mate and on seeing it is instinctively drawn toward it. Rational, that.

While going home I stopped in front of the Atheneum and heard the "Aethopians" perform one piece. The "bones" seemed to be wielded by a "scientific nigger's" hand. They rattled like — anything, almost.

Sunday, August 1

Rose about 7. Came to store. Washed all my body and made my toilet.

As by printed notices distributed last evening, George Truman, a minister from the Society of Friends from Philadelphia, held a meeting at the City Hall commencing at 10:30. I attended. Two of them were present. They sat with their hats on waiting for the motion of the Holy Ghost within them. Presently one of them, a young man about thirty-five, thin and cadaverous, rose, doffed beaver and stated some of the fundamental points of belief of the Friends. Did not believe it the part of man, as man, to call or choose a person for the minister of God. Disbelieved in a mercenary, hired priesthood, in praising God by the harmonious note, with voices, when the heart was not attuned to his praise, nor as a general thing in vocal, audible prayers. "Prayer is the soul's sincere desire" and it is known to God as well in thought as by expressed words. (Certainly)

The other rose after the first sat down and occupied the rest of the morning. . . . He was an older man dressed in a sack coat and vest buttoned straight to the chin, save near the top, white neckerchief and erect collar. Quaker style but fashionable at this time. He descanted in support of their tenets, against all rites and ceremonies, baptism, Lord's Supper, etc., against studying the Greek and Hebrew, theological seminaries, etc. Said in conclusion that if any had acquired one *friendly* feeling, he was well repaid for being a listener. About one hundred or more were present. Very good order was kept and all seemed interested.

P.M. staid at the house. Read from Sir Walter Scott's *Demonology and Witchcraft*. Considered witches mentioned in Scripture merely as "poisoners" (a synonymous Hebrew term) and pretenders to ability to work miracles by supernatural agency. . . . Read some in *Childe Harold*. Encountered some of the most exquisitely poetical passages I have ever met with. Such as the description of the Alpine storm, Canto 3; such as the last part of stanza 87, and a beautiful fancy is that in stanzas 74 and 75, same canto.

Strolled down by the Kenduskeag, where were four or five boys swimming. Watched their antics for a few moments, then left. Read from an old number of the *Lady's Book*. . . . After supper walked up to Uncle Samuel Foster's and got a piece of strawberry pye. . . .

Tuesday, August 3

Opened the store at 5. Traded about 3.50 before breakfast. Measured up seven or eight bushels of corn, which I found back-breaking work when done in a hurry. Father and William were down this A.M. Emma has the scarlet fever. Charles will come for me tomorrow. He brought down a book bought at Bugbee's auction for 9 cents, bound in cloth, entitled *The American Gentleman*.

Read some of the first parts which I liked well, but turned over to p. 233 on "Adherence to our Vocation" where the writer decries and severely censures the practice of composing or oratory by those who are not students by profession. . . . When this "itch for scribbling" affects the uneducated and unfit by nature to wield the pen, and persons write to the neglect and consequent detriment of their proper pursuit or occupation, I agree with him. But I contest the assumed position that mechanics or merchants should confine themselves to their business. No. Man's is a higher destiny. He should endeavor by writing, or otherwise to enlarge, cultivate and adorn his intellect. In this country where so few persons are able to subsist without labor, by far the greatest proportions are merchants, mechanics or farmers. These occupations contain necessarily very frequently those of superior talents and powers of mind. Should these "conceal their lights under a bushel" and leave formation of their and their country's literature to a favored few who may have studied or may be studying a little Greek or Latin? . . . Tacitly submit to a dependence on the "students by profession" for reading matter for their consumption, be dependent for information and ideas on them, thus becoming in a mental light virtually their serfs and vassals? Never let such a system of *literal* aristocracy be harbored here!

Saturday, August 21

Mirabile dictu. My dear cousin Winthrop arrived in the *Governor* from Boston this morning while I was out to collect a bill at Pitman's brass foundry. He left his traps at the store and stepped out. He and myself dined at Mr. Bright's and spent an hour and a half of the P.M. in perambulating the streets and viewing the *Lions,* of which *en passant* to a tyro there are not a few. . . . Went to Mr. Bright's in father's carriage — he was down — and got a bosom [a piece of hardware?] etc. Found C. B. Abbot's horse on the way to Glenburn. Carried him back to the Temperance House. Abbot offered me 3/ [/ referred to a shilling, six of which made a dollar] which, of course, I refused. If I had earned it, I should have taken it. Started for home at quarter of 5, I sitting on Winthrop's valise and driving.

Frances A. Colbath is out in the *Mercury* in a long deposition extenuating and vindicating herself from the charge of fornication. She acknowledges going into Walker's office to talk over "the difficulty" between Mrs. Walker and herself but says nothing improper was said or done. *I don't believe it.* Most any woman would, *if guilty,* perjure herself (more especially at the instigation of her friend and paramour) to re-establish a reputation.

Monday, August 23, Orono, Maine

This P.M. we rode to Oldtown. Crossed in the ferry. Set up two or three coppers for the Injin juveniles to shoot at with their bows and arrows. . . . Went into the grave yard. Some of the crosses at the head of the graves had carved out on them the figures of birds. Found one new-made grave and, while we were looking around, the bell in the Catholic Chapel began tolling. Concluding there was to be a funeral we left the yard and went over to the Chapel. We were refused admittance. We were told it was a Frenchman — "some Fraunchman" as they expressed it — who resided on the island. Presently there issued from the open door an Indian bearing a long cross with the image of Christ sculptured on it, about a foot in length, following him a man with a black cross, probably for the grave. Next a man with the coffin, covered with a white cloth, *under his arm.* Then, indiscriminately, the mourners and others. We left without following.

Went on board the *Governor Neptune,* the Oldtown and Passa-dumkeag steamer. She is a strange looking craft. Is flat-bottomed and very low built. Her boiler is about the dimensions of a cooking stove. She has a strange looking paddle wheel on behind. Her helm is rigged in the same manner as the sweep of a board raft — something like an oar made of a plank. Went into her cabin 12 by 15 and a snug and cozy little place. They were engaged in painting her. The fare to Greenbush is 25 cents, to Passadumkeag, 3/.

In the *Mercury,* Robert A. Colbath has a reply to his wife. He says his wife told him [Simon] Walker had done the thing often, when in his office at *that* time. Walker swore that on the time that she says they talked over the difficulty between Mrs Walker and herself, she went in after an umbrella. Richer than the other. Really liquorish.

Elder J. Adams delivered a "religious lecture" at the City Hall Sunday evening and at the close mentioned that he should play Richard III at the Atheneum on Monday evening and closed by the usual benediction. Monstrous, this uniting one's everyday trade with preaching and prayer.

Thursday, August 26

About half past 8 the whistles of the *Secor,* and the reiterated shouts of a multitude running toward Steamboat Wharf announced the advent of the Antiquarians [a segment of the Whig party]. We were at the time shutting the store and after closing I went to the wharf. Just before I got there I heard the report of the "mortars, taken at the battle of Jerico." When I arrived at the wharf, I found a large congregation and the *T. F. Secor* just riding in. She was brilliantly lighted and the brass band were striking up in their most glorious style while the Ancients were dancing around the deck in Indian file and high jollity. Some of them appeared most particularly *luminous.* Amidst reciprocating cheers from shore and sea, the steamer drew up. The plank was put ashore and, as soon as communication was opened, a concourse under the escort of John Goddard and the brass band poured onto terra firma, and marched up Broad St., crossed over to Vinton and Porter's, with band playing "Yankee Doodle" most enthusiastically, marched directly into his liquor room.

Oh then! were set on the counter the decanters of the red stuff and the yellow stuff; added thereto the sugar bowl, the tumblers and the spoons. Oh then! how they recounted the wonders discovered, among which were the horse that Richard in his exigency offered to exchange his kingdom for, which was on board the *Secor* tied, and the buoy to the anchor of Noah's Ark, discovered 12,000 ft. under Owl's Head. Oh then! how briskly and scientifically Vinton twirled a toddy stick. Oh then! how energetically John Goddard called on all around to participate in their orgies.

At length having got, many of them, most "essentially corned," Goddard raised his voice and his glass and said, "Let's do something Vinton and Porter *don't want* us to. Let's give the damn buggers three cheers and leave 'em." Then rang the glasses. Then the cheers arose. Then Goddard said, "Let's clear out." Then *exeunt omnes,* John and Lem Hudson at their head singing, "We're a band united in the Washingtonian cause," with the yells and the howls of the delighted boys and bystanders.

Saturday, September 11

There are but four or five wagons on the "stand" from the country. Yesterday but two, day before but two. Quite a contrast from the busy scenes we generally see, from twenty-five to forty wagons, horses heads turned toward the road, all in one long unbroken row on the right hand side of Main St., each surrounded by some six or ten of our citizens chaffering and haggling for the produce, butter, eggs, meat, etc., with which the wagons are laden. Also about as many two-horse wagons laden with shingles in the square, environed by purchasers of lumber with their large, savage looking chizels, prying open the bundles to see if the countrymen have attempted to "come Paddy" by putting the best outside, leaving the inside ones scoots. You will see of a morning many of these shingle buyers prowling along with gloomy, insidious, contracted brow, with slow and solemn step, their arms partly folded and their wicked looking instruments reposing in the crook of their left elbow. It would inspire a tyro with apprehension. It almost did me when I was a novice.

Dreamt last night of a meeting and conversation with J. H. Carleton, night before of Lord Byron, tonight probably of some other great literary. Dreamed also of my first real flame, Abigail.

Monday, September 13

John Lord has an advertisement in the *Whig* and *Mercury* to cure uncurables. Has taken an office in Granite Block, East Market Square. Among the maladies were *nervous affections* and *club feet.* O Moses! "Physician cure," etc. He preached this A.M. at the Congregational Church, and the young ones said they couldn't bear to look at him, he twisted his mouth and contorted his face so. Ah, the "nervous affections."

Mother will be forty years of age tomorrow. Dear Mother, I never yet till now knew how much I loved her. Absence is the true touchstone. I gave her as a present an old American dollar of the date 1795 with the injunction not to spend it. I had and could think of nothing else.

Tuesday, September 14

How mechanical a life I lead from morning early till 7 o'clock. Rise at half past 5, dress, come down to the store. Open door, remove shutters and open front window. Set out our "bee hive" (a something in that shape with "J. Bright Provision Store, Fruits and Groceries," painted on its four respective sides), a keg, hang up the signs against the door jambs, ("J. Bright Ship Stores," "J. Bright Family Groceries,") hang out three pails over the door, hang out a mat and mop on the spout, set out two quart boxes of salt, hang out the pasteboard tin-letter-stamped signs, "Rye Meal," "Oats," "Eggs," and "Butter," and then open the two back windows and the two windows upstairs, from which, leaving them open, I suspend two grass mats for show. This done I go down cellar and open the window there, after which I come up and fill the camphene and either two or three oil lamps, sweep out and sprinkle the floor, dust down when requisite. Then I wash and make my toilet and go to breakfast after journal.

I gave it to A. S. Adams good yesterday. He professes to be an antislavery man and yet said, at first, he wouldn't have the same familiarity with them as with others. Said in extenuation, "didn't like them, didn't like their smell." I asked him if it wasn't his duty as a Christian and as a consistent opponent of slavery to overcome this repugnance. He acknowledged it was and said he should try but it was impossible. I asked him why we here are so different from Southerners. By an article in the *Knickerbocker,* I see what I have often heard before: "I saw nothing of what we call prejudice against color in all my travels. In infancy the same nurse gives food and rest to her own child and her master's; in childhood the same eye watches and the same hand alternately caresses and corrects them; they mingle their sports in boyhood; and through youth up to manhood there are ties which link them to each other with an affinity that no time or circumstances can destroy." The Negro "seems essential to them — they are lonesome without them."

Such it is there. He said it wouldn't be popular here. That's the question. Why not? "We ain't used to them." Should not we become used to them, and is not this inconsistency a great obstacle to the general reception of antislavery principles?

Friday, September 17

Charles Stratton, Tom Thumb, fifteen years of age, 27 inches high, 15 lbs. in weight, has his picture the size of life in various attitudes on gaudy colored paper posted at the street corners.

Sunday, September 19

Killed two "ravin" distracted b-d b-gs on my bed this morning. Agreeable fellows they have proved to be as my feet can testify.

Wednesday, September 22

Father and Mother were down this P.M. to see Tom Thumb for principal object. They, particularly Mother, were in raptures. They had his Lilliputian visiting card, given at the door, "Gen. Tom Thumb," and they bought a gilt medal, on the obverse Victoria's head and bust with the words, "Victoria Regina," on the reverse Tom Thumb's likeness with the words, "General Tom Thumb, Weight 15 pounds." For this they paid 9d. Also a pamphlet, with his description, his song, his travels. This was 4d. He receipted in full to Mother with a kiss. The whole town is in a manner set crazy for him, the children especially. If a man is seen with a child, a troop of children collect round and eagerly scan it to see if it be Tom Thumb. I overheard two little girls talking about it and one explaining to the other how they got into the levee with a ticket. "Well," said the other triumphantly, "there's my singing school ticket." I sympathized with her disappointment when the other informed her of the true state of things. Went with Father and, after much looking around, selected a coat at Hunt's — a black broadcloth, price $10. We went and looked for Mother to go see it. We hunted Main St. in vain. By this time it was half past 6 and Bright had gone to tea. I was on nettles. At length we went and got the coat and I went up to Aunt Julia's, where we found Mother. . . .

Ten dollars! Quite a sum. The first broadcloth article of apparel he ever furnished me. Uncle Henry gave me, or rather Charles, an old coat and pair of pants which, after Charles outgrew, descended to me and which pants I now use as "handsome." I write with my shanks encased in a pair of Asa Walker's unspeakables.

Thursday, September 23

Dreamed of a battle being fought between the Mexicans and the Americans across the Kenduskeag, the temporary Rio Grande, which I judge resulted to the honor of American arms, inferring from the super-abundance of Mexicans which tumbled into the water on their, the east side. Also a woman swam from the Mexican to the American side. It was a particularly vivid dream. Rose at 6 exhausted from the nocturnal excitement, which was not, like the mesmeriser's sickness and pains, "all spiritual." It was like common excitement fatiguing to the body. . . .

Charles, Caro and Lyman [his sister and brothers] were down this P.M. to attend Tom Thumb's levee. I accompanied them. A large audience was in attendance. A case containing his presents was on the table. . . . He made his appearance in the hands of Barnum, raised above the crowd, and shouting in a childish but clear voice, "How do you do, *lad*-dies and gentlemen." My first emotion and which occurred to me several times after was of surprise that such a morsel, a mere crumb of humanity, could be the residence of a soul! Two feet, three inches! Then I was bewildered in wonder in regard to his physiological formation etc., etc. I shall enter into no details. . . . His frame was elegantly proportioned and extremely agile and for his size graceful in his movements. . . .

Barnum said that when Victoria showed him her picture gallery he [Tom] said it was "first rate" and wanted to know, pointing at the pictures of kings, who those "queer old chaps" were. . . . He sang "Lucy Lang" before Queen Victoria, who said it was the first time it was ever sung in Buckingham Palace. The General's personations of the Grecian statues, "One of the B'hoys," (with a long cigar and his hat cocked on one side), of Napoleon Bonaparte, Frederick the Great were fine. A leer, or rather a smile, was irrepressible on the General's part, which ill accorded with the serious mode of "Napoleon in Reverie." His songs were sung well, considering his sharp voice. His French Court dress passable, his Highland costume magnificent. In his case of presents was the watch presented by the Queen Dowager, the size of a quarter, and two or three little gold pistols, also a breast pin from the Queen of Spain representing Jim Crow and banjo in diverse colored stones. . . .

Friday, October 1

A veterinary surgeon is here. Advertises, "Horses mesmerized when undergoing severe operations. . . ."

Saturday, October 2

Opened the store at fifteen minutes past 6. Delayed sometime by the spilling of the nocturnal dish. I took hold to move it and a piece broke from the side spilling the fluid contents. I sopped it up as well as I could with some old New York *Mirrors*. "To what base uses," etc.

Major Thomas of the Army, Bright's brother-in-law, arrived today with wife and two sons. He realizes my ideal conception of a major. Short man, dapper legs, straight, thickset body, coat buttoned tight around, standing collar, brass buttons, flat cap, grizzled hair, spectacles.

Finished Vol. 1 of Coleridge's *Table Talk*.

Saturday, October 9

Surprising the ignorance of some paddies in relation to religion. One, Duffy, otherwise quite intelligent, was in the store last evening and referred me to *Galatians* 8:1 for the words of Christ, "Them that teaches any other doctrines than the Catholics have taught, let him be damned; let him go to hell." I got the Bible and there were but five or six chapters in *Galatians*.

He then said that that was "a Yankee Bible" and that *Galatians* was in the Old Testament. I asked him how Christ's words would be in the Old Testament when it was written before he came. Says he, "If the Apostles and the Pope didn't write it, who did?" "The Prophets." "Well, wasn't they Catholics?" with a triumphant grin as if he had established his first argument in regards to *Galatians*. . . .

Wednesday, October 13

Bright dismissed me this A.M. Settled up with him. Paid me 10.75$. 10.73$ was the balance due. . . . Was going to Woodbury's boarding place to carry a note with card and address. Saw in front of A. K. Norris' store in Elm block a large collection of men. The nucleus was a group as follows. A man on horseback, miserable looking, trowser's leg ripped up, bare legs protruding, grizzled red face, and wretched horse. Two shingle racks with ragged, squalid looking shingle weavers within. A jug of rum was passing among them, all drinking therefrom long draughts. Each drank two or three times before I left disgusted. There stood Hunt, the beautiful city marshal, looking on and enjoying the scene with gusto.

Thursday, October 14, Orono

Charles came down after me. Arrived at home about 12. Went to Forbes' to be cut for a broadcloth coat he is going to have manufactured. He was still out till 1 o'clock. At half past 12 Bright urged me to go to dinner but I was implacable. I knew Charles' "testy humor" about punctuality. We started just at 1 o'clock. A short distance from Uncle Theodore's our wagon wheel came off and left us in the lurch. We found the axle at the end was broken off where Charles ran against a wagon in Bangor. We were nearly opposite Jones' new house. I went in and got two or three nails and we patched up and drove along at a walk. Charles wanted to plug up and let it drag. It reminded me of the affairs we used to have at the old school, where we would sing out at every team, cart or carriage that passed that their "wheel was coming off." When we got to Dammers we whipped up though two small nails only held on the left hind wheel. . . .

When I got within sight of the village called by the sweetest of names, "Home," it caused a *good* sort of feeling. And yet when I came to particularize, as there lives Dennet, there Stinson, there Gould, there Baker, there MacDaniels, there Nat Lunt, did I feel my soul drawn thither by any kindly, friendly feeling? Decidedly the reverse, and a painful sensation usurped the place lately tenanted by the other. A sort of latent, inactive antipathy to nearly all Orono's denizens I have ever had.

CAPTAIN CHARLES C. DUNCAN
1821–1898

Captain Charles C. Duncan of Bath was a Maine worthy whose seventy-seven years spanned the great decades of Maine shipbuilding and transatlantic shipping and who deserves to be better remembered than he is. In those days, if you were born and raised in Bath and were ambitious, your future was almost sure to be in ships and shipping. Duncan was a ship's master at twenty-three, and in 1853, after fifty-eight transatlantic crossings, he went ashore in Brooklyn and opened an office on Wall Street as a ship broker. He fathered sixteen children. During the Civil War he was in England, trying to run a branch of his firm in Liverpool at a time when trade between Europe and America had come almost to a standstill. In 1864 one of his ships, the *Emma Jane,* named for his first daughter, was captured and burned off India's Malabar Coast by the famous Confederate raider the *Alabama.*

When the war ended, Duncan returned to Brooklyn to take on, among his other family and shipping activities, his role as the superintendent of the Sunday school of the Plymouth Congregational Church, which was led by the most famous preacher of the age, Henry Ward Beecher. (On Sundays, 2,500 people came to hear Beecher preach.) Beecher let it be known that he was planning to write a new life of Christ and was considering an absence from his pulpit to visit the Holy Land. Duncan had a better idea: charter a ship, invite others, especially members of the congregation, to join the voyage, and make leisurely stops at other ports of call along the way. This idea led to two significant cultural debuts of the mid-nineteenth century.

One was marine history's first luxury cruise. In 1867 Duncan's charter, the 1,900-ton side-wheeler *Quaker City,* carried seventy wealthy Americans on a five-month tour of the Mediterranean. (Beecher didn't go; he decided to write a novel instead.) The conception of the "Excursion," as it was called, was so new to the ports they entered that in Algiers Captain Duncan was asked by the harbor master whether his ship was a merchant vessel or a man-of-war. The answer: a yacht. Later, in Yalta, where the Americans were received by the czar, a Russian woman asked if the travelers were all related.

The other debut that will be forever associated with the Grand Holy Land Pleasure Excursion was that of the journalist and humorous lecturer from California who called himself Mark Twain. His San Francisco newspaper paid his fare of $1,250, the investment to be repaid by fifty letters written along the way. These letters became Samuel Clemens's first book, *The Innocents Abroad*. It was a smashing success. In writing it he found his public, the prosperous postwar American middle class, and his literary mission, to mock their not-so-innocent lives.

Ironically, Duncan suffered painfully for his brilliant invention of the luxury cruise. He, too, had gained prominence from the trip, and in one of his public lectures, he unwisely reported that when Mark Twain had come to sign on for the cruise he was drunk. Clemens took this comment as a challenge and began one of his bitter public quarrels, conducted in letters and interviews in the *New York Times*. Duncan had become in 1872 the first shipping commissioner of the Port of New York, a federal office created by Congress to protect the rights of sailors. He held the post for twelve years but was at last dismissed by a federal judge amid charges of malfeasance in office. Mark Twain's public vendetta against him helped, it appears, to set a hostile tone in the federal courtroom.

Near the end of his life Duncan began a personal memoir, from which these excerpts are taken.

Autobiography of
Captain Charles C. Duncan

"Mr. Nichols, I am five years old today, won't you give me two cents?" In writing one's life there's got to be a beginning and that is the very first utterance or incident in mine that I can remember. Mr. Jas. Nichols, the village shoemaker and a neighbor was standing on a ledge in the street in front of my mother's house and that house was a rough old affair located at the foot of South Street, corner of Water in Bath, Maine, on the west bank of the Kennebec River. As I said before, my memory from this day begins at this point. I remember that our family consisted of my mother, brother George, sister Elizabeth, sister Catherine, now Mrs. Davenport, and myself. Besides these my oldest brother William and next to him Samuel were sailor boys generally away from home. I remember being told that I was born on the fifteenth of May, 1821 in an old one story house on Washington Street opposite the then and present Methodist Meeting House, but of this although I was present on the occasion, I have no recollection whatever. Two elements are prominent in my first memories — they are my father and the Methodist religion. My father and mother lived estranged from each other. When he and my mother were first married, they were a prosperous and promising couple and I believe lived happily until after the six children comprising our family were born.

My father held public office, something in the Custom House I believe, and acquired some property. In an evil hour the habit of liquor drinking — a habit so common with rich and poor in the church and out of it, as to attract no attention whatever — fastened itself upon him. It swept away his reason — his property, his friends, and although naturally one of the kindest and most lovable of men,

The *Charles Crooker*

he became an object of disgust. His property vanished — with a few hundred dollars received, my mother bought the old house I have spoken of and gathered her children around her there. My father took up his abode with his sister, Mrs. Crocker and grandmother, Mrs. Arthur Sewell. All that I saw of him would be at times when he would be going through the streets in a liquor frenzy, followed and hooted at by boys, times when my mother would get me into the house and fasten the doors and windows. Such is my boyhood recollection of my father. . . .

I was sent to a school marm — private school, old Mrs. Cushing, teacher, to learn to chew gum and make spitballs. The disciplinary methods of the school were all concentrated in a "baster," an affair resembling a buckwheat cake with a handle two feet long screwed into one side of it. This was the old lady's assistant on all occasions and, on all places. I guess I didn't improve much there for my mother threatened to send me to the "Masters' " school, the town school taught by Mr. Littlefield, who wore green spectacles, black hair, pale face, and was a terror to the boys. I begged her to do so and she did and I at once became a favorite with the master. Often and often he would hold up little "Duncan" as a bright and shining example to the other boys. For a year or so, from eight to ten, I enjoyed and profited by my Town School — three months in summer, then three months in winter, after which for three or four years my boyhood went on part of the time at work and part of the time at school where grammar was taught. The summer that I was ten years old, an old Cape Cod schooner, the "Lady Hope," Capt. Ferris, was repaired at Houghton's Wharf near my mother's house. I shipped on her as cook to go up to Gardiner and load lumber and return. (That was my first marine service, I was gone three weeks and the Captain paid me seventy-five cents — all I earned, I think.)

After this I remember ships were being built every year, more or less, in the yards of Mr. Houghton and Mr. Trufant and the Crooker Brothers. And in one way and another, I managed to get employment about the shipyards. My mother took the carpenters to board, and by hard work managed to earn enough to keep soul and body together. As I said before, my brothers William and Samuel were at sea. William helped my mother in her struggle. Samuel became permanently absent. George was working in Mr. William Dunnell's blacksmith shop learning that trade. Catherine and Elizabeth worked in Mr. John Bovey's tailor shop. I got jobs in the shipyards. Sometimes shoveling salt out of the ships discharging — earning as much as ten cents a day, sometimes picking up and storing the big chips coming from the hewing of timbers, picking up tools and turning the grindstone and a hundred other things that a boy could be useful for — thereby earning a little change, and when having nothing else to do, with a bushel basket on my back carried home from the shipyards small chips which were readily given away and which we stored for winter fuel.

In this way we tided along two or three years, keeping the wolf from the door and with not much opportunity for schooling for me. Of course, I was growing older and stronger and found employment still in the shipyard with the caulkers for one season.

Then at fourteen, I went into my brother's blacksmith shop to work, intending to acquire that trade. I was not a very rugged boy — the iron work of several vessels was being done in the shop. We began work at daylight — sometimes at half past four in the morning and quit at dark. The days were long and the work hard for a young boy, and I remember sometimes to having discouraged feelings when my mother needed to call me to get up in the morning. However the only privation was schooling for — with mutual work we had plenty to eat and comfortable clothing. . . .

After working two years with my brother George, I discovered that being left-handed, I could not readily become a blacksmith and so decided to become a sailor. We were working on the iron work at that time of the ship "Glasgow" and I decided to make my beginning as a salt water sailor in that ship. I was duly enrolled — got a big chest — two stories — the upper filled with an ample sailor's kit and the lower story — a drawer with pies and pillow cases filled with cookies given to me by my good mother. And so on the 23rd of January, 1837, in a northwester which followed a heavy snow storm, weather bitter cold, ship filled with snow, the whole ship's company of strangers — we cast off from Crooker's Wharf and I took my first observation and experience on a cold Atlantic Ocean.

I had cut away now from boyhood life and all its memories and associations — from boyhood chums and friends — from the association of meetings — from the boys and girls parties that were current and my long and hard days work in the blacksmith shop, from my dear mother living all alone and from that which affected me more than one might think — my father. For within the last two years we had become very fond of each other. My heart went towards him in strong affection and he to me. He used often to come to the shop to see me and talk with me. I believed he had gotten over or was trying to do so, his habit of drinking and I got the idea that somehow, I was to open the door for him to restored life. I remember that one day just before I sailed he came into the shop and I handed him a new watch which I had saved money and bought for him. I said "Now, father, you won't be offended but this watch shall be the covenant between you and me. You will never while you hold it, cease resisting the temptation to drink and I will never cease my living watchful care". The old gentleman was good and affected — he took the watch — held it up to his ear to see if it were going, took my hand and left. I never heard of his having drunk liquor afterwards. The next object to be accomplished seemed to be to bring him and my mother together.

We were bound to Mobile in the Glasgow — besides officers, the ship had a crew of twelve able seamen and six green boys of which as Paul might say, I was the chief. We boys were set to shoveling snow off the decks as the ship sailed down the river and when the ocean was reached and the ship began to pay her respects to that great disturber, I found myself losing interest in snow and snow shoveling and wondering what was the matter with me, whether I was going to die or live on. Anyhow, I thought I'd better get out of sight and I

crawled away down into the fore peak and there in solitary wretchedness gave vent to my feelings. I think that I called myself a fool and
wished myself back in the blacksmith's shop or with my mother in
our plain old home or with my girl in the Methodist meeting or in
fact anywhere but where I then was in that little berth and attending
to the business that forced itself upon me. I wondered if I wouldn't
die soon — rather hoped so.

However all this wretchedness supreme passed away and in a day
or two, I found myself hazed around the deck by officers who seemed
to wonder what had been the matter with us boys, for the other boys
had had their taste, had worried through it so lank and forlorn as I
and were enjoying the same gentle encouragement as I was receiving.
I registered a vow then and there, that if I ever got to be an officer of
a ship having suffering seasick boys under my authority, I would treat
them mercifully, kindly and that vow in all later years, I kept. Of
course, all experiences to new sailors must be new and astonishing.
When I was informed a week later by one of the sailors who professed
to be my friend that Neptune was coming on board that night and was
going to chew all the green sailors but me, I was intensely interested
and so thankful that I had such a friend by whom I was to escape.

It was a fine night and when eight bells struck (eight o'clock) all
hands remained on deck — the watch whose right it was did not
go below. Presently "Ship Ahoy" came from a voice away over the
bow down upon the sea. "Hullo", "Hullo" responded the Captain through his trumpet. "Where are you from?". "Bath, Maine".
"Where are you bound?" "Mobile". "Have you any green hands
aboard?" "Yes, six". (I thought he should have said five, remembering my friend's promise.) "I shall come on board and initiate them."
"Very well, glad to see you." Then Neptune was seen, tall, bundled
up in oil-clothes, sea weeds and what not, climbing up over the bows.
He walked aft toward the quarter deck — sailors making the pas-
sage-way for him. He saluted the captain, inquired for the health of
the crew, apologized for the necessity of a short visit, because of the
many vessels coming along requiring attention, turned to the officers
and asked for the green hands and for shaving facilities. A large half
hogshead filled with water was standing near by, a bucket also filled
with tar and grease and other filth, a dirty brush was in it and an iron
scraper such as is used to scrape the pitch off of ships seams lay
across. The sailors were all around, the green hands were there
watching with great interest what was going on, each one had been
assured, as I had, that the others, not he, were to be shaved. "Who

comes first" said Neptune. The sailors grabbed a stout young country fellow and sat him on the edge of the tub, back to the water. "Your name" said Neptune. "Age" "Occupation before you came here?" "What made you come?" "Now give me your promise if ever you get out of this voyage, you never will try another. You never will sleep in a hard berth when you can get into a soft bed. You never will wear wet clothes when you can get dry. You never will eat hard bread when you can get soft". To all of these satisfactory replies were given. "You will now attend to being shaved". "Barbers, to your duty"! Instantly the big brush was dipped in the tar bucket, and the boy's face, mouth and ears besmeared with the tar. Another hand with the iron scraper attempted to scrape off that which had been put on. Then by a man at each shoulder, the victim was tipped backward under the water, lifted out and pushed away. And the "next" called for. I had seen enough: for this boy as he went away said "They promised me that I was not to be shaved!" I dodged down into the hold of the ship and hid myself away among the bales of hay stowed there. I heard the others being shaved. I heard "Charles" being called for and then I saw the lantern down in the hold hunting for "Charles", until the mate came down and ordered off the searchers fearing they would get the ship afire. I lay there all the next day and then appeared on deck much to the relief of everybody for it had come to be feared all over the ship that I had by fear or by accident come to harm. . . .

It is 1848. Charles Duncan is now master of the Swanton, *a ship built in Bath now engaged in the busy transatlantic trade. His freight may be American flour on its way to the victims of the Irish potato famine or tobacco going to Italy. Going west, the* Swanton *brings Carrara marble from Leghorn to Boston or, on this next voyage, 250 steerage passengers from Le Havre to New Orleans.*

From Boston (it was early fall) we discharged the ship and went to New Orleans, where we engaged another cargo of tobacco for London. . . . I went across by steamer to Havre, while the ship was discharging, for the purpose of getting a cargo back of passengers to New Orleans and succeeded and so after the ship was discharged in London, we sailed her across the Channel, went into Havre and then took on board a cargo of passengers, fraught with greater consequences to our country than any passengers that were ever landed upon its shores! For twenty days after leaving Havre, we had delightful weather, the ship and passengers were sweet and clean and perfectly healthful. The passengers were in excellent spirits, the ship had made good progress across the ocean and on the night on which I am now drawing the line, there was hot air, like steam came on board of us from the Southeast and started perspiration on everybody. No one knew where it came from, no one knew what it meant. We had on board about 250 steerage passengers. That night at about two o'clock, I was called to attend to a passenger sick in the steerage. We had no doctor on board and, since my business was to go, I went and the passenger died with Asiatic cholera as near as I could tell; shortly after I got there. I went back to my cabin and in an hour I was called to another one who also died shortly after I got to him. Instantly there was panic on board. We had cholera among our passengers. No one knew how it came or how long it would last. One and another were being taken and every one that was taken died. No doctor on board to consult — only medical books. There was terror for fear of contagion but really no danger — everybody on board was put under a course of medicine, camphor, supposed to be a sovereign preventive and from that hour until we arrived, the whole thought of our passengers and crew seemed to be the progress of the cholera. I was constant myself night and day in answering calls to the sick. Of course, there was worry and anxiety and great was the solicitude of the passengers, when as it often happened, I was so far exhausted as not to appear on deck. As I said before, everyone that was taken died; and from that time until we entered the Mississippi, a period of about 18 days, I think about 25 died and were buried at sea. We entered the Mississippi unmolested by quarantine guards or restraints.

Took a tow boat and started for the city. The ship should have been instantly detained at the mouth of the river in quarantine but this was neglected most unaccountably. I got on board a passenger steamer and started for the city. I think no one can imagine the relief that I found it when I stepped out of that ship infected by cholera, pursued by the groans and dying of the passengers, the care and responsibility of that whole ship's company — no one can imagine the relief I found it — to step on board that steamer, where there were no groans, no sickness, no dying. But that state of things did not last very long anywhere in that locality. I went up to New Orleans leaving the ship being towed up behind, and went direct to my consignee, Messrs. J. P. Whitney & Co., and gave them a true statement of the affairs on board my ship and I asked them whether I should call the ship into the levee when she came up and move her and land the passengers and say nothing about the cholera — or should I report her to the Board of Health, just as she was and have the ship quarantined over the river. Mr. Sumner, the managing partner said if I brought the ship in alongside of the levee, landed the passengers and said nothing about the cholera, most likely the whole thing would pass off — nothing would be known or said about it. Our passengers would assimilate with the population of the city and would create no unusual effect whatever. "But", said he, "if you report to the Board of Health what you have told me, how that cholera broke out on board your ship in mid-ocean, 25 or 30 have died of it, and that your passengers are still dying day by day, panic will sweep down upon us and will destroy the whole business of the city — say nothing about it!". . .

The next day but one after we arrived, the papers reported 90 deaths from cholera and the next day following more than 120. And then the dread disease took rapid hold of all the southern country. Up the Mississippi River, the Missouri and Ohio, all the low and marshy counties, thousands died of the dread disease. . . .

As soon as I got well enough, I settled up the voyage, installed Mr. Wood as Master and took out on an up-country boat for Pittsburg, Tenna. All the way up, there was the horrible groans of the dying of cholera to be heard. Nor did it leave us until we had passed Pittsburg and attained the summit of the Alleghany Mountains. The weather was cold when we got home (February) and my reputation as connected with the cholera had a long way preceded me. The good neighbors were not at all comfortable when I was around and most of them had a good deal rather I had not made them friendly calls. However, that unpleasant incident passed away and I enjoyed a delightful year at home. I was attached to the shipyard and my pay at a small rate was going on — the owners were having a small sized ship — the *Hannah Crooker* built for my old friend in the *Triumph*, Capt. Murray and another ship, the *Charles Crooker,* a larger one, being built for me. The building of both of which, it was my pleasant occupation to superintend. Capt. Murray's was completed first and he went off in it, still leaving me busy about my own. In due time, she was launched, completed, rigged and fitted for sea. When we came to preparing for sea, I suggested to the owners that it would be pleasant to have their consent to take my family along. . . .

In 1850, on his first voyage with his own ship and his family aboard, Duncan loaded a cargo of cotton in Charleston bound for Liverpool. The Charles Crooker *was nearly lost in a dense fog on the southwest coast of Ireland but at last moved up the Mersey River to Liverpool.*

Liverpool in those days, for American sailing ships was brisk and busy. It was 47 years ago — the "American flag covered the ocean" as the saying then was. Our ships were sought for to carry freight and were favorite conveyances of passengers. Few steamers crossed the ocean then — the old Cunard Line, for instance, that used to make rushing passages across the ocean in 14 or 15 days, their rates of passage were high; consequently American ships were caught up eagerly by passenger brokers and every day they were leaving Liverpool filled with passengers for New York or Boston.

Before our ship was half unloaded she was engaged for New York with a full cargo of goods in the lower hold and passengers in the between decks. We took about 500 passengers I remember and the whole "tween decks" was cleared out and filled up with berths from end to end. A row against either side and a double row along midships, running in two tiers and constructed 6 feet square and subdivided into berths 6 feet long and 18 inches wide by which each compartment was made to contain four persons. This was done in compliance with an Act of Congress that required that each passenger should be entitled to a separate berth of the dimensions named. It often happened that berths being constructed parallel with the sides of the ship and engaged by parties some in one part of the country, some in another, each berth identified with a number, that strange and unpleasant neighborhoods were formed in the sleeping quarters. An old lady and an old gentleman, for instance would be assigned to the two farther berths nearest to the sides of the ship. A young man and a young woman might be assigned to the two remaining berths and other equally unpleasant assignments in other berths made and in the going to bed and the getting up there would have to be climbing over and over each other — unpleasant, if not indecent. I will say in parenthesis that the attention of Congress being called to this evil, it was remedied by an amendment specifying that every berth should be located so that it could be reached without crossing any other berth and this was accomplished by thrifty passenger brokers by dividing the original 6 foot square berth athwart ships instead of fore and aft, so that they resembled long narrow drawers, the head against the side of the ship and the foot amid ships, so that the unfortunate passenger would need to crawl into his berth head first as into a hole. In practice, however, I will say that usually the large berths were engaged understandingly by families who took out the small subdivisions and filled the berth with their big mattresses and themselves.

While we were loading a young man from the broker's office came down on board saying that a clergyman was at a neighboring hotel and wanted to see me about arranging for a cabin passage. I went up and was introduced to him just as he was leaving the bar wiping his lips. "I understand, sir, that you desire to take passage in my ship to New York". "Yes, sir". "I am told you are a clergyman". "Yes, yes" said the clergyman. "I have a clergyman as a passenger on board already," I said, "a friend of mine". "Oh, well" said he, "he will not interfere with me and I shall not interfere with him". I excused myself, bade him good morning and told him I would send him my answer. I went outside the door and asked the clerk who was with me, if he would return and report to this "clergyman" that I would prefer not to take him.

Sailing day came and with our ship loaded deep and filled with passengers, we warped down to the dock gates, attached our hawser to a powerful steam tug in waiting and started for the sea and New York. Among the first that I saw among the passengers after we had got out, was the "clergyman" who I had refused to take. "Hello" said I, "you here". "Yes" said he, "You wouldn't have me in the cabin — I liked the looks of your ship and concluded I'd have to come along steerage". He was a Catholic priest, youngish man and proved invaluable during the passage in the influence he had among the passengers. He would drink with them — dance — play cards with them — was leader in all sports — would sit on the capstan head and play the fiddle but in matters of order and discipline he was a regular martinet and kept the whole 500 under thorough control.

There is no end to the interest to be had in watching the movements of passengers when first launched out of port on to the great ocean. Human nature asserts itself conspicuously in all its phases everywhere. The grouping of families, the caressing, the cursings — the billing and cooing of lovers — the supreme selfishness — the heroic endurance — the self-sacrificing kindness. But in the matter of cooking which I will allude to a little later on, it is curiously interesting. First out of the docks and going down the channel between the sand banks our passengers were all on deck and all astir — some bright and jolly — some sad and depressed. But as we got out to where the waves moved and our deeply loaded ship bowed to them on either side in passing, most all of them became thoughtful — then pale — then effusive. At last they disappeared. By nightfall there were none on deck, but deep and sad and heavy were the howlings and the moanings that came up from below. . . .

The passenger brokers supplied the passengers with cooking ranges placed on deck, and wood and water. The passengers took their provisions along themselves which the ship's officers took charge of and once every day everybody on board was supplied with food and water. Many were the episodes, funny and otherwise, at the cooking ranges while cooking was going on. Crowding for turns, moving away one another's utensils, "hooking" choice morsels. I remember once standing on the front part of the quarter deck seeing a man take off a pot from a nice place where it seemed comfortably enjoying itself, setting it back in the cold and in its place put his own frying pan, into which he put some slices of pork and broke some eggs. This dish took up the theme, went right on responding cheerily to the inspiration of the fire and soon sent up an odor that reached even my nostrils 40 feet away. Presently the woman came along — for it was a woman who owned the pot that had been taken off. She took in the situation at a glance and at a glance she identified the owner of all the mischief and in a moment she caught up the frying pan by the handle, gave it a whirl and brought it down, bottom up on the bare head of this man. Then she put her own pot back and resumed her cooking as if nothing had happened. . . .

We had sailed from Liverpool in March and most fortunately very shortly after sailing from Liverpool, a northeast wind took us (the northeast winds on that coast are clear, steady, strong and pleasant) and ran us up to the Western Islands — Azores — more than a thousand miles in less than a week. We thought we were going to have a short passage but alas! were disappointed. The wind changed, westerly gales prevailed, strong and severe. We could do nothing but tack, first one direction and then another — beaten back in every tack often losing spars and sails by the fury of the gales. In marking our position on the chart every day, I found that in 30 days from the time in which our fair winds left us until they returned again, we had not gained one mile! Many things happened though during those 30 days. I saw a ship at a distance one day, to the leeward with its foremast gone, broken off at the deck taking with it the main top-gallant mast, sails and yards. I ran for him to see if I could render some help and found it was an old acquaintance, the *William Jarvis* also from Liverpool, but he said we could render him no assistance. I wondered he had not gone into Fayal — close by — his ship being full of passengers, but he stuck to it and we parted company. They were disastrous days — for us those stormy 30 days — every day or every night some accident seemed to happen and we came to expect it. One day the tiller broke an iron and steel spring and necessitated sharp and skillful work to save the rudder. Then the main top-gallant mast rolled away when the ship was performing one of her Chinese Mandarin rolling-matches — then the jib broke — a stick as big around as any body, and always almost, the decks were so flooded by the breaking seas that the passengers, poor wretches, had to stop under deck and eat hard bread and uncooked food. . . .

Good weather and winds favored us for another third of our journey and enabled us to climb up to the banks of Newfoundland with nothing special to break the monotony of the voyage. We were becalmed here for a few days — caught a few fish. One of the ladies caught a big fellow by a hook through the tail. It took two men to pull him in. Then we made a little sport by selling him at auction.

Sundays were quietly observed — Mr. Morse preached in the forenoons and in the afternoons our Catholic priest went down in the steerage to tell his flock there was but a "plank between them and eternity!" which was his way of putting the gospel. There were no deaths on board, not even a case of sickness. Storms and trouble, however, returned again with the last one third of the passage. Crossing George's Shoals we were caught in a SWS hurricane which nearly stripped us of everything in the way of sails and spars. This same gale blew down in its circular course; while hitting us from the westward it struck Minot's Ledge Lighthouse near Boston from the eastward and blew it down and blew into Boston our friend the *William Jarvis* whom we had seen crippled and dismasted off the Western Islands more than a month before. The winds from the West had beaten us back and the same winds going in their circuit and from the eastward had beaten her along. In the midst of this fearful gale off George's Shoals, I was shocked in the evening to hear the cry that the ship was on fire and a bright light forward. It was not serious however. A frying pan had been capsized by the bumbling of the ship, burning fat had spilled out upon the deck upon chain cables down through the deck pipes and into the chain locker below, blazing as it went. It was easily extinguished and order restored. A week or so afterwards we worked our way into New York — a battered and bruised looking ship 56 days out from Liverpool but everybody healthy, hearty and strong. So ended the first voyage of the *Charles Crooker*.

HARRIET BEECHER STOWE
1811–1896

Harriet Beecher Stowe was a passionate, moralistic espouser of causes, a dedicated homemaker and mother to her seven children, and a hardworking genre novelist. She came by the first characteristic honestly, having been raised in a highly moral world. Her father, Lyman Beecher, was an evangelistic minister quick to proclaim good causes, her six brothers were ministers, and she married a biblical scholar, Calvin E. Stowe.

Her dismay at the miseries that slavery inflicted dated from her life in Cincinnati, a way station on the underground railroad, and her famous novel, *Uncle Tom's Cabin,* was written to express her outrage. It was her major and most influential work, as evidenced by Abraham Lincoln's words upon meeting her: "So you're the little woman who wrote the book that made this great war!" Mrs. Stowe backed other causes as well. While she was living in Maine, her aversion to liquor led her to support the boycott of wine at public dinners. Perhaps only coincidentally, Maine, in 1851, became the first state in the Union to enact Prohibition.

Uncle Tom's Cabin was written while Harriet Beecher Stowe was living in Brunswick, Maine. Her husband had been appointed to the faculty of Bowdoin College as Collins Professor of Natural and Revealed Religion, and in 1850 Harriet, with several of their children, was dispatched to set up housekeeping in a fine old house on Federal Street in Brunswick. She was thirty-nine years old, pregnant with her last child, and surprisingly cheerful about the trials inherent in making a new home for her family. The Stowes stayed on in Brunswick for two years.

In addition to *Uncle Tom's Cabin,* Mrs. Stowe wrote several novels set in a New England locale. *The Pearl of Orr's Island* (1862) is a

Maine novel and exemplifies Mrs. Stowe's merits — and deficiencies — as a writer. A strong moral tone and a pronounced sentimentality pervade this romance, yet her sense of the importance of local detail and of fully developed characters makes it a valid portrayal of life along the coast of Maine.

Uncle Tom's Cabin was first serialized in *National Era,* a weekly newspaper published in Washington, D.C., from 1847 to 1860. It was an abolitionist publication of considerable literary merit: John Greenleaf Whittier was a corresponding editor. Mrs. Stowe wrote two "Letters from Maine" for *National Era* in 1852. They extol the beauty of her Maine, allow her to indulge in a bit of whimsy about the creative writing process, and express her admiration and concern for the women of Maine.

Letters from Maine

To the Editor of *The National Era:*

The fashionable complaint of neuralgia has kept back from your paper many "thoughts, motions and revolutions" of the brain, which, could they have printed themselves on paper, would have found their way towards you. Don't you suppose, in the marvellous progress of this fast-living age, the time will ever come, when, by some metaphysical daguerreotype process, the thoughts and images of the brain shall print themselves on paper, without the intervention of pen and ink? Then, how many brilliancies, now lost and forgotten before one gets time to put them through the slow process of writing, shall flash upon us! Our poets will sit in luxurious ease, with a quire of paper in their pockets, and have nothing to do but lean back in their chairs, and go off in an ecstasy, and lo! they will find it all written out, commas and all, ready for the printer. What a relief too, to multitudes of gentle hearts, whose friends in this busy age are too hurried to find much time for writing. Your merchant puts a sheet of paper inside of his vest — over his heart, of course — and in the interval between selling

"Spinning"

goods and pricing stocks, thinks warm thoughts towards his wife or ladylove — and at night draws forth a long letter, all directed, ready for the post. How convenient! Would that some friend of humanity would offer a premium for the discovery!

The spiritual rapping fraternity, who are *au fait* in all that relates to man's capabilities, and who are now speaking *ex cathedra* of all things celestial and terrestrial, past, present and to come, can perhaps immediately settle the minutiae of such an arrangement. One thing is quite certain: that if every man wore a sheet of paper in his bosom, on which there should be a true and literal version of all his thoughts, even for one day, in a great many cases he would be astounded on reading it over. Are there not many who would there see, in plain unvarnished English, what their patriotism, disinterestedness, generosity, friendship, religion, actually amounts to? Let us fancy some of our extra patriotic public men comparing such a sheet with their speeches. We have been amused, sometimes, at the look of blank astonishment with which men look for the first time on their own daguerreotype. Is that me? Do I look so? Perhaps this *inner* daguerreotype might prove more surprising still. "What, *I* think *that*? I purpose so and so? What a troublesome, ugly machine! I'll have nothing to do with it!"

But to drop that subject, and start another. It seems to us quite wonderful, that in all the ecstasies that have been lavished on American scenery, this beautiful State of Maine should have been so much neglected; for nothing is or can be more wildly, peculiarly beautiful — particularly the scenery of the sea-coast. A glance at the map will show one the peculiarity of these shores. It is a complicated network and labyrinth of islands — the sea interpenetrating the land in every fanciful form, through a belt of coast from fifteen to twenty miles wide. The effect of this, as it lies on the map, and as it lives and glows in reality, is as different as the difference between the poetry of life and its dead matter of fact.

But supposing yourself almost anywhere in Maine, within fifteen miles of the shore, and you start for a ride to the sea side, you will then be in a fair way to realize it. The sea, living, beautiful and life-giving, seems, as you ride, to be everywhere about you — behind, before, around. Now it rises like a lake, gemmed with islands, and embosomed by rich swells of woodland. Now, you catch a peep of it on your right hand, among tufts of oak and maple, and anon it spreads on your left to a majestic sheet of silver, among rocky shores, hung with dark pines, hemlocks, and spruces.

The sea shores of Connecticut and Massachusetts have a kind of baldness and bareness which you never see here. As you approach the ocean *there,* the trees seem to become stunted and few in number, but *here* the sea luxuriates, swells, and falls, in the very lap of the primeval forest. The tide water washes the drooping branches of the oak and maple, and dashes itself up into whole hedges of luxuriant arbor vitae.

No language can be too enthusiastic to paint the beauty of this evergreen in these forests. The lordly spruce, so straight, so tall, so perfectly defined in its outline with its regal crest of cones, sparkling with the clear exuded gum, and bearing on its top that "silent finger" which Elliot describes as "ever pointing up to God" — the ancient white pine with its slender whispering leaves, the feathery larches, the rugged and shaggy cedar — all unite to form such a "goodly fellowship," that one is inclined to think for the time that no son of the forest can compare with them. But the spruce is the prince among them all. Far or near, you see its slender obelisk of dark green, rising singly amid forests of oak or maple, or marshalled together in serried ranks over distant hills, or wooding innumerable points, whose fantastic outlines interlace the silvery sea. The heavy blue green of these distant pines forms a beautiful contrast to the glitter of the waters, and affords a fine background, to throw out the small white wings of sail boats, which are ever passing from point to point among these bays and harbors. One of the most peculiar and romantic features of these secluded wood-embosomed waters of Maine is this sudden apparition of shipping and sea craft, in such wild and lonely places, that they seem to you, as the first ships did to the simple savages, to be visitants from the spirit land. You are riding in a lonely road, by some bay that seems to you like a secluded inland lake; you check your horse, to notice the fine outline of the various points, when lo! from behind one of them, swan-like, with wings all spread, glides in a ship from India or China, and wakes up the silence, by tumbling her great anchor into the water. A ship, of itself a child of romance — a dreamy, cloudlike, poetic thing — and that ship connects these piney hills and rocky shores, these spruces and firs, with distant lands of palm and spice, and speaks to you, in these solitudes, of groves of citron and olive. We pray the day may never come when any busy Yankee shall find a substitute for ship sails, and take from these spirits of the wave their glorious white wings, and silent, cloud-like movement, for any fuss and sputter of steam and machinery. It will be just like some Yankee to do it. That race will never rest till everything antique and poetic is drilled out of the world. The same spirit which yearns to make Niagara a mill-seat, and use all its pomp and power of cloud and spray and rainbow, and its voices of many waters, for accessories to a cotton factory, would, we suppose, be right glad to transform the winged ship into some disagreeable greasy combination of machinery, if it would only come cheaper. The islands along the coast of Maine are a study for a tourist. The whole sail along the shores is through a never-ending labyrinth of these — some high and rocky, with castellated sides, bannered with pines — some richly wooded with forest trees — and others, again, whose luxuriant meadow land affords the finest pasturage for cattle. Here are the cottages of fishermen, who divide their time between farming and fishing, and thus between land and water make a very respectable amphibious living. These people are simple-hearted, kindly, hardy, with a good deal of the genial broad-heartedness that characterizes their old father, the ocean. When down on one of these lonely islands, once, we were charmed to find, in a small cottage, one of the prettiest and most lady-like of women. Her husband owned a fishing-smack; and while we were sitting conversing in the house, in came a damsel from the neighborhood, arrayed, in all points, *cap-a-pie,* according to the latest city fashions. The husband came home from a trip while we were there. He had stopped in Portland, and brought home a new bonnet for his wife, of the most approved style, and a pair of gaiter shoes for his little girl. One of our company was talking with him, congratulating him on his retired situation.

"You can go all about, trading in your vessel, and make money," he said, "and here on this retired island there is no way to spend it so you must lay up a good deal."

"Don't know about that," said the young man; "there's women and girls everywhere; and they must have their rings and their pins, and parasols and ribbons. There's ways enough for money to go."

On Sunday mornings, these islanders have put out their sailboats, and all make sail for some point where there is a church. They spend the day in religious services and return at evening. Could one wish a more picturesque way of going to meeting of a calm summer morning? . . .

Bethel, Oxford County

. . . But while we have been writing, this Sunday river has been long past, and our road winds deeper and deeper among the blue mountains. There, now, we are fairly shut in; that great dark fellow in front of us, with his wall of black pines and forest trees, towering quite up to the sky — he is right across our path — no, here is a turn — and on we go, the old mountain seeming to glide politely to one side. Here we come to a little sunny interval again; soft, rich, meadow land, enclosed all round with solemn walls of mountain — tier above tier of tree and rock, where in good time our road will bring up against an impenetrable wall. Here is a little settlement of farm-houses. Here, by the side of a clear stream, and in a most charming grove of maples, birches, and other forest trees, rises the school-house of the settlement. One wonders, going by, whether these bright-eyed children are impressed and educated in a love of the beautiful and grand, by the scenery in which they are brought up. Do they ever look with wonder and awe, up the dark inaccessible walls that hang round the little sunny nook where they are born? Do they ever lie thoughtfully under these trees, and hear the gurgle of the mountain stream, and watch the bright fleeces of the heavy clouds that rest on the blue, smoky mountains and have strange wonderings and yearnings for anything that lies beyond? One would think that the grand solemnities of nature would stamp their seal on the young heart, and mould it into something characteristic and peculiar. Certain it is, that these nooks and hollows among the mountains produce a race of great intellectual activity.

You go into a plain farm house, where the furniture and all the appurtenances retain the most primitive simplicity — but be not surprised if you see Latin, Greek, and German books lying on the table. You look inquiringly, and are told perhaps of a certain Mary Ann or Maria, who is keeping school up at Umbagog, or some other impossible out-of-the-way place, whose books these are. *She* had long done using them — she got them when she first begun; now she has left them for Cynthia or Louisa, or some other fair successor in the family line, who is equally hardy and energetic in her attacks upon the tree of knowledge. Ten to one, you get a glimpse of said Cynthia, who proves a slender, blue-eyed girl, trimly dressed, with a pair of very pretty ear-rings in her ears, and an air of quiet composure, and *savoir faire* which shows you that she is princess of the blood in her own regions. You talk with her, and find she has a mind as sharp and bright and keen as one of the quartz crystals among her own mountains. She has been to the academy in the neighboring town. She has a fancy for drawing, and maybe shows you a crayon head or a landscape, which you did not expect to see just then — she wishes she could get somewhere where she could learn more about it — she has a cousin who paints in oils — she thinks perhaps, after she has taught a quarter or two, she will save enough to get to Portland, and take lessons of a master.

One is struck with the intellectual activity of the Maine women, wherever he travels among them. A friend of mine told me the other day that in one of the towns where he was visiting, in the clergyman's family, he was surprised to find the walls decorated with oil paintings which he thought it quite beyond the means of his friend to have purchased.

"Where did you get these paintings?" he asked.

"Oh, these! my wife painted them!" was the reply.

The same gentleman relates that at another time, when hospitably entertained in an obscure settlement, far out in the woods of Maine, being struck with the domestic talents and agreeable manners of his hostess, he entered into some conversation with her. Knowing that he was connected with the collegiate institution in Brunswick, she inquired with great interest after a young gentleman there, adding as an apology for her inquisitiveness, "I fell interested in that young man, for I fitted him for college."

My friend, of course, thought she alluded to some such fitting as knitting his stockings, making his shirts — and made a remark to that effect.

"Oh no," said the lady, composedly, "I mean that I taught him Greek and Latin, and so on, and of course I should wish to hear that he was doing well." It seemed to be quite an of course affair to her, nothing to what she could do. I can assure you, by the bye, that these women are yeoman housekeepers, and that you will never taste the Latin and Greek in sour bread or bad butter, or see the drawing and painting looking out of holes in dresses.

The fact is, that a sterile soil and a harsh climate, though not good for growing anything else, are first rate for raising *men and women;* and *men and women,* in the full, emphatic sense of the word, are the staple produce of Maine. The long cheerless winters here are powerful educators, both physically and morally — physically in the amount of oxygen and vitality which they force into the system, intellectually in the leisure which they force on one for intellectual pursuits. Apropos of the winters, I will relate an anecdote which I heard in my village under the mountains which might give some of our Southern friends a new idea of what a winter here is like.

Said one of our friends, whose house lies directly under the mountains — "Last winter the snow was banked up quite to the ridgepole of the house."

"Is it possible?" I exclaimed. "Why, what did you all do?"

"Tunnelled through it!" said my friend, composedly; "we had a tunnel some fifteen feet long to the road."

"And, pray, how long did it last?" said I.

"Well, about six months," said he.

"It made the house very warm, indeed," added his wife, "almost oppressive."

That was one view of a snow-bank that had never suggested itself to me. But I must add to what I said about the Maine women and girls, one drawback — one is impressed with it even in the most mountainous district — the want of an appearance of robust health. The young girls are fair, sparkling, intellectual-looking, but they are wanting in the physique. They look like forest flowers — very fair, but as if a breath might wither them. The mind seems altogether to have got the start of the body. The long winters may have something to do with this. For more than half the year the female sex in this climate are very much confined in-doors, in stove-heated rooms, generally very partially ventilated, as rooms in cold weather always are. Here they read, and study, and sew — and go out, at most only in pleasant weather — often only in sleighs with fathers or brothers to drive them, and the sleigh is a vehicle that gives no sort of exercise. Can we not see in this fact the reason for that predisposition to diseases of the lungs which is constantly the terror of every parent in New England, and which seals every year hundreds of her fairest for the grave? Think of the contrast between the stove-heated room, where one is kept almost at the point of perspiration, and the lungs constantly inhaling warm air, and the sharp, keen, cutting air that is breathed without. There is no remedy for this, but a hardier habit of life. A young girl in New England is never secure against consumption, but by keeping her physical vigor up to the highest point. She should go out regularly every day, in all weathers, and familiarize her lungs with the out-door atmosphere. She should fortify her skin with daily cold bathing, wear short walking-dresses, prefer walking to the sleigh, practice skating and out-door amusements, after the example of European ladies in a similar climate — and then the long winter will be to her as it is to the other sex, a discipliner and invigorator to the system, and not a constant enemy.

My letter is running to a great length. Adieu for the present.
H.B.S.

Two Literary Men Visit the Maine Woods

In the late summer of 1853, two leading members of the most illustrious generation of literary men New England has ever produced went to Maine in search of material. Each was on a visit to that special part of the New England territory, the Maine wilderness, and Maine's symbolic animal, the outlandish moose. James Russell Lowell was the first to arrive, on August 13, at Greenville on Moosehead Lake. One month later came Henry David Thoreau on his second visit to the Maine woods. Each in turn took the little steamer *Moosehead* to the head of the lake.

Lowell, with his young nephew Charles Russell Lowell ("Telemachus") and two guides, landed at the northwest carry and entered the west branch of the Penobscot. After a night in the woods he retreated to Kineo House, built five years earlier, and spent four comfortable nights there at $3 a night for each Lowell. Thoreau, with his cousin's husband, George Thatcher of Bangor, and an Indian guide, Joe Aitteon, landed at the northeast carry and spent five nights investigating the lower west branch of the river and its tributaries. Each party hoped to kill a moose. Each described the adventure in print: Lowell's version appeared in *Putnam's,* New York's new literary monthly; Thoreau's, in Boston's new *Atlantic Monthly,* James Russell Lowell, editor.

Lowell was a popular poet, a leading abolitionist, a Brahmin born and raised, and also, of course, a cosmopolitan. Two years after his visit to Maine, he would replace Longfellow as Harvard's professor of modern languages. He and his wife and their two young children had recently spent a year in Europe, most of it in Italy, where they had joined ten other Lowells currently spending the winter in Rome. His account of his trip to Moosehead was couched in the form of a letter to a friend in Italy to whom he explained that he had visited the European lakes celebrated in the works of Vergil and Scott but had neglected Moosehead, only two days away. He was as much a foreigner in Maine, he said, as his Italian friend would be.

For Lowell and tourists of his ilk, Maine can be imagined as New England's Far West, the moose replacing the buffalo and the Maine lumberman, the western hunter and trapper. The analogy puts Lowell in that other traditional role, the eastern tenderfoot who goes to the Maine woods bearing his bookish culture as lightly as possible, for he is, after all, a fellow American and a democrat.

Thoreau was coming to Maine after an absence of six years. He had interrupted his experimental life at Walden Pond in 1846 to travel by ship to Bangor, then by stagecoach, wagon, and canoe up the Penobscot to the challenge of climbing Mount Katahdin. His report on this present visit to, for him, a new part of the wilderness had been asked for by Lowell for the *Atlantic.* However, Lowell's editing of the manuscript caused a breach between the two men that never healed. In the essay "Chesuncook," excerpted here, Thoreau extolled the beauty and the "nature" of the Maine white pine tree with this sentence: "It is as immortal as I am, and perchance will go to as high a heaven, there to tower above me still." That transcendental praise was too much for Lowell and, without consulting Thoreau, he deleted it. Later, he claimed in his defense that the *Atlantic* was being charged by its orthodox Christian readers with impieties. The magazine's publishers, he said, needed protection against such an extreme religious position. Thoreau found Lowell's action cowardly and wrote to him: "I could excuse a man who was afraid of an uplifted fist, but if one habitually manifests fear at the utterance of a sincere thought, I must think that his life is a kind of nightmare continued into broad daylight." Lowell never answered the rebuke, and Thoreau never wrote again for the *Atlantic* while Lowell was editor.

Thoreau's three essays on Maine, published after his death as *The Maine Woods,* have never had the popular appeal of *Walden* or his political essays. They are detailed travel accounts that do not seem to make a book but read rather like notes for the book he always planned to write about Indians and the wilderness. The disparate materials, including his ambiguous relations with the Maine Indians whom he wanted so earnestly to understand, are not brought together in any structured plan. He is at his best when he is expressing his delight in being where he is — in a "bran-new country." Maine was the only place available to Thoreau where he could conceive of a region uninhabited by man: "We habitually presume his presence everywhere." And he was aware that the "tide of fashionable travel" had already begun to set in the direction of the wilderness.

In Maine, Lowell and Thoreau were human antipodes. "Wilderness," Lowell said, "was all very well for a mood or vacation, but not for a habit of life." Thoreau was in search of what he called, avoiding at all costs a religious word, "essentials." His most permanent conviction was his faith that man had a place in a natural, sacramental universe. He spent his days seeking those moments when he could identify himself with the earth and the materials of nature. In the Maine woods he hoped to find such moments.

A Moosehead Journal

JAMES RUSSELL LOWELL
1819–1891

Friday, August 12th, 1853. — The coach leaves Waterville at five
o'clock in the morning, and one must breakfast in the dark at a
quarter past four, because a train starts at twenty minutes before
five, — the passengers by both conveyances being pastured gregari-
ously. So one must be up at half past three. The primary geological
formations contain no trace of man, and it seems to me that these
eocene periods of the day are not fitted for sustaining the human
forms of life. One of the Fathers held that the sun was created to be
worshipped at his rising by the Gentiles. The more reason that Christians (except, perhaps, early Christians) should abstain from these
heathenish ceremonials. As one arriving by an early train is welcomed
by a drowsy maid with the sleep scarce brushed out of her hair, and
finds empty grates and polished mahogany, on whose arid plains the
pioneers of breakfast have not yet encamped, so a person waked thus
unseasonably is sent into the world before his faculties are up and
dressed to serve him. It might have been for this reason that my
stomach resented for several hours a piece of fried beefsteak which I
forced upon it, or, more properly speaking, a piece of that leathern
conveniency which in these regions assumed the name. . . .

Today has been the hottest day of the year, yet our drive has not
been unpleasant. For a considerable distance we followed the course
of the Sebasticook River, a pretty stream with alternations of dark
brown pools and wine-colored rapids. On each side of the road the
land had been cleared, and little one-storied farm-houses were scattered at intervals. But the stumps still held out in most of the fields,
and the tangled wilderness closed in behind, striped here and there

with the slim white trunks of the elm. As yet only the edges of the great forest have been nibbled away. Sometimes a root fence stretched up its bleaching antlers, like the trophies of a giant hunter. Now and then the houses thickened into an unsocial-looking village, and we drove up to the grocery to leave and take a mail-bag, stopping again presently to water the horses at some pallid little tavern, whose one red-curtained eye (the bar-room) had been put out by the inexorable thrust of the Maine Law [Maine's prohibition law, passed in 1851]. . . . As we trailed along at the rate of about four miles an hour, it was discovered that one of our mail bags was missing. "Guess somebody'll pick it up," said the driver coolly; "at any rate, likely there's nothing in it." Who knows how long it took some Elam D. or Zebulon K. to compose the missive, intrusted to that vagrant bag, and how much longer to persuade Pamela Grace or Sophronia Melissa that it had really and truly been written? The discovery of our loss was made by a tall man who sat next to me on the top of the coach, every one of whose senses seemed to be prosecuting its several investigations as we went along. Presently, sniffing gently, he remarked: " 'Pears to me's though I smell sunthin'. Ain't the aix het, think?" The driver pulled up, and, sure enough, the off fore-wheel was found to be smoking. In three minutes he had snatched a rail from the fence, made a lever, raised the coach, and taken off the wheel, bathing the hot axle and box with water from the river. . . .

There being four passengers for the Lake, a vehicle called a mud-wagon was detailed at Newport for our accommodation. In this we jolted and rattled along at a livelier pace than in the coach. As we got further north, the country (especially the hills) gave evidence of longer cultivation. About the thriving town of Dexter we saw fine farms and crops. The houses, too, became prettier; hop-vines were trained about the doors, and hung their clustering thyrsi over the open windows. A kind of wild rose (called by the country folk the primrose) and asters were planted about the door-yards, and orchards, commonly of natural fruit, added to the pleasant home-look. But everywhere we could see that the war between the white man and the forest was still fierce, and that it would be a long while before the axe was buried.

At a quarter past eleven, P.M., we reached Greenville, (a little village which looks as if it had dripped down from the hills, and settled in the hollow at the foot of the lake,) having accomplished seventy-two miles in eighteen hours. The tavern was totally extinguished. The driver rapped upon the bar-room window, and after a

"Rogers House, Phippsburg"

while we saw heat-lightnings of unsuccessful matches followed by a low grumble of vocal thunder, which I'm afraid took the form of imprecation. Presently there was a great success, and the steady blur of lighted tallow succeeded the fugitive brilliance of the pine. A hostler fumbled the door open, and stood staring at us but not seeing us, with the sleep sticking out all over him. We at last contrived to launch him, more like an insensible missile than an intelligent or intelligible being, at the slumbering landlord, who came out wide-awake, and welcomed us as so many half-dollars, — twenty-five cents for each bed, ditto breakfast. . . . The only roost was in the garret, which had been made into a single room, and contained eleven double beds, ranged along the walls. It was like sleeping in a hospital. However, nice customs curtsy to eighteen hour rides, and we slept.

Saturday, 13th. — This morning I performed my toilet in the bar-room, where there was an abundant supply of water and a halo of interested spectators. After a sufficient breakfast, we embarked on the little steamer *Moosehead,* and were soon throbbing up the lake. . . . There were three or four clearings on the western shore; but after passing these, the lake became wholly primeval, and looked to us as it did to the first adventurous Frenchman who paddled across it. . . . On all sides rose deep-blue mountains, of remarkably graceful outline, and more fortunate than common in their names. There were Big and Little Squaw, the Spencer and Lily-bay Mountains. It was debated whether we saw Katahdin or not, . . . and presently Mount Kineo rose abruptly before us, in a shape not unlike the island of Capri . . .

There were a couple of loggers on board, in red flannel shirts and with rifles. They were the first I had seen, and I was interested in their appearance. They were tall, well-knit men, straight as Robin Hood, and with a quiet, self-contained look that pleased me. I fell into talk with one of them.

"Is there a good market for the farmers here in the woods?" I asked.

"None better. They can sell what they raise at their doors, and for the best of prices. The lumberers want it all, and more."

"It must be a lonely life. But then we all have to pay more or less life for a living."

"Well, it is lonesome. Shouldn't like it. After all, the best crop a man can raise is a good crop of society. We don't live none too long anyhow; and without society a fellow couldn't tell more'n half the time whether he was alive or not."

This speech gave me a glimpse into the life of a lumberman's camp. It was there that a man would soon find out how much alive he was, — there he could learn to estimate his quality, weighed in the nicest self-adjusting balance. The best arm at the axe or the paddle, the surest eye for a road or for the weak point in a jam, the steadiest foot on the squirming log, the most persuasive voice to the tugging oxen, — all these things are rapidly settled, and so an aristocracy is evolved from this democracy of the woods. . . .

A string of five loons was flying back and forth in long, irregular zigzags, uttering at intervals their wild, tremulous cry, which always seems far away, like the last, faint pulse of echo, dying among the hills, and which is one of those few sounds that, instead of disturbing solitude, only deepen and confirm it. On our inland ponds they are usually seen in pairs, and I asked if it were common to meet five together. My question was answered by a queer-looking old man, chiefly remarkable for a pair of enormous cow-hide boots, over which large blue trousers of frocking strove in vain to crowd themselves.

"Wahl, 't ain't ushil," said he, "and it's called a sign o' rain comin', that is."

"Do you think it will rain?"

With the caution of a veteran "auspex," he evaded a direct reply. "Wahl, they du say it's a sign o' rain comin'," said he.

I discovered afterward that my interlocutor was Uncle Zeb. Formerly, every New England town had its representative uncle, ... some elderly man who, for want of more defined family ties, had gradually assumed this avuncular relation to the community, inhabiting the border-land between respectability and the almshouse, with no regular calling, but working at haying, wood-sawing, whitewashing, associated with the demise of pigs and the ailments of cattle. ...

By this time we had arrived at Kineo, — a flourishing village of one house, the tavern kept by 'Squire' Barrows. The 'Squire' is a large, hearty man, with a voice as clear and strong as a northwest wind, and a great laugh suitable to it. His table is neat and well supplied, and he waits upon it himself in the good old landlordy fashion.

Sunday, 14th. — The loons were right. About midnight it began to rain in earnest, and did not hold up until about ten o'clock this morning. "This is a Maine dew," said a shaggy woodman cheerily, as he shook the water out of his wide-awake, "if it don't look out sharp, it'll begin to rain afore it thinks on't." The day was mostly spent indoors, but I found good and intelligent society.

Monday, 15th. — The morning was fine and we were called at four o'clock. ... We were to paddle about twenty miles; but we made it rather more by crossing and recrossing the lake. ... Little islands loomed trembling between sky and water, like hanging gardens. ... About noon we reached the head of the lake and took possession of a deserted wongen [lumber camp shack], in which to cook and eat our dinner. No Jew, I am sure, can have more thorough dislike of salt pork than I have in a normal state, yet I had already eaten it raw with hard bread for lunch and relished it keenly. ... One of our guides had shot three Canada grouse, and these were turned slowly between the fire and a bit of salt pork which dropped fatness upon them as it fried. This accomplished we re-embarked. ... We paddled a short distance up a brook which came into the lake smoothly through a little meadow not far off. We soon reached the Northwest Carry, and our guide, pointing through the woods, said: "That's the Canady road. You can travel that clean to Kebeck, a hunderd and twenty mile," — a privilege of which I respectfully declined to avail myself. The offer, however remains open to the public. The Carry is called two miles; but this is the estimate of somebody who had nothing to lug. I had a headache and all my baggage, which, with a traveler's instinct, I had brought with me. . . . My estimate of the distance is eighteen thousand six hundred and seventy-four miles and three quarters, — the fraction being the part left to be travelled after one of my companions most kindly insisted on relieving me of my heaviest bag. . . .

The end of the carry was reached at last, and, as we drew near it, we heard a sound of shouting and laughter. It came from a party of men making hay of the wild grass in Seboomok meadows, which lie around Seboomok pond, into which the carry empties. Their camp was near and our two hunters set out for it, leaving us seated in the birch on the plashy border of the pond. The repose was perfect. Another heaven hallowed and deepened the polished lake, and through that nether world the fish-hawk's double floated with balanced wings, or, wheeling suddenly, flashed his whitened breast against the sun. As the clattering kingfisher flew unsteadily across, and seemed to push his heavy head along with ever-renewing effort, a visionary mate flitted from downward tree to tree below. Some tall alders shaded us from the sun, in whose yellow afternoon light the drowsy forest was steeped, giving out that wholesome, resinous perfume, almost the only warm odor which it is refreshing to breathe. The tame hay-cocks in the midst of the wildness gave one a pleasant reminiscence of home, like hearing one's native tongue in a strange country.

Presently our hunters came back, bringing with them a tall, thin, active-looking man with black eyes, that glanced unconsciously on all sides, like one of those spots of sunlight which a child dances up and down the street with a bit of looking glass. This was M., the captain of the hay-makers, a famous river-driver, and who was to have fifty men under him next winter. I could now understand that sleepy vigilance of eye. He had consented to take two of our party in his birch to search for moose. A quick, nervous, decided man, he got them into the birch and was off instantly, without a superfluous word. He evidently looked upon them as he would upon a couple of logs which he was to deliver at a certain place. . . .

After paddling a couple of miles, we found the arbored mouth of the little Malahoodus River, famous for moose. We had been on the look-out for it, and I was amused to hear one of the hunters say to the other, to assure himself of his familiarity with the spot, "You drove the West Branch last spring, didn't you?" as one of us might ask about a horse. We did not explore the Malahoodus far, but left the other birch to thread its cedar solitudes, while we turned back to try our fortunes in the larger stream. We paddled on about four miles farther, lingering now and then opposite the black mouth of a moose-path. . . .

Half past Eleven, P.M. — No sign of a moose yet. The birch, it seems, was strained at the Carry, or the pitch was softened as she lay on the shore during dinner, and she leaks a little. If there be any virtue in the "sitzbad," I shall discover it. . . .

Quarter to Twelve, — Later from the Freshet! The water in the birch is about three inches deep, but the dampness reaches nearly to the waist. I am obliged to remove the matches from the ground-floor of my trousers into the upper story of a breast-pocket. Meanwhile we are to sit immovable, — for fear of frightening the moose, — which induces cramps.

Half past Twelve, — A crashing is heard on the left bank. This is a moose in good earnest. We are besought to hold our breaths, if possible. My fingers so numb, I could not, if I tried. Crash! crash! again, and then a plunge, followed by a dead stillness. "Swimmin' crik," whispers guide, suppressing all unnecessary parts of speech, — "don't stir." I, for one, am not likely to. A cold fog which has been gathering for the last hour has finished me. I fancy myself one of those naked pigs that seem rushing out of market-doors in the winter, frozen in a ghastly attitude of gallop. If I were to be shot myself, I should feel no interest in it. As it is, I am only a spectator, having declined a gun. Splash! again; this time the moose is in sight, and click! click! one rifle misses fire after the other. The fog has quietly spiked our batteries. The moose goes crashing up the bank, and presently we can hear it chewing its cud close by. So we lie in wait, freezing.

At one o'clock, I propose to land at a deserted wongen I had noticed on the way up, where I will make a fire, and leave them to refrigerate as much longer as they please. Axe in hand, I go plunging through waist-deep weeds dripping with dew, haunted by an intense conviction that the gnawing sound we had heard was a bear, and a bear at least eighteen hands high. There is something pokerish about a deserted dwelling, even in broad daylight; but here in the obscure wood, and the moon filtering unwillingly though the trees! Well, I made the door at last, and found the place packed fuller with darkness than it had ever been with hay. Gradually I was able to make things out a little, and began to hack frozenly at a log which I had groped out. I was relieved presently by one of the guides. He cut at once into one of the uprights of the building till he got some dry splinters, and we soon had a fire like the burning of a whole wood-wharf in our part of the country. My companion went back to the birch, and left me to keep house. First I knocked a hole in the roof (which the fire began to lick in a relishing way) for a chimney, and then cleared away a damp growth of "pison-elder," to make a sleeping place. When the unsuccessful hunters returned, I had everything quite comfortable, and was steaming at the rate of ten horse-power a minute. Young Telemachus was sorry to give up the moose hunt so soon, and, with the teeth chattering almost out of his head, he declared that he would like to stick it out all night. However, he reconciled himself to the fire, and, making our bed of some "splits" which we poked from the roof, we lay down at half past two. I, who have inherited a habit of looking into every closet before I go to bed, for fear of fire, had become in two days such a stoic of the woods, that I went to sleep tranquilly certain that my bedroom would be in a blaze before morning. And, indeed, it was; and the withes that bound it together being burned off, one of the sides fell in without waking me.

A Moose Hunt

HENRY DAVID THOREAU
1817–1862

When I arrived [in Bangor on September 14, 1853] my companion that was to be had gone up river, and engaged an Indian, Joe Aitteon, a son of the Governor, to go with us to Chesuncook Lake. Joe had conducted two white men a-moose-hunting in the same direction the year before. He arrived by cars at Bangor that evening, with his canoe and a companion, Sabattis Solomon, who was going to leave Bangor the following Monday with Joe's father, by way of the Penobscot, and join Joe in moose-hunting at Chesuncook when we had done with him. They took supper at my friend's house and lodged in his barn, saying they should fare worse than that in the woods. They only made Watch bark a little, when they came to the door in the night for water, for he does not like Indians.

The next morning Joe and his canoe were put on board the stage for Moosehead Lake, sixty and odd miles distant, an hour before we started in an open wagon. We carried hard bread, pork, smoked beef, tea, sugar, etc., seemingly enough for a regiment; the sight of which brought together reminded me by what ignoble means we had maintained ourselves hitherto. We went by the avenue road, which is quite straight and very good, northwestward toward Moosehead Lake, through more than a dozen flourishing towns, with almost every one its academy, — not one of which, however, is on my General Atlas, published, alas! in 1824; so much are they before the age, or I behind it! The earth must have been considerably lighter to the shoulders of General Atlas then.

It rained all this day until the middle of the next forenoon, concealing the landscape almost entirely; but we had hardly got out of the

A Maine moose

streets of Bangor before I began to be exhilarated by the sight of the wild fir and spruce-tops, and those of other primitive evergreens peering through the mist in the horizon. It was like the sight and odor of cake to a schoolboy. He who rides and keeps the beaten track studies the fences chiefly. . . . I noticed occasionally very long troughs which supplied the road with water, and my companion said that three dollars annually were granted by the State to one man in each school district, who provided and maintained a suitable water trough by the roadside, for the use of travellers, — a piece of intelligence as refreshing to me as the water. That legislature did not sit in vain. It was an Oriental act, which made me wish that I was still further down East, — another Maine Law, which I hope we may get in Massachusetts. That State is banishing barrooms from its highways, and conducting the mountain springs thither. . . . We reached Monson, fifty miles from Bangor, and thirteen from the lake, after dark.

At four o'clock the next morning, in the dark, and still in the rain, we pursued our journey. . . . Already we had thought that we saw Moosehead Lake from a hill-top, where an extensive fog had filled the lowlands, but we were mistaken. It was not until we were in within a mile or two of its south end that we got our first view of it, — a suitably wild-looking sheet of water, sprinkled with small, low islands, which were covered with shaggy spruce and other wild wood, — seen over the infant port of Greenville, with mountains on each side and far in the north, and a steamer's smoke-pipe rising above a roof. A pair of moose-horns ornamented a corner of the public house where we left our horse, and a few rods distant lay the small steamer *Moosehead*, Captain King. There was no village, and no summer road any farther in this direction, — but a winter road, that is, one passable only when deep snow covers its inequalities, from Greenville up the east side of the lake to Lily Bay, about twelve miles.

I was here first introduced to Joe. He had ridden all the way on the outside of the stage, the day before, in the rain, giving way to ladies, and was well wetted. As it still rained, he asked if we were going to "put it through." He was a good-looking Indian, twenty-four years old, apparently of unmixed blood, short and stout, with a broad face and reddish complexion, and eyes, methinks, narrower and more turned-up at the outer corners than ours, answering to the description of his race. Besides his under-clothing, he wore a red-flannel shirt, woolen pants, and a black Kossuth hat, the ordinary dress of the lumberman, and, to a considerable extent of the Penobscot Indian. When, afterward, he had occasion to take off his shoes and stockings, I was struck with the smallness of his feet. He had worked a good deal as a lumberman, and appeared to identify himself with that class. He was the only one of the party who possessed an India-rubber jacket. The top strip or edge of his canoe was worn nearly through by friction on the stage.

At eight o'clock the steamer, with her bell and whistle, scaring the moose, summoned us aboard. She was a well-appointed little boat, commanded by a gentlemanly captain, with patent life-seats and metallic life-boat, and dinner on board, if you wish. She is chiefly used by lumberers for the transportation of themselves, their boats, and supplies, but also by hunters and tourists. . . . There were but few passengers, and not one female among them: a St. Francis Indian with his canoe and moose-hides, two explorers for lumber, three men who landed at Sandbar Island, and a gentleman who lives on Deer Island, eleven miles up the lake. . . . The explorers had a fine, new birch on board, larger than ours, in which they had come up the Piscataquis from Howland, and they had several messes of trout already. They were going to the neighborhood of Eagle and Chamberlain Lakes, or the headquarters of the St. John, and offered to keep us company as far as we went. . . .

We reached the head of the lake about noon. The weather had, in the meanwhile, cleared up, though the mountains were still capped with clouds. Seen from this point, Mount Kineo, and two other allied mountains ranging with it northeasterly, presented a very strong family likeness, as if all cast in one mould. The steamer here approached a long pier projecting from the northern wilderness, and built of some of its logs, — and whistled, where not a cabin nor a mortal was to be seen. The shore was quite low, with flat rocks on it, overhung with black ash, arbor-vitae, etc., which at first looked as if they did not care a whistle for us. There was not a single cabman to cry "Coach!" or inveigle us to the United States Hotel. At length a Mr. Hinckley, who had a camp at the other end of the "carry," appeared with a truck drawn by an ox and a horse over a rude log railway through the woods. The next thing was to get our canoe and effects over the carry from this lake, one of the heads of the Kennebec, into the Penobscot River. This railway from the lake to the river occupied the middle of a clearing two or three rods wide and perfectly straight through the forest. We walked across while our baggage was drawn behind. My companion went ahead to be ready for partridges, while I followed looking at the plants. . . . At the north end of the carry, in the midst of a clearing of sixty acres or more, there was a log camp of the usual construction, with something more like a house adjoining, for the accommodation of the carryman's family and passing lumberers. . . .

We now proceeded to get our dinner, which always turned out to be tea, and to pitch canoes, for which purpose a large iron pot lay permanently on the bank. This we did in company with the explorers. Both Indians and whites use a mixture of rosin and grease for this purpose, — that is, for the pitching, not the dinner. Joe took a small brand from the fire and blew the heat and flame against the pitch on his birch, and so melted and spread it. Sometimes he put his mouth over the suspected spot and sucked, to see if it admitted air; and at one place, where we stopped, he set his canoe high on crossed stakes, and poured water into it. I narrowly watched his motions, and listened attentively to his observations, for we had employed an Indian mainly that I might have an opportunity to study his ways. I heard him swear once, mildly, during this operation, about his knife being as dull as a hoe, — an accomplishment which he owed to his intercourse with the whites; and he remarked, "We ought to have some tea before we start; we shall be hungry before we kill that moose."

At mid-afternoon we embarked on the Penobscot. . . . After paddling about two miles, we parted company with the explorers, and turned up Lobster Stream, which comes in on the right from the southeast. This was six to eight rods wide, and appeared to run nearly parallel to the Penobscot. Joe said it was so called from small fresh-water lobsters found in it. . . . The kingfisher flew before us, the pigeon wood-pecker was seen and heard, and nuthatches and chick-adees close at hand. Joe said they called the chickadee "kecunnilessu" in his language. I will not vouch for the spelling of what possibly was never spelt before, but I pronounced after him till he said it would do. We passed close to a woodcock, which stood perfectly still on the shore, with feathers puffed up, as if sick. This Joe said they called "nipsquecohossus." The kingfisher was "skuscumonsuck;" bear was "wassus;" Indian Devil, "lunxus;" the mountain ash, "upahsis." This was very abundant and beautiful. . . .

After ascending about a mile and a half, to within a short distance of Lobster Lake, we returned to the Penobscot. Just below the mouth of the Lobster we found quick water, and the river expanded to twenty or thirty rods in width. The moose-tracks were quite numerous and fresh here. We noticed in a great many places narrow and well-trodden paths by which they had come down to the river, and where they had slid on the steep and clayey bank. Their tracks were either close to the edge of the stream, those of the calves distinguish-able from the others, or in shallow water; the holes made by their feet in the soft bottom being visible for a long time. They were particu-larly numerous where there was a small bay, or "pokelogan," as it is called, bordered by a strip of meadow, or separated from the river by a long peninsula covered with coarse grass, wool-grass, etc., wherein they had waded back and forth and eaten the pads. We detected the remains of one in such a spot. At one place, where we landed to pick up a summer duck, which my companion had shot, Joe peeled a canoe-birch for bark for his hunting-horn. He then asked if we were not going to get the other duck, for his sharp eyes had seen another fall in the bushes a little farther along, and my companion obtained it. I now began to notice the bright red berries of the tree-cranberry, which grows eight or ten feet high, mingled with the alders and cornel along the shore. There was less hard wood than at first.

After proceeding a mile and three-quarters below the mouth of the Lobster, we reached, about sun-down, a small island at the head of what Joe called the Moosehead Dead-water (the Moosehorn, in which he was going to hunt that night, coming in about three miles below), and on the upper end of this we decided to camp. . . . Though

I had not come a-hunting, and felt some compunctions about accompanying the hunters, I wished to see a moose near at hand, and was not sorry to learn how the Indian managed to kill one. I went as reporter or chaplain to the hunters, — and the chaplain has been known to carry a gun. . . .

At length . . . Joe laid down his paddle, drew forth his birch horn, — a straight one, about fifteen inches long and three or four wide at the mouth, tied round with strips of the same bark, — and standing up, imitated the call of the moose, — "ugh, ugh, ugh," or "oo-oo-oo-oo," and then a prolonged "oo-o-o-o-o-o-o-o," and listened attentively for several minutes. We asked him what kind of noise he expected to hear. He said, that, if a moose heard it, he guessed we should find out; we should hear him coming half a mile off; he would come close to, perhaps into the water, and my companion must wait until he got fair sight; and then aim just behind the shoulder. . . .

Again and again Joe called the moose, placing the canoe close by some favorable point of meadow for them to come out on, but listened in vain to hear one come rushing through the woods and concluded that they had been hunted too much thereabouts. . . . Once when Joe had called again, and we were listening for moose, we heard, come faintly echoing, or creeping from afar, through the moss-clad aisles, a dull, dry, rushing sound, with a solid core to it, yet as if half smothered under the grasp of the luxuriant and fungus-like forest, like the shutting of a door in some distant entry of the damp and shaggy wilderness. If we had not been there, no mortal had heard it. When we asked Joe in a whisper what it was, he answered, — "Tree fall. . . ."

When we awoke in the morning, (Saturday, September 17,) there was considerable frost whitening the leaves. We heard the sound of the chickadee, and a few faintly lisping birds, and also of ducks in the water about the island. I took a botanical account of the stock of our domestic domains before the dew was off, and found that the ground hemlock, or the American yew, was the prevailing under-shrub. We breakfasted on tea, hard bread and ducks.

Before the fog had cleared away, we paddled down the stream again, and were soon past the mouth of the Moosehorn. . . . We stopped to fish for trout at the mouth of a small stream called the Ragmuff, which came in from the west about two miles before the Moosehorn. . . . While we were trying for trout, Joe, Indian-like, wandered off up the Ragmuff on his own errands, and when we were ready to start was far beyond call. So we were compelled to make a fire and get our dinner here, not to lose time. . . . Joe at length returned, after an hour and a half, and said he had been two miles up the stream exploring, and had seen a moose, but, not having a gun, he did not get him. We made no complaint, but concluded to look out for Joe the next time. However, this may have been a mere mistake, for we had no reason to complain of him afterwards. As we continued down the stream, I was surprised to hear him whistling, "O Susanna," and several other such airs, while his paddle urged us along. Once he said, "Yes, Sir-ee." His common word was "Sartain." He paddled as usual on one side only, giving the birch an impulse by using the side as a fulcrum. I asked him how the ribs were fastened to the side rails. He answered, "I don't know, I never noticed." Talking with him about subsisting wholly on what the woods yielded, game, fish, berries, etc., I suggested that his ancestors did so; but he answered that he had been brought up in such a way that he could not do it. "Yes," said he, "that's the way they got a living, like wild fellows, wild as bears. By George! I shan't go into the woods without provision, — hard bread, pork, etc." He had brought on a barrel of hard bread and stored it at the carry for his hunting. However, though he was a governor's son, he had not learned to read. . . .

After passing through some long rips, and by a large island, we reached an interesting part of the river called the Pine Stream Dead-Water, about six miles below Ragmuff, where the river expanded to thirty rods in width and had many islands in it, with elms and canoe-birches, now yellowing, along the shore, and we got our first sight of Ktaadn.

Here, about two o'clock, we turned up a small branch three or four rods wide, which comes in on the right from the south, called Pine Stream, to look for moose signs. We had gone but a few rods before we saw some very recent signs along the water's edge, the mud lifted up by their feet being quite fresh, and Joe declared that they had gone along there but a short time before. We soon reached a small meadow on the east side, at an angle in the stream, which was, for the most part, densely covered with alders. As we were advancing along the edge of this, rather more quietly than usual, perhaps, on account of the freshness of the signs, — the design being to camp up this stream if it promised well, — I heard a slight crackling of twigs deep in the alders and turned Joe's attention to it; whereupon he began to push the canoe back rapidly; and we had receded thus half a dozen rods, when we suddenly spied two moose standing just on the edge of the open part of the meadow which we had passed, not more than six or seven rods distant, looking round the alders at us. They made me think of great frightened rabbits, with their long ears and half-inquisitive, half-frightened looks; the true denizens of the forest, (I saw at once,) filling a vacuum which now first I discovered had not been filled for me, — "moose"-men, "wood-eaters," the word is said to mean, — clad in a sort of Vermont gray, or homespun. Our Nimrod, owing to the retrograde movement, was now the farthest from the game; but being warned of its neighborhood, he hastily stood up, and, while we ducked, fired over our heads one barrel at the foremost, which alone he saw, though he did not know what kind of creature it was; whereupon this one dashed across the meadow and up a high bank on the northeast, so rapidly as to leave but an indistinct impression of its outlines on my mind. At the same instant, the other, a young one, but as tall as a horse, leaped out into the stream, in full sight, and there stood cowering for a moment, or rather its disproportionate lowness behind gave it that appearance, and uttering two or three trumpeting squeaks. I have an indistinct recollection of seeing the older one pause an instant on the top of the bank in the woods, look toward its shivering young and then dash away again. The second barrel was levelled at the calf, and when we expected to see it drop in the water, after a little hesitation, it, too, got out of the water and dashed up the hill, though in a somewhat different direction. All this was the work of a few seconds, and our hunter, having never seen a moose before, did not know but they were deer, for they stood partly in the water, nor whether he had fired at the same one twice or not. From the style in which they went off, and the fact that he was not used to standing up and firing from a canoe, I judged that we should not see anything more of them. The Indian said that they were a cow and her calf, — a yearling, or perhaps two years old, for they accompany their dams so long; but, for my part, I had not noticed much difference in their size. It was but two or three rods across the meadow to the foot of the bank, which, like all the world thereabouts, was densely wooded; but I was surprised to notice, that, as soon as the moose had passed behind the veil of the woods, there was no sound to be heard from the soft, damp moss which carpets that forest, and long before we landed, perfect silence reigned. Joe said, "If you wound 'em moose, me sure get 'em."

We all landed at once. My companion reloaded; the Indian fastened his birch, threw off his hat, adjusted his waistband, seized the hatchet, and set out. He told me afterward, casually, that before we landed he had seen a drop of blood on the bank, when it was two or three rods off. He proceeded rapidly up the bank and through the woods, with a peculiar, elastic, noiseless and stealthy tread, looking to right and left on the ground, and stepping in the faint tracks of the wounded moose, now and then pointing in silence to the single drop of blood on the handsome shining leaves of the Clintonia Borealis, which, on every side, covered the ground, or to a dried fern-stem freshly broken, all the while chewing some leaf or else the spruce gum. I followed, watching his motions more than the trail of the moose. After following the trail for about forty rods in a pretty direct course, stepping over fallen trees and winding between standing ones, he at length lost it, for there were many other moose-tracks there, and returning once more to the last blood-stain, traced it a little way and lost it again, and, too soon, I thought, for a good hunter, gave it up entirely. He traced a few steps, also, the tracks of the calf; but, seeing no blood, soon relinquished the search. . . .

About half an hour after seeing the moose, we pursued our voyage up Pine-Stream, and, soon, coming to a part that was very shoal and also rapid, we took out the baggage, and proceeded to carry it round, while Joe got up with the canoe alone. We were just completing our portage and I was absorbed in the plants, admiring the leaves of the aster macrophyllus, ten inches wide, and plucking the seeds of the great round-leaved orchis, when Joe exclaimed from the stream that he had killed a moose. He had found the cow-moose lying dead, but quite warm, in the middle of the stream, which was so shallow that it rested on the bottom, with hardly a third of its body above water. It was about an hour after it was shot, and it was swollen with water. It had run about a hundred rods and sought the stream again, cutting off a slight bend. No doubt, a better hunter would have tracked it to this spot at once. I was surprised at its great size, horse-like, but Joe said it was not a large cow-moose. My companion went in search of the calf again. I took hold of the ears of the moose, while Joe pushed his canoe down stream toward a favorable shore, and so we made out, though with some difficulty, its long nose frequently sticking in the bottom, to drag it into still shallower water. It was a brownish black, or perhaps a dark iron-gray, on the back and sides, but lighter beneath and in front. I took the cord which served as the canoe's painter, and with Joe's assistance measured it carefully, the greatest distance first, making a knot each time. The painter being wanted, I reduced these measures that night with equal care to lengths and fractions of my umbrella, beginning with the smallest measures, and untying the knots as I proceeded; and when we arrived at Chesuncook the next day, finding a two-foot rule there, I reduced the last to feet and inches; and, moreover, I made myself a two-foot rule of a thin and narrow strip of black ash which would fold up conveniently to six inches. All these pains I took because I did not wish to be obliged to say that the moose was very large. Of the various dimensions which I obtained I will mention only two. The distance from the tips of the hoofs of the fore-feet, stretched out, to the top of the back between the shoulders, was seven feet and five inches. I can hardly believe my own measure, for this is about two feet greater than the height of a tall horse. (Indeed, I am now satisfied that this measurement was incorrect, but the other measures given here I can warrant to be correct, having proved them in a more recent visit to those woods.) The extreme length was eight feet and two inches. Another cow-moose, which I have since measured in those woods with a tape, was just six feet from the tip of the hoof to the shoulders, and eight feet long as she lay. . . .

Here just at the head of the murmuring rapids, Joe now proceeded to skin the moose with a pocket knife, while I looked on; and a tragical business it was, — to see that still warm and palpitating body pierced with a knife, to see the warm milk stream from the rent udder, and the ghastly naked red carcass appearing from within its seemly robe, which was made to hide it. The ball had passed through the shoulder-blade diagonally and lodged under the skin on the opposite side, and was partially flattened. My companion keeps it to show to his grandchildren. He has the shanks of another moose which he has since shot, skinned and stuffed, ready to be made into boots by putting in a thick leather sole. Joe said, if a moose stood fronting you, you must not fire, but advance toward him, for he will turn slowly and give you a fair shot. In the bed of this narrow, wild, and rocky stream, between two lofty walls of spruce and firs, a mere cleft in the forest which the stream had made, this work went on. At length Joe had stripped off the hide and dragged it trailing to the shore, declaring that it weighed a hundred pounds, though probably fifty would have been nearer the truth. He cut off a large mass of the meat to carry along, and another, together with the tongue and the nose, he put with the hide on the shore to lie there all night or, until we returned. . . . This stream was so withdrawn, and the moose-tracks were so fresh, that my companions, still bent on hunting, concluded to go farther up it and camp, and then hunt up or down at night. . . .

But, on more accounts than one, I had had enough of moose-hunting. I had not come to the woods for this purpose, nor had I foreseen it, though I had been willing to learn how the Indian man-oeuvred; but one moose killed was as good, if not as bad, as a dozen. The afternoon's tragedy, and my share in it, as it affected the innocence, destroyed the pleasure of my adventure. It is true, I came as near as possible to come to being a hunter and miss it, myself; and as it is, I think that I could spend a year in the woods, fishing and hunting, just enough to sustain myself, with satisfaction. This would be next to living like a philosopher on the fruits of the earth which you had raised, which also attracts me. But this hunting of the moose merely for the satisfaction of killing him, — not even for the sake of his hide, — without making any extraordinary exertion or running any risk yourself, is too much like going out by night to some wood-side pasture and shooting your neighbor's horses. These are God's own horses, poor, timid creatures, that will run fast enough as soon as they smell you, though they are nine feet high. Joe told us of some hunters who a year or two before had shot down several oxen by night, somewhere in the Maine woods, mistaking them for moose. And so might any of the hunters; and what is the difference in the sport, but the name? In the former case, having killed one of God's and your own oxen, you strip off its hide, — because that is the common trophy, and, moreover, you have heard that it may be sold for moccasins, — cut a steak from its haunches, and leave the huge carcass to smell to heaven for you. It is no better, at least, than to assist at a slaughter-house.

This afternoon's experience suggested to me how base or coarse are the motives which commonly carry men into the wilderness. The explorers and the lumberers generally are all hirelings, paid so much a day for their labor, and as such they have no more love for wild nature than wood-sawyers have for forests. Other white men and Indians who come here are for the most part hunters, whose object is to slay as many moose and other wild animals as possible. But, pray, could not one spend some weeks or years in the solitude of this vast wilderness with other employments than these — employments per-fectly sweet and innocent and ennobling? For one that comes with a pencil to sketch, or sing, a thousand come with an axe or rifle. What a coarse and imperfect use Indians and hunters make of Nature! No wonder that their race is so soon exterminated. I already, and for weeks afterward, felt my nature the coarser for this part of my woodland experience, and was reminded that our life should be lived as tenderly and daintily as one would pluck a flower.

MAINE AND
THE CIVIL WAR

Maine and the Civil War

The story of Maine during the Civil War is the story of her sons marching south to fight and perhaps to die for the preservation of the Union. The personal history of two of her sons will stand here for all the others. The first is a young man from Saco who volunteered in August 1862 and fought for three years as an infantryman in the 17th Regiment. The second, a young college professor from Brunswick who also joined up in August 1862 and, without any previous military experience, was asked by Maine's governor to be colonel of the newly recruited 20th Regiment. He said he would be lieutenant-colonel until a real colonel could be found.

By the end of the war, Maine contributed to the Union army thirty-one regiments of infantry, three regiments of cavalry, one regiment of heavy artillery, seven batteries of light artillery, and seven companies of sharpshooters. Altogether, 73,000 Maine men bore arms (about 12 percent of the state's population); 8,792 died, 11,309 were wounded or discharged because of illness. Along the Maine coast a few "home guards" were stationed, armed with light artillery, to defend seaports and shipyards from possible attack by Confederate raiders from the sea. Only once did the enemy threaten. In May 1863, a crew of Confederate sailors, disguised as fishermen, entered Portland harbor in a ship they had captured offshore and escaped with an armed revenue cutter. They were overtaken and captured but not until they had blown up the ship.

The State of Maine was a Union stronghold. The great majority of her soldiers were volunteers, though the bounties paid by towns and the hiring of substitutes helped to fill company rolls. Long-held anti-

The 31st Regiment Maine Volunteers

slavery feeling and the supremacy of the state Republican Party were demonstrated in the election of 1856 when Hannibal Hamlin, an antislavery Democrat since Jackson's presidency, became Maine's first Republican governor. In 1860 he was elected Lincoln's vice president, and in that office stood for radical emancipation measures and the arming of Negroes. But there were nests of southern sympathizers, "copperheads," in some Maine towns and cities. Democratic newspapers in Portland and Bangor kept up a firm opposition to Lincoln and the war. Hatch notes in his *Maine, A History* that "in Kingfield a mob of about fifty men prevented the officer who was to distribute notifications to drafted men from entering the town." Later a Bangor man who expressed his approval of Lincoln's assassination was saved by police from a mob that looked to them like a lynch mob.

A more touching story comes down to us from a Richmond, Virginia, newspaper after the battle of Fredericksburg in December 1862:

Yesterday a rather prepossessing lass was discovered on Belle Isle, disguised among the prisoners of war held there. She gave her real name as Mary Jane Johnson, belonging to the Sixth Maine regiment. She gave as her excuse for donning her soldier's toggery, that she was following her lover to shield and protect him when in danger. He had been killed, and now she had no objection to return to the more peaceful sphere for which nature, by her sex, had better fitted her. Upon the discovery of her sex, Miss Johnson was removed from Belle Isle to Castle Thunder. She will probably go north by the next flag of truce. She is about sixteen years of age.

EDWARD CLARENCE PLUMMER
1863–1932

In the decades before the Civil War, the feelings in Maine about the continuation of slavery in the southern states followed a geographic pattern. There was a strong abolitionist sentiment inland, centered in the meetinghouses, which increased as the war grew near. But along the seacoast, where trade with the southern states flourished, abolitionist meetings both within and outside the churches often faced violent opposition. In the Congregational church in Brunswick, a visiting antislavery minister began one sermon in October 1838 by listing three obstacles that prevented the "Triumph of the Gospel": "intemperance, Sabbath breaking, and slavery." According to Hatch's history, "When that last word was heard, two wealthy shipowners and masters were quickly on their way out of the church, and another was prevented from following only by his daughter getting his hat."

It was probably inevitable that, with Maine's long history of seizing every economic opportunity the world's oceans offered, in 1849 the last recorded American slave ship should have sailed from Portland. The historian of the voyage, Edward Clarence Plummer, explains that he learned this story of the brig *Bonita* from the ship's second mate many years after the event.

The Slaver

Whatever submerged truths might reveal, the State of Maine's last vessel to engage in the African slave trade, so far as actual records show, was the brigantine *Bonita*. This craft was truly typical of a class of vessels which had been produced by the combined effects of stern laws, rigidly executed against offenders, and the resulting great profits to be had from any successful voyages in that prohibited trade — built for the greatest possible speed and of a size permitting them to hide in small creeks or shallow rivers until those mighty guardships, which the United States and England then were maintaining as a patrol along the African coast, could be evaded, a slave mart reached, a cargo of human beings secretly secured, and a dash across the Atlantic attempted.

The terrifying dangers of the slave trade, which traffic Congress had declared to be piracy and in its law of 1820 had enacted that "any person being of the crew of any vessel [engaged in the slave trade] shall be adjudged to be a pirate and shall suffer death," had been accentuated by a decision of the United States Supreme Court which, in the case of the *Butterfly* in 1840 (United States *vs.* Morris), had held that the mere finding in a vessel of the fittings usually carried by slavers was sufficient to condemn the craft as a slaver and the crew as being engaged in this trade, even though it was admitted that no slaves ever had been on board and it is a curious fact that the same Chief Justice Taney who, inspired by a desire to put into the law terrors which Congress had omitted, thus gave what was then quite generally considered to be a strained construction of the statute, and who, therefore, received the highest possible praise from all Abolitionists for his "humanity and enlightened judicial wisdom," was the same Chief Justice who a few years later brought upon himself and the Supreme Court such unmeasured condemnation from those same, and many other, people, because of his decision in the "Dred Scott" case.

The feeling that this judge and the court had stretched the law beyond the real intent of Congress and had made possible the punishment of innocent parties who might be engaged in the legitimate African trade, but caught under circumstances which could be said to indicate guilt, produced a corresponding disposition on the part of the general public to "wink" at attempted violations of that particular statute. Thus it was that when the little *Bonita* fitted out in August, 1849, for a voyage to Africa, the fact that beneath her cargo of cottons, rum, and that mixed lot of goods generally carried to the "West Coast," lay planks and timbers suitable for building the slave deck and "shooks" for twenty-five "leagers" or great water casks was ignored by such private citizens as chanced to know of these things — and the government officials, of course, were easily avoided. Public sentiment had not at that time reached the advanced position which made the average citizen recognize that it was any part of his duty to obstruct violations of that particular law.

The *Bonita* was commanded by Capt. John Scott, who had served on the slaver *Porpoise* of Portland, Maine, when that craft was made famous by the trial of her master charged with this offense, and when the court had incidentally brought out the methods by which the letter of the law could be avoided. He knew all the perils of the trade, the type of craft best suited to the business and the methods best calculated to make such an illegal venture a success.

In spite of the fact that death was the penalty they must defy in entering upon such a voyage, there was no difficulty in securing the necessary crew, for the high wages and the premium of five dollars to be paid each man for every slave safely landed, attracted plenty of adventurous seamen, who trusted to skill and luck to escape the watchful guardships.

Like many of her class, the *Bonita* carried the single stick foremast of a topsail schooner, so that she could assume a plain "fore-and-aft" rig whenever it seemed best or set broad square sails when running before the wind, thus not only disguising herself by changes in her display of canvas but enabling her to assume the most advantageous rig on every point of sailing. She had been thoroughly overhauled, hull and rigging put into the best possible condition to fit her for a race where death might be the penalty for those who failed to bring her in a winner, and started on her voyage with a crew full of confidence that no ocean patrol would be a match for them.

Having been sighted by but one guardship, which was easily eluded, the *Bonita* reached the African coast in safety and slipped into a small inlet just north of the Congo River, there to wait until the frigate then watching that broad entrance to the slave marts should be called away by some suspicious craft coming across the horizon.

This did not mean much delay, for vessels were to be sighted frequently in those waters; and as soon as the guardship had become a mere patch of white in the distance chasing an anticipated prize, the little brigantine, as the *Bonita* then was, slipped into the mouth of the great slave river.

There the wind failed, but this change did not mean material delay — lack of wind was only one of those many contingencies which the slave traders of those days provided for. Out went long sweeps at which the men worked with a will, sending their sharp craft swiftly through the water until, at nightfall, she approached Punta da Lenha, and she ran into a long winding creek near the head of which an American trader had established a slave corral.

This man, originally from Maine, had been on the coast for some fifteen years, had handled thousands of slaves, was secure in the friendship of all those great chiefs who brought their prisoners, and sometimes people of their own tribes, to market and was known to the master of the *Bonita*. Familiarity with the business had caused this trader to look upon these enterprises as purely commercial matters where meddlers had stuck in statutes that had no real excuse for being, and he evidently considered himself a successful dealer in choice cattle.

He had enclosed an acre of grassland with a high stockade and at the time of the *Bonita*'s visit had about fifteen hundred slaves on hand. These people appeared to be quite content with their condition — it was very seldom that one of them attempted to escape. They were well fed, as, of course, the interest of the owner dictated; they had nothing to do and that was highly satisfactory to them all; they probably realized that to attempt to return to their native wilds meant re-capture or death, and as the visitors entered the big pen they saw every manifestation of animal comfort among the prisoners there.

In the middle of the enclosure was a vessel of burning opium, the fumes from which permeated the air of the corral. In this drug the blacks took great delight. Running to the opium container, they would inhale deep breaths of its fumes with every manifestation of intense satisfaction, after which they would sink upon the ground in a half unconscious condition to enjoy at their ease the effects of this odd intoxication. As the visitors appeared, some of the livelier of the slaves gathered grinningly about them, and engaged in a lively scramble for some of those bright beads which the owner threw among them much as coins are sometimes thrown among street urchins. Clearly the owner of the corral was on good terms with his prisoners; but then, as he remarked to the captain, it was money in his pocket to keep his "crew happy."

A satisfactory bargain having been struck, scouts were posted on two commanding elevations as guards against surprise, the cargo was quickly unloaded, the slave deck laid, thus making a broad floor in the hold of the vessel just above the keelson, and the big room thus formed under the main deck was divided by a partition to separate the women from the men. Then the slaves began to march on board.

One by one the blacks came over the vessel's side. At a motion of the physician who stood at the gangway, they either entered the hold of the ship or, being thought too old or sickly, stepped aside to be returned to the corral, for the risks of this traffic were too great to permit of any vessel carrying other than a first class cargo. Meantime the great water casks, each holding two hundred gallons, were being set up and filled, large quantities of cracked corn, the principal food for these slaves, procured and added to the quantity of dried beef which the brig had brought for this purpose, and at last the *Bonita* was ready to start on her voyage to Brazil with two hundred and fourteen slaves on board.

The watchers having reported the coast clear, the *Bonita* got under way and was rowed into the river down which she proceeded under sail, favored by the current and a light breeze blowing over her starboard bow. At the foremast head was a lookout keenly watching for any suspicious sign, and as the mouth of the Congo was reached, a second man joined him on the cross-trees to make doubly sure that no enemy was near.

But at that time the mouth of the Congo was free from all craft, the horizon showed an unbroken line; so far as the eye could reach the shore appeared to be deserted. So the *Bonita* promptly entered the open sea.

But no sooner had she left behind that possible shelter of the river than the square-cut sails of the United States frigate *Essex* appeared coming from behind that promontory south of the Congo where, it appeared, the shrewd captain had hidden in the hope of catching some craft in the manner he now had actually done. This warship was readily recognized, for she had made herself a terror to the slavers from the moment she had reached this station, her commander being known as a man who would "carry the sticks out of her" before he would permit his ship to be left behind by one of these fugitives. Every man in the *Bonita*'s crew understood at once that this was literally a case of "neck or nothing" for them, with a most unpleasant accent on the "neck," and they entered the contest with every nerve at breaking tension, for the warship had made return to the Congo impossible.

Down came those long slender yards which had given her the character of a brigantine, up went the big foresail's gaff that completed her schooner rig, and then, with every sheet hauled aft, the little racer began shooting away to windward, a course which also took her off shore. On this point of sailing, the fore-and-aft rig of the *Bonita* gave her a marked advantage over the square-rigged warship, because it was possible for the fugitive to sail closer to the wind than her pursuer could "point," and before the chase was half an hour old, it was clear that the *Bonita* was gaining. But the *Essex,* as usual, hung to its task her master cherishing the hopes that some change in conditions might make possible a capture. That this naval officer was not acting without judgment became manifest during the latter part of the afternoon when the *Bonita,* having passed from that vast area of sea affected by the Congo's flood, found the wind increasing in force and a heavier sea running. Then the great size of the warship began to tell, she began to lay practically the same course that the little schooner was holding, unhampered by those rising waves which knocked the *Bonita* from crest to crest and checked her speed.

At five o'clock it was seen that the *Essex* was gaining and the *Bonita*'s skipper resorted to short tacks as an expedient to delay the pursuit, the three lower sails of his craft shifting themselves with the motion of the helm, while the many sails of the warship required the handling of a hundred sheets; but this trick failed to produce advantageous results, because the *Essex* had met it before and volunteers from the gun crews gladly joined the seamen at their tasks so that there were abundant men for every rope and as the schooner tacked that vengeful cloud of canvas behind her shifted likewise with magic swiftness — the frigate would not be delayed.

Three times the *Bonita* tacked, but she gained nothing by the maneuver — and the wind was increasing in its strength. When the *Essex* had drawn within a mile of the little slaver she failed to tack at the instant the *Bonita* changed her course and a moment later the bow chaser of the warship spoke. It was a long range for those days, but the gun had been elevated well, and while the shot failed to reach its mark it came dangerously near the flying vessel. Then that old expedient of dropping overboard slaves was tried in the hope of interrupting pursuit. Two of the older women were brought on deck and before they understood what their fate was to be they had been secured to either side of an empty cask, which would serve to keep them afloat and pitched into the water, directly in the track of the pursuing ship. Anxiously the *Bonita*'s crew watched the frigate, and when they saw her hold her course, leaving the helpless slaves to perish a howl of rage and despair burst from their lips. But the skipper's sharp orders brought from them an instant response. Half a dozen other slaves were soon secured to a plank and, struggling fiercely in spite of their bound condition, pushed over the vessel's side. It was sunset, but the floating heads were clearly visible upon the water and all knew that the lookouts on the *Essex* had seen these victims dropped. Then the *Bonita* tacked once more. The *Essex* held her course and as it was seen that her master apparently intended to tack ship at the point where the castaways were floating with the chance of saving them while his ship was in stays, the *Bonita*'s master ordered the crew to prepare to swing the square-sails again into position on the foremast — to take the one desperate chance of running squarely before the wind, a course which would put the three masts of the warship in line with the wind and not permit of all that towering canvas drawing with full effect.

When it was seen that the *Essex* was almost upon the floating slaves and it was evident that all eyes would be on the helpless blacks whose flying rescue was about to be attempted, the yards of the *Bonita* were suddenly swung into place, and that vessel, which had been given a "rap full" and had imperceptibly been changing her course to where she was sailing with started sheets so as to get the greatest speed and also to get well off the *Essex*'s port bow before the slaver's intention had been understood by her pursuers, was squared away for a run down the wind.

Fortunately for the *Bonita* her maneuver had not been anticipated and only the bow chaser had been fired as the slaver doubled on her pursuer, the shot passing well astern. To trim the vessel for this part of the race the slaves were driven as far aft as possible in the hold, while two of them, handcuffed and fastened to ropes that they might not be lost should a following sea crash upon the vessel, were brought up and placed on the very edge of the stern to help lift that vessel's knife-like bow and prevent its burying and thus losing speed as the little craft fled from wave to wave.

The *Essex* was not delayed. Discipline and a tremendous force of eager men made possible an act of humanity with little loss in the movement of vengeful justice. Quickly she swung to resume the pursuit and the men swarming into her rigging gave notice that, despite the heavy wind, her commander proposed to risk his studding sails in a desperate attempt to win this defiant prize.

The master of the *Bonita* was not idle, however. As soon as it was seen that the vessel could stand such a press, he hoisted his main gaff-topsail, the halyards being led to the taffrail chock to aid in supporting the bending spar. Time and again as the scudding stern of the brigantine settled in the trough of a wave it seemed as if the following water must cover it, but the billows were not combing sufficiently to break upon her and she continued her flight for safety, holding the big warship in full play.

Shot after shot came from the *Essex* and twice the canvas of the *Bonita* was pierced but her spars and rigging escaped injury, while the strong New England duck refused to rip in spite of the rents made in it by those cannon balls. Slowly the darkness settled, the big sails of the warship grew indistinct while her persistent guns showed bursts of angry flame instead of spouted smoke as they sent their deadly missiles through the night to cripple the flying craft. Long after her sails had become invisible and when even the night glass failed to reveal the *Essex,* the *Bonita* held her course. The slaver knew that somewhere in that enshrouding darkness was the grim old warship booming along in relentless pursuit, and that a single error of judgment on his part meant capture and the noose for him whatever chance there might be of a less severe penalty for his crew. Finally, having slackened his main sheet until the boom was against the shroud, he lashed that spar to the starboard rigging and changed his course two points to the starboard.

It was a shrewd, as well as a bold, trick, for he knew that the master of the *Essex* understood as well as he that it was impossible for him to jibe that great sail in such a wind as was then blowing, and that, therefore, he must continue before it, or trim down for the port tack — the only change of course to be made by the schooner with safety under those circumstances.

When the *Bonita* had run under these conditions for more than an hour, the lashing of the main boom to the starboard shrouds, preventing that great sail from jibing to port where it naturally would be with the wind coming over her starboard quarter and still nothing was to be seen of her pursuer, the gaff-topsail was stowed, the vessel brought into the wind and jibed, when, taking the breeze over her starboard beam, she headed off to the westward. Meanwhile the blacks were released and sent below and the ship resumed her normal condition.

The morning showed a vacant sea — the *Bonita* had escaped her pursuer.

During the days that followed sails were repeatedly sighted, but no real danger developed and the coast of Brazil was made in safety.

Entering the Para River the cargo was delivered by night to the trader whose business there was well known to every slaver, but who seemed never to be suspected by the public authorities — at least his vessels always escaped molestation. But the *Bonita* never returned to Maine. Her master was content to load a small cargo and proceed to Savannah, where she was sold, he preferring to take no more chances in a craft which he knew the *Essex* had so closely examined and was sure to recognize if they should ever meet again. As Scott made a handsome profit from this successful venture, he was enabled to purchase a captain's interest in one of those brigs which was then doing such a thriving trade between New England and the West Indies, and this trade he followed until he retired from the sea.

JOHN WEST HALEY
1840–1921

John West Haley was born in Biddeford, Maine, a descendant of the early settlers and proud of his heritage. Although he did not finish grammar school, he was a literate man and a careful and ironic observer.

Haley served in the Civil War as part of the 17th Maine from August 1862 until the regiment was mustered out in June 1865. The journals he kept describe his experiences with insight, humor, and despair. Two are daily accounts and a third, "Old Battlefields Revisited," reflects on the war days in general. In a roster of the men in his company, he describes himself as "Below criticism. Poor fighter. Attained successful mediocrity as a soldier. Present all the time." His personal history belies this sardonic description. In a war where disease, desertion, and death took an appalling toll, "present all the time" was no mean feat. While Haley may have backed into the war rather than rushing in with a burst of patriotic fervor, once in he stayed — through perseverance and great good luck. Although suffering from serious illness, Haley managed to keep his good humor, his compassion for the victims of the war on both sides, and his insightful and often acerbic view of the officers and men who fought with him. The 17th Maine did well. After the battle of Fredericksburg they were admitted to the Order of the Red Patch, the symbol of the bravery of 3rd Brigade Commander Kearney and his men, and subsequently wore this emblem on their caps. Haley was proud of his compatriots: "Our troops from Maine prove themselves as good as the best, and that is the record they have received from all who have commanded them."

After the war, Haley returned to his job at the Saco Water Power Shop but soon moved on to other occupations, including a stint on a

Recruits for sale

local newspaper. Offered the position of librarian at the Dyer Library when it opened in 1891, he remained there for twenty-eight years. Ill health, a legacy of the war, plagued him, but he was active as a historian, genealogist, and promoter of education and tried his hand at poetry, painting, and philosophy as well. His last gift to the town was his effort on behalf of a war memorial in Saco; it is unusual in that it honors the soldiers of all wars and the women who supported them. Haley's major memorial is, of course, *The Rebel Yell and the Yankee Hurrah,* the lively and poignant journals that have recently been edited by Ruth Silliker of Saco.

Haley's enlistment into the Army of the Potomac was hardly a glorious patriotic gesture. Like so many other young men of his time, he was fearful and uncertain of the commitment he was about to make. His journal tells of the roundabout way in which he became a member of Company I, 17th Maine Volunteer Regiment.

A Volunteer from Biddeford

In 1861 I concluded I had a duty to perform but hesitated about embarking on this troubled sea. I feared I lacked those qualities which soldiers so much need. And so that year passed and still the matter stood status quo. In the summer the president called for a large number of men, of which 300,000 were for three years and about the same number of nine-months men. A very intimate friend became fired up under this call, also some other friends, five of us in the same class in Sunday School, and we were getting hot under the collar. Our teacher, although one of the best of men, was a bitter opponent of the war and labored hard to knock the war spirit into a cocked hat. So we concluded to enlist, but waited still. My friend sounded his parents out and they neither denied nor affirmed. All at once they decided to give their consent if I was going — they never thinking I would — and all the time my going depended on his getting their consent, which I thought they would never give. A high school teacher had just opened a recruiting office, whither my friend sped to enlist August 5, 1862. As soon as morning dawned, he sought my society and informed me of what he had done. While it was brought home to me with an almost paralyzing shock, no grass was allowed to grow under my feet and my name was promptly plastered onto the roll of those who would answer father Abraham's call. This was

August 7. And thus the soldier life began for us until death overtook us or the war ended. . . .

Camp King, Cape Elizabeth August 6–22, 1862

I had *no* inclination for the business, but once committed in a momentary spasm of enthusiasm to serve under certain circumstances, which I never expected to occur, I found myself face to face with the alternative of going or showing a white liver by backing out. I decided to do as I had agreed and enlisted for "three years, unless sooner discharged." *Shot* or *starved* should have been added to the contract.

Given time for reflection, I had a thousand fears and misgivings. I moved in a dazed sort of way and couldn't believe I had done such a thing. Naturally timid and shrinking, it seemed impossible that I had, even for a moment, thought seriously of going into the service. I consoled myself with the thought that I should, if I lived, have a chance to see some of the country and *might* witness a battle, which I greatly desired, only I wished to be a safe distance from it — a mile at least.

August 6th was the day of enlistment. Ed Eastman was the recruiting officer and William Hobson was captain of the company. Our examination passed off all right. We were accepted and ordered to hold ourselves in readiness to report in Portland whenever they desired our company. And they desired it much sooner than we anticipated — the very next day.

August 7th

We were examined again thoroughly, found to be "sound and kind" and were then mustered into the state service by Captain Joe Perry. So another step was taken, and having nothing else to do, we were turned out into the field to run about like a flock of sheep, as long as we didn't run away. I grew homesick for the first time in my life, experiencing a feeling akin to being in solitary confinement. We have not been assigned to any company; we have no quarters as yet; nearly all who are in camp are strangers.

Company I, to which we are to belong, is composed almost entirely of men from York and Cumberland counties, with a few "Oxford bears" sandwiched in. Most of the men are scholars to a greater or lesser degree: sixteen graduates of high schools, nine collegians, two clergymen, and one lawyer. In addition to all this erudition, a decidedly moral tone pervades the company; there are not less than thirty who are really pious, and quite a number whose spasmodic bursts are noticeable because of their violence as well as their obtrusiveness.

It may be inferred, and justly so, that patriotism prompted most of these men to enter the service. As far as my own case is concerned, I lay claim to but very little of what goes by that name. Love of a change, an overwhelming desire to see the country (with certain considerations already named) furnished the key to my conduct.

But here I am, however I came. . . .

August 8th–10th

The first tap of the drum found us on our pins and ready for anything except a return to our beds. Sleeping on the soft side of a plank is a strong incentive, and we were not long in dressing as we had retired with everything on but our boots. For an hour or more after we turned out there were no exercises of a military character. Breakfast was announced, and we fell in with a cheerful alacrity. It was a slight improvement over supper: salt horse retired in favor of fresh beef, sage tea was displaced by coffee of a good degree of strength. We also had bread, accompanied by a villainous substance masquerading as butter. It proved a sorry apology for the real thing, having the tokens of age and being tall-flavored.

We find everything subject to one condition: we can eat, drink, or wash when we can find the wherewithal to do so. Our first duty each morning is to wash, when water is to be had, then to punish a quantity of soft bread, coffee, and meat. Our second duty is very much like the first, and so is the third. A few men vary the order of exercises, inasmuch as they indulge in only *one* meal, which lasts all day. It is also alarming, as we fear it might result in famine later. But idleness is conducive to hunger most assuredly and if they were not gourmandizing, there is no knowing how much worse they might be doing.

We cannot drill as there seems to be no one who knows enough about it to teach us. Several days of this regime have so disgusted and sickened us that we have lost all enthusiasm over the war and desire to depart for home although we have not fired a gun, nor have our officers drawn their "cheese knives" in defense of the Union. By the end of the third day, our military ardor had so abated that a thermometer which stood at fever heat on Wednesday would have been found at or below zero on Saturday as the mercury congealed.

On August 9th those of us from Saco and Biddeford were allowed a short furlough. Most of us had come away so suddenly as to have left our affairs unsettled. As there was a fair chance that many of us would not look upon our native town again, we did what was equivalent to making our last will and testament. Bidding goodbye to friends passed off jolly enough, as no one hinted even at the bare possibility that we should not come back. And *we* didn't propose to throw a pall of gloom over the matter. It might be four years and it might be forever. Who can tell?

August 11th

Received the princely sum of $55.00, which the town has voted to give those who enlisted. The men of means showed themselves to be exceedingly liberal. Men must be forthcoming, even if it takes a draft to do it, and it is touching to see the number of persons who are ready, even anxious, to sacrifice their relatives on the altar of their country. This "spontaneous" uprising of people should teach the South!

Fifty five dollars is a most generous sum for a man's head. Such high appreciation is almost enough to die for. The state also decided to do the handsome thing and so it came down with the magnificent sum of $45. The general government gave $25 and one month's wages in advance, making about $140 in all. Here is richness, and we consider ourselves very wealthy. I would feel better, though, if we had brought at least as much as the festive negro is worth at auction. . . .

One thing was gained by our furlough. We found better accommodations waiting us: straw beds and a blanket for each man. We have also been assigned to our company, which is Company I, under Captain William Hobson, First Lieutenant P. S. Boothby, and Second Lieutenant J. O. Thompson.

These appointments have no reference to the fitness of the candidates. None has any military knowledge to boast of. Captain Hobson was a schoolteacher, Boothby a hotel clerk, and Thompson a Methodist preacher of more assurance than piety, more breadth of beam than learning. . . .

As we are now officered and our noncommissioned officers appointed, we have commenced drilling. The paucity of military knowledge of both officers and privates renders this pretty dull music. One of our sergeants, who claims to be better posted than the average, was corrected so many times by a private that, in sheer desperation, he begged the latter to assist him. This the private refused to do but offered to take over the entire exercise. . . .

The 18th was the day of our muster into the United States service for three years. The mustering officer was Major Gardiner, a full-blooded West Pointer who has a crushing hatred for all volunteer troops. How we lived through this day, I know not. Somebody surely has formed a conspiracy to see how much the back can carry and not break, how much the flesh can suffer and not die. Several men fainted and fell from the ranks of dress parade but we managed to stand for hours while one company at a time was inspected. We found mustering into the service by a West Pointer a slow, painful performance. Red tape stuck out all over him like porcupine quills. It was with difficulty that he could get near enough to hand us our guns. He stood off and threw them at us. This, we learn, is not intended as a special token of disfavor; it is simply the West Point style.

The inspection continued, every detail undergoing the closest scrutiny. Our West Pointer was determined to find fault with something or somebody. By the time the first three companies were inspected, the rest of the regiment was flat on the ground, except for Jim Jose. He stood as a monument of endurance and folly. If it be not folly to thus punish oneself currying favor with some official snob, then I don't know what constitutes folly.

The ordeal was finally over and only one man was given permission to retire from service, but he has declined. He enlisted to escape domestic tyranny and has no desire to return.

We engage in drilling and otherwise preparing for the business before us. We have some company from Saco — wives, mothers and sisters who come in on some pretense or other almost daily. On Sunday the ladies of Portland made us a dinner of pies, cakes, cold meats, and other luxuries not mentioned in commissary supplies. We have not suffered for anything thus far, due to our Saco friends, but this does not prevent us from appreciating the Portland ladies' attentions. In the afternoon the Reverend Lovering of Park Street Unitarian Church came out and gave us a flowery discourse in which he was pleased to inform us that "all who died in defense of the flag had a sure passport to heaven." This is all very well for talk, but the Reverend evidently doesn't care to try it on. I feel that death is one of those things to which distance lends enchantment, so notwithstanding Mr. Lovering's bland audacities of speech and fine-spun theories, I don't care to cultivate a closer acquaintance with the hollow-eyed monster. It never does furnish much satisfaction to listen to these cowards who talk of pluck but are so destitute of the quality themselves. Why shrink from that which is so desirable as the glory of war? I am just perverse enough to want to share it.

August 20th

Drilling and readying for the move we know will come ere many days. Anywhere for a change! We are sick of this inactivity and its concomitant state of mind. It has been rumored that we are going to Annapolis to a military school for three months and are then to be quartered in the forts around Washington. This is a nice prospect and promises immunity from danger and the exposures incident to life in the field. At night we learned we should leave these diggings on the morrow. Our feelings are highly paradoxical: we want to go and we don't want to. Although we dread it, we have a curiosity to know our fate.

There wasn't a great deal of rest for anyone this night. Singing and carousing went on from dewy eve till daylight. About 3 A.M. there was a general turnout, and a most outrageous din and confusion commenced. Our orders are to move at six, and we set ourselves to getting ready. The glare of the burning beds and the gyrations around them, and all the confusion of breaking camp compares favorably with the popular idea of the place of "future uneasiness."

Haley and his company were not bound for Annapolis after all. Instead, they were shipped by train to Stonington, Connecticut, then by steamboat to Jersey City, thence overland to Philadelphia, where they were wined and dined by the citizenry. Haley commented, "It was with many regrets that we turned our backs on the City of Brotherly Love at midnight, when we took cars for Havre de Grace and the long, long road to Dixie."

Haley's war was to be fought primarily in Virginia. The first major battle in which he took part was at Fredericksburg, in December 1862.

December 11th

While it was yet dark we were suddenly startled by the boom of a cannon, quickly followed by another. These were the prelude to an ever-memorable battle.

Instinct told us what was coming. The shudder that passed over our frames as we answered to the roll call on this chill December morning was not altogether the result of the weather. We knew it was the "cannon's opening roar," and the long expected and dreaded day had come at last. The ball had opened and we should soon be dancing. By the time it was fairly light, we had orders to move immediately. By 7 o'clock the cannonade had become a roar, and the city was enveloped in a cloud of smoke and mist.

Our guns on Stafford Heights opened on the doomed city, and there was an almost continuous line of fire from Mrs. Scott's Hill on the right to Pollock Mill on the left. We soon started, and had an idea that we were to advance over the river at once so we began to brace ourselves for the shock. Mingled fear and curiosity filled our bosoms as we moved along. Curiosity to see a battle and to know how we should act in our first fight. Lurking under it all, the fear that we should fall in the fray. I am sure that some of us actually wished ourselves at home.

We didn't cross the river immediately but turned off to the left and marched down the river to a place called the Brooks Farm. Here we hauled up, listening to the terrible roar of nearly two-hundred guns belching fire and destruction on the city. Burnside was carrying out his threat to lay Fredericksburg in ashes if the Confederate forces didn't evacuate it within forty-eight hours of his ultimatum.

The shelling of the city was not for the purpose of destroying property, but to dislodge the Rebels occupying the houses and stone walls near the river, thus preventing our troops from laying pontoons. But the shelling didn't dislodge them, and so no progress was made in crossing. Finally a crew crossed over in pontoons and eliminated the sharpshooters, and the troops were soon driving the Rebels through the streets and lanes of Fredericksburg toward the heights in rear of town. A running fire was kept up through the forenoon. At the same time, shelling was maintained and a large portion of the city was rendered useless. One third of it lay in ashes. The firing was kept up all day at intervals, and after dark the sky was lit by the glare of shells.

We passed the day on the Brooks Farm, and for us it was a day of terrible suspense. Nothing could be seen because of the mist and smoke enveloping the city, but we could hear the firing and cheering as one regiment or brigade after another crossed the river and entered into the fray — the deadly fray. And when I use this phrase it is not idle chatter. There is a meaning to it which the soldier comprehends. . . .

As we laid there hour after hour hearing all this, our imaginations ran riot and we expected every moment to be ordered in. It was not an easy matter to keep our men within hailing distance, so eager were they to catch a glimpse of what was going on. Up to noon there had been no battle, only the fighting in the streets. After sunset we moved down into a piece of pine woods and bivouacked for the night. We had no news of what our army had accomplished and were in a state of appalling uncertainty. . . .

December 12th

Didn't move for the day. Kept out of sight of the Rebels until after dark, when we moved down into a grove of oaks not far from the river. This movement was owing to our division (Birney's) having been borrowed by Franklin as a reserve, ostensibly, but actually to further his designs against Hooker. Franklin thus weakened Hooker. He also intended to throw this little force over the river instead of his own larger one.

We were allowed to build only the very smallest fires and to make no noise. We didn't know just how near we were to the enemy, this being a new section of country to us, and it was dark and overcast so we couldn't tell anything as to our whereabouts. I made coffee and then retired with dismal forebodings. What is before us? Possibly this might be my last night on earth. Even worse, ere the setting of another sun I might be mangled and bleeding. Such thoughts crowd in upon me and prevent me from sleeping.

December 13th

A memorable day for some of us. We were out betimes and soon had the coffee kettle simmering and the pork sizzling. We had our grub and then laid around awaiting orders. A portion of Franklin's corps was engaged with the enemy over the river, and we were ordered across to support them, not knowing whether the entire Grand Division was there or not. Great was our surprise, as we emerged from the woods and came in sight of the river, to see no less than four lines of troops lying on the ground while a comparatively small force engaged the enemy.

We pushed over the river and moved up the old stage road to Richmond and came to a front near a fine residence, the Barnard House. On the side of the road, next the house and in lieu of a fence, were an embankment and a ditch. We couldn't take advantage of them then, although under severe fire, for we had something else to do. The small force sent over earlier by General Franklin had accomplished prodigies of valor and had pierced Lee's lines. At that moment, had it been supported by another division, there is no doubt a lodgement could have been effected. But they looked in vain for support and were compelled to fall back.

As they neared our group at the old stage, or river, road, the Rebels in hot pursuit, we came to a front and fixed bayonets. As soon as the Pennsylvania Bucktails, who were in front of us, cleared out, we charged on the advancing Southrons, giving them a volley as we moved. Shot and shell fire flew in all directions, reminding us of what an old nigger once said under similar circumstances: "See dar, Hell has laid an egg."

We were soon the recipients of as many of these favors, or "eggs," as we could attend to, and they kept us ducking and dodging in a lively and bewildering manner. The first in our company to receive an injury was Sergeant John Libby. A fragment of shell smashed his hip. He took it coolly and patiently, although judging from the nature of the wound, it must have been very painful. He smiled and tried to appear unconcerned, but it was a ghastly effort. He was carried to a brick house in rear of us used as a hospital. . . .

Our regiment formed in the road to dispute the further progress of Johnny Reb. The first volley from our guns compensated somewhat for the havoc the Rebels had made in the ranks of the Bucktails, who were now thoroughly demoralized. They were out of ammunition and forced to fall back and save themselves, if possible. There was no order in the manner of their coming off. Each was taking his own time and motion. Some, with broken legs, were carried on the shoulders of others who had been hit in the head or otherwise disabled. But for such timely assistance from their comrades, many must have been left on the field to the mercy of an exultant foe. . . .

Our regimental loss was twenty, Company I lost one. We were now ordered to lie down, but not willingly, as we had more curiosity than fear and wanted to see what was going on. General Berry paced back and forth in the rear of us, an old slouched hat pulled over his eyes. He ordered us to keep down, out of sight and out of range: "Boys, don't expose yourselves any more than you can help. You'll have a chance to see all you want to. The State of Maine is looking at you and expects every man to do his duty today."

This little speech stirred us wonderfully, way down to the bottom of our boots, making us wish we were back at home. Some of us still stood up and tried to peer into the Rebel lines, whereupon General Berry ordered, "Lay down, men! Lay down! I am here to take care of you, and I'll do it if you will let me and will obey my orders." . . .

Night soon settled over the scene of carnage, and after getting something to eat we laid on the ground, but not to sleep. Our ears are continually saluted with the cries of the wounded left on the field to the mercy of weather and Rebels, their sufferings heightened by cold and thirst. Who can depict such horrors? These wretched men lay crying, groaning, and begging for water and help in the most agonizing manner, and we unable to rescue them. The rustle of a leaf or the crackling of a twig might send a shower of Rebel bullets into our ranks. We had an illustration of this soon after settling down. Something caused the pickets to commence firing, and it increased to such an extent that it was feared a general engagement might be the result. We got up and packed our things and put our knapsacks up in front of our heads as a breastwork, much like the ostrich hiding its head and leaving the rest of its carcass exposed. (We learned better the longer we stayed in the show.) I was mortally scared and could not imagine what I should do on picket on such a night. It is a dreadful night even for old and tried soldiers.

A reconnoitering party passed along our front about the time the row was ending. Although close to our line, and with the pickets in front, one of this group displayed the most ridiculous fright. He dodged and ducked in a most comical manner. Each time, this affected the others. The officer in command of the squad drew his revolver and threatened to transfer its contents to the fellow's head. This proved to be a good remedy for the soldier's nerves. . . .

This day has been a most exciting and eventful one. It was our regiment's first experience under fire, and a whole lifetime has been crowded into it. It was expected that we should show the white feather. This formed no part of our plan; still, no man can tell as he sits in the chimney corner whether he is a brave man or a coward. In accordance with this belief, a couple of New York regiments were placed in rear of us to keep us in line. But, horrible to relate, our gallant support soon struck out and left us to do as we chose. All efforts of their officers were utterly unavailing, and they fled from the presence of the enemy. On the contrary, our regiment behaved so well it merited the encomiums of General Berry.

December 14th

It being Sunday, we made no demonstrations, and the enemy, also of a devotional turn, made no disturbance until afternoon. As we are suspicious that they might attempt to get a hold on our flank, it was deemed necessary to throw back our left so that our flank rests on the Rappahannock. After this a flag of truce was sent to protect our men who went out to bury the dead and bring in the wounded. The Rebels thronged the works opposite and gave us an idea of the number of our opponents. Most of them are clad in blue, so it is a plain case that our dead have been contributing largely to the Rebel wardrobe. The truce was limited by the Rebels to two hours, consequently we didn't even get all the wounded, and the defunct ones were left unburied.

Officers, Union and Rebel, found time to meet on the picket line and wet their whistles, then separated. As our stretcher-bearers were bringing in a wounded man, a Reb picket discharged his piece and one of our men was minus a toe. Perhaps this was accidental, but we chose to regard it as an exhibition of treachery. After the truce ended, the pickets resumed firing incessantly till darkness put an end to it.

I have almost forgotten to describe an occurrence during the truce. A. P. Hill, one of the ablest Confederate generals, sent his compliments to General Berry and begged to say, "I have never seen a brigade so skillfully handled on a battlefield." This was not an unmerited compliment, only it wasn't General Berry's brigade that he had handled so well, it was simply the 17th Maine. The way we had double-quicked down the old Richmond turnpike under fire, come to a front and delivered a volley, and then charged, is not easily surpassed.

After dark we drew rations of corn or rye (in a liquid state), though we would have much preferred it in palatable pork. There are times when whiskey is needed, this being one of them, for it is damp and cold. We have been worked hard and are nearly used up. We have also come to the conclusion that we should be relieved. We have been here over forty-eight hours and are well aware that there is nearly a whole grand division lying on the northern bank of the Rappahannock, which has not participated in the fight at all.

The 17th Maine went on to fight at Gettysburg and to march endlessly across Virginia, often retracing their steps, building camps and breaking them, skirmishing with the enemy in small battles as well as engaging in the major ones. They coped with inadequate food and illness, exhaustion, desertion, and death. The regiment had left Portland with 1,040 men; by July of 1864 only 200 were left.

Haley was dismayed by military disarray, drunken officers, and the lack of planning or coordination that exposed the troops to unnecessary danger. Haley himself was not wounded, although a bullet pierced his trousers, but he suffered severely from liver disease, dysentery, and other miseries caused by the Spartan living conditions.

The fighting intensified in 1864. The battles of the Wilderness, Po River, Spotsylvania, Cold Harbor, and finally Petersburg took a terrible toll of the men from Maine. The cold winter months were a respite of sorts, but life was miserable and uncertain for both armies.

Incredibly, during lulls in the fighting, Rebels and Yankees often socialized and swapped. Haley recorded:

> There is a brisk trade in tobacco in this neighborhood. The Rebs seem to have an unlimited supply of it, which they gladly trade for anything to eat. The news literature of the day is exchanged as well. We split a stick, insert the paper in the slit, and toss it across to the Confederate lines. (When there is any news that might encourage the other side, however, we cut it out before the exchange is made.) There is perfect freedom in this place. We go in and out as we please, and there seems to be an era of good feeling inaugurated, which if allowed to grow unchecked would shortly end this war.

By early 1865, the tide had turned against the South. Savannah, Charleston, and Richmond had fallen, and in the final battle for the 17th Maine, Petersburg was regained. April brought news of the surrender at Appomattox, and the two weary armies laid down their arms. Haley's regiment began the long journey home on foot, finally arriving back in Maine on June 8.

It is all over now, and I can only regard it as a hideous dream — the smoking ruins, the sodden field, the trailing banner, the slaughtered thousands and wailing families, the roar of cannon, the Rebel yell and the Yankee hurrah have all passed away and we again return to peace.

June 10th–11th

Returned to Portland from Saco and prepared to be mustered out of service. This day Uncle Sam refused to feed or clothe us any longer, so we were thrown on our own resources. Pending our release, though, we were put under guard and given mouldy bread and rotten pork, which were promptly stamped into the mud. After this we acted so badly that they were glad to hurry up and get rid of us.

Just before noon we marched to Portland and turned over our guns and equipment (those of us who were not foolish enough to buy them). After this, we hung around waiting for the paymaster. He didn't get to Company I before midnight. Those of us from Saco had a stage waiting to convey us home, where we arrived about 2 A.M. on Sunday, June 11th, 1865 — a happy set of mortals.

Haley's journals also include the following roster of Company I, with his private comments on many of the men who served with him.

ROSTER OF COMPANY I, 17TH MAINE REGIMENT

Below are the names of the original members of the company and their military standing.

*Captain William Hobson   Successively promoted to Brev. Brigadier General. Wounded April 6th, 1865.

*First Lieutenant P. S. Boothby   Didn't see much service. Promoted as adjutant of regiment. Dead.

*Second Lieutenant J. O. Thompson   Promoted captain of Company K. Resigned at or near Brandy Station, latter part of 1863, on account of conscientious scruples — alleged.

Sergeants

*S. S. Richards   First Sergeant. Wounded at Po River, May 11th, 1864. From Saco. Promoted Captain.

*F. C. Adams   Second Sergeant. Wounded at Gettysburg and Wilderness. From Saco. Promoted captain.

*J. C. Libby   Third Sergeant. Mortally wounded December 13th, 1862. Died a few days after. From Biddeford.

*C. C. Cole   Fourth Sergeant. From Oxford. Promoted captain. Very fine soldier.

*O. D. Blake   Fifth Sergeant. Retired to hospital and was returned later, reduced to the ranks. From Biddeford.

Corporals

*C. J. Goodwin   First Corporal. Promoted to first sergeant.

*S. C. Jenness   Second Corporal. Reduced to ranks.

*A. C. Parkhurst   Third Corporal. Remained in field short time.

*C. H. Parcher   Fourth Corporal. Promoted lieutenant, Company K.

*J. Boothby   Fifth Corporal. Died from homesickness.

*E. F. Tibbetts   Sixth Corporal. Not with us after Chancellorsville.

*A. A. Robertson   Seventh Corporal. Killed at Gettysburg.

*J. M. Paine   Eighth Corporal. Reduced for desertion.

Musicians

*J. P. Atkinson   Died at Fort Stanton.

*W. H. Atkinson   Remained till term expired.

Teamster

*Edward Sweetser   Died at Fort Stanton.

Privates

*Allen H. Abbott   With provost guard most of the time.

*Levi D. Allen   Deserted in Virginia, from Fort Stanton. Not recovered.

*Robert Benson   Wounded at Locust Grove. Company cook, generally, when not employed as officer's cook.

*Thomas Brand   Wounded at Gettysburg. Promoted to sergeant. Away sick considerable.

*T. C. Bradbury   Rheumatic. Promoted to sergeant. Present about all the time.

*Aug. F. Bradbury   Rheumatic. Present or accounted for most of the time.

*Stephen Bradbury   Wounded in Wilderness. Sick considerable.

*Cyrus Buker   Company cook, generally. Fell over a shadow and was disabled.

*James M. Brown   Away much. Loved rum more than country.

*James B. Brown   Died at Sandy Hook, Md. June 1863.

*I. M. Boothby   Discharged without seeing much service.

*J. C. Blaisdell   Present most of the time. Had an uncommonly brave appetite.

*Thomas Blaisdell   Away much after the first year.

*Thomas S. Clark   Hostler, also great facial contortionist and whisky guzzler.

*James S. Clark   Noted only for gluttony. Could eat four men's rations.

*Zenas Chase   Officer's cook. Also proprietor of "Zena's Spoon."

*F. S. Deland   Brought away but few scalps. No active service.

*T. W. Emerson   A bloodthirsty brave — in his mind.

*Daniel Foss   Discharged at Camp Pitcher on account of sickness.

*Charles E. Goodwin   Rheumatic. Killed in the Wilderness, May 6th, 1864.

*J. H. Goodrich   Well. Killed at Chancellorsville, May 3rd, 1863.

*Newhall Guptill   Well. Died at Camp Pitcher.

*Isaac Grant   Strong aversion to fighting. Face indicated conviviality.

*John Grant   Did better. Stayed nearly all the time. Killed in the Wilderness, May 6th, 1864.

*Joseph Hill   Wounded at Locust Grove, November 1863. Didn't return.

*Daniel Hill   Died of fever at Camp Pitcher, January 1863.

*John Haley   Below criticism. Poor fighter. Attained successful mediocrity as a soldier. Present all the time.

*W. S. Hodston   Rheumatic. Wounded April 6th, 1865. Good soldier. Shot in the lungs.

*S. J. Harmon   Stout. Very noisy, ignorant and absent-minded. Wounded in the Wilderness. Died at Fredericksburg, May 1864.

*A. J. Hodge   Transferred to battery. A notoriously coarse person. Good riddance.

*H. G. Holmes   Away about half the time. Always had a spasm of virtue when under fire.

*Mell Irish   Rupture and varicose veins. Better mimic than soldier. Clever person. The poor farms are filled with them.

*Ed Jaques   Discharged on account of sickness from Fort Pitcher. Very free and easy at expense of others.

*C. A. Jordan   Wounded at Gettysburg in leg. Did no further service.

*J. W. Jose   Wounded at Petersburg. An excellent soldier. None better or braver.

*Ambrose Kenney   Deserted on the "Mud March", January 20th, 1863.

*J. W. Kendrick   Wounded twice. Promoted twice. A great sufferer, in his mind.

*J. A. Kilham   Varicose veins. With the teams and provost much of the time. Killed at the North Anna, May 23rd, 1864.

*George Kimball   Wounded at Gettysburg. Present most of the time thereafter.

*J. E. Leach   Rheumatic. Pig with the same snout as Kenney. They took flight together and were seen no more.

*George W. Libby   Discharged early in the term. Don't know any cause.

*John G. Libby   Killed at Chancellorsville, May 3rd, 1863. Good fellow and good soldier.

*H. H. Libby   Alias "Hardbread." Had an insatiable appetite for hardbread. Sick much but showed excellent *grit*.

*F. A. Mitchell   Mortally wounded at Gettysburg. A good soldier and a good man.

*M. McGrath   Teamster, with all the instincts of the craft, including great piety when near the front.

*J. McKenny   Played out years "before the war, sah." Put in Ambulance Corps and hit in the toe.

*Moses Moody   Died of smallpox and came near to scaring another man to death with it.

*Hiram Patterson   Varicose veins. Promoted to corporal, for reasons best known to officers.

*William Perry   Varicose veins. Hostler for doctor. Was himself a pack mule when on the march.

*T. Perkins   Very shaky in action. At some other times very drunk. Wasn't built right inside for a soldier.

*W. H. Pillsbury   A *prodigious* eater. And not very well most of the time but very religious.

*Ben Ross   Teamster. Not violent as a patriot, except at the mess table.

*Walt Rounds   Met with various and sundry ills. A very good soldier. Promoted twice.

*G. S. Richardson   Piles. A great wit, and aggravator of simple ones. Would make a mule whicker.

*Eliphaz Ripley   Died from an excess of green peaches and other causes known to himself.

*John H. Roberts   Mortally wounded at Spotsylvania, May 12th, 1864. A good soldier.

*Charles F. Sawyer   Another good one. Slightly wounded at Locust Grove, November 29th, 1863.

*John H. Simpson   A most eccentric person. Dirty as he was brave.

*Jarry F. Smith   Company cook. Died at Camp Pitcher, January 1862.

*Owen Stacy   Promoted sergeant. Hit in the heel at Gettysburg. An excellent soldier, very odd.

*Al Smith   Good record, Killed in the Wilderness, May 6th, 1864.

*T. B. Sanders   Fought two battles and then hunted a soft place for the rest of his term.

*J. F. Sweetset   A good fellow and soldier. Killed in the Wilderness, May 5th, 1864.

*Benjamin F. Small   Discharged with very limited experience as a soldier.

*Josh W. Small   Most always sick. Suspected of eating soap and other choice edibles.

*Edwin Small   Most nerve of any man in the company. Didn't know fear, or had a great facility for concealing it.

*W. A. Small   Last and least of the Smalls. Liver all bleached out. Had "left his girl behind him."

*W. E. Strout   Good man. Died young, before eating many rations.

*Josiah H. Sturtevant   An ornament to any company. Was transferred to colored regiment as an officer.

*George Tasker   Killed in the Wilderness, May 6th, 1864. Not especially energetic.

*S. G. Usher   Promoted lieutenant. A very mysterious person. Mortally wounded April 6th, 1865. Died *whispering*.

*W. S. Waterhouse   Promoted corporal. A good soldier. Wounded in the lip at Spotsylvania, May 12th, 1864.

*George Whitten   Rheumatic. Taken prisoner at Chancellorsville. Away two or three times.

*Lewis G. Whitney   Killed in the Wilderness, May 6th, 1864.

*C. M. White   Served about half his time and then procured a discharge.

*David A. Wentworth   Killed in the Wilderness, May 6th, 1864.

*John Wentworth   Didn't stop with us long, or take many chances.

*Thomas R. Warren   An old man and a tough one. Served long and well. Knocked out lots of *boys*.

*John Wildes   Consumptive. A scrawny old maid. Looked like an Egyptian mummy. Tough as a boiled owl. Discharged.

*William Lamberton   If he was good for anything but lying and swearing, there is a gross omission in the records.
*Nahum Pillsbury   A remarkably good feeder and somewhat given to *pie*ty.

GENERAL JOSHUA LAWRENCE CHAMBERLAIN
1828–1914

General Joshua Lawrence Chamberlain is the heroic figure who dominates Maine's Civil War history. Modern interest in his life and times appears to be growing. His account of the final campaign of the Army of the Potomac was republished in 1974. His house in Brunswick is being restored and made into a memorial to his civil and military careers.

Chamberlain had an extraordinary military career. His promotion from colonel to brigadier general was the only battlefield promotion Grant ever made. The Congressional Medal of Honor recognized his defense against superior forces on the extreme left flank of the Union armies at Gettysburg — which historians describe as the turning point of that three-day battle. As the Army of the Potomac was beginning its final campaign, which led to Lee's surrender, Chamberlain was promoted to brevet major general for leading his infantry troops, even though his horse was shot from under him. When Grant soon afterward gave Chamberlain the signal honor of receiving the surrender of Lee's troops at Appomattox, he was rewarding one of his most indestructible and brilliant field commanders. Twice Chamberlain was wounded so seriously that he was reported as dead. At Petersburg, after a ball had ripped through his lower trunk, "leaving a streak of daylight" from hip joint to hip joint, he was out of the war for five months. He nearly died of pneumonia and was hospitalized with malaria, yet after the war he lived a vigorous public life and died at the age of eighty-six.

Chamberlain's mother had intended her eldest son to be a minister, not a soldier. He grew up on a hundred-acre farm in Brewer when the Bangor area was fast becoming the lumbering center of the Atlantic world. He prepared for Bowdoin at a military academy in Ellsworth, his father's choice. Since Greek, an entrance requirement for Bowdoin, wasn't taught there, the young Chamberlain learned it in six months by memorizing the grammar book. His Bowdoin career was filled with academic honors, including Phi Beta Kappa. After graduating in 1852, he entered the Bangor Theological Seminary and three years later was ready, he thought, to be ordained and become a missionary. Instead, he was invited to teach logic and "natural theology" at Bowdoin, where he stayed for six years, until the war began. The college offered him a year's leave of absence to study languages in Europe, but Chamberlain's conscience told him that he must resign from the faculty and join the war, of whose righteous purpose he was entirely convinced.

Chamberlain returned to Bowdoin after the war but within a year became restless. When the Republican party asked him to run for governor, he accepted and was elected by the largest majority in Maine's history. He was reelected three times — a term was one year — and, though not as regular a party man as the Republicans would have liked, he stood for what we would now call progressive programs: the land-grant college at Orono, a hospital for the insane, a reform school for young offenders. He worried about Maine's failure to make rapid economic progress and about its declining population. He urged that Swedish immigrants be invited to take up free land, that public funds be invested in new industries, port facilities, and railroads. Young people, he pointed out, were leaving Maine, new immigrants not settling here. In his last inaugural, in 1870, he sounded most nearly like a contemporary politician: "What this state needs is capital — money in motion, whether gold or currency. Our material is stagnant, our industry crippled, our enterprise staggered for want of money, which is power." He did not get the money, but he got part of his program, including the Swedish immigrants. New Sweden was founded in 1870.

In 1871 Chamberlain was asked yet again to return to Bowdoin, this time as president, and so began his third career, as a reforming educator. His reforms soon had a radical effect on student life and the curriculum. Formal prayers before breakfast were discontinued; evening prayers except on Sundays were abolished. New science courses and a new Bachelor of Science degree were introduced. Chamberlain wanted Bowdoin to accept the challenge of the times, and he even spoke of the unreality of life in an all-male college environment, with "woman banished and hence degraded, so that to admit her to a place in higher education is thought to degrade a college."

But his program to develop student character by organizing the

General Joshua Lawrence Chamberlain

student body into an infantry battalion and dressing them in military uniforms ended in a revolt. In the program's second year, the junior class refused to report for drill and was sent home; the sophomores and freshmen followed, and they were all given ten days to return or be expelled. All but three returned. At the end of the year military drill was made optional; a few years later, it was abolished.

After two years, Chamberlain found that "a spirit seems to possess the college with which I cannot harmonize." But the trustees refused to accept his resignation. Three years later he offered again to resign, and still he was asked to stay. At last, in 1883, ill health forced his retirement, but he remained close to the campus and continued to lecture on political science and constitutional law. Between 1855 and 1885, he taught every subject in the curriculum except mathematics and physics.

Chamberlain had continued to serve his state and nation in public missions, representing Maine at the Centennial Exposition in Philadelphia in 1876 and his country as the U.S. Commissioner to the

Paris Exposition in 1878. As major general of the state militia, he prevented by his reputation and personal force a crisis in state government after a disputed election in 1880. He then moved in new directions, especially into business in Florida and New York. He settled down at last in Portland when he was awarded a federal post as surveyor of the port, even turning that job into something more than a sinecure. He continued to write about the war for popular magazines — "Through Blood and Fire at Gettysburg" for *Hearst's* was typical — and to stir audiences, especially veterans' groups, with his oratory until his death in Brunswick.

The address that follows was recorded by a member of the audience at the Bowdoin Club in Boston on May 3, 1901. Chamberlain's mention of General Howard refers to the evening's second speaker, O. O. Howard, another Bowdoin man who also graduated from West Point. He, too, had a distinguished military career and became prominent in establishing educational opportunities for former slaves. Howard University carries his name.

Appomattox and the Surrender

I do not know how much you remember about the state of things that led to Appomattox. . . . We had broken up the whole right flank of Lee's lines. He was all broken up, nothing to do but get away, if he could, to North Carolina, where he thought he could effect a junction with Joe Johnston or get up in the mountains. He was going to get off by one or the other of the routes. He had been very much pressed for supplies, and his army was almost starving. . . . We were following on Lee's rear, pressing hard every day. . . . Two corps of Meade were present, and they with Sheridan's cavalry were to outflank Lee, and that is what we did for several days, four to eight days, kept him away from that crossing to the south side of the Appomattox River. It was the evening of the ninth; we had made a terribly hard march, had every obstacle on the road, a twenty-nine mile march of it. It was about two o'clock in the morning when we halted, halted not because we had reached any particular goal. . . . We halted because anatomy and physiology stopped us. Human endurance was exhausted. Sheer exhaustion of that march and firing; firing by day and marching by night, five of the eight days. . . .

We were not long going to sleep. However, not two hours had we been lying there in that way, ready to march at a moment's notice, the horses' girths loosened a little, but the riders slipped the bridle rein over the horses' necks, lay down under the horses' noses, and went to sleep. Scarcely had the first broken sleep begun when my sentinel comes and touching my shoulder, "Orders, sir!" I awake. The cavalry officer dismounted, comes up, and the sentinel strikes a match. I get up on my elbow and read the brief, thrilling note from Sheridan, one of those manifold orders sent to each of the infantry commanders along that line. It reads like this, "I have cut across the enemy at Appomattox Station on the south side of the road. Captured five of his trains. If you can possibly push your infantry up here tonight we will have great results in the morning. . . ."

In three hours we had reached Appomattox Station where Sheridan wrote his note, and there were his trains. He had left the rebel supply trains standing in their tracks. Sheridan was not there. Why? Because he had filed off with his cavalry sharp to his right, right to the Appomattox River. . . . It was not necessary to leave orders to follow. We did follow and took up the double-quick from that point. We can hear the sharp ring of that artillery that goes with the cavalry and ever and anon the sharp boom of some heavier cannon showing that there are some other troops up there — the heavier guns, then the light artillery, and soon the crack of the cavalry carbines and the unmistakable roar of the infantry — you see, that meant the enemy. There is no mistake about it. Sheridan is square across the rebel retreat and with that glorious cavalry line has held at bay there whatever is left of whatever has reached the front of the proudest army of the Confederacy.

I must stop to mention one rather striking incident in the rush to the front. For the first time in my life my eye caught the glimmer of black soldiers trotting along our left, eager for the front, faces all lighted up. The sight thrilled me. Was it patriotic justice or was it the irony of history or of fate, those black men pressing their way to the front, eager to get into the fray which was to make a white man's republic a free country? It was a thrilling sight. . . .

With the first and second brigade of the First Division I dashed there on the double-quick. . . . First thing I caught sight of was Sheridan's battle flag waving out there in the battle smoke. Soon I saw right in it, wrapped in smoke, that figure, that intense form, that countenance, that expression, rider and horse, both of them (that splendid horse, you know, which turned the tide of battle as they sang "In the Shenandoah Valley"), rider and horse, swarthy and terrible to look at, black as the cannon smoke above their heads. Of course I ride up to Sheridan; what I got for greeting was a grim smile and an impetuous wave of the hand — not one word, I understood it. He knew I would. I push out and formed forward of the line, in line of battle. I advanced past Sheridan and his guns and the cavalry and took the battle out of their hands. Stonewall Jackson's Corps is the center. At the bugle call they rally, formed their ranks, and swept like a most beautiful cloud around our right. . . . Of course we had to engage the Stonewall Jackson Corps. When they recognized this infantry which they knew so well on so many a well-remembered field, I could feel the shock in their minds. They did not fight so hard, made quite a show of fighting but were receding and, of course, the more they receded the more we pressed on. . . .

. . . the Stonewall Jackson Corps relinquished their namesake and retired a little over the crest. I was eager to push up the crest when General Ord himself rode up. He said, "Don't develop your lines on that crest and draw the destructive fire of the enemy. They will sweep you from it in an instant." That was a very positive order, but it was an extremely awkward place to be in on that slope. The crest cut off our vision. We did not know what there was behind it. I was troubled. I wondered why that order had not come from the regular general; I did not understand that at all. I heard that light battery coming up too, which stirred me up a bit; then I bethought myself of Grant's last words in the confidential order: that a general officer, when he had got things going, might push things. I thought that was about the time. Then Sheridan, who rode off to the rear of his cavalry, rode up to me with that black face of his and brought his two palms down like the crack of the carbine, "Now smash them, General, smash them!" (and two more words General Howard will not permit me to add, Sheridan said.)

I was young and I was very rash and very imprudent and became very unmilitary, rode close to my first line and used some very unmilitary language: "Forward, let 'er go! Forward to the top." We swept on! In a very few minutes the crest was ours! On the crest of the hill, now belted by that cordon of steel, our troops see down in the hollow below us the remainder of that magnificent far-boasted Army of

Northern Virginia, counterpart and companion of ours in war. Thrilling thoughts took possession of us at the sight. It brought every foot to an involuntary halt, but with a devout joy in our hearts we dashed forward on the hope of the consummation.

I am in two lines of battle. I ride between and push my two lines forward. We are already in the main street of Appomattox Court House. The right of our lines is diagonally across it, and the men are fighting in the houses and wild with excitement. . . . I was very apprehensive about my right, as I had crossed the road and my right flank stood towards the rebel flank. Longstreet was coming with his corps. . . . I could see in the glimpse between oak trees his formation of squadron front preparing for the charge. Although I was soldier enough to wonder why he was going to do that, I saw coming out from that dusky line two horsemen riding at full speed straight for me. I did not know whether they were going to call on me to surrender. I saw, waving, a white flag. I wondered at a white flag from that part of the field. I soon saw that the flag was a towel. I wondered still more where on earth in either army they got a towel and one as white as that. I saw a Confederate aide-de-camp. Soon I recognized Colonel Whitaker, chief of Custer's staff, who had joined the flag of truce. He rode over to me and said a rebel flag of truce was being made and that Longstreet and Gordon were there and [had] said, "For God's sake stop that line of infantry!" They rode up. Whitaker is very excited, tremendously excited. He exceeds his instructions, I rather think. The first thing he shouts out is, "This means unconditional surrender." "What is your authority?" "Major Brown of General Gordon's staff. Major Brown said, 'General Longstreet desires a cessation of hostilities until he can hear from General Lee as to the proposed surrender. . . .' " You may imagine how that word struck me, saying that Longstreet wanted to hear from Lee about the proposed surrender. "Sir," I answered, "that matter exceeds my authority; I am but a general officer here. You must find my superiors. General Ord is the superior officer over on the left. . . ."

Well, I did not know what to do. A flag of truce had come and passed me — whether to halt, cease firing — but I supposed I should obey somebody's orders. . . . Just then my heart stopped still, for a cannon shot came from the battery beyond, beyond the town, passed through the breast of a gallant and true young officer I had summoned to my side from the 185th New York Regiment, and takes off the legs of another. It struck me with a panic, but now that the flag of truce was in there we knew what must come of it. It seemed too costly a peace offering. The order comes now to cease firing and to halt. There was not much firing to cease from.

A truce is now agreed upon until one o'clock in the afternoon. Nobody had a right to talk about surrender. . . . Longstreet came up pretty soon and half a dozen of the rebel officers, and on our side a number of corps and division commanders, and I was honored with an invitation to go there myself. We were chaffing each other there, having all kinds of fun, why we did not do so and so at Gettysburg and Antietam, etc, everybody cheerful but Sheridan; he was just about as cross as a bear. He did not believe in the flag of truce. He was not very slow in saying so. He thought it would be just like the [defeated] men to attempt to get away, and he told General Merritt to take some cavalry and go on the Lynchburg Pike, and if there is any maneuvering, stop it. In the midst of this pleasant talk we hear a sharp ring of horse artillery and pretty soon a great din of musketry. Gordon jumps up and looks inquiringly at General Sheridan. He said, "For my part, I don't understand that." Sheridan says, "Oh, never mind. I know all about it. Let 'em fight. . . ."

One o'clock comes — no word from Lee. The truce had come. I think Lee had authorized Longstreet to ask for a truce till one o'clock. Nobody had any right to extend the time. Nothing to do but to resume hostilities. We shook hands and parted. I was ordered to return to my command. We took up arms, made a proper front and stood waiting. In a few minutes comes this strange order: "Prepare to make or receive an attack in ten minutes." I advanced my lines to some good ground and was prepared to make or receive an attack, but, gentlemen and ladies, something else had come to pass in the meantime. I was out and between the two lines when I became aware, possessed of one of those strange feelings of another world surrounding me, some visions of the night as in the times of old, times of prophets, aware of a presence — I was not seeing with my mortal eyes. I turned square around and there my eyes fell upon a wonderful figure, a man venerable and imposing in form, in bearing, magnificently dressed with an elegant gray uniform, superbly accoutered, magnificent sword with the hilt glittering with diamonds, superbly mounted, with an expression of intense emotion as if he were repressing heartbreaking thoughts. Who else, of course, but Robert E. Lee! and seen for the first time, between my two lines, he had ridden up the road that came between my two lines, riding from Appomattox. I looked, stood as if transfixed, thoughts came over me of all those years, the man whom we had confronted so long, whom we had often feared and sometimes pitied, the man who was in our thoughts so many times and, I don't but I might say, in our hearts, when on the retreat we saw what care he took of his men. I am almost willing to say we nearly loved him for that, but there was another figure in a few minutes, wholly different in its aspect, sitting on his saddle looking like a born master not only of horses but of men and a countenance which did not quite conceal tremendous emotions. I am seized with an admiration almost equal to that with which I looked at Lee, for what thoughts were in the souls of those men that day, appointed for such a service on which the destinies of the country hung, no longer free, those two men, no longer considering how they could best make their way against the other or wield their tremendous forces to overcome the other.

We sat in our places, still in this maze of thought and feeling, when there comes flying out from Appomattox Court House an order borne by gallant aides, shouting to the air, "Lee surrenders!" The shouts and uproar that arose I never heard before or since from the Confederate side, and they kept up nearly all night. One reason was that they had supper that night, which was something of a rarity, for we had divided equally with our vanquished foe, now that we found them famished. We were short rationed too, very short rationed; had not anything to eat, you might say, but those supplies we captured out of the rebel train the night before. But I remember General Gordon saying at the conference that his men were famished over there, and Longstreet came over with tears on his cheeks, saying, "For God's sake, have you anything to eat? Let my poor fellows have it!" Forty thousand rations went over to our famished foe! (Applause)

Orders were being given to go into camp, and the terms and the details were being arranged for the surrender. . . . On the night of the second day I was summoned to headquarters. . . . I was called for and told . . . what the ceremony was to be, that the rebels had begged to stack their arms where they were and we to get their arms afterwards. But the entire Confederate Army, it was decided, must come out, officers and men, and lay down their arms and colors with due ceremony before some representative part of our troops.

I was told it had been determined that I was to be in command at the final scene. I think I was the general officer on that field. I did not quite understand that. I want to confess to you that I was not entirely unaware of that being something of a distinction. . . .

We came out in the morning, forming our line of battle on the principal street of the town . . . to receive the arms and colors of the surrendering army. We see them not a mile away, breaking their camp and folding their little tents. I bethought myself that it would not be improper to pay them some respect, not to the Confederacy but to the surrendered Confederacy laying down the power and the will to hurt the dear old flag of ours. I sent down an order to come successively to the "Carry arms!" not to "Present" — that would be too much. At the signal of my bugle they did that. General Gordon was leading the whole rebel army with his Stonewall Corps. I saw him coming with his chin on his breast. He heard the rattle of our men coming to the carry and looked up and understood its meaning, straightened up, wheeled his horse facing me, and gently touching the spur, made the horse rear high in the air so that his horse and himself made a bow of salutation, bringing his sword to his boot toe, then gave the command for the men to give the salutation as they best may. They come by successive divisions to rest, halting about twelve feet off, fix bayonets, stack arms; then slowly removing their cartridge boxes and leaving them on the stacks, lastly, reluctantly with an agony of expression on the face, they furl their battle-stained, blood-stained flags and lay them down, some of the men rushing frantically from the ranks, kneeling over their flags, pressing them to their breasts with burning tears and burning kisses, and then the Star-Spangled Banner waved alone upon the field. (applause)

All day it takes — not a sound of trumpet, nor roar of drum, nor even a cheer or whisper of vainglory escapes the lips of a single man of our army. We could not look in those brave, bronzed faces, thinking of the battles we had been through. I wish I had time to tell you what those men were. We could not look into those brave, bronzed faces we had met on so many fields where glorious valor made the very earth glorious under their feet, and think of such a thing as hatred and mean revenge. Oh no, that was not our part! We were the appointed instruments to a divine decree that such things in the course of human history cause the steps to be taken in the enfranchisement of man. No, it was our glory only that the victory we had won was for others, for these very men before us, as well as for ourselves and ours. Our joy was a deep, far drawn, unspoken satisfaction. We seemed to be in the presence of some mighty angel appointed for human destinies, perhaps with the power of correcting errors and even of forgiving sins, and aught we knew, accepting sacrifice and crowning martyrs for the sake of man, which is the sake of God. (applause)

THE MAINE WOODS

JOHN S. SPRINGER
1811–1852

John Springer's *Forest Life and Forest Trees* is a conscientious depiction of the lumbering days in the Maine woods during the early and middle nineteenth century. Like Thoreau's *Maine Woods*, it is a classic. Springer had proper reverence for the noble pine tree and firsthand knowledge of the pleasures and perils of lumbering, based on his experiences on the St. Croix and Penobscot rivers.

His book spells out the characteristics of the indigenous trees, describes the great Maine river valleys, and tells of life in a lumber camp and on the river drives when the winter's accumulation of logs was moved down to the sawmills using the free, if extremely hazardous, transportation afforded by Maine's brooks, lakes, and rivers.

John Springer was born in Robbinston, Maine, and attended the Maine Wesleyan Seminary. He spent most of the 1820s and '30s in the woods and then became a Methodist minister in Massachusetts. After seven years of preaching, he became a shop owner in Boston and began writing about his forest experiences; his book was published in 1851, one year before his death. He was a careful writer, with a formal, moral style that seems to fit the preacher more than the lumberjack.

The River Drive

Having completed our winter's work in hauling logs, another period commences in the chain of operations, "breaking up," moving down river, and making preparations for "river-driving."

The time for breaking up is determined by various circumstances; sometimes an early spring, warm rains, and thawing days render the snow roads impassable for further log hauling. In other cases, when it is the intention to take the teams down river, where lakes and rivers are to be crossed on the route, it is necessary to start before the ice becomes too weak to bear up the oxen. Sometimes scarcity of timber renders an early removal necessary, while in those instances where it is concluded to turn the oxen out to shift for themselves, on browse and meadow grass, we haul as long as it can be done, esteeming every log hauled under such circumstances clear gain.

Breaking up is rather a joyful occasion than otherwise, though camp life, as a whole, is very agreeable. Change is something which so well accords with the demands of our nature, that in most cases, when it occurs, its effects are most exhilarating. Under such circumstances, after three or four months spent in the wild woods, away from home, friends, and society, the anticipation of a renewed participation in the relations of life, in town and country, creates much buoyancy of feeling. All is good nature; every thing seems strangely imbued with power to please, to raise a joke or to excite a laugh.

Whatever of value there may be about the premises not necessary for the driving operation, is loaded upon the long sled; the oxen being attached, the procession moves slowly from the scene of winter exploits, "homeward bound," leaving, however, a portion of the crew to make the necessary preparations for river-driving.

After several days' travel, the neighborhood of home is reached; but, before the arrival in town, some little preparations are made by the hands for a triumphant entrée. Accordingly, colors are displayed

Saw-mills on the Penobscot at Oldtown

from tall poles fastened to the sled, and sometimes, also, to the yoke of the oxen, made of handkerchiefs, with streaming pennants floating on the wind, or of strips of red flannel, or the remains of a shirt of the same material, while the hats are decorated with liberal strips of ribbon of the same material, and waists are sashed with red comforters, their beards being such as a Mohammedan might swear by. Thus attired, they parade the town with all the pomp of a modern caravan. The arrival of a company of these teams, ten or a dozen in number, sometimes amounting to forty or fifty oxen, and nearly as many men, creates no little interest in those thriving towns on the river which owe their existence, growth, and prosperity to the toils and hardships of these same hardy loggers. Each team is an object of special interest and criticism; and, according to the "condition" of flesh they are found in, so is the praise or discredit of the teamster in command, always making the amount of labor performed and the quality of the keeping furnished an accompanying criterion of judgment. This voluntary review, to the knight of the goad, is fraught with interest, as by the decisions of this review he either maintains, advances, or recedes from his former standing in the profession, and thus it affects not only his pride, but also his purse, as a teamster of repute commands the highest rate of wages.

Some twenty years since, these arrivals, and also those of the river-drivers, were characterized by a free indulgence in spirituous liquors, and many drunken carousals. Grog-shops were numerous, and the dominion of King Alcohol undisputed by the masses. Liquor flowed as freely as the waters which bore their logs to the mills. Hogsheads of rum were drunk or wasted in the course of a few hours on some occasions, and excessive indulgence was the almost daily practice of the majority, even from the time of their arrival in the spring until the commencement of another winter's campaign. I speak now more particularly of employees, though I calculate, as a Southerner would say, that many of the employers in those days had experience enough to tell good West India from New England rum. . . .

The business of *river-driving* is not so agreeable as other departments of labor in the lumbering operations, though equally important, and also, in many respects, intensely interesting. The hands left at the camps at the time the team breaks up, to make the necessary instruments for *river-driving,* are soon joined with the addition of such forces as are requisite for an expeditious drive. As in most labor performed there is a directing and responsible head, so is it in river-driving; here, too, we have our "boss."

As early as April, and sometimes the last of March, the high ascending sun begins to melt the snow on the south of mountain and hill sides, flowing intervales and lowlands, forming considerable rivers where at other seasons of the year the insignificant little brook wound its stealthy course among the alders, hardly of a capacity to float the staff of a traveler; but, at the period referred to, by a little previous labor in cutting away the bushes and removing some of the stones in its channel, it is made capable of floating large logs, with the occasional assistance of a dam to flow shoal places.

In brook-driving it is necessary to begin early, in order to get the logs into the more ample current of the main river while the freshet is yet up. In some cases, therefore, as a necessary step, the ice in the channel of the brook is cut out, opening a passage of sufficient width to allow three or four logs to float side by side. In forming a landing on the margin of such streams, the trees and bushes are cut and cleared out of the way for several rods back, and a considerable distance up and down, according to the number of logs to be hauled into it. To facilitate the sawing of the logs into suitable lengths for driving, as well as more especially to form bedpieces upon which to roll them into the brook in the spring, a great many skids are cut and laid parallel with each other, running at right angles to the margin of the stream. On these landings, in the spring, the water is from one to two feet deep, the cause of which is sometimes accounted for from the fact that in the autumn the water is quite low, and the ice, in forming, is attached to the grass and bushes, which prevent it from rising; the result is, that the whole is overflowed in the spring. Into the channel thus cut the logs are rolled, as fast as it can be cleared, by shoving those already in down stream, until the brook, for a mile or more, is filled with new and beautiful logs.

No part of the driving business is so trying to the constitution, perhaps, as clearing such a landing. It often occupies a week, during which all hands are in the water, in depth from the ankle to the hips, exerting themselves to the utmost, lifting with heavy pries, hand-spikes, and cant-dogs, to roll these massive sticks into the brook channel. The water at this season is extremely chilly, so much so that a few moments exposure deprives the feet and legs of nearly all feeling, and the individual of power to move them, so that it often becomes necessary to assist each other to climb upon a log, where a process of thumping, rubbing, and stamping restores the circulation and natural power of motion. This effected, they jump in and at it again.

When the water is too shallow on any part of a stream to float the logs, dams are constructed to flow the water back, with gates which can be opened and shut at pleasure; and either through the apertures of the gates or sluice-ways made for the purpose, the logs are run. This dam answers the same purpose in raising the water to float the logs below as above, on the brook. Shutting the gates, a large pond of water is soon accumulated; then hoisting them, out leaps the hissing element, foaming and dashing onward like a tiger leaping upon his prey. Away the logs scamper, reminding one of a flock of frightened sheep fleeing before the wolf. Some logs are so cumbersome that they remain unmoved, even with this artificial accumulation of water. In such cases, embracing the moment when the water is at its highest pitch, in we leap, and thrusting our hand-spikes beneath them bow our shoulders to the instrument, often stooping so low as to kiss the curling ripples as they dance by. In this way, sometimes by a few inches at a time, and sometimes by the rod, we urge them over difficult places while, in connection with the annoyance of very cold water, broken fragments of ice mingle in the melée, imposing sundry thumps and bruises upon the benumbed limbs of the enduring river-driver. . . .

Logs are now driven down streams whose navigation for such purposes was formerly regarded as impracticable — some from their diminutive size, and others from their wild, craggy channel. There is

Logjam

a stream of the latter description, called *"Nesourdnehunk,"* which disembogues into the Penobscot on the southwest side of Mount Ktaadn, whose foaming waters leap from crag to crag, or roll in one plunging sheet down perpendicular ledges between two mountains. On one section of this stream, said to be about half a mile in length, there is a fall of three hundred feet. In some places it falls twenty-five feet perpendicularly. Down this wild pass logs are run, rolling, dashing, and plunging, end over end, making the astonished forest echo with their rebounding concussion. . . .

In many cases logs are hauled on to the ice of the lakes, streams, and rivers, instead of being left upon the banks or landing-places. When hauled on to the lakes, they are laid together as compactly as possible, and inclosed in a "boom", which is made by fastening the ends of the trunks of long trees, so as to prevent them from scattering over the lake on the breaking up of the ice. A strong bulk-head or raft is constructed of the logs, with a capstan or windlass for the purpose of warping the whole forward in a calm or when the wind is ahead. In this operation, two or three men take an anchor into the boat, to which, of course, the warp is attached, when they row out to the extent of the rope, let go the anchor, and haul up by working the windlass. Sometimes a tempest breaks up the boom, and the logs are scattered, which gives much trouble, and not unfrequently causes a delay of one year before they reach the mills.

On Moosehead Lake, at the head of the Kennebeck, a steam tow-boat has recently been built, which has proved very serviceable to lumbermen in towing rafts to the outlet. Probably the time will come when the business of other large lakes in Maine will require the services of similar boats. . . .

No employment that I am aware of threatens the life and health more than river-driving. Many a poor fellow finds his last resting-place on the bank of some wild stream, in whose stifling depths his last struggle for life was spent, where the wild wood skirts its mar-gin — where, too, the lonely owl hoots his midnight requiem. I have visited many spots that were, from facts called up by retrospection, lonely and painfully silent, but have never been so spell-bound, so extremely oppressed with a feeling of sadness, as while standing over the little mound which marked the resting-place of a river-driver on the banks of a lonely stream, far away from the hearth of his child-hood and the permanent abodes of civilization. The silent ripple of the now quiet stream (for the spring floods were past), and the sighing of the winds among the branches of trees which waved in silence over the unconscious sleeper, rendered the position too painful for one predisposed to melancholy. When in those wild regions we have the misfortune to lose one of our number, after the body is recovered, we place it in a coffin composed of two empty flour barrels. One is passed over the head and shoulders, the other receives the lower extremities; then the two are brought together and fastened, his grave-clothes generally being some of his common wearing apparel. Seldom, if ever, does the voice of prayer rise over their bier under these circumstances; in silence the corpse is committed to its rude burial, while now and then a half-suppressed sigh is heard, and the unbidden tears steal down the sunburned cheeks of his manly associ-ates. Events of this kind generally come suddenly, though, when in dangerous circumstances, they are often anticipated. After such an occurrence, an air of sobriety pervades the company; jokes are dis-pensed with, the voice of song is hushed, and for several days the deportment of the men is characterized with a degree of cautiousness unusual, except when reminded by some such impressive example of the frailty and uncertainty of human life. But with most the impres-sion soon wears off, and their accustomed cheerfulness is regained; their exertions are marked with the same daring as before the acci-dent, or as though a life had never been lost in the business. . . .

On the falls, and the more difficult portions of the river, sometimes immense jams form. In the commencement, some unlucky log swings across the narrow chasm, striking some protruding portions of the ledge, and stops fast; others come on, and, meeting this obstruction, stick fast also, until thousands upon thousands form one dense breast-work, against and through which a boiling, leaping river rushes with terrible force. Who that is unaccustomed to such scenes, on viewing that pile of massive logs, now densely packed, cross-piled, and interwoven in every conceivable position in a deep chasm with overhanging cliffs, with a mighty column of rushing water, which, like the heavy pressure upon an arch, confines the whole more closely, would decide otherwise than that the mass must lay in its present position, either to decay or be moved by some extraordinary convulsion. Tens of thousands of dollars' worth lay in this wild and unpromising position. The property involved, together with the exploits of daring and feats of skill to be performed in breaking that "jam," invest the whole with a degree of interest not common to the ordinary pursuits of life, and but little realized by many who are even familiar with the terms *lumber* and *river-driving*. In some cases many obstructing logs are to be removed singly. Days and weeks sometimes are thus expended before the channel is cleared. In other cases a single point only is to be touched, and the whole jam is in motion. To hit upon the most vulnerable point is the first object; the best means of effecting it next claims attention; then the consummation brings into requisition all the physical force, activity, and courage of the men, more especially those engaged at the dangerous points.

From the neighboring precipice, overhanging the scene of operation, a man is suspended by a rope round his body, and lowered near to the spot where a breach is to be made, which is always selected at the lower edge of the jam. The point may be treacherous, and yield to a feeble touch, or it may require much strength to move it. In the latter case, the operator fastens a long rope to a log, the end of which is taken down stream by a portion of the crew, who are to give a long pull and strong pull when all is ready. He then commences prying while they are pulling. If the jam starts, or any part of it, or if there be even an indication of its starting, he is drawn suddenly up by those stationed above; and, in their excitement and apprehensions for his safety, this is frequently done with such haste as to subject him to bruises and scratches upon the sharp-pointed ledges or bushes in the way. It may be thought best to cut off the key-log, or that which appears to be the principal barrier. Accordingly, he is let down on to the jam, and as the place to be operated upon may in some cases be a little removed from the shore, he either walks to the place with the rope attached to his body, or, untying it, leaves it where he can readily grasp it in time to be drawn from his perilous position. Often when the pressure is direct, a few blows only are given with the ax, when the log snaps in an instant with a loud report, followed suddenly by the violent motion of the "jam" and, ere our bold river-driver is jerked half way to the top of the cliff, scores of logs, in wildest confusion, rush beneath his feet, while he yet dangles in air, above the rushing tumbling mass. If that rope, on which life and hope hang thus suspended, should part, worn by the sharp point of some jutting rock, death, certain and quick, would be inevitable.

The deafening noise when such a jam breaks, produced by the concussion of moving logs whirled about like mere straws, and the crash and breaking of some of the largest, which part apparently as easily as a reed is severed, together with the roar of waters, may be heard for miles; and nothing can exceed the enthusiasm of the river-drivers on such occasions, jumping, hurraing, and yelling with joyous excitement. . . .

From the foregoing account, which is really believed to come short of the reality, the reader will be enabled to form some estimate of the dangers, hardships, and deaths encountered by thousands in the lumbering operations — a business which is hardly supposed to possess any peculiarities of incident or adventure above the most common pursuits of life. How little are the generality of mankind disposed to consider as they should, that for much which contributes to their comfort and ease, many a hardship has been endured and multitudes of individuals have been sacrificed.

JOHN BURROUGHS
1837–1921

John Burroughs, the first well-known nature writer in America, was born into a large farm family near Roxbury, New York. As a child, he was attracted to the natural world around him, and he developed that interest into a writing career of some fifty years' duration. His collected works fill twenty-three volumes, and his graceful style, which strikes a balance between the popular and the academic, made him a nationally known and respected figure.

Ralph Waldo Emerson was an early influence on the young Burroughs. Indeed, the first essay Burroughs submitted to the *Atlantic Monthly* sent its editor, James Russell Lowell, to Emerson's collected works to verify its originality. A further insult was the *Poole's Index* reference to the unsigned piece which credits Emerson, not Burroughs, as its author.

Burroughs also came under the influence of Walt Whitman. The two met and became great friends while Burroughs was spending ten years as a treasury clerk in Washington, D.C. Later, he wrote a biography of the poet.

Burroughs, an enthusiastic traveler, observed the natural world around him wherever he went. He camped in Yosemite with his fellow naturalist John Muir and in Yellowstone with Theodore Roosevelt, and he journeyed to the Caribbean and to Europe. But his home base was the foothills of the Catskills, where he lived at "Riverby," on the Hudson, for most of his adult life.

The following piece, taken from an article written for the *Atlantic Monthly* in 1881, tells of Burroughs's journey to the woods and lakes of Maine. He came not only as a naturalist, observing the plants, rocks, and animals around him, but also as a sportsman and hunter. He and his party fished for trout, shot loons and ducks, and hunted

John Burroughs

for moose and bear. Conservation was not uppermost in the minds of naturalists at that time; even their profligate use of birch bark might be frowned upon today. Nevertheless, Burroughs had a fine time in Maine, and he tells us much of the uses of birch bark, of canoes, and of the geology of the upper Kennebec.

A Taste of Maine Birch

The traveler and camper-out in Maine, unless he penetrates its more northern portions, has less reason to remember it as a pine-tree State than a birch-tree State. The white-pine forests have melted away like snow in the spring and gone down stream, leaving only patches here and there in the more remote and inaccessible parts. The portion of the State I saw, the valley of the Kennebec and the woods about Moxie Lake, had been shorn of its pine timber more than forty years before, and is now covered with a thick growth of spruce and cedar and various deciduous trees. But the birch abounds. Indeed, when the pine goes out the birch comes in; the race of men succeeds the race of giants. This tree has great stay-at-home virtues. Let the sombre, aspiring, mysterious pine go; the birch has humble every-day uses. In Maine, the paper or canoe birch is turned to more account than any other tree. Uncle Nathan, our guide, said it was made especially for the camper-out; yes, and for the woodman and frontiersman generally. It is a magazine, a furnishing store set up in the wilderness, whose goods are free to every comer. The whole equipment of the camp lies folded in it, and comes forth at the beck of the woodman's axe; tent, water-proof roof, boat, camp utensils, buckets, cups, plates, spoons, napkins, table-cloths, paper for letters or your journal, torches, candles, kindling wood and fuel. The canoe birch yields you its vestments with the utmost liberality. Ask for its coat and it gives you its waistcoat also. Its bark seems wrapped about it layer upon layer, and comes off with great ease. We saw many rude structures and cabins shingled and sided with it, and hay-stacks capped with it. Near a maple-sugar camp there was a large pile of birch-bark sap-buckets, — each bucket made of a piece of bark about a yard square, folded up as the tinman folds up a sheet of tin to make a square vessel, the corners bent around against the sides and held by a wooden pin. When, one day, we were overtaken by a shower in traveling through the woods, our guide quickly stripped large sheets of the bark from a near tree, and we had each a perfect umbrella as by magic. When the rain was over, and we moved on, I wrapped mine about me like a large leather apron, and it shielded my clothes from the wet bushes. When we came to a spring, Uncle Nathan would have a birch-bark cup ready before any of us could get a tin one out of his knapsack, and I think water never tastes so sweet as from one of these bark cups. It is exactly the thing. It just fits the mouth, and it seems to give new virtues to the water. It makes me thirsty now when I think of it. In our camp at Moxie we made a large birch-bark box to keep the butter in; and the butter in this box, covered with some leafy boughs, I think improved in flavor day by day. Maine butter needs something to mollify and sweeten it a little, and I think birch bark will do it. In camp Uncle Nathan often drank his tea and coffee from a bark cup; the china closet in the birch-tree was always handy, and our vulgar tinware was generally a good deal mixed, and the kitchen-maid not at all particular about dish-washing. We all tried the oatmeal with the maple syrup in one of these dishes, and the stewed mountain cranberries, using a birch-bark spoon, and never found service better. Uncle Nathan declared he could boil potatoes in a bark kettle, and I did not doubt him. Instead of sending our soiled napkins and table-spreads to the wash, we rolled them up into candles and torches, and drew daily upon our stores in the forest for new ones.

But the great triumph of the birch is of course the bark canoe. When Uncle Nathan took us out under his little wood-shed, and showed us, or rather modestly permitted us to see, his nearly finished canoe, it was like a first glimpse of some new and unknown genius of the woods or streams. It sat there on the chips and shavings and fragments of bark like some shy, delicate creature just emerged from its hiding-place, or like some wild flower just opened. It was the first boat of the kind I had ever seen, and it filled my eye completely. What wood-craft it indicated and what a wild free life, sylvan life, it promised! It had such a fresh, aboriginal look as I had never before seen in any kind of handiwork. Its clear yellow-red color would have become the cheek of an Indian maiden. Then its supple curves and swells, its sinewy stays and thwarts, its bow-like contour, its tomahawk stem

and stern rising quickly and sharply from its frame, were all vividly
suggestive of the race from which it came. An old Indian had taught
Uncle Nathan the art, and the soul of the ideal red man looked out of
the boat before us. Uncle Nathan had spent two days ranging the
mountains looking for a suitable tree, and had worked nearly a week
on the craft. It was twelve feet long, and would seat and carry five
men nicely. Three trees contribute to the making of a canoe beside
the birch, namely, the white cedar for ribs and lining, the spruce for
roots and fibres to sew its joints and bind its frame, and the pine for
pitch or rosin to stop its seams and cracks. It is hand-made and home-
made, or rather wood-made, in a sense that no other craft is, except
a dug-out, and it suggests a taste and a refinement that few products
of a civilization realize. The design of a savage, it yet looks like the
thought of a poet, and its grace and fitness haunt the imagination. I
suppose its production was the inevitable result of the Indian's wants
and surroundings, but that does not detract from its beauty. It is,
indeed, one of the fairest flowers the thorny plant of necessity ever
bore. Our canoe, as I have intimated, was not yet finished, when we
first saw it, not yet when we took it up, with its architect, upon our
metaphorical backs and bore it to the woods. It lacked part of its
cedar lining and the rosin upon its joints, and these were added after
we reached our destination. . . .

Our first glimpse of Maine waters was Pleasant Pond, which we
found by following a white, rapid, musical stream from the Kennebec
three miles back into the mountains. Maine waters are for the most
part dark-complexioned, Indian-colored streams, but Pleasant Pond
is a pale-face among them both in name and nature. It is the only
strictly silver lake I ever saw. Its waters seem almost artificially white
and brilliant, though of remarkable transparency. I think I detected
minute shining motes held in suspension in it. As for the trout, they
are veritable bars of silver until you have cut their flesh, when they
are the reddest of gold. They have no crimson or other spots, and the
straight lateral line is but a faint pencil mark. They appeared to be a
species of lake trout peculiar to these waters, uniformly from ten to
twelve inches in length. And these beautiful fish, at the time of our
visit (last of August) at least, were to be taken only in deep water
upon a hook baited with salt pork. And then you needed a letter of
introduction to them. They were not to be tempted or cajoled by
strangers. We did not succeed in raising a fish, although instructed
how it was to be done, until one of the natives, a young and obliging
farmer living hard by, came and lent his countenance to the enter-

prise. I sat in one end of the boat and he in the other, my pork was the same as his and I manoeuvered it as directed, and yet those fish knew his hook from mine in sixty feet of water and preferred it four times in five. Evidently, they did not bite because they were hungry, but solely for old acquaintance' sake. . . .

Moxie Lake lies much lower than Pleasant Pond, and its waters compared with those of the latter are as copper compared with silver. It is very irregular in shape; now narrowing to the dimensions of a slow moving grassy creek, then expanding into a broad deep basin with rocky shores, and commanding the noblest mountain scenery. It is rarely that the pond-lily and the speckled trout are found together, — the fish the soul of the purest spring water, the flower the transfigured spirit of the dark mud and slime of sluggish summer streams and ponds; yet in Moxie they were both found in perfection. Our camp was amid the birches, poplars, and white cedars near the head of the lake, where the best fishing at this season was to be had. Moxie has a small oval head, rather shallow, but bumpy with rocks; a long, deep neck, full of springs, where the trout lie; and a very broad chest, with two islands tufted with pine-trees for breasts. We swam in the head, we fished in the neck, or in a small section of it, a space about the size of the Adam's apple, and we paddled across and around the broad expanse below. Our birch-bark was not finished and christened till we reached Moxie. The cedar lining was completed at Pleasant Pond, where we had the use of a *bateau,* but the rosin was not applied to the seams till we reached this lake. When I knelt down in it for the first time, and put its slender maple paddle into the water, it sprang away with such quickness and speed that it disturbed me in my seat. I had spurred a more restive and spirited steed than I was used to. In fact, I had never been in a craft that sustained so close a relation to my will, and was so responsive to my slightest wish. When I caught my first large trout from it, it sympathized a little too closely, and my enthusiasm started a leak, which, however, with a live coal and a piece of rosin, was quickly mended. You cannot perform much of a war-dance in a birch-bark; better wait till you get on dry land. Yet as a boat it is not so shy and "ticklish" as I had imagined. One needs to be on the alert, as becomes a sportsman and an angler, and in his dealings with it must charge himself with three things, — precision, moderation, and circumspection. . . .

One day we made an excursion of three miles through the woods to Bald Mountain, following a dim trail. We saw, as we filed silently along, plenty of signs of caribou, deer, and bear, but were not blessed with a sight of either of the animals themselves. I noticed that Uncle Nathan, in looking through the woods, did not hold his head as we did, but thrust it slightly forward, and peered under the branches like a deer, or other wild creature.

The summit of Bald Mountain was the most impressive mountain top I had ever seen, mainly, perhaps, because it was one enormous crown of nearly naked granite. The rock had that gray, elemental, eternal look which granite alone has. One seemed to be face to face with the gods of the fore-world. Like an atom, like a breath of to-day, we were suddenly confronted by abysmal geologic time, the eternities past and the eternities to come. The enormous cleavage of the rocks, the appalling cracks and fissures, the rent bowlders, the smitten granite floors, gave one a new sense of the power of heat and frost. In one place we noticed several deep parallel grooves made by the old glaciers. In the depressions on the summit there was a hard, black, peaty-like soil that looked indescribably ancient and unfamiliar. Out of this mould, that might have come from the moon, or the interplanetary spaces, were growing mountain cranberries and blueberries, or huckleberries. We were soon so absorbed in gathering the latter that we were quite oblivious of the grandeurs about us. It is these blueberries that attract the bears. In eating them, Uncle Nathan said, they take the bushes in their mouths, and by an upward movement strip them clean of both leaves and berries. We were constantly on the lookout for bears, but failed to see any. Yet a few days afterward, when two of our party returned here and encamped upon the mountain, they saw five during their stay, but failed to get a good shot. The rifle was in the wrong place each time. The man with the shot-gun saw an old bear and two cubs lift themselves from behind a rock and twist their noses around for his scent, and then shrink away. They were too far off for his buckshot. I must not forget the superb view that lay before us, a wilderness of woods and waters stretching away to the horizon on every hand. Nearly a dozen lakes and ponds could be seen, and in a clearer atmosphere the foot of Moosehead Lake would have been visible. The highest and most striking mountain to be seen was Mount Bigelow, rising above Dead River, far to the west, and its two sharp peaks notching the horizon like enormous saw teeth. We walked around and viewed curiously a huge bowlder on the top of the mountain that had been split in two vertically, and one of the halves moved a few feet out of its bed. It looked recent and familiar, but suggested gods instead of men. The force that moved the rock had plainly come from the north. . . .

We stayed a week at Moxie, or until we became surfeited with its trout, and had killed the last merganser duck that lingered about our end of the lake. The trout that had accumulated on our hands we had kept alive in a large champagne basket submerged in the lake, and the morning we broke camp the basket was towed to the shore and opened; and after we had feasted our eyes upon the superb spectacle, every trout, twelve or fifteen in number, some of them two-pounders, was allowed to swim back into the lake. They went leisurely, in couples and in trios, and were soon kicking up their heels in their old haunts. I expect that the divinity who presides over Moxie will see to it that every one of those trout, doubled in weight, come to our basket in the future.

ROBERT SMITH
1905—

Nearly 90 percent of Maine's 33,000 square miles is forested. That single fact has dominated Maine's economy since early colonial times, for wood and its products — from building boards to ships' masts, from newsprint to toothpicks — are the state's major industry. The figures for 1989 show a total product value of more than $4 billion for wood-derived paper products and nearly $1 billion for lumber. This great natural resource has historically called the industrial tune for the State of Maine.

In pre-Revolutionary times, lumbering and the milling of wood were done on a limited scale: single sawmills operated on the lesser coastal streams, with the owner cutting the trees and running his own mill. Maine was the site of the first two such mills, built in Berwick and York in 1634. The longest, straightest pines were always marked with the king's arrow and reserved for the Royal Navy to use as masts — a source of some resentment among the Maine lumbermen. As the more easily accessible trees were felled, lumbering became more complex, requiring more capital, land, and labor to bring the cut logs out of the deeper woods. Cooperative associations were formed, and river driving served to transport the logs to the mills. Special boats, called batteaus, helped maneuver the great masses of logs downriver, and special tools, such as the peavey, enabled the log drivers to control their logs in the water. In the nineteenth century, cut lumber was used primarily for ship timbers and spars and milled for planks and boards. Smaller products, such as barrel hoops, shingles, and clapboards, also came from this resource. Lumber was king, and it was generally accepted that the entrepreneurs had preeminent rights to the waterways used to transport the logs. Canals, dams, and sluiceways were built for this purpose, and any other use of the great

Camp at Russell Pond

rivers, the Kennebec, the Penobscot, and the Androscoggin, took second place.

The end of the nineteenth century saw an expansion of lumbering with an infusion of out-of-state capital, an increasing use of the rivers for hydropower, and a shift in emphasis to the use of pulpwood for making paper. In the early part of the eighteenth century, Massachusetts, of which Maine was then a part, encouraged the manufacture of paper from rags in Maine by granting sole production rights for ten years to one Daniel Henchman and his associates. Paper mills were built in Falmouth and Stroudwater, presumably under contract with Henchman. But the manufacture of paper from wood did not become a major industry until the late 1880s. The great spruce forests and abundant water resources of Maine contributed to the preeminence of the pulp and paper companies here today.

A considerable body of lore evolved around the various aspects of lumbering in Maine: ballads, stories, and firsthand accounts of life in the woods abound. The hardships of pulpwood operations in the twentieth century are forthrightly presented by Robert Smith in his memoir *My Life in the North Woods,* which describes his days as a clerk for the McCormick brothers' logging camp near Rangeley during the Depression. The big paper companies contracted out the logging operations to the likes of Tim and Wallace McCormick, who worked their men hard. Smith was responsible for the wangan (company store) as well as the bookkeeping, which always seemed to end up with the hapless young "Dutchmen" — actually Canadians of German descent — paying back to the McCormicks most of their wages in board and keep. Smith was also kept on call as needed in the cookhouse and in the woods, so he soon became familiar with the entire operation and with the mean-spirited men who ran it. These passages tell what life in this camp was like and explain something of the dangers inherent in the hard work of getting logs out of the woods.

Smith has written more than forty books of both fiction and non-fiction. A resident of Lenox, Massachusetts, he contributes articles to the *Berkshire Eagle*.

The McCormick Brothers' Logging Camp

Tim by this time was far off in the woods, where, according to the informal arrangement that seemed to exist between the brothers, he spotted out roads for the choppers to follow and generally oversaw the swamping of the roads and the piling of wood where it would be accessible to the teams that would start hauling when the snow grew deep. Harold and I knew, from having watched his plodding figure move through the woods, axe on shoulder, as we stood far off unseen on a knoll, that Tim often took himself a half mile south of our works to where some summer resident had long before built a small spring-house in the woods. Under the skimpy shelter here, Tim would light his pipe, out of the wind, and sit quietly puffing blue smoke for an hour or more.

Wallace meanwhile labored without letup in the dooryard, and when Tim would return from the woods, Wallace seemed to make an extra show of hustling about his own chores — just as if Tim were the schoolmaster and Wallace but a small boy who had been set some

Lumber camp crew

tasks to complete for punishment. Wallace was a deft man with an adze, with which he would hew out sleds to be fitted with steel runners. He could shape the steel with forge and anvil and hammer, fix it to the sled, and bolt it tight, with the bolts I had brought him. When the lake was open he had run the motorboat to fetch the freight, had landed and stored it. He ordered the supplies, paid the bills, brought the horses in on a scow and rationed their feed — as he rationed that of the dollar-a-day boarders, the lumberjacks themselves.

Indeed, there was not a man in the camp who did not work harder than Tim did. But Tim did a special penance that Wallace avoided. Tim took his meals with the rest of us, in the cook camp, dipping his meat out of the common pot, drinking the ink-black tea, and sharing the pans of dark-boiled potatoes and cabbage. The food provided, for a dollar a day, was but barely fit for human fodder. Only two full meals were served in the camp, for the woodsmen carried their lunches with them into the woods, where they built fires to boil their tea or coffee.

The meat served at supper (dinner was the name of the noonday meal) was always some form of beef butts. These were purchased in small wooden boxes that, to look at them would not have weighed over forty pounds. But the little boxes weighed a hundred pounds apiece; the meat they contained had been so compressed — the juice having been squeezed out for soups before it was marketed — that it had acquired the specific gravity of lead, or something close to it. I know when I first set out to pick up a box, consigned to our camp, from the railroad station platform, my first tug had not even budged it. Several gawky adolescents of my own age and general appearance, who had been watching me, burst out laughing then. This drove me to such a surge of effort that I hoisted the box with one quick heave right to my shoulder and walked off with it, leaving all the laughers (I imagined) undone.

But putting even small chunks of this beef into the stomach required determination of a different caliber entirely, and it was more than I could summon, after I had swallowed the stuff once or twice. The meat was cooked up in a pot full of lard substitute, dug out of wooden pails with a greasy paddle, and set to bubbling on the stove. When it was "done," the whole mess was turned out into pannikins that were set about the long board tables for the men to dip into. If you waited too long to take your share, the grease would have turned back into a gray-white solid that neither Harold or I could quite manage to consign, unmolten, to our insides.

The boiled potatoes, set out in pannikins like the beef, were always the color of waterlogged snow, for they had remained too long in the pot after being taken off the fire. They were edible, however, as the cabbage was. Some of the Dutchmen even found the stomach to flavor their potatoes with the grease from the meat. It perhaps need not be said that there were always two or three lumberjacks laid out in the barroom, suffering from diarrhea of varying virulence.

The drinks were tea, coffee, evaporated milk, and water fetched from the spring in buckets. The cookee, carrying either the teapot or the coffee pot or the water pitcher, walked up and down the aisles between the tables and filled the pannikins as requested. There were no handles on those "cups," so many of the men drank with their thumbs immersed in their drink. The tea could not be distinguished from the coffee by looking at it or smelling it. Both were black and bitter as tar. But there was always a string wound around the handle of the teapot, so the cookee would know what he was carrying. Most of the men would mix their drinks without regard, taking tea first, then filling the pan with evaporated milk before the tea was quite gone, then taking water on top of the remnants of that mixture, to which sugar had been liberally added at the start. There was little talk at the table, except as the men called out to remind the cookee that a pan was empty, for every man devoted himself to eating, which was almost the only recreation the camp afforded.

Harold and I found ourselves eventually living on cabbage, turnips, potatoes, cookies and tea, with bacon in the morning that had many of the qualities of rock salt, but that was at least more palatable than the beef. The others, even Tim, who had surely known better fare, consumed whatever they found before them, not always without complaint, but always with appetite. When they found some dish difficult to stomach, there was always a jar of molasses to garnish it with and render it sweet enough to swallow.

The boarding arrangement was difficult for me to understand. In all other live-in jobs I had known about, the "found" — that is, the board — was included in the wage. But here the woodsmen seemed to own the status of independent contractors. They received two dollars and forty cents for a cord of spruce or fir, cut four feet long and piled "at the stump" — that is, along the woods road they themselves had to swamp out of the forest. A woods cord in that day measured four feet deep by eight feet long by four feet and four inches high — the four inches being allowed for "loose piling." It was, however, just a means of slicing a tiny bit of extra profit from the woodsman's wage, for the lumber company, when it sold the wood, granted the buyer no extra lagniappe for loose piling. The woodsmen also rented their tools from the subcontractor — the McCormicks — so in addition to the dollar a day that was subtracted for their board, a fee for "use of tools" was also figured in, the fee varying, depending on the length of time the man had worked. Occasionally, when a man was paid off who seemed less woods-smart than the others, the crafty brothers would credit his tools back at a price somewhat less than they had been charged out. Tim would pick up the returned axe and weigh it carelessly in his hand as if looking for a place to discard it.

"Look at that," he would growl. "Not worth a shit now!" The saw and the sledgehammer (listed as a "swedging hammer") would likewise be cried down, and the whole lot taken back at less than half what they went out for. Then the two or three dollars for "use of tools" would be subtracted as well, while the tools, after a few passes with a whetstone, a file, and a dirty cloth, would be charged at full price to the next man.

It became clear to me that the McCormicks were really running a sort of boarding house and rental service, as well as taking a profit on the wood. They also sold, of course, candy and clothing to the workmen out of the wangan, and sometimes apples and playing cards, so there was many an extra penny turned from those stingy wages. The men were required to swamp out their own roads — that is, cut the stumps down so that the snow would cover them and the sleds could ride over them, clean out the brush and pile the tops out of the way, leaving a way clear of brush, stumps, and saplings where a horse-drawn sled could haul a load. The main roads, called two-sled roads because they had to be wide enough for a rack set on two sleds and drawn by two horses, were swamped out by men hired at day rates. The piecework lumberjacks had to stamp their wood too, marking each stick on both ends with a small stamp axe that bit a cold brand into the wood designating the company to which it belonged. The Brown Company, with whom the McCormicks held a contract, used a letter H as their timber mark. Inasmuch as the mark also had to be cut into some timber with an axe, it was desirable to use a mark that could be made with straight axe strokes — an H or an E or an I or a Y. The smaller sticks, with the mark indented at each end, could be identified if they strayed from the drive and lodged on a riverbank or became mixed with wood destined for another mill. The boom logs, cut twenty to thirty feet long, had their brands cut into their bark with an axe — and an able man with an axe could mark an H in three quick strokes. It was also a relatively easy matter for a practiced eye to judge the cubic contents of a log at a glance, a skill in which I prided myself. The lumber mills that shared these waters used them as if they held private title to lakes, rivers, and brooks, and could dam them, jam them full of wood, or turn them loose to suit their own needs and God help those who might thereby be discommoded. In my day, and for long afterward, vacationers, hikers, fishermen, hunters, birdwatchers, and campers were mere nuisances to a lumber company, folk who sometimes had to be chased away from a stream, waved away from a towboat that was drawing a boom full of pulp down a lake, or warned to take their canoes out of water being used for driving pulpwood to the mill.

No one dared question the right of the almighty lumber companies to treat all the waters of the state of Maine as their own preserve. Even at the paper mill, the entire river might be used to wash the waste away, rendering the river for miles below undrinkable, unswimmable, and unbearable. To the people who dwelt in modest homes along the banks, the presence of a noisome stream was simply one more of the prices men paid for being poor.

The McCormicks themselves had been raised poor but they had only scorn for men who had remained that way. The young Nova Scotians they imported to work in the woods were all of German origin, inhabitants of a tiny corner of Lunenburg County, where Germans had settled more than a century earlier, and they all wore names like Ernst, Aulenbach, Wentzel, and Veinot. In our camp there may have been five Aulenbachs and none claimed kinship with any of the others. Indeed, when I mistakenly suggested to one yellow-haired young Aulenbach that another Aulenbach, also yellow-haired, and also built square as a woodbox, might be his brother, he angrily corrected me. But there was no question that all were damn poor. Their pants were heavily patched and their boots too often worn right through. Nearly every one of them, when he had been in camp two weeks or more, used up a share of his scant earnings in the wangan, buying new pants and "rubbers" to last him through.

A lumberjack "tried on" his pants by closing his fist and shoving his forearm inside the waistband. If the pants fit the forearm tight, then they were the right size. One fellow, laughing as he chose a pair to fit, kept demonstrating his need by lifting one leg and showing how his current pair were completely gone on the inside, from crotch to knee. That any man should exist in such penury aroused open contempt in both the McCormicks. They were soft-spoken as could be in dealing directly with the men, but out of their hearing, they spoke in disgust of the way the Dutchmen ate, slept, washed, and relieved themselves.

Their manner of performing most of these simple tasks was largely dictated by the facilities the McCormicks provided them. But there was no doubt they had all been brought up in homes where the only plumbing was installed at the well, where all natural needs were attended to outdoors, and where laundering was a luxury. Here in the lumber camp, they all slept, half clothed (they'd have frozen otherwise), under a lumpy fat "comforter" made of horse blankets sewed together and stuffed with cotton waste, in a straw-filled bunk, two men together in a bunk about three feet wide. The straw, of course, frequently crawled with live creatures, which moved freely from one body to another all up and down the double row of bunks. The barroom, or sleeping quarters, and the cookshack were all of a piece, a long low building made of used boards covered with tar paper. A door and a high sill, over which sleepy lumberjacks frequently stumbled, connected the two large rooms.

Some twenty yards above the bunkhouse, out of sight behind a clump of alders, a pit had been dug and a lean-to shelter rigged over it, open at the sides, with a long pole stretched across the pit at just the right height for a man, standing on a narrow strip of planking on the edge of the pit, to lean back and hook his arms over. There was room for three or four men at a time. This was the spot provided for defecation. It stunk to the skies. Tattered bits of newspaper or advertising circulars, used as toilet paper, formed a sort of carpet on the planking or blew out to adorn the brush and snowbanks all around. There was a bucket of loose earth at hand to be tossed into the pit atop each new deposit, but few men out in the zero cold of an evening paused to perform this office. "Ain't as if they was *human*," Wallace would snarl occasionally when he chanced near the place and shrugged off its foul condition.

The kitchen staff consisted of cook and cookee who slept in two bunks behind the stove. The cookee's assignment was to cut stovewood and keep the woodbox filled, to start fires, to wash pots and pans, to set the table, serve the food, keep the floor clean, and the sugar bowls filled, and put oil in all the lamps. It was also his duty to waken the whole camp in the morning, at half past five, and to call them all to meals. This he did with the traditional wailing cry that cookees had sung out over pitch-dark dooryards since men first gathered in gangs to fell trees and bring them to market.

"Turn a-a-a-a-a-out!" he would call, first into the sleeping barroom, where the fire had died to a few blinking coals, and then out across the yard to wake up the office crew. The sound of this strange cry, disembodied as the call of a distant loon, and echoing like a loon's across the dark empty lake and against the wooded mountain, is one that haunts me still. It rose and fell like the cry of a sailor at sea, seeming, despite its throatiness, as gentle as music. "Turn a-a-a-a-a-out!" I would hear it first, muffled as in a dream, inside the walls of the barroom, and then, some thirty seconds later, instant and clear, just across the yard from our door. It would be black dark. The sound of men thumping about in the barroom to pull their boots on would follow instantly. Harold, who could reach out to the table without leaving his bed, would, after three or four attempts, set a match to spluttering into flame, and would light the small lamp, suddenly isolating our little cobwebbed world from the vast cold night. Then, after a few quiet curses, he would hop out in his socks to open the stove door, set the drafts, shove in new wood, and get the fire to pulsing.

We had wash water in a kettle on the stove and a small basin to wash in but often we would first take a turn trudging, with boots unlaced, out to the small, snugly boarded shithouse that was our very own, with a hole in the seat and a board cover to go over it. It would sometimes be just cracking dawn, so that I could make out the men who stood outside the barroom door, all facing the east in a semicircle like worshippers, and all urinating solemnly into the snow.

Tim McCormick, whose scorn for his fellowman was more caustic than his brother's, or at least expressed more openly and more often, found frequent excuse to share his conviction that all the young Dutchmen were engaged, night after night, in "whetting." That was Tim's word for masturbation, an activity that Tim, like practically every other two-fisted male alive in that day, devoutly believed led to cowardice, distaste for outdoor labor, muscular flabbiness, loss of appetite, and eventual homosexuality. There seems hardly any doubt that these young men — but one or two of whom had gone more than a short stride past thirty, all of whom owned less worldly wisdom than a modern eight-year-old, who were largely married and all vigorous and emotionally stable, and every last one of whom lacked the brass to offer a half-day's pay to one of the scrawny whores who operated semiprofessionally in Oquossoc — certainly required and undoubtedly found some occasional sexual outlet. There was no homosexuality in the camp. If there had been, it could not have remained secret even half a day. And the brothers McCormick would have rooted it out as they would have driven out a thief — by instant violence and consignment to a cold hike across the ice. . . .

Hauling began when the snow was so deep that it would hide a horse right to his ears. The teamster, drawing two trailing loads of bundled pulp sticks to break out a road, would ride on the second bundle, far enough behind so as not to slide up on the horse's rump if the beast should balk at the steepness of a sudden ram down. Once a good road had been broken on the downgrade, the loaded racks would be drawn down more directly to the shore, to be emptied out on the frozen lake.

Men would stand then along the road, which would gradually turn slick and shiny, and would fork hay out on the sled track, to help keep the loads from "sluicing" — running away, that is, impelled by their own weight, and carrying the team with them. Spreading the hay was an endless job, for each sled would gather up the hay into windrows as it slid over it, then it would all have to be spread out over the track more or less evenly to help brake the team that followed. On the steepest grade the pace of the sled had to be slowed by means of a length of bridle chain hooked around underneath the sled iron in what was known as a bear-trap hitch, which could be knocked loose with one blow of an axe, so the sled could run freely once it reached level ground. On many jobs where the grade was dangerously steep, snub lines were used to hold back on the rack full of pulp as it coasted down behind the team. These were long ropes, hitched to the back sled and wound around a tree trunk. A wooden brake would be driven into the trunk just above the coil of rope, so that it could be pushed down against the rope to keep it from unwinding too rapidly. The man who stood at the end of the rope and worked the brake, or fed the snubbed rope to the tree trunk by hand, had to stay constantly alert lest the rope escape and unreel around the trunk in a smoking fury, allowing a rack of pulp to smash into the hapless team and send it to destruction.

The McCormicks would never have trusted me with any such job and I wanted none of it anyway, for I would have lived in terror with that burden on my conscience. Instead, I was set to loading pulp at the top of the grade, yanking the sticks off a pile with a needle-sharp pulp hook, and tossing them up into the rack to be piled snugly together. This was a frantic enough task for me, who had never wielded a pulp hook more than casually, and who was given to stumbling and sliding about in my desperate efforts to keep pace with the teamsters. Actually the job of yanking the half-frozen sticks off the pile and heaving them to the bed of the rack was twice the job of piling them and most of the teamsters acknowledged this. But in every such crew there was always at least one hand ready to seize any chance to flaunt a spoonful of authority. One skinny, shock-haired young man always drove up toward me wearing a smirk, as if he were savoring in advance his delight at putting me down. He always pretended to bear my slowness and awkwardness with extreme patience — patience that was being tried to its outer limits. Most people in the woods converse in loud shouts anyway, but this lad, whose name was Jack Scott, invariably bellowed out his comments to me so that everyone within a quarter mile could hear them. Jack was no favorite of anyone, for he was given to outbragging every man in camp. There was no hunting ground, no matter how remote, nor any pond or stream, in whatever hidden corner of nowhere it might lie, that he had not fished in or trod upon, no game he had not bagged, no willing lady he had not himself enjoyed, nor any boss he had not taken the measure of. Whatever strange accident might have befallen any of his associates, the very like, if not something far stranger, had happened to Jack. And all the marvels of nature that other men had set eyes upon, Jack had seen them all before they did, or soon after.

So Jack, despite his unvoiced appeal to all the other teamsters to come share his distress at my failings, never won any sympathy from his mates. Indeed, one of the Rangeley teamsters, Walter Hamm, invited Jack one time to try swapping jobs with me and Jack allowed solemnly that By God no man was going to load *his* team but himself, being as *he* was the man had to *answer* for it if there was anything wrong. At this Walter chuckled darkly; I was comforted thereby and even dared look Jack in the eye and second the invitation.

Poor Jack, as it happened, had something wrong to answer for before the second week of hauling was out. It was a bright cold morning, and the road was all ice as he brought his smoking team up to gather his first load. I watched the nodding horses pull the empty rack up abreast of the pulp pile, and I took care to avoid Jack's eye, for I knew he would be offering me his look of weary resignation before he even had to deal with me. My glance fell instead on the icy chains that trailed alongside the forward sleds and I waited to see Jack hop out and hitch them in place. Instead, Jack merely clambered into the bed of the rack and let go a yell:

"Well, Jesus Christ, clerk! Ain't you done dreaming? You'd oughta get your sleeping done on your *own* time!"

Because I had heard this identical jibe from him more times than I wanted to count, it hardly raised a welt on my vanity.

"You going to hitch the bridle chains first?" I asked him.

Jack did look mildly abashed, for the better part of a second, but he recovered himself at once.

"Don't you fret yourself about my bridle chains, young feller!" he shouted. "You handle your end of the contract and I'll be able to handle mine a damn sight better!" I had already dug the point of my pulp hook into the nearest stick and I began to swing the rough bolts of wood one at a time up onto the rack, where Jack, still protesting to the wide woodland that I would do my own job better if I would be pleased to butt out of his, grabbed them up and arranged them in rows.

My part of the job always left me drawing in deep painful drafts of zero air, convinced that I could not pick up one more stick, nor even hold the pulp hook another two seconds at the end of my aching arm. Unable, or at least unwilling in Jack's presence, to pause long enough to comfort my numb face, I worked with tears running unchecked clear down over my chin and with my nose building a puddle on my upper lip. So when I saw the load start off at last, while Jack flailed his whip and shouted, "Git up in that goddamn collar!" I saw, and yet I did not see, that the bridle chains still trailed unhitched alongside the sled. That is, I observed that they had not been hitched, but I was too done in to tell myself about it.

It was not until the sled had mounted the slight rise and started on the steep downgrade that the meaning of the loose chains registered.

"Hey!" I hollered. "Hey! The chains!"

But by this time Jack too had begun to yell.

"Whoa! Whoa!" he screamed, as he felt the overloaded sleds pick up speed beneath him. I began to run after the team, as if I might catch hold of the rack and by main strength keep it from sluicing. But it was already moving faster than I could and Jack's wild yells had become wordless sounds of terror. Yet he clung to the suddenly slackened reins and waved his useless whip even as the loaded rack, now completely out of control, drove into the rumps of the terrified team and swept them on.

Harry Ernst, who had entered the main road just two or three rods ahead with his own team, turned back to see the source of the racket. He made one vain and frantic effort to whip up his horses to clear the way, then leapt out into the snow, where he sank to his waist. His team plunged partway into the snowbank and stuck there. Jack, too, then leapt for safety, still hanging tight to his whip. The thundering load of pulp drove the two horses straight into the rack ahead and seemed to crush them into the jumbled wood. A shaft splintered, with a crack like a felled tree. Pulp was spilled out of the rack and hid itself in the snow. The horses screamed like human creatures in awful pain and struggled wildly to get free. The near horse, as he tossed his head, flung a stream of blood into the snow, where it scattered in bright red gobbets, like spilled marbles.

Two dozen men gathered from everywhere, some floundering through the drifts, some scrambling along the icy way. Tim Mc-Cormick, his face suddenly gray, pounded up the slope, mouth wide-open and eyes aflame. He joined the others in the desperate effort to cut the trapped horses loose. The near horse, free of his harness and pawing wildly at the dumped sticks of pulp, stumbled at last into the snow, where he sank to his belly and stood there mournfully wheezing, his muzzle an oozing red mass, like a blood-soaked sponge. The other horse seemed to be struggling vainly to free himself from a trap. Even when the tugs and belly strap had been unbuckled, he kept pawing with one hoof at the pulp sticks beneath him, while one front leg was held fast. Harry Ernst found a way through the scattered pulpwood and splintered poles to get at the anchored hoof and he let out a yell of dismay.

"Jesus Holy Christ!" he hollered. "See what this poor fuckin critter done to hisself! He's driven that shaft right through his fuckin hoof!" Harry clambered out to find an axe and set out to cut the horse free. When the horse was led out at last, it wore a long splinter of wood, three inches thick, stuck right through the cleft in its front hoof and protruding six inches in front. "Never touched no flesh!" Harry exclaimed breathlessly. "Didn't cut him a bit!"

Foolishly, with his open mouth pouring white smoke, Tim Mc-Cormick seized hold of the splinter and tried to yank it by main strength free of the horse's hoof. But it stuck as if it had grown there.

"You ain't going to get that out that way," Harry told him. "Only way is to cut into the hoof. You may have to pare it down some."

But Tim kept trying, gasping out curses in a sort of fiendish whisper, for he was nearly spent from running up the slope. After one final yank, which almost cost him his mittens, Tim sat right down on the ice and rocked himself back and forth, eyes shut, like a man knocked down in a fight. Breath scraped in and out of his throat but he had none to spare for talking. Harry stood over him.

"You feel all right?" he said. Tim waved one hand weakly, then shook his head and spat.

"Out of breath," he gasped.

The whole crew by this time had gathered about the scene, to help move the wreckage off the road, and to rescue the buried pulpwood from the drifts. Jack Scott, wearing clots of snow all down his front, from his hat to his trousers, and still carrying his useless whip, stumbled down toward where Tim was sitting. Jack was pounding the air with his whip and shaking his head to the same rhythm.

"I swear to *God!*" he was crying to any ear that would attend him. "I swear to *God,* I had them bridle chains *hitched.* Must be someone *knocked* them. Or . . ." He slid a glance toward me, as he appraised his chances of shifting the blame to my back. "I swear to *God,* they was *hitched* when I was *loading!*" He seemed very near to weeping. His mouth kept twisting as if he were in pain.

Harry Ernst stood up from where he had been bending over Tim and turned to face Jack Scott.

"You're a fucking liar already," said Harry, as calmly as if he were reporting on the weather. "Clerk was yelling to you about the chains when you come over the rise."

Jack's expression of studied bewilderment dissolved as if he had been struck in the face. His chin went limp and his mouth hung open. Only a faint sound came forth as his breath tried to catch its balance: "I . . . I . . ."

Tim had got himself to his feet at last. He wiped spittle from his lips and made a gesture with one mittened hand as if he were tapping Jack, who was yards away, in the chest.

"Never mind that," Tim gasped. "You . . . you just . . . get the hell down to camp and let clerk figure your time."

Jack had his mouth back in working order now. His face went very white. "Jesus Christ Almighty, Tim!" he wailed. "You got to give me a chance!"

But Tim had used all the breath he could spare. He clung to a corner of the devastated rack and kept his eyes closed. He did not seem to hear Jack at all and eventually Jack started back to camp, with me a few strides behind, and Jack explaining to me and to the empty woods and to himself how unfairly he had been dealt with. In the office camp, while I fished up the book to figure his time, Jack kept his tear-filled eyes fixed on my face and talked as if he and I were both privy to the fact that it had been he — Jack Scott — and none other, who had warned of just such a disaster as this.

"I don't know how many times I told Tim . . . Hell, you must have heard me say it Christ knows how many times . . . I told him to get rid of that Christly beartrap hitch! Christ! I don't *like* that goddamn hitch. You seen what can happen coming over that rise when I knocked into some fuckin stump or something and that hitch just come undone! You seen that yourself! You know Jack Scott don't load up without he's got them bridle chains hitched! You ever know me to load up without I had them bridle chains hitched?"

I dared not add to Jack's misery by answering him truthfully, so I pretended to find some scribble I had to squint at to decipher. But Jack hardly left room for an answer. "I like that old-*time* hitch," he declared breathlessly, "where the teamster hung right on to the bridle chain. Then if anything went wrong you knowed it right off. These goddamn beartrap hitches, they've lost more hosses! I've seen it! I've seen more good hosses lost from using them fuckin beartrap hitches. Not only in this country but over in Magalloway, back along. Save *time!* Shit! You ever try to knock a beartrap hitch loose when she's all iced up under the sled? Why I've spent as much as twenty minutes trying to knock one of them bastards loose with an axe. Had to crawl right under the sled to get at her! I told them what could happen. But oh, no! They know better. Some of these big brains down to Berlin. They ever try driving a two-sled rig in the woods? Like Hell! But you can't tell *them!* Well, now you seen what happens!"

Having satisfied himself that his reputation had been repaired, Jack had become nearly his old self again, no longer bent half across the desk to beseech my sympathy, but sprawled in his chair and waving one red hand shoulder-high to decorate his speech. I had made out the company order in his name and I pushed over the slip on which I had done my figuring, pointing out the deductions for tobacco and other trifles. Jack, half smiling, with an almost scornful expression, hardly took time to read them but picked up his order and folded it small to fit it into his purse.

"Well, now they seen what can happen," he said, with his voice back in his chest once more. "Maybe next time they'll *listen* when somebody that knows his business tries to tell them something. They won't take the word of a teamster! All right, now they lost a hoss!"

Jack would not wait until the men had returned to camp and someone might have given him the ride back to Oquossoc to which he was entitled. He obviously had no stomach for touting to any other teamster the virtues of the old-time hitch. He'd *walk* out, by Christ!

"Why, shit," he told me. "I've *swum* acrost bigger puddles than this."

And off he went, floundering through thigh-deep drifts to reach the roadway the tote team from the storehouse had broken out to travel down the lake to the village. The cook and the cookee both came out of the cookshack to look after Jack, unbelieving.

"Hey!" the cook cried. "Whyn't you wait till one of the other fellers gets back to give you a lift?" But the cook was not used to shouting — indeed he talked hardly at all — and his thin voice seemed to fade into a whisper before it reached halfway out to Jack. So we watched him until at last he found the road, shook snow off his trousers, then set off southward, with his straw suitcase tied to his shoulders like a backpack, a shabby and forlorn little figure on the wide white lake. I could not even rejoice at his going.

MARITIME MAINE

ROBERT CARTER
1819–1879

The coast of Maine is a summer sailor's paradise. Its 3,500-mile shoreline of bays and inlets, coves and river mouths, is punctuated with some three thousand islands, from small barren ledges to the mountainous 1,200 square miles of Mount Desert, and offers the cruising yachtsman an almost infinite variety of courses to set and harbors to visit. Cruising the Maine coast has always been a major drawing card for tourists.

One of the earliest records of such a pleasure trip was the journal kept by Robert Carter of his cruise from Boston to Mount Desert in 1858. With two friends — the "Professor," who was interested in marine biology, and the "Assyrian," who seemed to be primarily interested in circumventing Maine's 1851 Prohibition law — Carter chartered the 33-foot sloop *Helen* with a crew of two for $7.50 a day.

These gay blades had a fine time of it, and Carter's journal, *A Summer Cruise on the Coast of New England,* gives a free-spirited account of their trip: the beauty of the coast, the challenge of catching most of their meals from the ocean, their encounters with foul weather at sea and, in the section on Maine, with down east folk of all varieties on shore.

Carter himself was a literary and journalistic gadfly, a prodigious reader with an encyclopedic memory. He wrote poetry and novels and served as an editor or correspondent for newspapers in Boston, New York, Washington, and Rochester, New York. His involvement with the antislavery Free Soil party led him to organize a convention in Massachusetts in 1848 at which a platform was drafted and the name Republican chosen. It was one of several similar political meetings convened that year to protest the Kansas-Nebraska Act and led to the formation of the Republican party.

Politics and journalism aside, Carter's joy in his summer cruise and his whimsical observations provide a timeless record of the pleasures of sailing along the Maine coast.

Casco Bay, The Power of Melody, The Haddock, Jewell's Island

No July morning was ever finer than that on which we bade adieu to Portland, and turned our little sloop toward the nearest of the countless isles of Casco Bay. As the gentle breeze swept the *Helen* slowly over the sparkling waters, we spread on the top of the cabin the charts of the coast of Maine with which our good friends in Portland had provided us and fell to diligent study of our proposed route.

Casco Bay extends from Cape Elizabeth on the west, to Cape Small Point on the east, a distance of about twenty miles. It is an indentation in the coast whose greatest depth does not exceed fifteen miles. Beside Portland, at its western end, there are three or four flourishing towns on the shores of the bay; and embosomed in its waters, if the popular account be true, are no less than three hundred and sixty-five islands, a compliment to the days of the year which is also attributed to Lake George, Lake Winnipesaukee, and several other bodies of water. Without vouching for the exact number, it is doubtless safe to say that there are at least three hundred isles and islets, besides many bold and picturesque headlands and peninsulas, so that scarcely anywhere else in the world can you find a more varied or more lovely commingling of land and water.

The shores of the islands and the promontories are mostly covered with woods of maple, oak, beech, pine, and fir, growing nearly to the water's edge and throwing their shadows over many a deep inlet and winding channel. It is impossible to conceive of any combination of scenery more charming, more romantic, more captivating to the eye, or more suggestive to the imagination. No element of beauty is want-

Schooner under tow on the Saco River, 1911

ing. Many of the islands are wildly picturesque in form, and from their woodland summits you behold on one hand the surges of the Atlantic, breaking almost at your feet, and on the other the placid waters of the bay, spangled by gems of emerald, while in the distance you discern the peaks of the White Mountains.

For several hours we sauntered, rather than sailed, through this enchanted and enchanting fairyland, steering hither and thither as caprice impelled, or as the perpetually-changing views attracted. At length the Skipper, whose taste for the picturesque was yet undeveloped, and who beside was sufficiently familiar with beauties of the bay, began to hint that it was time to think of dinner, and that a few fresh fish would lend additional grace to that ceremony. We anchored in deep water, in a broad channel called Hussey's Sound. The Pilot kindled his fire in the furnace at the companion-way, and we baited our lines and began to fish.

For more than an hour we fished without a bite. We suggested to the Skipper that our lines were not cast in pleasant places, and that we had better shift our ground. But that worthy, who had an innate repugnance to hoisting the mainsail oftener than he was obliged to, held for some moments silent and mysterious communion with the sky, the water, and the neighboring shores, and then confidently predicted that the fish would soon bite. Having considerable faith in his penetration into the whims and ways of our finny friends, and suspecting that in this instance his judgment was based upon observation of the state of the tide, we patiently pursued our sport, if sport it could be called.

The Assyrian, who was prone to easy postures, had been for the last half-hour lying on his back with his hands clasped on the top of his head, and his feet, about which he had fastened his line, protruding over the low rail of the sloop. He now began to sing a song which began:

> The grasshopper sat on the sweet-potato vine,
> Up came the turkey-gobbler and yanked him off behind.

The second stanza, intended to show the careless security of the grasshopper, was next sung:

> The grasshopper sat on the sweet-potato vine,
> Up came the turkey-gobbler and yanked him off behind.

Then followed the third stanza, illustrating the trickery of the turkey-gobbler:

> The grasshopper sat on the sweet-potato vine,
> Up came the turkey-gobbler and yanked him off behind.

This elegant ditty was interrupted by a bite which nearly "yanked" the minstrel into the water. He rolled over and scrambled to his feet with remarkable agility, exclaiming, as he hauled in his line, "A halibut at last, I think!" To catch a halibut had been for some time the main object of the Assyrian's ambition, and the farther east we went the more confident he became that every large fish he hooked would prove to be the prize. I observed, however, that the old Pilot, who always grew excited at the prospect of halibut, after one eager glance at the line, turned with indifference to his furnace, on which he had a large iron pot bubbling with water, all ready for a cod or haddock, or even for a pollack if nothing better could be got. There was evidently no hope of halibut yet.

The capture proved to be a skate — a flat, broad brown-backed monster, with a dirty-white belly, a tail like a monkey's and a spade-shaped snout with powerful teeth. He was very large — about three feet in length — and it required a good deal of careful management to get him aboard without breaking the cod-line. The creature was very angry, and furiously lashed the deck with its tail, squeaking and writhing in a droll manner.

The capture of the skate did not materially improve our prospect of dinner, for though the Professor proposed to cook the creature, the Pilot would not hear of such an abomination. In vain he was assured that it was a favorite fish in the markets of London, Paris, and Edinburgh; in vain I cited to him the Rev. Badham's assertion that all skate is eatable, though not all equally good; in vain the Professor assured him that Galen, in his treatise on ailments, particularly recommends the flesh of the skate as agreeable in flavor and light of digestion. His objections were immovable. At length the Assyrian, who had a bad habit of inventing quotations, recited to him an imaginary passage of Aristotle about the obstinacy of fishermen with regard to the edible qualities of the skate.

"Damn Aristotle!" responded the old fisherman; "don't you suppose I know what fish are fit to eat?" With the aid of the Skipper, he tossed the monster overboard, and seizing a line, he said he would soon give us something worth cooking. Sure enough, in a few minutes, he pulled up a haddock weighing about seven pounds — as we judged by the eye, for we were too anxious for dinner to delay his transfer to the pot by putting him to the test of the steelyards.

As cooked by the Pilot, we pronounced the haddock excellent; and after dinner we raised the anchor, hoisted sail, and cruised idly among the islands till near sunset, when we put into a delicious little cove — narrow, deep, and shady — on Jewell's Island. As we glided in, an old fisherman who resided on the island came alongside in his dory to have a little chat, and gave us a magnificent lobster, which went immediately into the pot for supper. After coming to anchor, we all went ashore in our boat, except the Pilot, who was detained on board by his duties as cook; to explore the island, witness the sunset, and get milk, eggs, and butter from a farmhouse near our landing-place.

The island, which lies about ten miles east of Portland, seemed to be fertile and well cultivated. The farmhouse was built on elevated ground, and the view of the sunset and of the island-studded bay was superb. Fresh and sweet were the eggs and milk and butter with which we returned to our sloop, and very jolly the supper we had in the little cabin. The evening was pleasantly cool, and the Assyrian, remarking that boiled lobster was not wholesome unless well qualified with something acid, availed himself of the Pilot's steaming teakettle and brewed a pitcher of hot lemonade with a strong infusion of whiskey, which he administered to each of us in proper doses, as a sure preventive against any ill effects from our supper.

The yachtsmen spend a few more days in Casco Bay before setting sail for Boothbay Harbor.

A Storm off Cape Seguin, Boothbay, The Coast Survey Schooner

We sat long at table that day, and when we went on deck about three o'clock it was raining, and the wind was beginning to blow pretty hard. We made sail at once in the direction of Boothbay, but in the course of a couple of hours the wind rose to a gale. The sea grew very rough, and almost every minute a wave would break over our vessel and, sweeping along the deck, deluge the cockpit with water. We closed the cabin to keep it dry, and, gathering at the stern, watched the sea, not without anxiety. The air was so thick with mist that we could see nothing but the raging waves around us, and could not tell where we were going, though the sloop was plunging along at a fearful rate, her bows almost continually under water and her mast opening wide cracks at every tug of the sails. There was considerable danger of the mast's going overboard. In that case we should have been completely at the mercy of the waves, on a coast every inch of which was rock-bound, so that, if our vessel struck, she would be pounded to pieces in ten minutes.

We drove madly along, the grim old Pilot at the helm, and the anxious Skipper, arrayed in oil-skin to shed the wet, clinging to the mast and keeping a sharp lookout ahead. Suddenly the mist rose and rolled away before a sweeping blast, and then we saw Seguin light-house, and knew where we were. It was a superb and terrible sight — these wild reefs with the waves foaming and flashing over them, directly in our course. It was growing late, and the gale was on the increase. The sea was white with foam on the surface, but the great waves, as they came leaping and roaring at us, had a black and angry look not pleasant to behold. Our aged Pilot, as he sat clutching the helm, his hat drawn tightly over his brows to keep it from blowing off, glanced uneasily from time to time at the laboring and groaning mast, whose wide seams were alternately opening and shutting, but he said nothing. He had weathered many a harder gale, though never in so poor a craft. The Assyrian, clinging to the cover of the cabin for support, and with strong symptoms of seasickness in his face, at length broke out as a whooping billow swept over us, soaking him from head to foot:

"I say, Skipper, this is coming in rather strong. Can't we put in somewhere?"

The Skipper had been for some minutes watching a large schooner about a mile ahead of us, and coming aft, said that it was hardly possible to weather Cape Newagin in such a storm, even if our mast held, about which he had great doubts. The schooner ahead of us was running for shelter into Sheepscut Bay, where there was an excellent harbor and we could easily follow her in. The Pilot, after an emphatic reference to "that damned old stick," as he called the mast, assented to this opinion, and our course was accordingly changed to the northward.

Following the lead of the schooner for several miles, we reached about nightfall a beautiful and perfectly sheltered harbor, which the Skipper called sometimes Southport and sometimes Abenacook. There were a few scattered houses on the shore, but nothing that could be called a village. We anchored in the midst of a number of vessels which had, like ourselves, sought refuge there from the gale, though all except the schooner that we followed had put in earlier in the day. The storm, as we afterwards learned, raged all along the coast, and did considerable damage to the shipping.

The weather had grown so cold as to be uncomfortable even in our snug cabin, and so, after hastily swallowing some supper, we stripped off our wet clothes and turned into our berths long before our usual hour.

I lay awake half the night listening to the rain pattering on the deck, and when we arose next morning it was still pouring hard. It was so cold that the seamen got the stove out of the fore-peak, and we soon had a fire in the cabin, to which the rain confined us all the forenoon. The schooner we had followed into this harbor was bound for Boothbay, and after dinner got underway and passed into Townsend Cut, a passage of some miles in length leading into Townsend Harbor, as the port of Boothbay is called. We followed, and, the rain having ceased, had a delightful sail through a most singular strait — narrow, like a river of moderate size, and bordered on both sides by meadows green to the water's edge, with occasional groves ringing the banks. We should have had no suspicion that this passage was not a river had it not been for the seaweed growing on its rocky edges.

We reached Boothbay in the course of an hour, and came to anchor a short distance off the town, which seemed to be of considerable size. The Assyrian immediately put on his shore clothes, and getting the Skipper to row him to the nearest wharf, went in search of lemons and whiskey. After a protracted absence he returned disconsolate. Lemons he had got, but whiskey was not to be obtained for love or money; the place, he said, was drier than the Sahara. He brought us, however, letters and papers, so that his visit was not altogether fruitless.

As we sat reading the papers, a boat from the town came alongside with one man in it, a respectable looking person, who produced an empty bottle, and asked if we could let him have a little brandy, for which he would pay. His wife, he said, was sick, and the doctor had prescribed brandy, but none was to be had in the town.

The Assyrian's sympathies were touched by this appeal, and he gave the man a couple of bottles of ale, assuring him that he would have been welcome to brandy if we had not unfortunately run out of everything of the sort. He was still expressing his admiration of the stranger's devotion when we were hailed by a boat approaching from another quarter of the town. This, too, contained a single individual, and he too produced a bottle, and, strange to say, he likewise had a sick wife for whom the doctor had prescribed brandy.

The Assyrian's eyes began to open. "I say, my dear fellow," he remarked to the man in the boat, "are all the women in Boothbay sick, and has the doctor prescribed brandy for all of them? You're the second chap that has been here within ten minutes with the same story. Hadn't you better call a town-meeting, and confer together, so as to have a little variety in your pretenses?"

The man laughed, and explained that, as no liquor could be bought in town, the only way they had to get it was by buying it of vessels in the harbor. They had found the pretense of sickness useful in inducing their visitors to violate the law by selling to them.

Shortly after this fellow left us, the Professor, who had been studying the craft in the harbor through the telescope, pointed out a schooner at some distance which he recognized as the United States Coast-Survey vessel, the *Hassler,* and said he knew one of her officers.

The Assyrian snapped his fingers in delight. "I know one too," he said, "and a right good fellow he is. Let us go on board. We shall find something there to wet our whistles with, I know."

In a few minutes we were all in the dory, and the Skipper rowed us alongside the schooner. We were cordially received by the three officers on board, and found the Assyrian's prediction amply verified. As we sat in the cabin, whose spaciousness seemed magnificent compared with that of the *Helen,* I was startled by the sudden appearance at my elbow of an ebony complexioned individual, bearing a tray containing decanters, glasses, lemons, and a pitcher of hot water. How he had got into the cabin was inconceivable, for he certainly had not descended by the only visible entrance. His coming, so sudden and so noiseless, made me think of the genie of the lamp that waited on Aladdin. But though he came in so questionable a manner, "the prince of darkness was a gentleman." Placing the tray before us, he vanished as silently as he came — behind a curtain.

We spent a merry evening, and on parting, our friends on the *Hassler* invited us to dine with them on board the schooner next day, remarking, by way of enticement, that their steward had been to market that afternoon, and had brought back a fine leg of veal. We accepted the invitation, and got back to the sloop a little before midnight. To celebrate the discovery of the *Hassler,* we fired off, before we turned in, all our remaining rockets, blue-lights, and Roman candles.

The next morning (Sunday) was serene and mild. After breakfast, two of the officers of the *Hassler* came to visit us in their cutter, and the Assyrian proposed, that as we were going for the first time in several weeks to have a Christian dinner, we should all go to church. To this reasonable proposal we agreed, and, dressing ourselves in our best clothes, went ashore in man-of-war style with the United States officers. After rambling awhile on the beach, we went in search of a meeting-house. A very deaf old fellow, whom we made to understand by much shouting what we wanted, conducted us to a sort of garret, where we found a small and singularly hard-favored congregation, who greeted our entrance with a stare which was prolonged throughout the whole service. Presently the minister entered, and he too fixed his eyes upon us as we sat in a row on a back bench, and seldom removed his gaze, except when he shut his eyes to pray.

It was a Methodist meeting, and notwithstanding the homeliness of the place and the people, the sermon was sound discourse, full of practical good sense. The Assyrian listened with devout attention, and, when we came out, declared that he could now eat the fatted calf with a good conscience. Re-embarking in the cutter, we were soon on board the *Hassler,* where dinner was speedily served by the mysterious gentleman in black, who came and went in the most absolute silence.

After dinner, we adjourned with our cigars to the deck, and spent the afternoon in conversation, which was prolonged by jest and story far into the evening. Tea was served on deck, soon after sunset, by the speechless African, whose silence to this day I know not whether to ascribe to absolute dumbness or to his sense of discipline. At length we bade our friends farewell, and returned to the *Helen* about 10 o'clock. The night was so fine and the air so warm that we lingered on deck till after midnight. Our parting command to the skipper was to get under way at daylight and make sail for the nearest large town to the eastward.

WILLIAM HENRY BISHOP
1847–1928

Commercial fisheries have always been an important part of Maine's economy. The early explorers discovered this rich resource, and the various fisheries have developed — and fluctuated — ever since. The market for salt mackerel was greatest at the end of the nineteenth century: in 1880 there were some eighty vessels in the Maine mackerel fleet and the catch weighed in at more than 131 million pounds. Spotters sighted the fish swimming on the surface, purse seines were set to encircle them, and the fish were cleaned, soaked, and salted down immediately after being brought on board.

Like all fisheries, the mackerel market has been affected by such variables as weather, demand, government regulation, foreign competition, and changes in fishing technology — to say nothing of the unpredictable quantity each year. The transition to power boats and refrigeration spelled the end of the salt mackerel bonanza and the beginning of a market for fresh fish. This market has diminished in recent years as people's taste for fish has turned toward halibut and swordfish: the 1986 mackerel catch was down to 330,000 pounds.

W. H. Bishop, a turn-of-the-century travel writer, was born in Hartford, Connecticut. After graduating from Yale in 1867, he set about making a career of writing about his journeys in this country and abroad. He contributed to the *Atlantic Monthly* and *Harper's New Monthly Magazine* and published several collections of short stories and travel tales. His style was humorous, sometimes sardonic, and reflects his energy and curiosity about the people and places he saw.

"Fish and Men in the Maine Islands," a two-part work that appeared in *Harper's* in 1880, told of one Middleton's experiences as he toured Maine, seeking to learn about the people, the places, and the various fisheries operating off the coast in those days. Incidentally, the peppery red seed to which Middleton refers is in fact a living organism, a copepod, which does indeed menace the unwary fish handler.

Mackerel Fishing off Monhegan

All this time Middleton was making little personal acquaintance with "the fleet," and the mackerel, the object of its quest, and the staple of the coast fishery. He pushed on, therefore, in search of it, going from Deer Island to Mount Desert Island.

On the charming mountainous isle which fashion has so liberally taken into favor, the greater part of the active population was drafted to the service of the summer hotels. The young women went as waitresses, in which capacity they netted "tatting" in the intervals of their duties, and devoured with undisguised admiration the toilets of the city belles; and the men as porters, drivers, and hostlers. Still a bolder portion of the men refused to yield to the blandishments of these spiritless new occupations, and cured their fish and went their voyages as usual. At Manchester's, at the mouth of the long Somes Sound, which stretches up like a noble river of clear deep green water among the mountains, he came upon an important establishment where herring were smoked. A myriad of the small fish hung like bronze pendants, slowly turning to gold in an atmosphere of white smoke from a smouldering fire of logs, which, when a door was opened upon it, looked like imprisoned fog. When the smoke had circulated thus among them for a month, and they were turned to the purest, most finely burnished gold — no mere resemblance, but the thing itself — they were done.

Further up the coast he came upon a crew ready to set off in a long, sharp, white seine-boat, heavily loaded down with barrels of water and general traps, and riding as steady as a steamer. They all belonged in the same place, and had been put ashore at the completion of the trip by their vessel, which was to lay to for them off the mouth

Harpooning swordfish

of their cove on her return and was now due. Middleton had a mind to join them. The chief authority was aboard the vessel, of course; but he inquired, "Where is the mate?"

"We're all mates, and scarcely any cap'n," they said, in a jovial way, "and the cook is the best man."

They said if he would put up with what they had (he had previously heard that this was very good indeed, and that an added cause of the decline in the fishing interest was the epicurean tastes of the employes), he might go with them, and see their manner of life to his heart's content, as far as they were concerned, and they believed the captain would make no exception. But when they had rowed to meet the vessel, nearly to the Great Cranberry, and it was not yet in sight, and having in mind strongly the inconvenience of getting back in case of refusal — for which contingency he had brought an attendant in an extra dory — he asked again if there was doubt as to the captain, an entire change of sentiment appeared. It was not manifested in a Chesterfieldian but in a boorish way, which Middleton hoped was not characteristic of the Maine islander at large. Certain new sullen spokesmen, who had interposed no objection before, now spoke up, and their opinion prevailed. They thought there *was* doubt about the captain — pretty decided doubts. Whether so or not, there was about *them*. They were opposed to it — that was how it was. They had no more room aboard than they wanted for themselves.

The hilarious ones of before had no opposition to offer to this, being apparently, on reflection, of the same mind. Nor had they any comments regretful or otherwise; and so, amid a stolid silence, Middleton took to his skiff with his attendant, and with an hour's hard pulling was again upon the shore.

From this disappointment resulted the cruise heretofore referred to, some thirty miles to sea, to the desolate light of Mount Desert Rock, off which the fleet was credibly said to be lying. It was made in a hired jigger, manned by its skipper, the artist of the truthful pictures accompanying this account of Middleton's journeys, and himself.

They had continual sunshine, and considerable periods of calms, in which the most singular mirages rose up around them. An island below the horizon came and piled itself over one upon it. Low islands in the middle distance appeared to have precipitous walls a hundred feet high; light-houses came where none were, and when you looked the next moment, were gone, and the land with them. Then drifts of curious white fog came in, not creating a chilliness in the atmosphere, but holding the sunshine in luminous suspension, and crystallizing on the clothing in little needle points more like a powder, yet enveloping them completely, and cutting off surrounding objects. The ancient compass in the jigger's binnacle had a way of sticking where it was while her course might be altered a dozen points, and once the skipper, jumping excitedly to the tiller, saved her from dangerous reefs near Bass Head Light, to which the screaming of sea-fowl and the noise of surf close by were the first intimation of approach.

The Rock was a bare lonely bank of granite, with no habitation upon it but its light, in which four men, a woman, and a child pass their time with such philosophy as they can. A luxuriant slippery seaweed draped the rounding ledges with the semblance of verdant grass, but on actually going ashore, the only vegetation was a little dog-weed, and fifty poor hills of potatoes, by actual count, distrib-

Off duty, at Monhegan

uted wherever a space for five or six plants together could be found among the chaotic stones.

They saw the sun set upon it, as warm as on a tower of Torcello, and the moon rise, nearly at its full, behind it. And lying off it at night, with only a solitary haker for a consort, taking his turn on the watch in his nautical capacity toward morning, Middleton saw all the stars shine in their splendor, traced the unhampered constellations, divined mysterious things in the long fields of rock-weed drifting idly past, saw the fins of a sinister cruising shark, and heard from time to time the stertorous blowing of a whale in the distance.

But the desired fleet, after all, was not at the Rock, and though they sailed twenty miles one way to the Bank of Comfort, and as much the other to the Isle au Haut, it still did not appear. It had doubled on them it seemed, in the night, and following the schools of fish, had worked westward toward Matinicus and Monhegan. Upon this, Middleton believed he could do no better than go to Monhegan also. By various detours and conveyances, stopping at Castine to moralize on the departed maritime greatness of Oakum Bay, passing down by stage from Rockland twenty miles to Herring Gut, and from there fifteen miles by water, in the boat of a fisherman of Bremen Long Island (to distinguish it, in the multiplicity of Long Islands, from Friendship Long Island, its neighbor), he made his way thither.

Monhegan is still accurately described in the words of Captain John Smith, who came to it on his cruise in the year 1614: "A round, high isle, with little Monanis by its side, betwixt which is a harbor where our ships can lie at anchor." He made a garden here, he tells, "on the rocky isle, in May, which grew so well it served for salads in June and July."

There is a white light-house on the back of the round high isle. Half way up the hill toward it, from a fringe of gray fish-houses at the water's edge, climbs the weather-beaten little settlement, in which all the habitations of the island and its whole population are concentrated. The school-house is at the top of the buildings. Then comes a space of debris of igneous rock like the scoriae of a volcano, the color of ploughed ground, on which is railed off a bare little grave-yard, visible from all directions.

The little harbor was speckled with small boats when Middleton came in and the schooner *Marthy,* which "smacked" fresh fish regularly to Portland, and a freighter, purposing to go in to Herring Gut to paint, were lying there at anchor. The small boats were tied to the tall stakes, more common as the Bay of Fundy is approached, with crosses on the top, which at low tide give the appearance of a melancholy kind of marine grave-yard too. It is not a common kind of harbor. It is a deep channel between Monhegan and Menana (as Monanis is now called), open at the outer end, and partly closed at the inner by a rugged black ledge called Smutty Nose. On Smutty Nose is reared a tall pole, part of a disused apparatus for communications between the light-house and the keeper of the fog-whistle on Menana, which has the air of a jury-mast rigged as a signal of distress. In southeast gales a formidable surf drives in through the passage, and it is then by no means so agreeable a place of anchorage. In a wild night of rain, wind, and pitch-darkness of 1858, the whole contents of the strait, fourteen fishing vessels, besides the flotilla of boats, were piled upon Smutty Nose in a mass.

There was a shark's forked tail nailed to the principal spile of the wharf, as hawks are nailed to farmers' barn doors. The fish-houses had a warm yellow lichen, such as grew also on some of the high cliffs of the outer shore on the weather side, and over the doors of some of them, by way of decoration, were name-boards picked up from castaway boats, as "Rescue," or "Excalibur." The principal activity clustered around two little sand beaches, the only ones on the island, which would be set down, by a voyager coming to it as a new land, as quite the ideal and providential sort.

The greater part of the male population, stalwart, rawboned men in flannel shirts, well-tanned canvas jackets, and big boots, came down to meet him. When they had gratified their curiosity about the newcomer, they went back, and threw themselves down at the top of the first rise of the slope, among the houses, in the nonchalant attitudes which were their normal condition when the fish were not schooling. A philosophic bearded man from the mainland, come to pass the summer here, was calking his boat, drawn up on the stocks near by, and joining in their gossip. Occasionally one of them took up a battered telescope, which always lay there in the grass, or against the neighboring wood-pile, and swept the horizon with it.

Monhegan was the most remote and primitive of all the Maine islands. It had no direct connection with the mainland, and no post-office. Such mail as came to it was brought over by some casual fishing-boat from Herring Gut, where it had accumulated. The bearer, sitting on a rock or the gunwale of a boat on one of the little beaches, distributes their letters to the group flocking around him, from the old newspaper in which he has tied them up for safe-keeping. There were plenty of sheep, but little agriculture, no roads, nor use for any except to haul a little wood from the other end of the island in winter. In this service cows as well as the few oxen were put under the yoke.

There were hollyhocks, camomile, and dahlias in some of the small door-yards, but these could not redeem the shabbiness of a growth of white-weed knee-deep along all the straggling paths of the hamlet, to which no one had public spirit enough to take a sickle. Though but a mile long, the centre and eastern end of the island had still the most virgin and savage air. Gorges containing the whitened bones of ancient cedar-trees and wet morasses barred the way. The low, thick resinous groves, too, were impenetrable, except for some dark burrows like lairs where the sheep had gone through. Long gray moss, like the drift of some deluge, hung from the branches of the spruces; but the carpet was of an overluxuriant, vivid kind, more suggestive — though starred with scarlet bunch-berries — of death and decay even than the grave-yard on the slope. . . .

Monhegan had a glorious open out-look, somewhat too rare in the other Maine islands, where impertinent satellites, of which the map gives little idea, are continually cropping up to destroy the desirable effect of space. From an elevated point Middleton could follow the sea all around, and shoreward a distant blue island or two lay in the high-lifted horizon like a cloud over the tops of the pines. But he liked most to lie on the brim of the outer cliffs, the High Heads, and White Heads, that rose one hundred and fifty feet straight from the angry breakers, and look off upon the wide ocean expanse, scattered with sails as if with a flight of butterfly moths. Timid groups of sheep looked on with curiosity at him from the vantage ground of neighboring hillocks. He was often the companion here of the look-out watching for the schooling of fish in the interest of the nonchalant group on the grassy bank below.

The fleet was here at last. He came to know it well, both far and near, and the leading traits of the much-badgered mackerel, the object of its pursuit. The islanders fished with the fleet, pulling out in their seine-boats from their island, as if it were only a steadier kind of schooner like the rest. It was a schooner that never rolled, on which they had all they made, without a division with shippers and underwriters, and to which they returned at night to their families and firesides.

Middleton was impressed by the singular procession moving up the Atlantic coast every year, and speculated about it from High Head as if from a peculiarly advantageous point for observing a pageant passing wholly under his eye. "It could be made a fine decorative frieze of," he said, "full of moral lessons besides." It could be a kind of natural-history Odyssey or Nibelungen, or a hemicycle of important submarine deeds, for another Delaroche — the allegory of the Mackerel on his way through life, his hopes and his fears, his virtues and vices, his friends and his enemies, his triumphs and disasters.

The mackerel began their migration, he learned, or at least the first were taken by the fleet which went south after them, in deep water, about sixty miles below the capes of Delaware, early in March. They arrived on the Maine coast about the first of June, followed closely by the vessels, which were presently strung all along from Cape Ann to Cape Sable. Late in September, they began to work to the southward, not schooling on their return, and by the middle of November hardly one would be found to the northward of Boston Bay. This, at least, was the habit of our American mackerel, which were looked upon as a distinct nation, with no affiliation with that which comes in over the Grand Banks, spawns on the Magdalen Islands, and remains in Canadian waters all winter. They seemed to come up along the coast, and strike inshore all about the same time, and the first notice of their arrival was often their appearance in the weirs on the bays and inlets.

An advance guard preceded the main body often by a week or ten days. A mysterious live seed, of which Middleton could only hear that it was red, excessively hot, like pepper, and floated in the water, was thought to be the mackerel's principal inducement to come into the bays. He was passionately fond of it, and when it was ripe he was there, though it was a most reckless dissipation, for it was said that it was so hot that it would burn its way out of a fish in a few hours, and it burned the hands of the fishermen in dressing such as had eaten it.

A multitude of smaller marine creatures were fond of the red seed also. The tiny pilot-fish, perhaps a kind of fugleman for the mackerel, but more likely his prey, like the rest, came first; then shoals of herring, shrimp, squid, menhaden. The round, limpid jelly-fish called the sun-squall, occurring sometimes almost numerously enough to stop the way of a boat, sought it. Woe to them all! They can snatch but a furtive joy; the fierce mackerel follows them up, devouring them as they fly. The only visible bits of solidity in the organism of the limpid sun-squall are the few red seeds, which it seems not even to have the pleasure of digesting. The mackerel ruthlessly tears him in pieces for them, and the sea is strewn with the remains of unhappy sun-squalls.

"Did the picture stop here, how little deserving would the mackerel be of sympathy!" mused Middleton. "And indeed, after all this, he is not one to call forth too much sympathy in any event; but the Nemesis that pursues him is terrible. The procession consists of the mackerel, his prey, *and his enemies.* Now here he is, as one might say, a wild young prodigal, in his laced coat of green and silver, pursuing every mad whim and selfish pleasure, and blinded by his folly to the yawning pitfalls and omens of danger all about him. Or he may be looked upon as a Belchazzar sort of person, drunk with insolent pride, while at the very moment the Mede and Persian are battering at the gate. Mene, mene, tekel, upharsin! Thou are found a palatable article by many tastes, and thou shalt be weighed in the balance. The sinister shark is on thy track; the porpoise lunges from the right; dogfish, blue-fish, black-fish, from the left; the mackerel-gull swoops down from overhead; the solemn whale cruises in thy wake, ready to dive below a school and blow it into the air, and though prevented by an unfortunate arrangement of the jaws from taking in the splendid gulps that might be imagined, does it very liberal justice; and lastly comes the great schooner of inexorable man, the merchant, to whom all the other enemies are as nothing, and snares thee in lots of five hundred barrels in a day."

A quaint apparent exception, and the only one, to the universal rule of rapine in the great procession was a little bird somewhat larger than a sandpiper — the sea-goose, so called. It sits over a mackerel school, and accompanies it in its course, whether out of an amicable sentiment of companionship, or as a rival for the mysterious peppery seed, is not quite certain.

It could well be believed that these voracious pursuers sometimes conflicted among themselves. The dogfish and sharks, ravening to get at their prey when in the nets, bit or tore through, and released them by the barrel. The sharks came up around the boats of fishermen, and by frightening away the game, prevented all their operations. It was necessary to strike them with a shark-knife in a peculiar way, otherwise they would not make off and cease their annoyance. One day a fisherman, having no weapon handy — a heavy gun exploding a shell in the carcass is the one most in use for this service — thrust an oar down the throat of a whale, which came up beside his boat, and broke it off, upon which it retreated, and left him in peace.

To devour and be devoured was by no means a matter confined to the mackerel and his relations. Cod, haddock, and hake gorged themselves on herring and every smaller fish. The blue-fish chased the porgies with such peculiar animosity that it quite depended upon their choice of position whether porgies should even make an appearance on the coast at all or not. They drove them in one day near Herring Gut in such wild alarm that they lay ankle-deep on the sands, and had to be buried to prevent an epidemic.

"Faugh!" said Middleton, "I'll have no patience with them. Not one spark of kindly feeling, not one scintilla of ordinary human — that is, of consideration. It never seems to occur to a fish that he is not to murder anybody, for his comfort of the moment, any more than that he is not to flap his tail." And he went down to the port to experiment with a method of harpooning sword-fish from a seat fixed up in the bowsprit of a schooner, which he was promised an opportunity soon of trying.

The population of the islands generally was of genuine Yankee stock, only beginning to be mixed a little where the quarries brought in a new element. At one place was a "portugee" of the Western Islands. He had sailed out of Gloucester, as do plenty of his countrymen, as a cook, married his gallant captain's daughter, settled down to the shore, and was pronounced "a real good feller." There were a number of cases of insanity, and consumption was a definite scourge. Crimes were few and far between, being confined principally to a little thieving of fish from one another's flakes, unless the record were enlivened by some such bold exploit from without as that of a marauding negro who rifled the principal store at Monhegan one night, and carried off the entire contents in his cat-boat. He was pursued by a fast sloop, ran on a bar at the Isle au Haut, and there was for a time the best of reasons for expecting his capture. By desperate exertions, however, he got over the bar in time, leaving it as an impediment in the way of the heavier-draught sloop, made off down to Long Island, and then further east, till he was inside the Canadian line, and secure from pursuit. . . .

If a Monheganer was ill, it was a matter of thirty miles' sailing at least to bring him a physician to attend him. If he died, he was borne up to the grave-yard on the hill on the shoulders of his associates, and at the next arrival of a minister from the main a discourse was pronounced over him. To such occasions, too, were postponed marriages of consideration; but in minor cases the couple put off somewhat by stealth to the main, and kept the affair rather quiet till the knot was tied. Persons who had savings invested them by preference in vessel property. If they amassed any considerable sum, they were apt to move to the main, and embark in a business in some way connected with fish, as the keeping of a market.

The women were often out on the hillside mending the great nets damaged in service. In winter they sometimes had knitting bees, at which they replaced the nets of a comrade carried away and destroyed perhaps by fouling a ship's anchor. In winter, too, the residents coasted down the light-house hill; flooded a small valley lying just by the houses, and skated and ran an ice-boat on it.

The slight government of the island (plantation in form, and not yet a town) was languidly administered, and offices were avoided, not sought. It was necessary to elect a treasurer (in place of one who had positively refused to serve), and to provide funds for the payment of the glossy-haired teacher, in the neatest of calico dresses with a frill at the throat, from a high school on the main, whose term was drawing near its close. The meeting was set time after time, but nobody came, not even the officer who called it, all having regularly hurried off to the water in pursuit of fish.

Mackerel and mackerel only was the object of their ambition. It seemed almost an object in itself, apart from what it would bring. In confirmation of this view there was an account of a case, in the good old times, which Monhegan not less than the world in general has enjoyed, when a group was assembled to divide profits amounting to upward of fourteen hundred dollars on recent ventures. Suddenly the signal for mackerel was given. Careless of the business in hand, they caught up a few bills each at random, and put off hurriedly to sea, and the children picked up afterward more than six hundred dollars around the fish-house where this had taken place.

There were three seine-boats, owned in shares by their crews, as the custom was. No one on the island could be oblivious of their movements. Its whole life centred round them. They set off for their first trip before daylight, and the voices and knockings at the door in the darkness that summoned the men awakened the settlement. At noon and evening the careful housewife had the old spy-glass often at her eye, and knew how to regulate the laying of the cloth, and the lifting of the cover of the boiling pot, to the dot of an i, by their rounding the point at the harbor mouth. But it was their departures by day, after considerable spells of inaction, that were the most animated, and Middleton was glad to be able to share the contagion.

The look-out had been sitting a long time on the cliff, as like a blasted stump in appearance as a man. Suddenly he jumped to his feet, shouted, and came running down. The heavy-booted, flannel-shirted, lounging men knew what it meant, and were down at the beaches and in their long swift boats instantly. Each strove for the lead. How they leaped through the water under the strokes of the bending hickory!

Amos has it. No, it is William Henry. No, it is "Cap" Trefeathering, and Middleton is with him.

Seven men throw their weight upon the oars, some standing, some sitting. The Cap, aloft on the poop, surveys the watery field, and directs the course with a long steering oar down to the slight rippled patches which to the experienced eye denote the schooling fish. The great seine, one hundred and fifty fathoms long and twenty-four wide, an apparently chaotic heap of corks and twine, well sprinkled with salt for preservation, is piled aft, and two veteran hands stand by to pay it out. A boy rows in the dory astern.

The schools are exceedingly shy. The art is to anticipate, if possible, their direction, and meet them with the net. Even then they will dive directly under it, and disappear. The first school is missed, the second, the third, the fourth. The fifth is of great promise, but a single gull comes and poises over it to pounce upon a victim. "I wish I had a gun for that fellow," says the Cap, and having none, he swings his hat and screams shrilly; but meanwhile the fish have gone down, and the heavy net must be dragged grumblingly in again without results.

Their flocks and herds look down at them at first from the cliffs as they toss in the breakers, but, with many disappointments, they are presently eight to ten miles off from shore. All the boats of the fleet are out around them, full of men, as if meditating some warlike descent on the coast. The cloud of fast yacht-like schooners is tacking and standing off and on in every variety of pose. Dark figures in their tops and shrouds look out for schools; others fling over bait of ground porgies from boxes along the sides, to "toll" them up for easier capture. Among the rest are two of the singular "porgy steamers" turned to mackereling, in which veterans predict their career will be brief, saying they will roll too much, and their fires be put out.

The seas are heavy, and in the crowded boats, particularly those of the middle distance and the contracted horizon, as they rise on a gloomy wave, with all their figures notched momentarily against the sky, before sinking from sight as if ingulfed, Middleton finds a hundred noble and gallant aspects. What an ineffable contrast, this free, breezy, stalwart life, to the cramping and tameness and fetid exhalations of city shops!

Yonder, again, is a promising school; there are fifty barrels in it if there is a fish. Give way all! The *Fidelia*'s boat sees it too, and so does the *Watchman*'s, the *Excalibur*'s, the *Wild Rose*'s, and that of the *Light of the Age,* and all race for it. But the Cap and Middleton are there first and have the *pas.*

Over with the net! The dory holds one end of it while the seine-boat rows around the school. Swash! swash! go the corks, and draw a long, agreeable curve on the water. The two ends are brought together, and the net pursed up. "Bagged, by the great horn spoon!" cries an excited share-holder; and they go to dipping the fish out with a scoop-net, and loading the dory as full as it will hold.

There were bankers and grand-bankers among the seiners or in the harbor from time to time, for this was well out in the route of all of them. Middleton transferred his flag from one to another as pleased him, like Perry at the battle of Lake Erie. The vessels outwardly, as a rule, were trim and ship-shape; within, cleanliness or squalor depended upon the individual taste of the captain. Apart from an occasional "pink-stern," there was little picturesqueness in the hulls, and — since the American fisherman despises the picturesque economy of tanned sails, leaving that to benighted Canadians and French of the Bay of St. Lawrence — almost as little in the upper works.

The routine of affairs on all was much the same. There was breakfast at four in the morning, and three more meals in the course of the day, regulated by the exigencies of the work. Besides that, a substantial lunch table stood all day in the forecastle. The cook appeared, indeed, from the financial point of view, to be the best man, since he had a liberal salary in addition to a share of the catch, while the rest depended on the catch alone. In fishing, all hands often took to the boat, leaving only the cook aboard. When they had made a successful cast, they signalled the schooner with an oar. She ran down to them, the seine was made fast to her side, and the fish dipped out on the deck, where they were rapidly dressed and thrown into barrels of brine, one school being disposed of before another was sought, owing to their easy deterioration.

At night the island went early to its slumbers, and only the lighthouse on the hill kept watch. It dazzled the eyes if one looked up, and rendered the darkness more profound. On evenings of a heavy atmosphere slow rays went round and round from it, separating the mist like vast knives. But the fleet at night, with its numerous lanterns (green to port, and red to starboard), and watchmen on deck, was like a little floating city. There was no commodore and no regular organization, yet accidents from collision were rare. They laid their heads all one way, by a tacit agreement. At midnight they reversed, and beat back upon their course. The schools worked nearer the top at night, and their presence was betrayed by a phosphorescent "firing" in the water, so that it seemed something almost like insensate folly that this, instead of the day, was not the favorite time. But attention to the subject showed that the nets fired the water too, and gave a warning much more than counterbalancing the advantage. The desirability of a calm understanding of what you are going to do before you attempt to do it was brought to view by this discovery, and also the evident intention of nature to interpose a certain degree of hardship between the prize and the methods of securing it.

Reflecting thus as he was "smacked" back to Portland, soon after, as part of the burden of the *Marthy,* Middleton felt that these lessons alone, notwithstanding they might be learned elsewhere, if they were invariably observed and acted upon, were much more than sufficient to repay a desultory jaunt among the fish and men of the Maine islands.

DOROTHEA MOULTON BALANO
1882–1951

Dorothea Moulton Balano was a spunky farm girl from Minnesota whose enthusiasm for travel and curiosity about her world made her a natural for life at sea. Typically, she came to her role as a skipper's wife in a roundabout fashion. She was teaching school in Puerto Rico in 1911 when she accepted an invitation from a friend to accompany her as chaperone aboard her fiancé's ship, which was sailing back to Boston. The friend was seasick most of the trip, and by the end of the voyage Captain Fred Balano was engaged to Dorothea Moulton. The *Boston Globe* took note of the impending event.

A Romance of the Sea

The wedding of Capt. Fred B. Balano, commander of the four-masted schooner R. W. Hopkins, and Miss Dorothea Moulton of Dawson, Minn., which will probably occur today, will be the culmination of a romance that had its origin under tropical skies. . . .

The schooner Hopkins was towed across the harbor yesterday from the Boston molasses dock at South Boston, where she had just finished discharging a cargo of molasses, to East Boston and will receive a new coat of paint and be made spic and span for the bridal trip. . . .

The bridal couple will make their honeymoon trip on the schooner to Porto Rico, where the vessel will take on a shipment of molasses. The captain and his bride will have ample time to visit their friends in Porto Rico and have planned to journey to the little school at Utuado. . . .

The captain's quarters on the Hopkins have the appearance of a well appointed flat. The main cabin is furnished with costly rugs and draperies, an upright piano and attractive furniture. Capt. Balano's home is in Port Clyde, Me.

Dorothea Moulton Balano

The wedding took place in 1911 and Dorothea, in the tradition of the time, moved aboard Fred's ship, the *R. W. Hopkins*. She had a strong stomach and was ready for adventure.

Her lively journal tells us of her life aboard ship, the ports they visited, and the storms they weathered, both at sea and in the marriage. (She was a reader and an opera buff, but his interests were simpler and earthier, which made for a constant element of conflict in their relationship.) Dorothea also wrote, somewhat acerbically, about Captain Balano's home of Port Clyde, Maine. The *Hopkins* was a Maine-built schooner; Fred, who came from a line of seagoing men, owned shares in her and in several other vessels. Port Clyde, which used to be known (to Dorothea's dismay) as Herring Gut, is in Muscongus Bay, near the granite-quarrying islands of Penobscot Bay, and was an important port for fishing boats and cargo schooners. Its residents were an insular group and baffled the outgoing Dorothea.

Dorothea continued to sail with her husband and their two young sons as sail turned to steam. World War I intervened. Fred commanded transports to France and Dorothea became involved in war activities at home. Afterward, Dorothea spent more time on shore; her last voyage with Captain Fred was in 1927. He then took a shore job in New York, and the couple split their time between New York and Maine. Dorothea was busy with her children and her musical interests, so it fell to her older son, James, to edit and publish this journal.

Life Aboard the *R. W. Hopkins*

The Hopkins *is en route from Puerto Rico to Baltimore with a load of molasses.*

Sunday, July 2, 1911

Fred heaved his old shoes overboard to bring wind. A sacrifice to Neptune? It's a tradition going back, I know, and I must spend some time in re-studying ancient history to see what I can find about Greek and Roman seamen making their sacrifices to get a fair wind. Isn't it enchanting?

Calm, calmer, calmest. Shall we ever arrive off the Chesapeake for Baltimore? I doubt it. Patience, my girl.

Monday, July 3, 1911

A little wind. Thanks to the shoes? We are slowly approaching Cape Henry. Apropos of my being a crew member, the joke Fred likes best is one about the colored gentleman before the judge who asked, "Have you any occupation?"

"Yassuh."

"What is it?"

"I's the proprietor of a laundry."

"You are? What's its name?"

"Eliza Ann."

I wonder if Eliza Ann received any wages; I don't. But now my dear, sweet handsome husband with the most beautiful nose says I'm to be part owner of the *Hopkins*. He's getting me a few sixty-fourths when we arrive. I'll have the dividends for pin money, he says. Pin-money be damned! I'll see an opera or two, or should I say hear an opera?

Tuesday, July 4, 1911

Towed up the bay with the *Governor Powers* alongside. Riverview Park in the afternoon. Iced drinks for a change. . . .

Thursday, July 6, 1911

Shopped with Fred. Got an icebox for the vessel. Selected a hat and the darlingest pair of blue slippers you ever saw. Fred brought me the daintiest sweet peas and a bunch of yellow coreopsis and some pretty red and white sweet williams. Mrs. Kent came on board in the afternoon and we visited. She is a veteran at sea and sea captains. She said to stand firm and I'd be surprised at how they give in. . . .

Wednesday, July 12, 1911

I complain about feeling ill, but when Fred gets really sick he says nothing. Wasn't Captain Kent a Godsend. He told me Fred must be watched for his stinginess. Imagine a downeaster saying that! But then it takes one to know one. He sailed as mate with Fred's father, Captain J.W. of the *Mabel Jordan* and now the *Margaret Thomas*, and tells about Fred as a boy on board. He had a little red tricycle which his father let him ride even in rough weather along the deck. Fred's mother sailed with her husband for over ten years and then said: "I've served my time and I'm going down home because my home suits me fine." The next trip she wrote her husband that he must have planned the plumbing in their new big house when he was in Rio de Janeiro because the water pipes froze by early December. Captain Kent said she was in Maine even when she was in Rio, refusing strawberries in December because they were out of season. Once, when her husband was too sick to handle the ship and the mate couldn't navigate, she brought the *Mabel Jordan* home to Thomaston from Martinique all by herself. She surely did "serve her time." . . .

Excerpt from April 10, 1912, when Dorothea's relations with her mother-in-law had taken a turn for the worse.

It reminds me of the story they tell about her back in Port Clyde, the one of her and the parson who came to call on Sunday and sat with her in the parlor, open that day only. Says the parson, distraught with the heavy silence: "Nice sheep you got out in the yard, Mrs. Balano." Says she, "They look all right on this side." Careful Caroline, she's called, hanging on to not every penny but every word, as well. If that's how to accumulate money, I'll settle for a garret in Paris with hard cheese and watered absinthe.

Returning from a run to Jacksonville, Florida.

Saturday, September 16, 1911

Heading in the wrong direction, running for Nova Scotia as fast as this wind will take us. Too cloudy, dark and foggy to haul up for tricky Boston Bay. Then, near noon, with the wind decreasing, we hauled in a bit more westerly, then sou'west and finally heard Cape Cod's foghorn: a blast lasting eight seconds. Very foggy. The mate said: "It's clear overhead, Captain." The Captain said, "We ain't goin' that way, not just yet."

With all the running abouts, handling sails, I marvelled at one crew member, a little, squat San Blas Indian Fred picked up off Panama. While the West India blacks and the Matthews County boys from Virginia would climb up and down the ratlines to shift the gaskets and lines for the topsails, little Jackson calmly walked from mast to mast on the stays, ninety feet above the deck, his broad, bare feet manipulating the narrow stays as though they were padding along a forest trail.

Very calm now and thick of fog. Soundings gave us fifty-five fathoms at one P.M. The bottom is rocky and broken, like me.

Am too discouraged and so permeated with this deadening pea-soup fog that I can't do anything; even letters are a bore. . . .

Monday, September 18, 1911. (Boston, would you believe it?)

Anchored off Baker's Island last night. Sailed in early this A.M. Hired a launch to set me ashore from the stream and spent all day in Boston. Returned on board by launch in the early evening just as the tug was docking the *Hopkins*. Shopped furiously all along Washington Street and up at Houghton's. We're going to Maine, so must get busy on my new suit. Shall never forget the last time in Thomaston when the ladies gave me the party. I asked Fred what to wear. He said call the hostess, cousin Thankful, and ask. I did. She said, "Oh, just anything." I was suspicious, but helpless until Central, the telephone operator, who waited for Thankful to hang up, said "Cousin Dorothea, I want you to know, so's you won't feel odd, that every one of those girls are going to be all dressed up in their best bib and tucker."

Wednesday, September 20, 1911

Thirty years old today. My villainous but darling boy gave me a present of twenty-five dollars. Wasn't that lovely after I had spent so much money in Boston?

Took the steamer to Belfast and back down to Rockland. Up early to cross the Rockland wharf and catch the little white steamer *Monhegan,* one of Captain Archibald's, for Port Clyde. Sailed out around impressive, high Owl's Head and down the Muscle Ridge Channel past the picturesque fish weirs off Ash Point. Saw seven schooners waiting for paving-block cargoes in Long Cove. Tenants Harbor was loaded with two masters. Then on around Mosquito Island we raced, and off Marshall's Point where suddenly opened up the charming village of Port Clyde. How dreadful to call it Herring Gut! No wonder Mother B. was instrumental in having it named Port Clyde. She also got Horse Point Road changed to Pleasant Street, she says, but apparently that change did not stick. Cousin Alice Balano Davidson dropped in on us from Tenants Harbor, and it was good to see her. She was so kind to us at her home in Melrose where we were married. Her father, Captain John Balano, was lost at sea. Fred says he never wanted to do deep-water but had set his course for being a barge skipper on the Gowanus Canal in Brooklyn, where he could have a daily paper and fresh milk. . . .

Returning from Rio de Janeiro.

January 13, 1912

At night under the moon I walked the after deck and brought my thoughts back to what I think makes Fred tick. In Port Clyde I noticed a bawdy, jolly, lusty Elizabethan remnant now mixed with, but not thoroughly blended with, the Baptist code of conduct, which has been superimposed. The downeasters are not a colloid or a solvent into which the basics have lost their identity. One moment the lust comes out; the next moment it settles to the bottom of a crude mix and on top appears the righteous element. One moment the preacher is ridiculed as a "sky-pilot"; the next he is revered in the parlor on Sunday as the arbiter of who shall be saved.

One moment Fred and his sea-going peers from Maine are like the Squire in Fielding's *Tom Jones,* ready to roll in the hay with anything that can accommodate their lust; the next moment they boast of the stained window they gave the chapel. Their Sunday go-to-meeting faces are shed as quickly as their blue serge suits and become goatish leers of pure corruption. The village is loaded with Lowells, Conants, and other old Puritan names, the descendants of the boys sent down-east from Plymouth and Boston and Salem to fish for the greater glory of those Lowells and Conants who stayed home and went to Harvard. The downeast cousins don't write much poetry, but their low brows outsmart the fish and their broad bottoms, low-slung to make good ballast for the dories, are more practical than the high brows of their sou'west relatives. If east met west, they could hardly communicate unless the talk was of herring. But amongst the villagers of Herring Gut are the Simmonses of black-eye "gypsy" stock, their ancestors said to have been rounded up by the agents of the Hano-verian kings and shipped as good riddance from around Bremen to Bremen, Maine, and the dour Scots-Irish who were brought over by the old English stock to man the quarries, the Lowells and Conants remained free of the enticements of emotional religion. . . . The Low-ells, Conants, Huppers and Trussells keep what little religion they have strictly unemotional. If they are overheard humming a hymn, it is not "He walks with me and He talks with me," but something a bit less emotional, such as "Let the lower lights keep burning, send a gleam across the way. Some struggling seaman you may rescue, you may save." That hymn may have been written by one who wanted to entice seamen to be "saved" in a religious manner, but the descen-dants of the old English look upon it as strictly a lighthouse-keeping job to aid the sailor, whereas the emotional descendants of the Ger-mans and the inheritors of Celtic underhanded rebelliousness against the English both cling to the feverish hope that supernatural allies will compensate for their lack of "git-up-and-git." Fred inherits the individuality and strong independence of his English ancestors, but there has rubbed off on him, as on his mother and all the Huppers and Trussels, a bit of the wild and orgy-prone proclivities of the Germans and Celts, a sensuousness that is the other extreme of "holier-than-thou" religiosity. It is an addition to the old English Elizabethan jollity, and it results in what I'd call the third type of Maniac, aside from the coast and swamp categories, the sex Maniac.

January 25, 1912 (37–27 West Longitude, 0–09
North Latitude. Little headway.)
Ironed, of course, embroidered and mended, of course. Then came the deluge. We had just gone to bed around midnight when there

came a white squall. I thought this craft would sink. Immediately I remembered, in my panic, that I had questioned Fred about carrying no ballast and his telling me that the southern seas this time of the year were kind. Well, we nearly turned turtle. Fred dashed madly on deck in nothing but what God gave him as a birthday suit. Dawson's mate, Smith, was at the wheel. If Dawson had been on watch, it might not have happened as he has an eye for squalls. But neither Smith nor the mate saw the monster coming, as they should have. The mate was all confused and shouted to let the topsails down. That was like feeding a whisper to a gale. Fred acted magnificently. He let go the spanker sheet to cut down the force of the wind upon us. Then he let go the spanker topsail. It started to rain torrents. The wind moderated. But this vessel rode along on her port side, the port rail under water, too long for comfort. If Fred had not relieved her, the ship would have surely tossed her sails into the water and, wetting them, would have turned over.

Later Fred told the mate not to let a squall strike him like that again so suddenly and so unpreparedly. "If you let that happen again, I'll throw you overboard," he said. If Fred did throw him overboard, no one would ever know what happened to him in that dark pandemonium. Such is life at sea, and I suppose the mate will not be around next trip. Then Fred told me always to remember that he never said any such thing. "Landsmen wouldn't understand," he said. . . .

The Hopkins *stopped at Barbados, then sailed for Jacksonville, Florida, to load railroad ties bound for Boston.*

March 26, 1912. (Boston, would you believe it! I can't, quite.)

Such luck! Last week was simply awful, enough to cure the worst case of sea fever, but not mine. Gales and the highest seas I ever saw. The *Hopkins,* light and tiddly, would climb up a solid mountain of water, up and up until her jib boom was invading the heavens, right straight above us; then down, down, plunging downhill into the depths on the other side of continuous mountains, until she shuddered and shook and submarined half her length. And me trying to wash clothes! It might have been terrifying if we all had not known that she was a Thomaston-built schooner, put together by the best men in the trade, such as Oliver Ames, the Washburns, the Lermonds, with old techniques absorbed from years of building them for the typhoons, gales and hurricanes that confronted, for hundreds of years, the sea-going men of the "Town That Went to Sea."

KENNETH ROBERTS
1885–1957

Kenneth Roberts was a Maine man, a writer of historical novels about the colonial and Revolutionary periods in New England. He was a staunch defender of his state; "Don't Say That About Maine!" was written in response to the English historian Arnold Toynbee's patronizing comments about the state. *Trending into Maine,* from which the following sea story is selected, is a collection of essays with the common theme of the wonders of Maine and Roberts's very personal relationship to the state.

In this tale Captain Daniel Dudley, a retired sea captain who had been a master of full-rigged ships in the China trade, was the proto-type for Booth Tarkington's character Captain Francis Embury in his novel of early days in Kennebunkport, *Mirthful Haven.* Roberts writes that "those so fortunate as to have the friendship of Cap'n Dudley were occasionally treated to strange tales — so strange, in-deed, as to raise doubts, sometimes, in the minds of those who heard them. The Cap'n was well aware of the doubts, even when they weren't expressed, but he never seemed to take offense at them. In fact, he was apologetic about some of his stories, and freely admitted that they didn't sound right; but he had to tell them, when he told them at all, just as they had happened to him. Not even to make them sound more, let us say, reasonable could he alter them."

When Tarkington stopped by one day, Captain Dudley showed him his treasures, brought back from voyages all over the world, including a "small meteorite that he had, himself, seen fall in a mandarin's garden as he sat feasting close by. 'Had it dug up right away, still hot, he did, and gave it to me the minute he saw me look at it. Knew how to make presents, those men did, so't you couldn't refuse 'em, no matter how selfish you felt about takin' them.' He returned the meteorite to a shelf of the wide and high glass-fronted cabinet wherein were chunks of yellow sulphur the Captain had brought up from the craters of smoking volcanoes, bits of petrified wood, spider-like dried vegetable growths from the depths of tropical waters, dried sea-horses, orange-colored starfishes, groups of delicate shells, and dozens of specimens, large and small, of contrasting varieties of coral."

Seamen and Sea Serpents

The meteorite to which Mr. Tarkington referred was the most prominent of all the articles in the Cap'n's favorite glass-fronted corner cupboard. It was an irregular lump of rock the size of an ossified tomcat, and when the Cap'n lectured to favored visitors on the contents of the cabinet, as he often did, he frequently avoided mentioning the meteorite until specifically requested to explain it. Even then he seemed reluctant.

Mr. Tarkington and I once took General Charles G. Dawes, who was Vice President at the time, to call on the Cap'n and hear the full details of the occasion when the Cap'n saw the sea serpent. Of all the Cap'n's stories, the one about the sea serpent was the most difficult to extract; but we hoped that in view of General Dawes's exalted position, the Cap'n could be persuaded to overcome his reticence.

No sooner had the Cap'n begun to explain the contents of his cabinet than the General tapped the lump of rock and said "What's this?"

The Cap'n was uncomfortable. He took the rock from the cabinet and pointed out iridescent patches on its surface. "See those?" he asked. "Some say those are opals, but I don't know."

"Where'd you get it and what is it?" the General asked.

"Well," the Cap'n said, "I say it's meteorite, but people that know about meteorites, they say it aint, and they ought to know."

The General picked it up, hefted it and shook his head. "Too light for a meteorite," he said. "No signs of fusing."

Kenneth Roberts

"Yes," the Cap'n said sadly, "that's what the meteorite fellers say. They say it's too light: aint got the right kind of stuff in it for a meteorite. Fellers that've seen meteorites all over the world, they've looked at it, and they say it aint."

"What do they think it is?" the General asked.

"They don't know," the Cap'n said. "They don't know *what* it is, only they're sure it aint a meteorite."

"And yet you keep on thinking it is one?" the General asked.

"Why yes," the Cap'n said. "Yes, I do."

"What makes you think so?" the General asked.

"Well," the Cap'n said, "I was having dinner with a mandarin out in China one night when there was a flash and a howling sound and a big smack, not more'n thirty yards from where we was sitting. Well, the mandarin, he called his servants and sent 'em over where the smack came from and there was a hole in the ground, like a cannon ball makes when you drop it in mud. The mandarin, he told his servants to dig in the hole, and they done so, but when they got to the bottom of the hole, they found a piece of rock too hot to handle. Well, I went back to my ship, and the next morning the mandarin sent this here rock out to me. Still hot, it was. This is it."

"*Hm*," the General said. "I see."

"Now what would *you* think it was, General?" the Cap'n asked.

"Well," said the General, "it certainly doesn't look like a meteorite. It's not heavy enough."

The Cap'n replaced the debatable stone in the cabinet. "Yes," he said, "there aint any doubt there's something wrong with it; and if I hadn't seen it come down myself, I wouldn't take any stock in it. Sometimes I kind of wish it hadn't never been dug up."

Mr. Tarkington broke the meditative silence. "We were telling General Dawes about the time you saw the sea serpent," he said.

"Pshaw!" the Cap'n said uncomfortably.

"How big was it?" the General asked.

"This here," the Cap'n said, taking a gray chunk from the cabinet, "this here's a piece of pumice from Krakatoa. Prob'ly you gentlemen don't remember Krakatoa, but those of us who was to sea when it happened, we remember it, by James, and we wont never forget it. No *sir!* That was in '83, that was, in August, and we was a hundred seventy-two miles from her when she blew up — Bong! We could hear the noise she made just as if she'd been around the corner — sounded like the whole world had blew up in one great big bang! And ashes! Why they was so thick it was darker'n midnight, and we had to keep the riding lights and cabin lamps *and* galley lamp burning day and night. And waves! Why the waves that come along that calm sea, pushed up by that explosion — why, they kept a-hitting us and a-hitting us — fifty feet high, some of 'em! No *sir,* there aint any seaman that'll forget Krakatoa in a hurry. Just solid with floating pumice, the sea was, for days and days. So much of it we had to heave to, because it cut through the copper on our bends — pumiced it right off; and if we'd kept on, it'd a' cut through our planking. That's when I took this piece aboard. Picked up tons of the stuff to give away to cap'ns I'd meet when I got farther north. I'd a' taken more aboard if it hadn't been for the snakes."

He shook his head and cautiously turned the pumice over and over in his hands, as if he still suspected it of harboring a snake.

"You saw snakes on the pumice?" General Dawes asked.

"Snakes!" the Cap'n said. "There was millions of 'em — millions! There was a sheet of pumice over the ocean; and everywhere on it, as far as you could see, there was snakes. There wasn't a square yard of that pumice that didn't have a snake on it — a snake four feet, five feet, six feet long, all purple and yellow and bright colors — water snakes, they was, blew up by the explosion." The Cap'n looked regretful. "Well, we couldn't take chances with water snakes, on account they being so poisonous. Rattlesnakes, coral snakes, cobras — why they're plumb harmless compared to water snakes."

"Indeed," the General said. "Indeed! You surprise me."

"Yes," the Cap'n said, "they're the worst snakes there is. You let one of 'em bite you, and you'll be dead before they can get to the medicine chest. Maybe you've heard of this Captain Marryat that wrote books."

"Yes indeed," the General said. "I've read his books."

The Cap'n was frankly pleased. "You don't say! Well, Cap'n Marryat had a son that follered the sea — promising young feller, too. He got bit by one of those sea snakes and died inside of five minutes." He put the piece of pumice back in the cabinet, locked the door with an air of finality, and politely ushered us into the next room.

"It was some time after Krakatoa that you saw the sea serpent, wasn't it?" Mr. Tarkington asked.

"Yes, it was," the Cap'n said. "It was in the summer of 1891, eight years afterward, but pshaw! I aint going to tell about that!"

"Why not?" the General asked. "It sounds interesting."

"Oh, it aint that," the Cap'n said, "only I hate to tell it, because every time I do, everybody thinks I'm just a damned liar. Don't seem to me as if they should, because my land! if they'd seen all those snakes on the pumice, they'd a' figured there'd have to be some awful big ones hiding under water. It stands to reason, now don't it, that if there's millions and millions of 'em six feet long, there must be a lot of old, old ones that's certainly sixty feet long and maybe a few awful old ones that's six hundred feet long. There aint nothing unreasonable about that, is there?"

"The Cap'n isn't implying that the one he saw was six hundred feet long," Mr. Tarkington told the General.

"No, he wa'n't quite that," the Cap'n said defiantly; "but it wouldn't surprise me a mite if there *was* some that was six hundred feet long — not after seeing the millions of 'em we saw after Krakatoa blew up."

"Where was it you saw this sea serpent?" General Dawes asked.

"It was the twenty-eighth day of July, 1891," the Cap'n said, "and I was cap'n of the *Hannah W. Dudley*, 1128 tons, and our noon reckoning showed us to be 71 South 104 East in the Indian Ocean, heading up for Sunda Straits. A little after two bells in the first dogwatch, just about an hour before pitch dark, the lookout let out a yell and before he more'n got it out of his mouth I saw what he was yelling at, and so did everybody else on deck, because it was the biggest snake's head and neck ever I hope to see, and it was sticking right straight up out of the water just abreast of our port fore chains, not more'n three fathoms away, and it was turning its head from bow to stern as if it was mighty curious about what we was, and didn't want to overlook nothing on our decks. I guess its head stuck twelve feet above our bulwarks, and I don't mind telling you, gentlemen, that it gave me pretty much of a start."

"How big was its head and what color was it and could you see its eyes and did it have a mane?" the General asked.

The Cap'n laughed abruptly. "See its eyes! That snake was so close, you'd a' thought you could lean over the bulwarks and kiss him if you'd been feeling in the mood. You know them thin flat Spanish kegs that hold about ten gallons? Well, that was about the size of this critter's head, and it was smooth, though there was some stuff on the back part of its neck that looked like brown rockweed, and might a' been, for all I know — same color, it was, and it laid kind of flat, the way rockweed does on a ledge when it's out of water. He had little peeny-weeny eyes, no bigger'n an elephant's, and he kind of looked like he had eye-trouble."

"After it had looked around your decks what did it do?" the General asked.

"He didn't do nothing," the Cap'n said. "He just put his head flat down on the water and moved it around as if he was looking straight down into the ocean to see what things looked like down there. You kind of got the feeling he was interested in pretty near everything."

"I suppose the crew was frightened," the General asked.

"Frightened?" the Cap'n said. "No! They wa'n't frightened. We carried two eight-pounders forward, in case any of those Malays or Chinks took a notion to board us, the way they used to do sometimes and the men was possessed to run one, an eight-pounder, back to a mizzen port and give that snake a charge of cannister shot. Well, sir, I put my foot down! 'S'pose you miss,' I told 'em, or s'pose you just cut him up a little and make him mad. Aint he going to rare up and whack that head of his around our decks? He'd make a nice mess out of our rigging, wouldn't he, and 'twouldn't surprise me none if he ripped our courses and lower topsails all to ribbons and maybe broke the legs of a few of you. No *sir!* I told 'em. 'Don't you go to interfering with that snake in no way at all! Don't throw nothing at him,' I told 'em, 'and don't even holler at him. Just leave him be,' I told 'em.

"Well, they left him be, and I climbed over onto the port cathead so to be sure just where his head lay, so I could get his measurements as accurate as I could to enter in the log. Well, his head was four paces forward of the cathead and when I climbed back onto the deck and ran aft, the last part of his tail that I could see lying in the water was flush with the taffrail, and that made him one hundred and twenty-one feet long, provided it was the end of his tail we was looking at, on account the *Hannah W. Dudley* was one hundred and thirty-one feet long on deck. All those water snakes we saw in the Straits of Sunda, their tails most generally hung down a little at the tip when they laid quiet in the water, the way this one was doing. But anyway, that's the way I logged him — one hundred and twenty-one feet."

SMALL-TOWN LIFE

SARAH ORNE JEWETT
1849–1909

Sarah Orne Jewett's place in Maine's literary history is secure. A writer of regional fiction, she was an exemplar of skilled observation and sensitive reporting on her part of Maine and the people who lived there.

She was born in South Berwick, just up the Piscataqua River from Portsmouth, New Hampshire. Her grandfather was a sea captain. Her father, a country doctor, was the major influence on the young Sarah. She often accompanied him on his rounds, learning early and intimately about her neighbors. *A Country Doctor*, written in 1884, is a fictional account of those times.

Her early plan to follow her father into medicine was abandoned both because of her tenuous health and because she recognized that medicine was a closed field for women. Instead, influenced by Harriet Beecher Stowe's *Pearl of Orr's Island,* she began writing and at eighteen sold her first piece to a Boston weekly.

Jewett was a fine craftsman and a more sophisticated regionalist than most of her peers. She was a hard worker who took her writing seriously. A voluminous reader, she maintained a correspondence with several other authors as she produced novels, short stories, works of history, children's books, and poetry. Her subjects were usually women, the often lonely people of fading small towns in Maine, and with great compassion she depicted their manners, their strengths, and their foibles. Her advice to the young Willa Cather in 1908 tells us something of how she felt about the business of writing:

> . . . in short you must write to the human heart, the great consciousness that all humanity goes to make up. Otherwise what might be strength in a writer is only crudeness, and what might be insight is

only observation; sentiment falls to sentimentality — you can write about life, but never write life itself.

To work in silence and with all one's heart, that is the writer's lot. He is the only artist who must be a solitary, and yet needs the widest outlook upon the world.

Jewett wrote of rural Maine with insight and humor. In *The Country of the Pointed Firs,* perhaps her finest and best-known work, she gives us the town of Dunnet Landing, evoking the sights and scents of this small coastal village and deftly recreating the warm and simple people who live there. Rich in detail and with a true sense of the local dialect, these stories go straight to the heart of the world that absorbed Jewett during her long career. "The Town Poor" is a chapter from this collection of loosely connected stories.

The Town Poor

Mrs. William Trimble and Miss Rebecca Wright were driving along Hampden east road, one afternoon in early spring. Their progress was slow. Mrs. Trimble's sorrel horse was old and stiff, and the wheels were clogged by clay mud. The frost was not yet out of the ground, although the snow was nearly gone, except in a few places on the north side of the woods, or where it had drifted all winter against a length of fence.

"There must be a good deal o'snow to the nor'ard of us yet," said weather-wise Mrs. Trimble. "I feel it in the air, 't is more than the ground-damp. We ain't goin' to have real nice weather till the up-country snow's all gone."

"I heard say yesterday that there was good sleddin' yet, all up through Parsley," responded Miss Wright. "I shouldn't like to live in them northern places. My cousin Ellen's husband was a Parsley man, an' he was obliged, as you may have heard, to go up north to his father's second wife's funeral; got back day before yesterday. 'T was about twenty-one miles, an' they started on wheels; but when they'd gone nine or ten miles, they found 't was no sort o' use, an' left their wagon an' took a sleigh. The man that owned it charged 'em four an'

"East Machias Post Office"

six, too. I shouldn't have thought he would; they told him they was goin' to a funeral; an' they had their own buffaloes an' everything."

"Well, I expect it's a good deal harder scratchin', up that way; they have to git money where they can; the farms is very poor as you go north," suggested Mrs. Trimble kindly. " 'T ain't none too rich a country where we be, but I've always been grateful I wa'n't born up to Parsley."

The old horse plodded along, and the sun, coming out from the heavy spring clouds, sent a sudden shine of light along the muddy road. Sister Wright drew her large veil forward over the high brim of her bonnet. She was not used to driving, or to being much in the open air; but Mrs. Trimble was an active business woman, and looked after her own affairs herself, in all weathers. The late Mr. Trimble had left her a good farm, but not much ready money, and it was often said that she was better off in the end than if he had lived. She regretted his loss deeply, however; it was impossible for her to speak of him, even to intimate friends, without emotion, and nobody had ever hinted that this emotion was insincere. She was most warm-hearted and generous, and in her limited way played the part of Lady Bountiful in the town of Hampden.

"Why, there's where the Bray girls lives, ain't it?" she exclaimed, as, beyond a thicket of witch-hazel and scrub oak, they came in sight of a weather-beaten, solitary farmhouse. The barn was too far away for thrift or comfort, and they could see long lines of light between the shrunken boards as they came nearer. The fields looked both stony and sodden. Somehow, even Parsley itself could be hardly more forlorn.

"Yes'm," said Miss Wright, "that's where they live now, poor things. I know the place, though I ain't been up here for years. You don't suppose, Mis' Trimble — I ain't seen the girls out to meetin' all winter. I've re'lly been covetin' " —

"Why, yes, Rebecca, of course we could stop," answered Mrs. Trimble heartily. "The exercises was over earlier'n I expected, an' you're goin' to remain over night long o' me, you know. There won't be no tea till we git there, so we can't be late. I'm in the habit o' sending' a basket to the Bray girls when any o' our folks is comin' this way, but I ain't been to see 'em since they moved up here. Why, it must be a good deal over a year ago. I know 't was in the late winter they had to make the move. 'T was cruel hard, I must say, an' if I hadn't been down with my pleurisy fever I'd have stirred round an' done somethin' about it. There was a good deal o' sickness at the time, an' — well, 't was kind o' rushed through, breakin' of 'em up, an' lots o' folks blamed the selec'men; but when 't was done, 't was done, an' nobody took holt to undo it. Ann an' Mandy looked same's ever when they come to meetin', 'long in the summer, — kind o' wishful, perhaps. They've always sent me word they was gittin' on pretty comfortable."

"That would be their way," said Rebecca Wright. "They never was

"Noonday Meal, West New Portland, Maine"

any hand to complain, though Mandy's less cheerful than Ann. If Mandy'd been spared such poor eyesight, an' Ann hadn't got her lame wrist that wa'n't set right they'd kep' off the town fast enough. They both shed tears when they talked to me about havin' to break up, when I went to see 'em before I went over to brother Asa's. You see we was brought up neighbors, an' we went to school together, the Brays an' me. 'T was a special Providence brought us home this road, I've been covetin' a chance to git to see 'em. My lameness hampers me."

"I'm glad we come this way, myself," said Mrs. Trimble.

"I'd like to see just how they fare," Miss Rebecca Wright continued. "They give their consent to goin' on the town because they knew they'd got to be dependent, an' so they felt 't would come easier for all than for a few to help 'em. They acted real dignified an' right-minded, contrary to what most do in such cases, but they was dreadful anxious to see who would bid 'em off, town-meeting day; they did so hope 't would be somebody right in the village. I just sat down an' cried good when I found Abel Janes' folks had got hold of 'em. They always had the name of bein' slack an' poor-spirited, an' they did it just for what they got out o' the town. The selectmen this last year ain't what we have had. I hope they've been considerate about the Bray girls."

"I should have be'n more considerate about fetchin' of you over," apologized Mrs. Trimble. "I've got my horse, an' you're lame-footed: 't is too far for you to come. But time does slip away with busy folks, an' I forgit a good deal I ought to remember."

"There's nobody more considerate than you be," protested Miss Rebecca Wright.

Mrs. Trimble made no answer, but took out her whip and gently touched the sorrel horse, who walked considerably faster, but did not think it worth while to trot. It was a long, round-about way to the house, farther down the road and up a lane.

"I never had any opinion of the Bray girls' father, leavin' 'em as he did," said Mrs. Trimble.

"He was much praised in his time, though there was always some said his early life hadn't been up to the mark," explained her companion. "He was a great favorite of our then preacher, the Reverend Daniel Longbrother. They did a good deal for the parish, but they did it their own way. Deacon Bray was one that did his part in the repairs without urging. You know 't was in his time the first repairs was made, when they got out the old soundin'-board an' them handsome square pews. It cost an awful sight o' money, too. They hadn't done payin' up that debt when they set to alter it again an' git the walls frescoed. My grandmother was one that always spoke her mind right out, an' she was dreadful opposed to breakin' up the square pews where she'd always set. They was countin' up what 't would cost in parish meetin', an' she riz right up an' said 't wouldn't cost nothin' to let 'em stay, an' there wa'n't a house carpenter left in the parish that could do such nice work, an' time would come when the great-grand-children would give their eye-teeth to have the old meetin'-house look just as it did then. But haul the inside to pieces they would and did."

"There come to be a real fight over it, didn't there?" agreed Mrs. Trimble soothingly. "Well, 't wa'n't good taste. I remember the old house well. I come here as a child to visit a cousin o' mother's, an' Mr. Trimble's folks was neighbors, an' we was drawed to each other then, young's we was. Mr. Trimble spoke of it many's the time, — that first time he ever see me, in a leghorn hat with a feather; 't was one that mother had, an' pressed over."

"When I think of them old sermons that used to be preached in that old meetin'-house of all, I'm glad it's altered over, so's not to remind folks," said Miss Rebecca Wright, after a suitable pause. "Them old brimstone discourses, you know, Mis' Trimble. Preachers is far more reasonable, nowadays. Why, I set an' thought, last Sabbath, as I listened, that if old Mr. Longbrother an' Deacon Bray could hear the difference they'd crack the ground over 'em like pole beans, an' come right up 'long side their headstones."

Mrs. Trimble laughed heartily, and shook the reins three or four times by way of emphasis. "There's no gitting round you," she said, much pleased. "I should think Deacon Bray would want to rise, any way, if 't was so he could, an' knew how his poor girls was farin'. A man ought to provide for his folks he's got to leave behind him, specially if they're women. To be sure, they had their little home; but we've seen how, with all their industrious ways, they hadn't means to keep it. I s'pose he thought he'd got time enough to lay by, when he give so generous in collections; but he didn't lay by, an' there they be. He might have took lessons from the squirrels: even them little wild creatur's makes them their winter hoards, an' menfolks ought to know enough if squirrels does, 'Be just before you are generous:' that's what was always set for the B's in the copy-books, when I was to school, and it often runs through my mind."

" 'As for man, his days are as grass, — that was for A; the two go well together," added Miss Rebecca Wright soberly. "My good gracious, ain't this a starved-lookin' place? It makes me ache to think them nice Bray girls has to brook it here."

The sorrel horse, though somewhat puzzled by an unexpected deviation from his homeward way, willingly came to a stand by the gnawed corner of the door-yard fence, which evidently served as hitching-place. Two or three ragged old hens were picking about the yard, and at last a face appeared at the kitchen window, tied up in a handkerchief, as if it were a case of toothache. By the time our friends reached the side door next this window, Mrs. Janes came disconsolately to open it for them, shutting it again as soon as possible, though the air felt more chilly inside the house.

"Take seats," said Mrs. Janes briefly. "You'll have to see me just as I be. I have been suffering these four days with the ague, and everything to do. Mr. Janes is to court, on the jury. 'T was inconvenient to spare him. I should be pleased to have you lay off your things."

Comfortable Mrs. Trimble looked about the cheerless kitchen, and could not think of anything to say; so she smiled blandly and shook her head in answer to the invitation. "We'll just set a few minutes with you, to pass the time o' day, an' then we must go in an' have a word with the Miss Brays, bein' old acquaintance. It ain't been so we could git to call on 'em before. I don't know 's you're acquainted with Miss R'becca Wright. She's been out of town a good deal."

"I heard she was stopping over to Plainfields with her brother's folks," replied Mrs. Janes, rocking herself with irregular motion, as she sat close to the stove. "Got back some time in the fall, I believe?"

"Yes'm," said Miss Rebecca, with an undue sense of guilt and conviction. "We've been to the installation over to the East Parish, an' thought we'd stop in; we took this road home to see if 't was any better. How is the Miss Brays gettin' on?"

"They're well's common," answered Mrs. Janes grudgingly. "I was put out with Mr. Janes for fetchin' of 'em here, with all I've got to do, an' I own I was kind o' surly to 'em 'long to the first of it. He gits the money from the town, an' it helps him out; but he bid 'm off for five dollars a month, an' we can't do much for 'em at no such price as that. I went an' dealt with the selec'men, an' made 'em promise to find their firewood an' some other things extra. They was glad to get rid o' the matter the fourth time I went, an' would ha' promised 'most anything. But Mr. Janes don't keep me half the time in oven-wood, he's off so much, an' we was cramped o' room, any way. I have to store things up garrit a good deal, an' that keeps me trampin' right through their room. I do the best for 'em I can, Mis' Trimble, but 't ain't so easy for me as 't is for you, with all your means to do with."

The poor woman looked pinched and miserable herself, though it was evident that she had no gift at house or home keeping. Mrs. Trimble's heart was wrung with pain, as she thought of the unwelcome inmates of such a place; but she held her peace bravely, while Miss Rebecca again gave some brief information in regard to the installation.

"You go right up them back stairs," the hostess directed at last. "I'm glad some o' you church folks has seen fit to come an' visit 'em. There ain't been nobody here this long spell, an' they've aged a sight since they come. They always send down a taste out of your baskets, Mis' Trimble, an' I relish it, I tell you. I'll shut the door after you, if you don't object. I feel every draught o' cold air."

"I've always heard she was a great hand to make a poor mouth. Wa'n't she from somewheres up Parsley way?" whispered Miss Rebecca, as they stumbled in the half-light.

"Poor meechin' body, wherever she come from," replied Mrs. Trimble, as she knocked at the door.

There was silence for a moment after this unusual sound; then one of the Bray sisters opened the door. The eager guests stared into a small, low room, brown with age, and gray, too, as if former dust and cobwebs could not be made wholly to disappear. The two elderly women who stood there looked captives. Their withered faces wore a look of apprehension, and the room itself was more bare and plain than was fitting to their evident refinement of character and self-respect. There was an uncovered small table in the middle of the floor, with some crackers on a plate; and, for some reason or other, this added a great deal to the general desolation.

But Miss Ann Bray, the elder sister, who carried her right arm in a sling, with piteously drooping fingers, gazed at the visitors with radiant joy. She had not seen them arrive.

The one window gave only the view at the back of the house, across the fields, and their coming was indeed a surprise. The next minute she was laughing and crying together. "Oh, sister!" she said, "if here ain't our dear Mis' Trimble! — an' my heart o' goodness, 't is 'Becca Wright, too! What dear good creatures you be! I've felt all day as if something good was goin' to happen, an' was just sayin' to myself 't was most sundown now, but I wouldn't let on to Mandany I'd give up hope quite yet. You see, the scissors stuck in the floor this very mornin' an' it's always a reliable sign. There, I've got to kiss ye both again!"

"I don't know where we can all set," lamented sister Mandana. "There ain't but the one chair an' the bed; t' other chair's too rickety; an' we've been promised another these ten days; but first they've forgot it, an' next Mis' Janes can't spare it, — one excuse an' another. I am goin' to git a stump o' wood an' nail a board on to it, when I git outdoor again," said Mandana, in a plaintive voice. "There, I ain't goin' to complain o' nothin', now you've come," she added; and the guests sat down, Mrs. Trimble, as was proper, in the one chair.

"We've sat on the bed many's the time with you, 'Becca, an' talked over our girl nonsense, ain't we? You know where 't was — in the little back bedroom we had when we was girls, an' used to peek out at our beaux through the strings o' mornin'-glories," laughed Ann Bray delightedly, her thin face shining more and more with joy. "I brought some o' them mornin'-glory seeds along when we come away, we'd raised 'em so many years; an' we got 'em started all right, but the hens found 'em out. I declare I chased them poor hens, foolish as 't was; but the mornin'-glories I'd counted on a sight to remind me o' home. You see, our debts was so large, after my long sickness an' all, that we didn't feel 't was right to keep back anything we could help from the auction."

It was impossible for any one to speak for a moment or two; the sisters felt their own uprooted condition afresh, and their guests for the first time really comprehended the piteous contrast between that neat little village house, which now seemed a palace of comfort, and this cold, unpainted upper room in the remote Janes farmhouse. It was an unwelcome thought to Mrs. Trimble that the well-to-do town of Hampden could provide no better for its poor than this, and her round face flushed with resentment and the shame of personal responsibility. "The girls shall be well settled in the village before another winter, if I pay their board myself," she made an inward resolution, and took another almost tearful look at the broken stove, the miserable bed and the sisters' one hair-covered trunk, on which Mandana was sitting. But the poor place was filled with a golden spirit of hospitality.

Rebecca was again discoursing eloquently of the installation; it was so much easier to speak of general subjects, and the sisters had evidently been longing to hear some news. Since the late summer they had not been to church, and presently Mrs. Trimble asked the reason.

"Now, don't you go to pouring out our woes, Mandy!" begged little old Ann, looking shy and almost girlish, and as if she insisted upon playing that life was still all before them and all pleasure. "Don't you go to spoilin' their visit with our complaints! They know well's we do that changes must come, an' we'd been so wonted to our home things that this come hard at first; but then they felt for us, I know just as well's can be. 'T will soon be summer again, an' 't is real pleasant right out in the fields here, when there ain't too hot a spell. I've got to know a sight o' singin' birds since we come."

"Give me the folks I've always known," sighed the younger sister, who looked older than Miss Ann, and less even-tempered. "You may have your birds, if you want' em. I do re'lly long to go to meetin' an' see folks go by up the aisle. Now, I will speak of it, Ann, whatever you say. We need, each of us, a pair o' good stout shoes an' rubbers, — ours are all wore out; an' we've asked an' asked, an' they never think to bring 'em, an' " —

Poor old Mandana, on the trunk, covered her face with her arms and sobbed aloud. The elder sister stood over her, and patted her on the thin shoulder like a child, and tried to comfort her. It crossed Mrs. Trimble's mind that it was not the first time one had wept and the other had comforted. The sad scene must have been repeated many times in that long, drear winter. She would see them forever after in her mind as fixed as a picture, and her own tears fell fast.

"You didn't see Mis' Janes's cunning little boy, the next one to the baby, did you?" asked Ann Bray, turning round quickly at last, and going cheerfully on with the conversation. "Now, hush, Mandy, dear; they'll think you're childish! He's a dear, friendly little creatur', an' likes to stay with us a good deal, though we feel 's if it was too cold for him, now we are waitin' to get us more wood."

"When I think of the acres o' woodland in this town!" groaned Rebecca Wright. "I believe I'm going to preach next Sunday, 'stead o' the minister, an' I'll make the sparks fly. I've always heard the saying, 'What's everybody's business is nobody's business,' an' I've come to believe it."

"Now, don't you, 'Becca. You've happened on a kind of a poor time with us, but we've got more belongings than you see here, an' a good large cluset, where we can store those things there ain't room to have about. You an' Mis' Trimble have happened on a kind of poor day, you know. Soon's I git me some stout shoes an' rubbers, as Mandy says, I can fetch home plenty o' little dry boughs o' pine; you remember I was always a great hand to roam in the woods? If we could only have a front room, so 't we could look out on the road an' see passin', an' was shod for meetin', I don' know's we should complain. Now we're just goin' to give you what we've got, an' make out with a good welcome. We make more tea 'n we want in the mornin', an' then let the fire go down, since 't has been so mild. We've got a *good* cluset" (disappearing as she spoke), "an' I know this to be good tea, 'cause it's some o' yourn, Mis' Trimble. An' here's our sprigged chiny cups that R'becca knows by sight, if Mis' Trimble don't. We kep' out four of 'em, an' put the even half dozen with the rest of the auction stuff. I've often wondered who'd got 'em, but I never asked, for fear 't would be somebody that would distress us. They was mother's, you know."

The four cups were poured, and the little table pushed to the bed, where Rebecca Wright still sat, and Mandana, wiping her eyes, came and joined her. Mrs. Trimble sat in her chair at the end, and Ann trotted about the room in pleased content for a while, and in and out of the closet, as if she still had much to do; then she came and stood opposite Mrs. Trimble. She was very short and small, and there was no painful sense of her being obliged to stand. The four cups were not quite full of cold tea, but there was a clean old tablecloth folded double, and a plate with three pairs of crackers neatly piled, and a small — it must be owned, a very small — piece of hard white cheese. Then, for a treat, in a glass dish, there was a little preserved peach, the last — Miss Rebecca knew it instinctively — of the household stores brought from their old home. It was very sugary, this bit of peach; and as she helped her guests and sister Mandy, Miss Ann Bray said, half unconsciously, as she often had said with less reason in the old days, "Our preserves ain't so good as usual this year; this is beginning to candy." Both the guests protested, while Rebecca added that the taste of it carried her back, and made her feel young again. The Brays had always managed to keep one or two peach trees alive in their corner of a garden. "I've been keeping this preserve for a treat," said her friend. "I'm glad to have you eat some, 'Becca. Last summer I often wished you was home an' could come an' see us, 'stead o' being away off to Plainfields."

The crackers did not taste too dry. Miss Ann took the last of the peach on her own cracker; there could not have been quite a small spoonful, after the others were helped, but she asked them first if they would not have some more. Then there was a silence, and in the silence a wave of tender feeling rose high in the hearts of the four elderly women. At this moment the setting sun flooded the poor plain room with light; the unpainted wood was all of a golden-brown, and Ann Bray, with her gray hair and aged face, stood at the head of the table in a kind of aureole. Mrs. Trimble's face was all aquiver as she looked at her; she thought of the text about two or three being gathered together, and was half afraid.

"I believe we ought to 've asked Mis' Janes if she wouldn't come up," said Ann. "She's real good feelin', but she's had it very hard, an gits discouraged. I can't find that she's ever had anything real pleasant to look back to, as we have. There, next time we'll make a good heartenin' time for her too."

The sorrel horse had taken a long nap by the gnawed fencerail, and the cool air after sundown made him impatient to be gone. The two friends jolted homeward in the gathering darkness, through the stiffening mud, and neither Mrs. Trimble nor Rebecca Wright said a word until they were out of sight as well as out of sound of the Janes house. Time must elapse before they could reach a more familiar part of the road and resume conversation on its natural level.

"I consider myself to blame," insisted Mrs. Trimble at last. "I haven't no words of accusation for nobody else, an' I ain't one to take comfort in calling names to the board o' selec'men. I make no reproaches, an' I take it all on my own shoulders; but I'm goin' to stir about me, I tell you! I shall begin early to-morrow. They're goin' back to their own house, — it's been standin' empty all winter, — an' the town's goin' to give 'em the rent an' what firewood they need; it won't come to more than the board's payin' out now. An' you an' me'll take this same horse an' wagon, an' ride an' go afoot by turns, an' git means enough together to buy back their furniture an' whatever was sold at that plaguey auction; an' then we'll put it all back, an' tell 'em they've got to move to a new place, an' just carry 'em right back again where they come from. An' don't you never tell, R'becca, but here I be a widow woman, layin' up what I make from my farm for nobody knows who, an' I'm goin' to do for them Bray girls all I'm a mind to. I should be sca't to wake up in heaven, an' hear anybody there ask how the Bray girls was. Don't talk to me about the town o' Hampden, an' don't ever let me hear the name o' town poor! I'm ashamed to go home an' see what's set out for supper. I wish I'd brought 'em right along."

"I was goin' to ask if we couldn't git the new doctor to go up an' do somethin' for poor Ann's arm," said Miss Rebecca. "They say he's very smart. If she could get so's to braid straw or hook rugs again, she'd soon be earnin' a little somethin'. An' may be he could do somethin' for Mandy's eyes. They did use to live so neat an' ladylike. Somehow I couldn't speak to tell 'em there that 't was I bought them six best cups an' saucers, time of the auction; they went very low, as everything else did, an' I thought I could save it some other way. They shall have 'em back an' welcome. You're real wholehearted, Mis' Trimble. I expect Ann'll be sayin' that her father's child'n wa'n't goin' to be left desolate, an' that all the bread he cast on the water's coming back through you."

"I don't care what she says, dear creature!" exclaimed Mrs. Trimble. "I'm full o' regrets I took time for that installation, an' set there seepin' in a lot o' talk this whole day long, except for its kind of bringin' us to the Bray girls. I wish to my heart 't was tomorrow mornin' a'ready, an' I a-startin' for the selec'men."

MARY ELLEN CHASE
1887–1973

In colonial times, when the Province of Maine was a part of Massachusetts, religion played a central role in village life. A kind of theocracy was in place, with the meetinghouse as the primary social institution. The middle of the seventeenth century found Maine bound by a Massachusetts law that mandated local tax support of a minister, including his lodgings, for he was an official of the town, even if his church had not yet been established. The prevailing religion of Massachusetts was Congregationalism, and soon the Congregational church replaced the Anglican as the dominant faith in Maine. The later emergence of Baptists, Methodists, Quakers, Catholics — from the Irish and French-Canadian immigrants — and others served to dilute the Congregational strength, but the First Parish Church of Blue Hill remained strong and in Mary Ellen Chase's time, the late nineteenth century, was still a focal point of town life.

As a girl, Mary Ellen met Sarah Orne Jewett and was inspired to become a writer. After graduating from the University of Maine and doing advanced work and teaching at the University of Minnesota, Chase returned east to Smith College, where she taught for thirty years.

Her interest in religion manifested itself in works about the Bible as literature and in a biography of the Reverend Jonathan Fisher, the pastor of the church at Blue Hill from 1796 to 1846. Fisher was a man of many talents: diarist, farmer, architect, painter, theologian; Chase called him the "Leonardo da Vinci of his time and place."

Like Jewett, Chase was a careful observer of the land and people around her, and her family and their life in the coastal town of Blue Hill formed the basis of her novels about the region and the autobio-

Mary Ellen Chase

graphical *A Goodly Heritage*. There, her affectionate portrayal of her family's observation of the Sabbath shows her use of lyrical prose, attention to detail, and sensitivity to the nature of family relationships.

The Lord's Day in the Nineties

I

To all Protestant communities in rural New England during the nineties (and in the State of Maine there was almost no distinctly rural community which was not wholly Protestant) Sunday was unmistakably the Lord's Day. That we were glad and rejoiced therein cannot be claimed with the same degree of certainty. Foretaste, perhaps even foreboding, of Sunday began with our Saturday dinner, which was invariable. It consisted of salt fish boiled in a cloth bag and in a pot well filled with potatoes. This sustenance, commonly known in New England as "Cape Cod turkey," was served with a generous supply of hot pork scraps floating in a bowl of equally hot grease. Strangers to Maine ways who came to our table often had to be shown how to shred the fish on their plates, how to mash their potatoes, how to pour upon the mixture the pork gravy. Under my mother's cooking the result was not only palatable but delicious. This meal had originated many years before because it made possible the Sunday dinner without undue labour on that day. In the afternoon the large remainder was made into fish-balls and set in a cool place to await the morrow.

Another foretaste of Sunday came, in our large family, immediately after dinner was cleared away. By two o'clock the weekly bathing began. Before the turn of the century no house in Blue Hill possessed a bath-room. Ours, the first in town, was installed when I was seventeen, and its exciting installation followed a law-suit of several years' standing in which we became involved because of our inordinate desire for a water supply of our own. There was no town water supply; indeed, there is not to this day; and one paid dearly both financially and emotionally for any rebellion against wells, cisterns, or pasture springs.

The weekly bath, therefore, was fraught with inconvenience and difficulty; nevertheless, in all well-regulated families, the omission of it was inconceivable. Although in the warmest weather the sea proved helpful, a salt water bath by tacit consent of all the "best people", was looked upon with suspicion as not fulfilling the requirements either of cleanliness or of moral and religious duty. Custom and time alike had prescribed a washtub by the kitchen stove; and time and custom in the nineties were not lightly set aside.

One by one we scrubbed ourselves, or were scrubbed, the odour of the warm soap-suds mingling with the smell of the beans in the oven. One by one we arrayed ourselves or were arrayed in clean underwear and fresh, well-mended stockings. If we finished early, we were encouraged to play at temperate games, to spend an hour at a neighbour's house, or to read quietly in our corners of the library. Riotousness on late Saturday afternoons was frowned upon; it was too much like jocularity after the performance of a sacred rite. On Saturday evenings it was with a sense of corporate decency and order that we gathered around the supper table — a sense which modern plumbing with all its comforts cannot produce.

Sundays in all seasons dawned soberly. Toys of all kinds had been put away in closed drawers or in the corners of the stable. To allow a sled or a cart in the driveway was unthinkable. After a somewhat later breakfast of warmed-over beans and brown bread, we prepared for church and Sunday school, warned of such necessity by the nine o'clock bells which pealed alternately from the twin white steeples on opposite hills. In earlier years my mother, for the sake of family integrity, forsook her Baptist heritage and accompanied her husband, mother-in-law, and children to the Congregational church.

Our family left the house shortly after 10:15 as we must be ascending the church steps by the time the sombre tolling of the last bell began just before the half hour. My father always walked a bit ahead of the rest of us. In all seasonable weather he wore a top hat and a black frock coat, and he carried a gold-headed cane. My mother, often flurried a bit by her morning's undertaking, always had very pink cheeks as she brought up the rear. The appearance of us children varied only with the change from fall and winter to late spring and summer. We each had one best costume and we wore it. My father having a passion for blue serge, which he bought by the bolt, our winter dresses were often fashioned from this material, my mother cleverly disguising one frock from another by bands, braids, pipings, and divergence in pattern. In the summer we wore white or sprigged muslins and wide leghorn hats. The blue serge of my brothers did not change with any season although occasionally it was alleviated by trousers of white duck. We went silently down the country road, skirting a wide field on the right filled with violets, or daisies, or goldenrod, and climbed the hill to the church. At the door we met my grandmother, whose sedate and solitary progress had been accomplished earlier since she liked to confer with her friend, the sexton, over the morning lesson assigned to the minister's Bible class.

Our pew was taxed to its capacity to hold us in the nineties, and as years elapsed we spilled over into another. We had certain rules which we followed in regard to occupation and behaviour during the long morning service. Children up to the age of six were encouraged to sit on crickets [footstools] throughout the sermon and to draw or look at pictures; from six to ten years they might read their Sunday-school books; from ten on they must sit quietly and at least pretend attention. During the hymns, the responsive reading and the long prayer all of whatever age must listen and participate in so far as each was able. My father not infrequently annoyed my mother after the sermon had gone on for three-quarters of an hour by turning in his corner seat at the outside of our pew to look at the great circular clock which hung below the choir gallery; but if we perchance followed his bad example, we were admonished by a shake of her head or, for that matter, of his own.

Although church provided in the nineties no such dramatic possibilities as it had promised in the days of the Reverend Jonathan Fisher, it was not entirely bereft of excitement. Once my brother Edward, deep in his Sunday-school book, and forgetful of his surroundings, laughed aloud in the midst of the sermon. This act, however, which my father singularly enough allowed to go unreproved, was as nothing compared to the consternation and embarrassment which he caused us all on one memorable day. Seized by a spirit of defiance and of rebellion unknown among us, he had on the morning in question purposely hitched himself in his white duck trousers around on the grass of the lawn until their seat was a sight to behold. Our hearts stood still as my father, issuing from the house, beheld this proof of insurrection. But instead of the swift retribution which we expected, my brother was forced to walk to church and to stand, during the Doxology and the hymns, on the highest cricket, his pants in full view of the congregation. The mortification which we as a family experienced on that devastating occasion can never be minimized or forgotten! Surely one cannot pay singly for his own transgressions!

My grandmother also afforded drama, now amusing to recollect but then embarrassing to undergo. As she grew older and the deafness which crept early upon her became more acute, a certain practice of hers was a source of no little confusion. Since she contributed fifty dollars yearly to the support of the minister, an amount almost unheard of in those days and equalled only by a certain well-to-do parishioner, Mrs. Harriet Morton by name, she made it an unchangeable rule to place no offering at all in the contribution plate. Her generosity and her habit alike being well and favourably known to the entire community, she was upheld by public sentiment. Imagine then her distress when her rival in good works developed suddenly and without fair warning the custom of giving also some coin as the plate was passed. Not to be undone, my grandmother prepared with reluctance but with commendable spirit to do the same; her refusal, however, to give one jot or tittle more than her neighbor was destined sorely to test the ingenuity and the peace of mind of the grandchild who sat next to her.

Mrs. Morton sat across the aisle and one pew ahead of our own. The task of the child next to my grandmother was to ascertain the amount of the coin which she drew from her black reticule and placed upon the plate and to communicate its size to my grandmother before the arrival of the deacon who collected the alms on our side of the church. This information was not so difficult to procure as it might have been in view of the fact that our respective pews were at the extreme front; but the conveying of it required no little ingenuity. It was usually given by signs, one finger signifying a nickel, two a dime, the full hand (a gesture very rarely displayed!) a quarter. But as my grandmother grew older and more hard of hearing, the nervousness engendered by this trying situation increased until, forgetting her deafness, she would say in a voice perfectly audible to the entire congregation, though unheard by herself, "How much did Hattie Morton give *this* morning?" I regret to say, moreover, that neither her voice nor her intonation was strictly in keeping with the ideal atmosphere of a Christian edifice.

After all, the most unalloyed, if less exciting, drama occurred every Sunday morning when my father made his contribution. This was a never failing source of pride to us; for as coins were drawn from pockets and from purses, my father invariably procured from one small pocket at the bottom of his waistcoat a new one-dollar bill and laid it upon the plate. The amount and the occasion alike were too momentous to allow comment at any time. We should have liked to know how he obtained always a new note, how he managed to afford such a prodigious offering. But we never asked, only remained secure in the social and financial distinction which his weekly act conferred upon us.

I do not know that the church service itself engendered much religion within us. The sermons were long and abstruse, and, even as I grew older, I do not recall any which meant much to me. But the solemnity of the occasion, the observance together of a custom, the sense of well-being and of well-doing — memories of these I would not be without. Details, too, impressed themselves on my mind and in my imagination to bring later their longer, richer consequences: the black shadows of birds passing and repassing behind the coloured glass of a memorial window; the sunlight lying in bright, precise figures across the pulpit steps; the order and beauty of the white panelled pews with their polished, mahogany railings; the words and the imagery of old hymns. Most of all I remember verses of the Bible as they were read by the singularly beautiful voice of the old pastor whom I knew throughout my childhood. Sometimes the sonorous quality of the words themselves quite apart from their sense stayed long with me:

"Wherefore, seeing we also are encompassed about by so great a cloud of witnesses. . . ."

"The former treatise have I made, O Theophilus. . . ."

"Now faith is the substance of things hoped for, the evidence of things not seen."

Once when I was hardly ten I was startled, aroused from my wandering thoughts, by the awful discovery, the stupendous announcement, that someone had actually *seen* the Lord. This was the prophet Isaiah in the year that King Uzziah died; but for the moment, so convincing was his voice, I felt sure it was our minister himself — that in his black coat and white linen necktie he, the Reverend Ebenezer Bean, had been before that great throne, high and lifted up, in that train which filled the temple. As he read, I felt a tingling sensation down my back, the tiny hairs rising in my excitement. In one of those inexplicable feats of memory, the words were stamped henceforth indelibly upon my mind.

"Above it stood the seraphim; each had six wings; with twain he covered his face, and with twain he covered his feet; and with twain he did fly.

"And one cried to another saying, 'Holy, Holy, Holy is the Lord of hosts. The whole earth is full of His glory.' "

II

After Sunday-school, which followed hard upon church, we came home either to change our dresses or to cover them with large aprons and to await the Sunday dinner. There was no possible surprise engendered by this anticipation, for we knew precisely what we were to have. Fishballs browned in a spider formed the dinner proper. They came on the table garnished with parsley and interspaced with hard-boiled eggs cut in white and yellow circles. With them were served raw onions in vinegar and large plates of beautifully browned and buttered toast, each plate being covered ceremoniously with a spotless white napkin. For dessert there were always preserves of some sort and cake. This dinner had been for many years a custom in the family, since its preparation was so slight as to make no one miss church on account of it and since its actual cooking could be accomplished on Saturday.

Unlike many other children even as late as the nineties we were not forbidden to read anything we liked on Sundays; indeed, we were encouraged to spend many a Sunday afternoon with our books. Often, too, during the six months she spent yearly with us, my grandmother told us sea stories. This occupation, because of her own dramatic personality, partook of the nature of a rite rather than of a pastime. It was performed on summer days in the apple orchard, my grandmother sitting in a low red chair beneath a black silk parasol. Other children of the neighbourhood stood about with us, like attendant acolytes in an entranced circle while her voice rose and fell, now in tales of shipwreck, now in many-hued pictures of Cadiz by moonlight, of the strangely-coloured birds of the South Seas, of fish flying through green waves touched with sunset. Quite different and far less appealing was the Junior Christian Endeavor meeting which in my childhood was held in the vestry of the church at three o'clock. This we always attended, reciting Bible verses memorized for the occasion. We were also encouraged to make "testimonies," not of our religious experience, for excepting in rare cases of early conversion we were not supposed to have "experienced" religion, but of our childish aspirations toward that state of Grace. Before or after this meeting, depending upon the season, we often went on our family drive. If that entertainment for some reason or other were lacking, we walked, occasionally with reliable friends of our own age. The favourite place of these Sunday rambles was the cemetery. Whether the day had actually engendered within us a kind of pensive melan-

choly which was satisfied by such a retreat, I do not know. Perhaps
the beautiful location of the spot above the bay with the Mount
Desert hills tumbling to the southward had quite as much to do with
our choice. But that we chose to walk there often I have undeniable
proof in that the dead of my native village, after many years' absence,
are more familiar to me than are the living!

On rainy or snowy Sundays there was always the Bible game, the
answer to every green card of which by the time I was thirteen I knew
by heart. There was also the spelling match designed especially for
Sabbath enjoyment. My mother occasionally on stormy Sundays
made candy for us while my father took an afternoon nap. More
frequently she popped corn, allowing us our share in this delightful
operation, so that when my father returned to Creasy or the *Iliad* by
the library table he might find a yellow bowl of well-salted puffed
kernels at his elbow. In the evening as we grew older we might attend
the seven o'clock prayer meeting with my grandmother, although this
finish to the day was never insisted upon by our parents.

But the one unalterable rule of the household was that we were to
do no manner of week-day work other than that absolutely necessary. My mother could not have brought herself to touch her great
sewing-basket even to sew on buttons or to mend a sudden rip.
Clothes were carefully inspected on Saturday to forestall any such
trying emergencies. Indeed, there seemed to exist in those days an
especial Nemesis which brooded over the performance of any sort of
handiwork on Sunday. Perhaps an incident which occurred when I
was twelve and which made a lasting impression upon me will serve
as an adequate illustration of this sinister viewpoint.

The measles, rampant in the village, smote at once all of us children, then numbering five. It being winter time, the question of caring
for us in rooms decently warm for sickness engaged my anxious
mother, who finally decided to move all her patients downstairs and
to convert the parlour and the library into a hospital. The nature of
the epidemic was severe, and the convalescence correspondingly
slow. What to do with five fractious children, all peeling and itching
at the same time, constituted a major problem. We could not read,
and even although my mother could set aside household cares long
enough to read to us, it was not easy to entertain all by means of the
same book. We were forbidden to get out of bed because of drafts or
to keep our arms sufficiently from under our bed-clothes to cut paper-
dolls or to play games. In the midst of these manifold perplexities my
father returned on Saturday from some days at holding court in the

county seat, bearing with him my mother's salvation in the shape of five knitting-machines and a quantity of yarns in safe and soothing colours.

To all middle-aged readers of these pages such knitting-machines will bring familiar remembrance. They were small circular objects, a little more than an inch in height and an inch and a half in diameter, painted blue, red, or green. A round hole in the centre was surrounded at equal intervals by curved steel uprights like imbedded wire hairpins. Two strands of yarn were wound about these, and the knitting began by means of a hairpin, the lower strand being lifted over the higher to the inside edge of the uprights. In due course of time there formed within the hole and was drawn below it a small circular tubing of yarn, which after much knitting might form horse reins or a cord for one's mittens. The use of these machines was very popular in my childhood, although in late years I have hunted for them in vain.

When my father entered our well-populated sick rooms on that late Saturday afternoon and displayed his timely gifts, we were jubilant. Here at last was something to do. Propped on pillows and still extremely well covered, we could, with safety, ply our knitting and thus occupy many tedious hours. My mother also was visibly relieved. Busy hands could not scratch, and busy minds would not be so likely to engender the desire to scratch and to merit thereby the necessary reproofs.

But even with pleasure so near at hand anxiety seized us all. With the lamps already lighted, knitting that evening was out of the question. Could knitting-machines be used with safety and decorum on the Lord's Day? Simultaneously, the question sprang to the lips of all of us. My father, often inadvertent in his replies and quick decisions, answered immediately in the affirmative in spite of the obvious hesitation of my mother. Alas! He was forced to eat his words! My mother might, in view of the fortnight she had endured, have been won over to his point of view; in fact, she was visibly yielding when my grandmother appeared upon the scene.

Now my grandmother was, as has been said, an eclectic in religious matters. Her theology, if, indeed, she possessed anything so erudite, neither deterred nor frightened, neither solaced nor confirmed her. But even in her delightful and volatile mind there existed certain deeply-rooted convictions, just as in her soul there burned with a steady glow certain invincible aspirations, fed daily by the inexhaustible fuel of custom, tradition and practice. Knitting on Sunday, even as a prescription against ill-health and peevish dispositions, had never for one moment been condoned within the precincts of her home and she was morally and emotionally unable to sanction it.

The five knitting-machines stood in a row on the library mantel all through an interminable Sunday. That much she was willing to allow. Credit should also be given for her generous attempts to amuse us. She read for hours, and, after we tired of books, told us innumerable sea stories, rehearsing the familiar ones with expert embroidering and from her abundant and rampant imagination inventing new ones, which doubtless had small basis in literal truth. And on Monday she was ardent in her promotion of our knitting, winding the skeins of yarn into balls for us after she had placed each on the back of an appropriate chair.

It is difficult, indeed, today when tenseness of thought and of action has almost annihilated intensity of conviction, to find in my grandmother's unequivocal stand anything except amusement. In Mr. Samuel Eliot Morison's satisfying book, *Builders of the Bay Colony,* he praises the Puritans not for the nature of their religious beliefs and principles, but for the ruthless fervour with which they held to them. Perhaps, indeed, my zealous, fruitless search for ten cent knitting-machines as gifts to my nephews and nieces can be easily explained. Surely in these days of electric trains and aeronautic inventions of every sort most children would scorn so sedative a pleasure as knitting even on their emancipated Sundays. Is not, therefore, the reason for my continued quest only that I may rediscover from my whimsical and humorous contemplation of such a symbol something of the moral force behind my grandmother's ultimatum in the year 1898?

LURA BEAM
1887–1978

Lura Beam, a sea captain's daughter, was born and raised in Marsh-field, near Machias, Maine. She went on to Barnard College, in New York City, and to the University of California at Berkeley, preparing for a career as an educator and social reformer. She taught black children in the South in the early years of this century and later wrote a book about her experiences, *He Called Them by the Lightning*.

In 1953 Beam returned to Marshfield, which she described as "a cold country; not always in bloom, yet to a child the looks of life were endless flowers." She set about the business of recording life in this village of 227 residents during the period from 1894 to 1904. As she recalled it:

> I lived in this town until I was twelve years old, and I was related to one household in every three. . . . The hamlet impressed me in child-hood as a place of wonder and beauty. It held all the world of pity, terror, love, faith, and fate. The adults appeared strange, good, dig-nified, beautiful, marvelous. Perhaps the neighborhood was not with-out examples of evil, but that a child never knew of them was a happy way of starting life.

Lura Beam acknowledges her indebtedness to Sarah Orne Jewett, whose *Country of the Pointed Firs* she read while in high school. *A Maine Hamlet,* an observant and detailed account of her Marshfield days, is her own, however, full of information about the culture and daily life of this small town written in a straightforward, unsentimen-tal prose. This chapter describes her grandparents' lives and, by inference, the wonderful combination of spare living and simple pleasures, sternness and love, that could be found in the towns of Maine in those days. Lura Beam was the village scribe in the best sense of the word.

Man and Woman

The land was a passion, magical in its influence upon human life. It produced people; nothing else at all, except trees and flowers and vegetable harvests. Life ran back and forth, land into people and people back into land, until both were the same.

The two with whom the hamlet's story begins were truly of the land's forming: their origins, upbringing, education, occupations, and course of life were its gifts.

On summer evenings at twilight, I used to sit at the window in Grandma's sitting-room, between Grandma and Grandpa. She rested in a black Boston rocker stenciled on the back with a fruit pattern in green and gold. A little round table beside her held her Bible, a kerosene lamp, her spectacle case, and Dr. Talmadge's sermon from the last Bangor Sunday newspaper.

Grandpa sat a little further back, just looking and talking about new peas and marsh hay to Grandma. He never smoked or drank, and it was only on winter evenings that he read *The Old Farmer's Almanac* or *The Union*. Both of them sat still, with intervals of silence. They had been up since five o'clock in the morning and had been on their feet all day. The smell of rose petals drying in spices for the winter rose jars filled the drowsy room.

I looked out of the window. The big front dooryard still had white roses. The mown fields where the crows walked dropped over the hill to the marshes where Middle River wound through the valley. Beyond, the roof tops of the town and the white spire of the Congregational Church showed among the trees and, to the east, the broad full darkness of the Machias River. Already the pointed tree tops on the horizon seemed black.

Inside the quiet room the rocking-chairs, the table with a red cover, the sofa, and the Franklin stove had been in the same places a long time. Grandma had made the rag carpet, the drawn rugs, and the chair cushions in log cabin design. She had collected the books in the hanging bookcase, the seashells, the picture of Adam and Eve standing by the Tree of Life, and the illuminated copy of the Lord's Prayer that hung over the mantel. Grandpa had built the fireplace cupboard where I kept my Noah's Ark, with the elephant, lion, tiger, giraffe and all the rest down to the hen and rooster, that had been my mother's when she was a little girl.

My grandparents were then about sixty-eight years old. Both represented well the pioneer Englishmen who had settled the Maine area, laid out the town, fought the Revolution, made the roads, suffered the Civil War, built the church, and filled the schoolhouse with children. They now seem to me to have been stubbornly British in character and temperament, like figures out of Thomas Hardy. They were the eighth generation from the first English ancestor who came to Massachusetts, and the fourth from the first settled in this Maine spot. They still lived on the original land grant given the settlement by the English Crown. His Revolutionary ancestors were buried five doors away, and hers in a neighboring hamlet.

They had the taste of this past in their mouths. They lived by the weather, by whatever came, and by what they could do with the whole body. They spanned the period 1828–1914, the last couple in the family to touch this rural American life in its undiluted form. All their children migrated and became urban. All their daughters would shiver when riding along little wooded roads, and sigh reflectively, "I hate the country."

The remarkable quality about Grandfather was his ability to adapt his occupation to local changes, an ability which he continued to have to extreme old age. His family was land-rich in lumber, and they had taught him their ways of abundance. When the lumber period ended and they became poor, he was the only one of nine children who continued in the same environment. This staying at home was made possible only by four major occupational shifts.

Grandfather was apprenticed as a young man to his father who was a lumber operator. He knew the great woods when the thick pines rose high and when men lived all winter in the lumber camps in the snow. He worked as a lumberjack on the Mopang and the Plantations and as a log-driver on the rivers. He could break a log jam. After the lumber cycle, he worked for years as a shipyard carpenter, helping build vessels. At off times, he built an ell on his farmhouse, a large barn, sheds and poultry houses, sleds and hayracks. The slopes

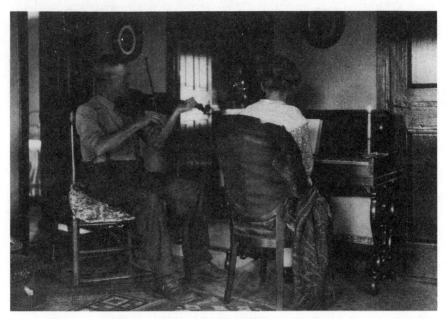

"Parlor Music (Melodeon and Fiddle)"

of his buildings were slow and graceful. Somewhere in him he had absorbed the Colonial builder's mastery of line and mass. After a while, the shipyard closed down permanently. Grandfather went to work in the town sawmill, and was steadily employed because he could do all five types of sawing operations. He had to drive two and a half miles to the mill, so he used to get up at half-past three in the morning. Three cows were fed, milked, and taken to the pasture half a mile away. Then he harnessed the gray mare Dolly and left, to be in time for the mill whistle at half-past six. In the afternoon, the process was reversed: drive home, go to the pasture for the cows, feed and milk them, come to supper about sunset, shut up the hens, and go to bed at eight.

Once, as a treat, I got up at four o'clock and ate breakfast with Grandpa by lamplight. Oatmeal with heavy cream, fried ham and eggs, fried potatoes, hot biscuits, and strawberry jam "from the upper field" were on the table, and his dinner-pail was ready. No one ever remarked that this was hard work for a man of sixty-five, but it must have been the reason why he later took to market gardening only, and got up at a Christian hour like five o'clock.

Grandfather hardly knew the word, but in old age he was a specialist. He went in for raising choice varieties of the very earliest farm produce — peas, potatoes, beans, corn, cucumbers, squash, berries and fruit. This was partly pride — he used to get prizes at the County Fair — in being the man who could best outguess the bugs and the weather. The rest of it was pleasure in making things grow. Once a week he carried a load of fresh fruit and vegetables, eggs and butter, to his customers in the town. Never to the general store; that would have been demeaning. He had to be enough in advance of the market to bring extra prices from selected families.

As my grandparents did it, market gardening was an artistic and scientific occupation. They got great satisfaction out of doing everything as well as they knew how. After Christmas they studied the catalogues and debated amiably about how much land should go into Early Rose potatoes, and where they should plant the corn. They were full of names and qualities of the various seeds, crop rotation, and the year's experiment with something new. *The Old Farmer's Almanac* and the moon were their tyrants. Root vegetables like potatoes and beets were planted two days before the full moon; peas, beans and other crops which bore their fruit above the ground, on the day of the new moon.

The preparations for market day were loving and guileless. Some of the finest berries and fruit were put on the bottom of every basket. Every measure was heaped on. Thirteen eggs made a dozen; leaves were laid around the strawberries; sprays heavy with blueberries were laid across the blueberry boxes; presents of fresh horseradish, currants, or an odd cucumber or cabbage were added. In the fall they gave everyone pumpkins for jack-o'-lanterns. Grandma packed these baskets and Grandpa looked them over. Then they looked at each other and he put her grocery list in his top inside pocket.

In winter the work routine was cutting wood. Grandpa cut on every fine day, enough to keep four stoves going, and cords and cords to sell. When I went with him we left early, wrapped in blankets. There were two sleds painted bright blue, usually hitched together like an automobile and trailer, but for smaller operations they were used separately. The wood road, only five or six feet wide between fir and hemlock, was so rocky it was passable with a team only in deep snow. When it opened into a clearing of tree stumps and woodpiles, circled with thick woods, I climbed down and began to play in the snow and make up games, while Grandpa cut trees all day long. When he cut birch for the fireplace, I peeled sheets of the birch bark to make canoes with, and to write letters on. At noon we sat by the fire and thawed out the frozen ham and biscuits, the doughnuts and apple pie, and heated the tea. Going home, we rode high on a load of logs the length of trees. The snow used to have a faint rosy radiance of light from the sunset sky.

Most of the work in Grandfather's life — lumbering, river driving, sawmill operations, carpentering, and haying — involved tools or machinery, or rushing bodies of water. He was a confident man. He never had either accident or injury.

When he was young, he used to conduct Singing School and Dancing School for the neighborhood at the schoolhouse. His copy of one of the songs, "The Mackerel Catchers," shows his thin, delicate handwriting, with curlicues at the tops of the capital letters. His daughters had opened dances with him and the family albums still have invitations to the New Year's Eve dances of the 1870's:

"— and Lady. Supper will be served at midnight."

He and Grandma went to dances until they were in their fifties.

When Grandpa was young and wore sideburns he was handsome; but better than handsome, he was a fine piece of structure, a man as good as a tree. In the first daguerreotypes he looked as if he could never be quenched. When he was an old gentleman he looked settled, but as if he had had possibilities, a bit like pictures of Thomas Carlyle. In winter when he drove his sleigh over the snow, he wore a sealskin cap and a very heavy overcoat. A buffalo-fur robe lined with red flannel was tucked around him. A long, knitted scarf shaded from rose to garnet, a piece of Grandmother's knitting, flew out behind. He was fiercely fond of horses. Winter driving must have been one of his big moments.

Loving and watching and speculating about horses was Grandpa's only recreation apart from his family amusements. He had no small vices, no liquor, no tobacco, no coffee, no eating except at mealtime, no personal luxuries — he usually sat in a straight chair — no hurry, ill-temper, or indolence. His serious expletives were "By gorry," and "By Godfrey," and his remonstrance to a child walking the fence above his cherished peonies was only, "Take care, Dardie."

The order was all but perfect on Grandfather's farm. The fields lay between sound stone walls, the house was always painted, the fields fertilized in turn, the gardens cultivated and sprayed for pests. The fruit trees were pruned, the crops rotated, the buildings kept in sparkling repair. Hardly a blade of grass was allowed to grow askew in his big dooryard, and he swept the barn floor the last thing every evening. His barn was neat enough for people to live in; the cows in their stanchions, the horse in a box stall, the harnesses hanging on their hooks.

When it rained he would saw wood, or spend the whole day in one of the sheds, mending harness, milking-stools, whiffletrees, and hoes. He always left the swallows' nests under the barn eaves, and he knew to a day when they would come back in spring. On every winter night his last trip to the barn was with Cyrus the Great under his arm. Cyrus was the big black cat who slept in the haymow and watched the mouseholes.

Grandfather was married when he was twenty-one. He brought his bride to her new home on the evening of June 21, 1851. The bride had been born in a neighboring hamlet. Her mother had died when she was eleven and her father when she was thirteen, and she had been the housemother for the younger children. This meant that she did housework for a good seventy years. No one ever heard her say she was tired of it.

They rented half a house in the town at first, but soon moved to the country home they lived in always. It was in the hamlet on the ridge of a hill with a superb view in every direction. A gift from Grandfather's father, it was originally a two-room rectangle downstairs with three little upstairs bedrooms, but they had added the ell, the barn, and all the buildings. When I first knew it, they had been working over the house and grounds for thirty years. Their homestead had grown to be an expressive and restful home among trees and flowers. It had an almost colonial charm. The chimney was large, the doorlatches iron, the floorboards very wide, the window panes small. Many furnishings had been made by hand, and others after patterns of good cabinetmakers. The parlor had a gray carpet, hooked rugs in flower and geometric designs, walnut and haircloth furniture, lace curtains, an organ, marble topped tables, Victorian lamps, a mirror set between two windows, seagrasses in silvered glass vases, and always the smell of rose leaves in spices.

Upstairs, the bedrooms had low slanting ceilings, white walls, rag carpets, big white beds, and the smell of lavender and sweetgrass. The grandparents slept downstairs in a maple fourposter, and the bureau and chiffonier were of the 1850 period. The stoves were the heart of the house in winter time, and even the guest room had one.

The kitchen faced the rising sun. It was painted white, as all the rooms were, but the floor was colonial buff and so were the Windsor chairs. The kitchen had a sofa, very hard but covered with flowery chintz, and a clock with a cheerful face. The woodbox was as large as the closets under the stairs, the stove huge, and the iron teakettle, always hot, puffed lazily.

The pantry, a room now lost to modern houses, was as large as a present-day two-car garage, and it served both as a storehouse and a place where food was prepared. The flour barrel, the white sugar barrel, and the brown sugar firkin were closed off behind the door. Under the shelves, big gray stoneware jugs with blue designs, from the Bennington, Vermont, potteries, held molasses and vinegar. Wall cupboards held the dishes — blue Staffordshire, old goblets, and pressed glass preserve dishes for best, and heavy white ware for every day. Milk was kept in yellow earthenware dishes, on shelves used for milk alone. Thick cream that skimmed in yellowy folds stood in stoneware crocks waiting for the weekly churning. In summer, everything to do with milk was moved downstairs to the cellar.

The woodshed beyond the kitchen was a splendid part of the house; it had all the evidences of country plenty. Enough wood to fill today's large living-rooms was stored to the ceiling; on the floor were piles of kindling. In barrels and chests were meal, corn, oats, fine-feed, and prepared foods for animals and poultry; on shelves, kerosene and tools. In summer the washing was done in the woodshed. In winter, sausages, head cheese, smoked hams, and dried herbs hung from the ceiling. All the root vegetables had their bins in the cellar. Over the woodshed was a child's paradise called "the Open Chamber." Dried camomile, tansy, pennyroyal, and mullein hung along the pillars, and the floor looked like a Curiosity Shop. Articles were stored in the order they had stopped being useful, so that the cradles and baby carriages were under the eaves and the carpetbags at the head of the stairs.

An old house in those days had delicious smells that have disappeared now, a mingling of wood fires, herbs, food and the smell of the wood itself. This house was built between 1825 and 1850; it was two miles from the log cabin that had been built for Grandfather's ancestor in 1763.

Around the dooryard, roses and old lilacs ranged; a bleeding-heart plant had grown as big as a barrel; a bush of lad's-love was feathery green, the flower beds ran the length of the house and had sweet-william, phlox, petunias, pinks, pansies, and ragged-ladies. Grandma could never resist a flower and fruit salesman. She grew pears and plums as well as apples, and red, black, and white currants, gooseberries, strawberries, and rhubarb. Just on principle, she had a corner for growing seed, and was always fussing with seed plants of parsnips, carrots, and carroway. Grandma could remember when toma-toes were called "Love Apples" and thought to be poisonous.

The family love for animals and growing things was big enough to include the inanimate. The best stones and ledges in the pasture were named. The backyard had a boulder as big as a Packard, aloof and distinguished in pale gray and rosy granite. This boulder was prized as a landmark and was called "The Monument."

The tax on the homestead and farm in 1900 was $9.94. It tells a good deal that this farm and the tax were in Grandmother's name. She was a woman dominant without having to make any claims. Whenever she praised her husband's skill as a woodsman, she added softly, "but no judgment about horses."

Grandmother was remarkably versatile. She had only to look at an emergency or a problem to be able to find a way out. She could duplicate any piece of handicraft of the day after examining it. None of her daughters had these abilities. Her life demanded such qualities and theirs did not, so she left them her industry, but took her inventiveness with her.

Grandmother was the last woman of her line to find complete personal expression in her home and in her native environment. All her daughters had to take jobs outside the home before marriage and shift to urban life. She had only the ancient functions of women, and she never went more than fifteen miles from her birthplace.

Her husband's free gifts to the village were for recreation in the Singing and Dancing Schools. Hers were for illness, birth, and death. She used to be nurse in sickness, midwife in childbirth, and layer-out of the dead. Her next door neighbor had twelve children and she told me she had helped with the first eleven. When she went to sit up all night with the typhoid patient who lived a mile away, she carried a large white apron, a little black bag of home remedies, and perhaps a cake for the family. As a colonial settlement this place had had no doctor for twelve years. Women learned by experience to handle colds, croup, convulsions, measles, mumps, grippe, whooping-cough, and cuts and sprains, and the tradition lingered.

Grandma had an excellent knack with her hands. She made her own carpets, rugs, quilts, pillows, and counterpanes. She cut and made frocks for the neighborhood children, and she made Grandpa's blue flannel tailored shirts, his nightshirts, and his flowing black silk ties — all without a sewing machine. She knitted the winter stockings, socks, hoods, scarves, and mittens for seven. Her hooked rugs, usually three-and-a-half by five-and-a-half feet — orange, rose, red, and pale violet flowers with pale green leaves, conventionalized on white and edged with gray shading into black — were the product of her recreation. She baked all the bread, pies, and cake eaten by the family for nearly sixty years, smoked the hams, and made the jellies, jams, pickles, and mincemeat.

Grandma was always making preserves or raspberry shrub, or cutting up old tablecloths to make napkins or rolling newspapers into lamplighter spills to save matches. She liked to dye cloth; it amused her to get a good color. She made salves and perfumes. Her balm-of-Gilead buds, kept in an alcohol solution, were for sore places and lameness. Her little red flannel bags, stuffed with herbs, were heated half a dozen at a time, and used as one would now use an electric pad.

She was very fond of reading. While she rested in the afternoon, she used to re-read her *Pilgrim's Progress,* some of Dickens' novels, a few others like Susan Warner's *The Wide, Wide World,* and some sentimental English stories about dukes and duchesses. She had no notion of harm coming to a child through reading, and I read *East Lynne,* a nineteenth century tear-jerker, and *Robert Elsmere,* then supposed to be a "radical" book about religion, in her house. She never sang when I knew her, but when a snowstorm was coming, she would quote:

> The sun that brief December day
> Rose cheerless over hills of grey. . . .

Of all the past, Grandmother talked most about the Civil War. Four of her brothers and brothers-in-law and three of her nephews had been in it. She said it was she who did not want Grandfather to go, because she was so afraid of being left alone with the five children. They scraped up the three hundred dollars to pay a substitute, and he stayed home. She seemed still to feel, in the Nineties, the post-war hardships, when flour was forty dollars a barrel, and the children had no more than an orange and a home-made doll or top for Christmas.

Recreation in this hard-working life was a different need from ours, because the couple were working at something of their own choice, at their own pace, and often they were accountable only to themselves. They never had a vacation. Their tension and relaxation came out of the weather and the seasons. When the thermometer went below zero, and when spring brought the mud to the wagon-wheel hubs, then their daily rhythm would change.

In winter, they gave or went to large family parties at Thanksgiving and Christmas. In summer, they drove out to have Sunday dinner with relatives, with me sitting on a hassock on the floor between them. Driving to the August Camp Meeting and the September Fair, I listened to long conversations about the people in every house we passed. They knew the grandparents of every couple, just whom everyone had married, and what the old ones died of. From the looks of a garden they could name the seed used in the planting.

Perhaps food had more of an aura than it has now. While eating, they used to recount the whole progress of the food they had raised from the seed to the table. Occasionally during every winter, a dish of Indian corn boiled in milk, or cornmeal mush served with cream was cooked. This was food associated with their childhood. The grandparents eating it would talk about their brothers and sisters, when they left for Minnesota and California, and how this one had liked mush, and another only venison. Except in summer, there was no fresh fruit except apples, but stewed fruit of many kinds belonged with every meal. There was always hot bread, and much more sugar, starch, and fat than are eaten now; more condiments, including some hot stuff called pepper-sauce; never salads; more eggs — a larger volume of food altogether. Only children drank water; tea was the beverage. In the Civil War, the family could not afford coffee and turned to tea; gradually they lost the taste for anything else. In those days, farm people hated milk. Cows were tyrants; cows, death, and taxes conquered all — but it was not necessary to drink them from a glass.

When I knew them, my grandparents never talked about religion, but both of them were members of the Congregational Church from their youth, and they attended it all their days. Grandmother would habitually and meditatively read her Bible. They both talked often and tenderly about the son they had lost at sixteen. In the bookcase there was an old book, *Bear Hunters,* which was marked half-way through, "Harley's last page." Grandfather used to quote the verse they had engraved on his tombstone. The letters cut into the marble in the engraver's odd spacing are still legible:

> For we know that if our
> earthly house of this
> tabernacle were dissolved
> We have a building of God
> an house not made with hands
> eternal in the heavens.

The grandparents used to laugh when they heard talk of wedding presents. No one gave them a wedding present; not even any food to

take to their new home. On that June morning, for their first breakfast, Grandmother made hot biscuits, opened a jar of cranberry sauce
she had brought from home, and they washed the food down with
hot tea. This was a puckery beginning, but both of them could digest
nails all their lives.

They were married for fifty-nine years, and were never separated
for a night, except when he was working in lumber camps, but she
had no engagement or wedding ring. After they had been married so
long that all their children were gone, Grandpa, on their wedding
anniversary, gave her a broad, heavily chased gold ring, and they
called it their "engagement" ring. About the same time he had made
up from gold nuggets a mining brother had sent home from Alaska,
a heavy gold circle, and this was the "wedding" ring. The rings came
after she had begun to look a little like Queen Victoria, always in
black with a bunch of violets nodding in her black bonnet.

Because my father was a sea captain away from home for almost
years at a time, the grandparents offered my first laboratory observation of marriage. I understood very early that these two were myste-
riously one. I also absorbed from the air the idea that there was some
balance of function in marriage. For instance, gossip used to say that
in a cold country, you could understand the balance of a marriage if
you knew which of a couple got up to start the kitchen fire in January.
We knew that Grandpa always got up first, and that this was the way.
We accepted it so definitely that we looked down on various respectable old gentlemen we saw at church, because they were known to
advise and to operate on the other theory. We also looked down on
husbands who called their wives "the Missus" or "my old woman"
because Grandpa always called Grandma "Mother" or "Susan."

They made all their garden plans together with evident enjoyment.
She prepared the seeds for his planting and he tended all her special-
ties in a little garden near the strawberry bed. But Grandmother never
worked in the garden except to pick fruit or vegetables for dinner,
and if she helped with the haying, it meant that rain was threatening.

My parents seemed to have but one purse, and they acted like one
person about it. It was a surprise to find that the grandparents had
two. Each of them had a small black leather purse that opened with a
snap. They were kept in the top bureau drawers in a house that was
never locked except when they went to town. But the bureau drawers
were separate, and so were the purses. Grandma had all the "butter
and eggs money." She used it to buy clothes, gifts, books, medicines
and flowers.

Since the grandparents were usually so near to perfection, I remember it the more when they put the apple of knowledge into my hands. On a hot day in August, Grandfather, pitching hay five feet above his head into the hayloft, lost his temper and struck the horse. Grandmother, above him in the loft, pitching hay above her head into the rear, poured out her thoughts about the abuse of animals. That evening they did not speak at the supper table. He passed her his teacup without saying anything, and she filled it and passed it back, also without saying anything. This made me shake; I heard thoughts louder than thunder. I was already nine years old. I kept away from the adults and puzzled alone about this schism. If Grandmother and Grandfather could be divided, nothing in the world was as I had supposed. I could almost have understood it better if the rift had gone on, but in a few days everything was as before. It took a long time to realize that people come out of their black moments.

They had five children and their theory was that the children should stay at home and go to school, or have an apprenticeship as long as possible, and at twenty-one leave for the city. Of the four who lived to maturity, two walked five miles a day in the 1870's to go to high school, crossing the river on ice in the winter. One girl became a teacher, two went to the Lawrence textile mills, one as a weaver and one as a spinner; the boy learned carpentry and went West. Later, all of them "married well," migrated to New York, Minnesota and California, and lived to share the roses, vacations, new suburban homes, the furs and matinées, and the trips abroad of the twentieth century's higher level of living. The childless couple willed $15,000 to the State University for Student Loans. The daughters carried on the parents' longevity and lived to eighty-six, eighty-eight, and ninety-nine years.

My grandparents were so balanced and calm in their sixties that I always wished I could have known them when they were young and dancing. The amount of work they did was enough to make any one pause. When I heard them quote the saying, "Root, hog, or die," I always supposed they had made it up. They must have begun house-keeping with candles, for we have their candlesticks and candle snuffers. They had a well only for a short time, until it caved in. After that, Grandpa brought all the water for cooking and drinking from a spring, up a grievously long hill. During the winter he had to carry enough for the cattle, since they never went out in the snow, and at intervals for the horse, too. Grandma did all her washing without a wringer, using water from the rain-barrel.

Grandfather had no farm machinery beyond a plow and a horse-rake, but using the latter he exchanged work with some farmers who owned a mowing machine. Neither of them ever had any paid help, except a few days' labor in haying time. They had come to terms with the monotonous repetition of much manual labor. When he dropped the seed corn into the hill Grandfather used to say:

> One for the blackbird,
> One for the crow,
> One for the cut-worm
> And two to grow.

The wife still did the washing and made the sausage, and the husband still swung the scythe in summer and the axe in winter, until they were past eighty. In old age they simply did less.

They had magnificent health, a hardiness beyond colds and indispositions. The only time I ever knew a doctor to come to the house in the seventeen years I lived with or near them, was when Grandma dislocated her shoulder while catching a hen. She used to say she had to "favor" her rheumatism, but she had only one illness in her long life. Grandfather had no illness until his quiet end from arteriosclerosis.

When Grandmother died, at eighty-two, Grandfather asserted himself violently against his daughters and said, "I shall pay no attention at all to you girls. I will not have Mother buried in the country. She shall be in the town, where the graves have perpetual care." So she was buried there, and he put up a double stone, of gray-white marble, ready for himself. The farm was sold for $1,150 and the furnishings for $100, because all of the children lived too far away to want anything. The widower's share, by the time a mortgage had been paid to the eldest daughter, was $174.64.

Grandfather always seemed lost after Grandmother's death. She had been his interpretation of life, and as soon as she was gone, there was pain he could never understand. In Grandmother's closet for her best clothes, her daughters found a little hoard of money, mostly in silver, about three hundred dollars. He said, "I never knew about this. Why, Mother knew every penny I ever had, and our bank account was in both our names." His children thought she had been saving for illness or for a surprise, but he always grieved because she had kept a secret from him.

He began a career of long visits to his children. All he really thought about New York was that it was too high. He could hardly bear to look out of an eighth story window. Every time he went downtown, he came back saying, "In that great street, not a soul to speak to, I never can stand it." After he had returned to Maine, he was taken up with his first great-grandchild. When he was eighty-four and she was three, he went shopping and bought a tiny gold locket and chain for her, saying, "I want she should remember me." He had never owned a watch until the last years. He came home from work all his life by the sun.

What I remember first about my grandparents is that they always wanted a child around. I passed from one lap to the other and barely knew I was changing. When I was four, while Grandma was trimming the Christmas tree, Grandpa was holding me and playing Cat's Cradle until the tree was ready. My parents were young enough to protect themselves; they could snap, "Run away and play, and don't bother me!" The grandparents never gave in. They were superhuman.

Walking with Grandpa in the woods one day, we came across a lake with many white waterlilies. He said, "Do you want them? I doubt if I could swim in that, it would be muddy; but if you do want them, I can knock together a raft and we can float there."

Grandma paid for my first painting lessons, and, after I had water colors and wanted oils, she gave me a big box of them on my eleventh birthday, at a time when it was a nuisance to order them from Boston. When I saw the paints, I felt myself growing tall and I said, "Now I have everything I want in the world." She said, "It is the first time I ever was able to satisfy anyone's last desire."

When I was away at school, the grandparents together sent me five dollars on my birthday, with the instruction, "Spend it all at once on something you want." This must have been a freedom in spending they had wanted, but never quite dared to take. They had no romanticism at all except a terrible faith in education. Once, when I found Grandmother lying on the sofa, looking out of the window, I asked, "What are you thinking?" She said, "I laid myself down here to think about how we would transplant the peonies, but I got to thinking about the stars. I was wishing I'd had the chance to learn astronomy and to know more about the wonders of the world."

They left their grandchildren the great gift of experience in human goodness and stability. When their eight-year-old great-great-grandchild first heard bits of their story, she said, "Oh, I want to know them. Are they really dead?"

EDWIN ARLINGTON ROBINSON
1869–1935

Maine's first poet of the modern age — some would say the nation's first — was Edwin Arlington Robinson, who was born in the small village of Head Tide. His father's lumber business soon moved the family to nearby Gardiner, which became the young writer's Tilbury Town, the theater of his first and many later poems. The family's fortunes became unstable, especially after the oldest son, Herman, lost most of his father's money speculating in midwestern lands. Another older son, Dean, got a medical education and became a country doctor but became addicted to morphine. At twenty-two, Edwin was lucky to begin at Harvard before the money ran out, allowing him only two years of college. But those years made the difference. They opened him to the great world of literature, and he learned that the poetry he had begun to write in Gardiner was good enough to appear in the *Harvard Advocate*. For the next four years he stayed in Gardiner with no clearer designs on the future than to write more poetry. Near the end of his life he said of his personal history, "I could never do anything but write poetry."

After three years at home he published privately a collection of poems, *The Torrent and the Night Before,* and a year later a second book — including most of the poems in the first — *The Children of the Night*. Both books went unnoticed, which the defiant young man had predicted in the first book's dedication: "To any man, woman or critic who will cut the edges of it — I have done the top." But the literary world was wrong not to notice. The poet had more to demonstrate than defiance. He had produced a new kind of straightforward, dramatic poetry in a style that wouldn't be seen in the works of other poets for another fifteen years; his was a "middle style" that "always keeps prose in view," as the best of his modern critics, Louis

O. Coxe, puts it. And he had found a subject that he once called "the slow tragedy of haunted men." In these first two books are included the portrait poems "Richard Cory," "Aaron Stark," "Cliff Klingen-hagen," "The Clerks," and "Reuben Bright," which have been the common coin of American poetry anthologies ever since.

These reports of human souls in travail have been traced by some readers to the declining fortunes of the people left behind in rural, small-town Maine. But it is the human condition, not social conditions, that spins these plots in Tilbury Town and elsewhere. Robinson belongs among the New England poets of introspection in the line of descent from Nathaniel Hawthorne and Emily Dickinson. Certainly Robinson had a sharp eye for the lonely and separated, but he included among his despairing subjects those compassionate observers who see too much and are anguished by the fate of their brothers and sisters. So tightly woven are some of the portrait studies that Robinson's readers need to puzzle them out. But the difficulties presented by the poet's seeming refusal to suggest a solution to a character's quandary must be read as part of the dilemma. The mystery of the world we must live in is the basis of the tragedy. The closest Robinson ever came to a hopeful statement of the matter was this:

> I've always told you it was a hell of a place
> That's why it must mean something.

Robinson's reputation grew slowly. In his fifties, his long narrative poems based on the Arthurian legends made him popular at last and brought him three Pulitzer prizes. But it is his short poems — some of them tough-minded declarative statements, others quiet meditations on small-town Maine people — that are still read and are most closely associated with Robinson's genius.

Mr. Flood's Party

Old Eben Flood, climbing alone one night
Over the hill between the town below
And the forsaken upland hermitage
That held as much as he should ever know
On earth again of home, paused warily.
The road was his without a native near;
And Eben, having leisure, said aloud,
For no man else in Tilbury Town to hear:

"Well, Mr. Flood, we have the harvest moon
Again, and we may not have many more;
The bird is on the wing, the poet says,
And you and I have said it here before.
Drink to the bird." He raised up to the light
The jug that he had gone so far to fill,
And answered huskily: "Well, Mr. Flood,
Since you propose it, I believe I will."

Alone, as if enduring to the end
A valiant armor of scarred hopes outworn,
He stood there in the middle of the road
Like Roland's ghost winding a silent horn.
Below him, in the town among the trees,
Where friends of other days had honored him,
A phantom salutation of the dead
Rang thinly till old Eben's eyes were dim.

Then, as a mother lays her sleeping child
Down tenderly, fearing it may awake,

He set the jug down slowly at his feet
With trembling care, knowing that most things break;
And only when assured that on firm earth
It stood, as the uncertain lives of men
Assuredly did not, he paced away,
And with his hand extended paused again:

"Well, Mr. Flood, we have not met like this
In a long time; and many a change has come
To both of us, I fear, since last it was
We had a drop together. Welcome home!"
Convivially returning with himself,
Again he raised the jug up to the light;
And with an acquiescent quaver said:
"Well, Mr. Flood, if you insist, I might."

"Only a very little, Mr. Flood —
For auld lang syne. No more, sir; that will do."
So, for the time, apparently it did,
And Eben evidently thought so too;
For soon amid the silvery loneliness
Of night he lifted up his voice and sang,
Secure, with only two moons listening,
Until the whole harmonious landscape rang —

"For auld lang syne." The weary throat gave out;
The last word wavered, and the song was done.
He raised again the jug regretfully,
And shook his head, and was again alone.
There was not much that was ahead of him,
And there was nothing in the town below —
Where strangers would have shut the many doors
That many friends had opened long ago.

The Clerks

I did not think that I should find them there
When I came back again; but there they stood,
As in the days they dreamed of when young blood
Was in their cheeks and women called them fair.
Be sure, they met me with an ancient air, —
And yes, there was a shop-worn brotherhood
About them; but the men were just as good,
And just as human as they ever were.

And you that ache so much to be sublime,
And you that feed yourselves with your descent,
What comes of all your visions and your fears?
Poets and kings are but the clerks of Time,
Tiering the same dull webs of discontent,
Clipping the same sad alnage of the years.

Cliff Klingenhagen

Cliff Klingenhagen had me in to dine
With him one day; and after soup and meat,
And all the other things there were to eat,
Cliff took two glasses and filled one with wine
And one with wormwood. Then, without a sign
For me to choose at all, he took the draught

Of bitterness himself, and lightly quaffed
It off, and said the other one was mine.

And when I asked him what the deuce he meant
By doing that, he only looked at me
And smiled, and said it was a way of his.
And though I know the fellow, I have spent
Long time a-wondering when I shall be
As happy as Cliff Klingenhagen is.

New England

Here where the wind is always north-north-east
And children learn to walk on frozen toes,
Wonder begets an envy of all those
Who boil elsewhere with such a lyric yeast
Of love that you will hear them at a feast
Where demons would appeal for some repose,
Still clamoring where the chalice overflows
And crying wildest who have drunk the least.

Passion is here a soilure of the wits,
We're told, and Love a cross for them to bear;
Joy shivers on the corner where she knits
And Conscience always has the rocking chair,
Cheerful as when she tortured into fits
The first cat that was ever killed by Care.

ROBERT P. TRISTRAM COFFIN
1892–1955

Ice was a natural product of the cold Maine winters. The big rivers — the Kennebec, Penobscot, and Sheepscot — froze early and stayed that way. The ice was there for the taking, and in 1824 the first shipment was cut and loaded onto a schooner bound for Baltimore — at a price of $700. By the middle of the century, great icehouses were being built along the riverbanks to store the cakes of ice, which was being shipped to Atlantic ports as far south as the West Indies. Dorothea Balano, in *The Log of a Skipper's Wife,* tells of sailing for Rio de Janeiro with "the usual Christmas cargo . . . ice, packed in sawdust, and topped off with barrels of apples."

Large companies were attracted to investing, and the business reached its heyday in the winter of 1879–1880, when nearly 1.5 million tons of ice were shipped out of Maine ports. In subsequent years, the ice companies formed a trust and by raising and fixing prices created resentment among customers. Hudson River ice proved easier and cheaper to harvest, and by the turn of the century the inevitable artificial production of ice had brought an end to ice cutting in Maine.

Robert P. Tristram Coffin was an unabashed admirer of his native state and an exuberant chronicler of its history and people. Born in Brunswick and raised on a saltwater farm in nearby Pennellville, he graduated from Bowdoin College, was a Rhodes Scholar at Oxford, taught briefly at Wells College, and then returned to Brunswick to teach at Bowdoin until his death.

Coffin wrote voluminously: essays, novels, biographies, histories, and poetry. *Strange Holiness,* a book of poetry, won a Pulitzer Prize in 1935. His piece on the ice industry depicts the nature and hazards of this short-lived enterprise and of a boy's wonder at the drama and the excitement of it all.

Robert P. Tristram Coffin

The Harvest of Diamonds

Today is a "diamond-dust day," as Maine people describe it, such a day as only middle Winter brings. There is terrific sunshine. There is terrific wind. Every snowdrift smokes at its edge with powdered diamonds that blind the eyes.

Such a day, when I was a boy many years ago, would have seen one of Maine's best harvests in full swing. It was a harvest that brought millions of dollars into thousands of homes. It was a harvest that took nothing out of the soil, nothing out of the state. Yet it was a heavy crop and weighted down a thousand schooners sailing the two greatest oceans, rounding Cape Horn and Good Hope.

It was ice. The harvest that electricity has almost erased from the world.

On such a Winter day as this, years ago, every road and railroad track leading to the Kennebec River would have been black with men, walking. They walked down from the upper part of the state, in from New Hampshire, up from Massachusetts. They walked railroad tracks because the railroads would not let them ride. For every man-jack of them was shod with steel, and the calks on his shoes would have cut the train floors to pieces. Those shoes were life to the wearers; men never stepped out of them all the weeks they worked. Those shoes cut the railroad ties to sawdust. The ends of all the sleepers, outside the rails, were worn down to the gravel when the ice season was over. Men's feet had worn the railroad out!

All Maine farmers, with their fields under snow and nothing to be gathered there, became, for five or six weeks, gatherers of squared diamonds cut out of the sparkling Kennebec and shipped across the continent and to the corners of the world to keep food and people cool in Summer.

The ice companies had to build huge sheds to house these harvesters at night, and furnish each man with a blanket. One man was told off to keep the single stove going. The other men lay down in wind-rows in their calked boots. They were packed in like sardines on the floor, and they had to turn over on the other side all at the same time. "Break joints!" was the cry, and the men rolled over in unison. The workers slept with their picks, too. They had brought them from home; they knew their potentialities and powers by heart. They had to, for their lives depended on the steel points they had sharpened. A dull point might mean a cold grave thirty feet deep. An ice cake handled wrong could break a man's back.

After a gigantic breakfast of meal gruel in the eating places of Gardiner, Richmond, or Bowdoinham, the men went out on the fields on the river that had been staked off with brush. There scrapers were dragging off the night's snow and frost or windscuff. Behind them came the ice markers, plows drawn by one horse, which lined off the field into a checkerboard of twenty-two-inch squares. Back of these the two-horse groovers came, one after the other, with teeth gradu-ated at a slant to cut a progressive cut, five inches, seven inches, ten, twelve, inches deep. These plows of the water were all made by the same firm: first *Gifford and Wood,* later *Wood and Sons.*

It was a great sight for a boy to see, the fine horses coming with plumes at each nostril, the plows ripping through the ice behind with sparks of ice flying, the brawny men holding the groovers' handles with their gates-ajar moustaches fringed with frosty breath. Not many such sights in the world this side of Homer!

So the fields were made ready, and the cakes took final form, standard the world over, twenty-two by forty-four inches, for the groovers took only every other mark in the cross-hatching the mark-ers had made when they grooved the field lengthwise. The cakes were ready now to be broken apart, each still dry and joined to all the others by the three inches of ice left unflawed at the bottom of the field and still capable of holding up all the ice-king's horses and all the ice-king's men. The river from Augusta to Bath was dotted with smoking horses and smoking men.

Now two husky sawyers cut a canal, only a bit wider than the lengths of the rectangles of ice, from the field to the icehouse on the bank where a steam engine worked an endless chain with oak lugs a dozen feet apart. The last diamond-cutting began. The breakers of diamonds, armed like Neptune with their three-pronged "busting-bar," started taking the field apart. The calkers went ahead of them and closed up the seams of the cakes remaining as each row of cakes

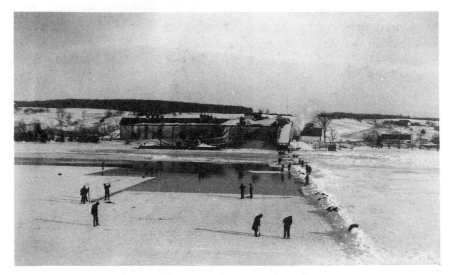

Ice harvest on the Kennebec, 1888

was broken free. For if the water got into the cuts, they would heal up, and all the grooving would have to be done over. The breakers walked along, striking here and there with their bars, the ice sighed, and long rows of diamonds broke off, submerged, and rose to the top of the water. Men with picks nosed these lines of squared jewels up the canal and floated them on to the house. At the foot of the run, two giants took turns "busting" the cakes apart. The engine chugged, the lugs caught the cakes, the cakes shot shining up in a long slant on the sky to the high door of the icehouse.

Some of these icehouses were larger than the chateaux of France. Six hundred feet long, some of them. With double pine walls upholstered with sawdust between. The runs could be extended upward as the houses filled towards their eaves. As each cake of ice plunged up into the house, it shot through a planer, gauged to cut all cakes to that particular day's thickness, so the tiers would be uniformly thick. The cakes leapt out of the planer upon the fan-tail, full of great momentum still. Here was the hot spot most boys loved to stand at. Here was the most motion, most speed and danger. The blue diamonds came in like things wicked and alive, they struck the oak fantail, and the switchers caught them delicately on their pikes, shunted them this way and that, with the speed of light, and let them roar on along the proper tracks that led to the tiers. The diamonds ran on their own power still till they reached the exact spot where the stowers wanted them to lie. They had to be humored in handling, for, in spite of their heft, they were fragile as glass and easily broken. The vast cathedral of ice was full of thunder as the ice cakes came running, full of the thunder of men's shouts as they coaxed the cakes in place.

The tiers rose fast. A space of two inches was left between the cakes. But when men and cakes touched the roof, a top layer, the "plugger," was put on crosswise with its cakes touching, to bind all together against warm weather. Marsh hay was heaped over the top. The house was sealed, full to the eaves. The army of men moved on, engine and all, to the next cathedral of Winter.

So the crop was garnered in. And Kennebec preachers thanked God for sending Maine zero weather, and some of them, I know for a fact, thanked God for keeping the rival Hudson unfrozen. Thaws and warm spells might come, but there was the Kennebec adage that "Winter has never rotted in the sky yet," and that other one, "Never too late to cut ice till the robins sing." And the farmers went back with fat wallets to their farms rejoicing and wearing the railroad ties down to the bone.

But when the ice broke up in the Spring, in those days of rich harvests, there would always be ten or so bodies of stout men picked up at the Kennebec's mouth, men with the calked boots still on their feet. The river took its harvest, too.

Spring brought the schooners. Vessels from Singapore, Yokahama, Batavia, San Francisco and Calcutta lay side by side at Iceboro and Swan Island in my river. The ice slid into their holds and was stanchioned firm and braced against the roll of the sea. And the schooners went off over the whole globe, and yellow men and black men and brown men who lived in perpetual Summer put sparkling Maine and Winter into their mouths, and wonder lit their eyes.

Today the great cathedrals are gone. Gone away into the smoke that took many of the icehouses till insurance companies refused to insure them, gone rotting into the ground beside caves still intact where the Abenaki Indians refrigerated their sturgeon and deer three hundred years ago. But now and then you can come upon tools made by *Wood and Sons* in Kennebec haymows, and you may fall in with an old man who had stood up on calked shoes with his spear in Maine's epic age, when Maine diamonds kept the whole world fresh and cool.

MAINE ARTISTS

Maine Landscape Painters

The very special natural beauty of Maine has long attracted both native artists and those from away. In colonial times, indigenous artists specialized in portraits, and itinerants painted designs on wagons and signs as well as depicting local people and scenery. By the nineteenth century, landscape painting had come into its own. Maine natives such as Charles Codman and Harrison Brown, and later Waldo Pierce and Marsden Hartley, developed careers that brought them lasting fame. But it was the out-of-state painters who were to make the most of Maine's landscape.

In 1844 the first of the great Hudson River School painters, Thomas Cole, came to stay at the newly emerging summer colony at Bar Harbor. His enthusiasm for Maine attracted his colleagues, and soon such painters as Thomas Doughty and Frederick Church were vacationing and painting in Maine. More and more artists were drawn to Maine's dramatic and often lonely coastline. They painted the mountains and islands, harbors and villages, in the summers and exhibited their work in Boston and New York in the winters.

The affinity of these various painters for Maine's unspoiled scenery has been the common thread among artists of different schools. Realists such as Robert Henri, George Bellows, and Rockwell Kent painted on Monhegan, the impressionists Childe Hassam on Appledore and Maurice Prendergast at Ogunquit, the luminist Fitz Hugh Lane on Penobscot Bay, the abstractionist John Marin on the coast. They may have taken different approaches, but transcending and uniting them all was the unchanging beauty of the Maine coast. While the early years of the twentieth century saw many of these painters

Visitors landing on Monhegan Island, 1911

working abroad, experimenting with "modernism," their later work reflects a return to more representational painting, with Maine as the common ground.

By the late nineteenth century, painters from away began to put down roots in Maine. In 1884 Winslow Homer had set up his studio in Prout's Neck and started to work on the paintings that were to have a profound influence on later artists from Kent to Wyeth. Later Hartley moved back to Maine, Marin bought property down the coast, the Wyeth family established itself in Port Clyde, and Marguerite and William Zorach settled in Georgetown. Art colonies developed on Monhegan Island and in Ogunquit, and art schools and the shared painterly experience attracted such well-known painters as Edward Hopper, Georgia O'Keeffe, and the Soyer brothers.

The landscape tradition in Maine continues. Fairfield Porter's luminous, pastel views of summer life on Penobscot Bay, Stephen Etnier's sunlit shore and harbor scenes, William Thon's semiabstract quarry and woods paintings, and Neil Welliver's pastoral forest pictures tell us that Maine's influence on landscape painters is a constant.

Some of those who paint in Maine also write about it. In addition to producing autobiographical material, Maine painters have been novelists, essayists, and poets. Here are samplings from the writings of two landscape painters, contemporaries: Rockwell Kent and Marsden Hartley. Although their painting and their writing reflect their different styles, each expresses the profound influence Maine has had on his art.

ROCKWELL KENT
1882–1971

Rockwell Kent was a fine painter and illustrator, a writer, an adventurer, and a political gadfly. Maine, and the time he spent on Monhegan Island, had an important influence on all of these facets of his life. Kent's trip to Monhegan in 1905 was his first adventure; he later traveled to Alaska, Newfoundland, Greenland, and Tierra del Fuego. His enthusiasm for the stark beauty of Monhegan and for the simple integrity of its inhabitants inspired many paintings and admiring comments in his autobiographies and heightened his sense of the importance of meaningful work and social justice for the common man. His fiery espousal of a variety of liberal causes kept him at odds with the political establishment all his life. His art, however, was strong and solid.

Kent was born into a family that respected art and encouraged his interest in painting. Yet he was a rebellious youth, difficult for his widowed mother to handle. He was sent to military school, then to the Horace Mann School in New York. After a period as an architecture student at Columbia University, Kent returned to his first love and studied painting with Robert Henri at the New York School of Art. He also worked with William Merritt Chase and Abbott Thayer. A compatriot of the members of "the Eight," he joined in their efforts to establish a more contemporary school of social realism in New York. Although the sales of his paintings were not enough to support the growing Kent family until well into the 1920s, occasional architectural assignments and an increasingly successful career as an illustrator filled the gap.

The following selections from Kent's last autobiographical work, *It's Me, O Lord,* tell of his first visit to Monhegan in 1905, when he boarded out and worked for Hiram Cazallis, the island well-driller.

"The Boatman," by Rockwell Kent

He returned in 1906 to build his own house; then, after a long absence, he came back in 1947 with his third wife, Sally. They repurchased and restored the house, and Kent found a renewed enthusiasm for painting on the island. His reception among the islanders, however, was colored by the publicity his political polemics had been receiving in the post–World War II era of McCarthyism, and in 1953 Kent again sold the house and left Monhegan for good.

Kent's voyages to cold and distant regions brought variety and vitality to his paintings and to the books he wrote about these places. His sense of adventure, enthusiasm for life, and joy in the beauty of his surroundings are reflected in the strong, massive forms and the striking light and color of his paintings. The Maine works exemplify Kent at his best.

Life and Art on Monhegan

Monhegan, Maine: a small island lying in latitude 43°-46′ North, longitude 69°-19′ West, about ten miles from the nearest mainland and twenty miles from Boothbay Harbor, the mail boat's port of departure.

At the moment of our story it is noon of a day in early June of the year 1905 and the Monhegan mail boat, the ancient, weakly-powered schooner *Effort,* lies at her Boothbay wharf in readiness, it would appear — the mail sack having just been tossed on deck and stowed below — to cast off and set sail. And, now, the lone passenger having stepped aboard, the motor starts, the lines are slacked and cast off by a loiterer on the wharf, and the *Effort,* slowly, heavily as though to justify her name, gets under way . . . it is daytime on this day of June, daytime at sea, and our traveller's eyes — our traveller, that's me — *my* eyes are already upon Monhegan as the land of promise, upon Monhegan already risen faint but clear on the far, sharp horizon of the ocean's deep blue plane.

Monhegan! We've reached the harbor's mouth; we've entered it; we've reached the wharf; we're moored; I've jumped ashore. My bag in hand I race up the hill and race along the road to the old Brackett House. Two minutes in my room to get out of — what did Miss Libbey call it? — my "stylish suit," and into an unstylish one; and like a puppy let out of his pen I'm off at a run to see, to climb, to touch and feel this wonder island that I've come to.

Hugging the harbor shore I reached the island's south-west end where the surf makes suds around the Washerwoman rock or breaks on Norman's ledge; then on to the gulley of Gull Rock, and over it to climb the smooth, bald, winter-surf-washed rock itself; and on again to Burnt Head; and then down and over a broad waste of boulder-strewn, bare granite ledges to climb the headland, Whitehead, and from its one hundred and fifty foot height look far out to sea toward Africa and England. It was so vast, so beautiful that clear blue day, with the green grass and dandelions at my feet! And Blackhead, its twin headland seen from there in all its mass and dignity of form, Blackhead, its dark face splotched with gleaming guano! Then on again over the intervening minor headlands and the gulleys tangled with the debris of fire and storm, and through such tangles up and over Blackhead; and down again — real climbing now to pass the rocky gorges — to the massive granite cube of Pulpit Rock. And then at last, like a quiet passage in a tumultuous symphony, a sheltered harbor after storm, the gentle, grassy slopes of Green Point, still thickly starred with the blossoms of strawberries to be. And the seal ledges and their happy denizens — sunning themselves or slithering and diving off the rocks as though in sport, the water dotted with their almost human heads. Then on to Deadman's Cove and its lone fish-house outpost of the settlement. And always, looking inland from the shore, there was the dark spruce forest, another world, a deeply solemn world that I should come to know.

The village of Monhegan in those days consisted of hardly more than twenty-five or, at the most, thirty houses, of which far the greater number were lived in by the year-round residents whose occupation was fishing and, in particular, lobster fishing. Being an old settlement, its white man's history dating from some years prior to the Plymouth landing, many of the houses, though not of great antiquity, had inherited the character and fine proportions of New England architecture at its best — although, in keeping with the island's wind-swept situation, they were simple and unadorned to the point of austerity. Besides the residences there was a store — an extended, unpretentious one-story affair, the little old red school house, painted white; the church — a fairly recent, fairly ugly, unobtrusive wooden structure; and last, and far from least, there were, unhappily, two hotels, big barn-like things, externally as uninviting as their tasteless insides warranted. But what are we to expect, we touring picture painters and summer tourists and visitors — "rusticators" they call us. Don't we invite just such monstrosities for our convenience? Don't *they*, perhaps, match *us*?

Unlike most New England villages, Monhegan had no plan, no straight, broad, elm-bordered avenue faced by the houses in their white fenced yards: there was no avenue, there were no trees, there were no picket fences. No one had ever "laid out" Monhegan; it just grew. And past the random houses wandered a narrow road, a track first worn there by the oxen of other days and now kept open by the one-horse, drop axle wagon that was the island's sole conveyance.

The harbor of Monhegan was formed by an adjacent smaller island, stark, treeless, whale-backed shaped Manana, and lay open to the south-west wind and seas. On the Monhegan shore of the harbor, and mainly clustered around the wharf and two small beaches, stood the fish-houses, most of them two-storied structures with runways leading to their lofts. Unpainted and weatherbeaten, they proclaimed to eyes — and *nose!* — the island's industry. So too did every foot of intervening ground occupied, as it was in summer, by drying-flakes for cod, and by the pyramids of lobster traps and heaps of painted buoys withdrawn for the season.

Monhegan: its rock-bound shores, its towering headlands, the thundering surf with gleaming crests and emerald eddies, its forest and its flowering meadowlands; the village, quaint and picturesque; the fish-houses, evoking in their dilapidation those sad thoughts on the passage of time and the transitoriness of all things human so dear to the artistic soul; and the *people*, those hardy fisherfolk, those men garbed in their sea boots and their black or yellow oil skins, those horny-handed sons of toil — shall I go on? No, that's enough. It was enough for me, enough for all my fellow artists, for all of us who sought "material" for art. It was enough to start me off to such feverish activity in painting as I had never known.

From breakfast until noon, from after lunch until suppertime, here, overlooking the village or the harbor, there, on the rocks or headlands; on fair days — how I loved them in their sharp, clear revelation of infinitude! — and on those so "artistic" days when fog made mystery mysterious, all day of every day I painted. . . .

The summer visitors to Monhegan were, in those days, relatively few. And although they were in general people of moderate means and, consequently, uninflated standards of living and of taste, although they were — or, since I was one — although we were good, decent, democratic people, it was both natural and inevitable that we should constitute ourselves a society somewhat apart from the indigenous Monheganers. Not that the natives — there is no stigma to the term in Maine — were anything but friendly: they were not. Proud men, they had no need to be. They went about their work, which was fishing; we artists went about ours, painting; and the others, the true "rusticators," worked hard at doing nothing.

There was, however, and happily, one interest that united us all: it was the ball games. Apart from the settlement, crowning the island's next to highest hill, stood the lighthouse and its two substantial houses for the keeper, the assistant, and their families. And nearby on that hilltop lay a fairly level, open field. It was our soft-ball diamond. If I have boasted of how hard I worked at painting, and told how hard the islanders would fish, it must be qualified by this: that, beginning in mid-summer, almost every afternoon at four, artists quit working, fishermen quit fishing, idlers quit idling; and all showed up to work at playing ball. Those were great games, warm friendly games, with none of us so good as to make the worst of us not good enough. And so, little by little I got to know the island men, and more and more, somehow, to envy them.

I envied them their strength, their knowledge of their work, their skill in it; I envied them their knowledge of boats and their familiarity with that awesome portion of the infinite, the sea. I envied them their worker's human dignity. . . .

The fact is that there on Monhegan Island, between and after days of work with maul and drill, with hammer and nails or at the oars, on days it blew too hard at sea, on Sundays, I was painting; painting with a fervor born, as I have said, of my close contact with the sea and soil, and deepened by the reverence that the whole universe imposed. What though my artist friends felt true concern at what they thought my waste of time. Just let the man grow up: his art will follow. And art being properly a by-product of living, how little would a man love life who loved art more! How little can the graven-image worshippers love God!

At any rate, life — not just as looked at but as lived — was to me so exhilarating and so infinitely beautiful that I could strive for nothing but, through experience, a greater share of it. If I could only recreate the world as I beheld and sensed or, even in some measure, understood it, let what I did be art or not, it was enough.

Art is not art until it has effaced itself. Only when the blue paint of a sky ceases to be just color — becoming as it were the depths of space — is that blue right and truly beautiful. Only when the green becomes the growing grass, or the earth-colors land and rocks, when indigo becomes the ocean, and the colors of a figure become flesh and blood only when words become ideas; when the sounds of music become images; only when every medium of the arts becomes transmuted into a portion of our living universe, only then is art consistent with the dignity of man.

Truly I loved that little world, Monhegan. Small, sea-girt island that it was, a seeming floating speck in the infinitude of sea and sky, one was as though driven to seek refuge from the impendent cosmic immensity in a closer relationship to people and to every living thing. I came to know each individual flower and bright-colored mushroom and toadstool that grew beside the woodland paths. I would watch them bud and blossom and be saddened when at last their petals fell; and be infuriated by some vandal's having trampled them. I won't say that I loved the rocks; I just respected them. And when I'd find some fellow's, some brother-artist's, palette scrapings on them, I'd read it as the measure of his miserable soul. . . .

1906

All of a certain lot or parcel of land situated on Horn's Hill, so called, in the Plantation of Monhegan, in the County of Lincoln and State of Maine, bounded and described as follows: — and continuing with a lot of mumbo-jumbo about old walls, and stakes in said old walls, and former stumps and former marks, and distances all vaguely "more or less" and square feet (14,400) "more or less," there is conveyed to me, "my heirs and assigns, to their use and behoof forever . . . with all the privileges and appurtenances thereto belonging" a piece of the Solar System's planet Earth, in the universe of the heavens. In short, I own a piece of land.

George Everett, the artist turned speculator in real estate who had bought Horn's Hill, had made a pretty map of it with building lots and streets and rights of way. But when it came to showing me my boundaries it wasn't of much use. "Your line would run about here," he would say, waving his hand toward an impenetrable thicket of alders, "and then sort of southerly to somewhere" — struggling through more alders and long grass — "to somewhere about here. That land, way over there, belongs to the Widder Albee."

"So if I put my house on this spot," I asked him, walking over to the remotest corner of my alleged property, "it would be all right?"

"Sure, sure," said he. "Your line's way over there somewhere."

So on that spot I built my house.

But we're getting far ahead of our story, for it was only April when I bought the land, and months would pass before I got to building on it. Meantime I went to work, for Hiram needed me. And within a few days I was swinging my hammer as easily as though I had been at it all my life.

And there was other work for me on Monhegan in the spring, for lobstering, the island's chief industry, was then in full operation, and would be until that time in June when the lobster season closed. Now Hiram Cazallis had a brother, George, a red-cheeked, roly-poly, healthy brother, as warm-hearted and good-natured a man as ever lived — and one of the most unlucky. Everyone liked George, and George liked everyone: so, naturally, George liked me. And, liking me, he gave me now and then a job.

In those days lobstering was conducted in dories manned, in general, by two. But there was one exception to this practice, and he was George Cazallis. George owned a fair-sized, cabined boat, the *Janet B.*, powered by a one cylinder, jump-spark marine engine. It was an old boat, an awkward boat to handle, but George, after his fashion, could handle it. He didn't need a man to share his work and profits with, but George liked company; and company for George on many a day meant me.

I had come to be pretty handy with small boats. I could row a dory or scull a skiff as well as the next man, and it followed that, once I got used to it, I liked the sea. Thank God, it took just once! It was a dead calm day, a fair, sunshiny day; and a long, mean, oily swell cradled and rocked the old *Janet B.* as she lay hove to while we were hauling traps. It was a hot day, for that season, a day just perfect for the incubation, ripening and hatching of every last, least, latent smell in that old tub: the gasoline with which the engine cockpit was saturated, the bilge water, the rotten, stinking, pickled-herring bait. Whew, what a nauseating stench that mixture made! "What's the matter with you?" asks George cheerily — damn him! "You're lookin' kinda green."

Actions, they say, speak louder than — at any rate my action answered him, and quick!

That utterance, that unburdening of myself, that blessed act of self-expression made me, and to this day has kept me well.

But nothing, somehow, could keep old *Janet B.* out of trouble. If the engine motor would start — and what exhausting turning of the heavy fly wheel it would take! — it was sure to conk out close to a windward shore. Two or three times we narrowly missed piling up on the rocks. But what should I care, I who could swim? George didn't; and he had never been in the water except the two or three times he had fallen in. Men warned me not to go out with George Cazallis. But maybe it was good for George that I did: my good luck overcame his bad. And, after all, is there any better school than that of experience?

I was with George the day of trap-setting the following late December or early January. For months every man had been working on his traps: repairing the old ones, replacing broken slats and worn-out heads; building and ballasting and rigging new ones; replacing broken toggles; painting the buoys, each man with his own, bright, distinguishing colors and marks. And then the readied traps would all be piled convenient to the landing beach, piled there like race horses lined up at the barrier. As the day for setting neared — a date unspecified but dependent on what was felt to be the market's peak — the tension grew. Some man would start, someone would try to jump the gun; but who? And when? One thing was sure; the break would come at daybreak or before; and every man slept with one ear listening for the tramp of rubber boots on the frozen ground. Then suddenly it happened. Lanterns moved about the beaches and the harbor like giant fireflies; there was the tramp of men, the thumping of traps as they were loaded into dories, the sound of oars in their tholes. They're off! — with every dory racing for the favorite grounds.

It was just dawn as the *Janet B.*, piled high with traps, headed out of the harbor. We had set a few traps before we reached the harbor's mouth; and there the heavy south-east swell began to set them for us. "Hop in the dory, boy," said George as the first trap slid overboard: "Pick up the trap and follow me."

By the time I had pulled the first trap into the dory, a couple more had been spilled; and by the time I'd picked these up, three more. The next thing was to catch the *Janet B.* She didn't wait. She'd stop, of course, while George set traps: she'd stop, and I'd pull frantically to catch up — only to have her start ahead again when I was maybe but a length or two away. Waiting tantalizingly as though for me, luring me on and on, only each time to run away again, she led me half way round the island before she let me catch her fleeing petticoats and pull myself aboard. Yes, life was chock full of small adventures when you sailed with George.

But, meantime, how about my piece of land, my building lot? What's happening there? In April and in May — besides the grass on Horn's Hill growing green, and the alders burgeoning, and the wild strawberries coming into bloom, and the migratory birds in hundreds fluttering about — just absolutely nothing. Oh, I had drawn my plans, and figured out my lumber. I had ordered it, and it had come. And Hiram and I and Hiram's horse had carted it up Horn's Hill to my land; and stacked it there. And the cement was there — well covered up; and the bricks for the chimney; and the shingles for the roof; and the nails. But you could no longer see them from the village for the way the grass and bushes had grown up.

And the carpenter who was to build the house was there; not on Horn's Hill, but on Monhegan. You could see *him* all right, for big Bill Orne stood six feet something high and was in daily evidence behind the counter of his store, or doing handy jobs of carpentry for this or that one near at hand. Bill wasn't a *great* carpenter by any means. Compared to Will Stanley, the island's Portland-trained carpenter and builder, Bill was just a plain wood butcher. But he was just the man to build my unpretentious house. And he was *quick,* quick at his work; not quick, as I found out, at starting it. He was a great tomorrow man; and Bill's tomorrows never came. At least they never came for me. And so it happened that when April's tomorrows had all slipped away, and May's, and June had come, my cup of toleration overflowed: I just got mad. To hell with Bill, I said. I'll build the house myself. And so, of wrath, was born a carpenter.

I wonder if it ever happens that somebody, suddenly and out of a clear sky, discovers that he knows much more than he had ever thought he knew. What a wonderful proud feeling it would be! I've never felt it. I wonder if it has ever happened to me to discover that I did in fact know just as much as I had thought. It's possible — though I don't recall it. But I do recall how, having studied architecture at Columbia University and having worked at it in the great city of New York, having made plans of houses and drawn the details of their construction, having — to get down to the case in point — drawn a careful plan and sections and elevations for my own little house, how, the minute it came to picking up my square and saw and hammer I discovered that I hardly knew the least thing about building a house. Fortunately, however, I didn't let that stop me. And so it happened that with one thing that I did leading to another, and so on in endless succession, and doing each thing in the way it struck me as needing to be done, I discovered that I was doing practically everything the right way, and that building, like most other enterprises of man, is mainly just a matter of common sense.

Of course I'd had experience with tools: that helped a lot. But if I hadn't had it I'd have learned. Then, too, I knew what good work was: once you know that, you can't or won't be slipshod.

I would have been well advised had I reared my house on a solid masonry foundation, and even better had I called upon the firm of Cazallis and Kent to blast me out a good cellar. But unfortunately my chief adviser at that time was, of necessity, my pocket book: it ordered locust posts, at the same time offering me the common-labor services of a good, hard working islander, Mr. Richards, who for some reason or other did little, if any, lobstering. So when I had driven my stakes and stretched my lines, Mr. Richards and I got to work setting the posts, digging for the chimney foundation, and building it; and in a very few days we were ready to lay the sills and floor joists.

The house was to be a diminutive affair consisting of a small living room and kitchen, a smaller bed room, a still smaller hallway, and two ample closets. And on one end was to be an open shed. It was to be as nearly New England in character as a young New York trained architect of that period could make it. That wasn't very near. But, aside from its aesthetic shortcomings, it was just exactly right for the self-serving, unmarried workman it was designed for. And what more could you ask of any house?

The rough floor laid, up went the corner posts, the plates, the studs. Next came the sheathing; then the attic floor, the rafters and the roof boards. Then the chimney. I'd never tried brick-laying, but it wasn't hard. With lines to guide me it went well: messy but straight. And, with Mr. Richards tending mason, it went fast.

Next came the roof shingles: that went slowly until I got the knack of it; a tap to fix the nail, one blow to drive it. So the roof went fast. And the first thing I knew I was sitting astride of its finished ridge looking down and off to the west — over the broad cranberry bog that lay at the foot of Horn's Hill, over the strip of village between the bog and the harbor, over the harbor at whale-backed Manana or, to the right of it, over ten or twelve miles of blue ocean to the dim blue mainland of the Pine Tree State of Maine. More proudly even than I'd ever ridden [my horse] Kitty, I now rode my house. This was my own, my native land, its vault of heaven, my lot, my house, *my* home! Now I could move in; for if the house was far from finished, so was I. It was right that we should grow up together.

I sent for a mail-order four-lid kitchen range, for pots and pans and "silverware." I bought a table and a cot and picked up a few chairs. I bought a lamp. My mother sent me blankets, pillows, linen. And while all these furnishings were on their way, I put the door and window frames in place and hung the doors and sash. Food I bought at the store, and oil for my lamp. And when everything was assembled and in order, I fetched my bag from Aunt Annie's, lit my stove and lit my lamp and from the little house on Horn's Hill let my light so shine that men might see my good work and, truly reading it as betokening a fellow human being's utter well-being and contentment, glorify our Father which is in Heaven.

I believe it was the following day when glancing up from my preparation of supper, I saw a long, lean, black-robed figure standing in my dooryard: it was the Widder Albee. I left my work, stepped out and greeted her.

Mrs. Albee was the owner of one of the larger of the two island hotels and of broad acres of Monhegan land. She was a woman of past middle age; but the process of time that can prove so beneficent to wine and human nature had somehow in her life gone wrong; Mrs. Albee had turned sour.

"Mr. Kent," said she in a voice as hard as carborundum, "I'd like to know what you mean by building your house on my land."

George Everett's words flashed to my mind: "It's somewhere here, and somewhere over there." *Somewhere,* but where? "Why, Mrs. Albee," I began, "George Everett said. . . ."

"George Everett!" she snorted back. "George Everett! What does he know! Here's where my line runs — from that tree — see that? Past here, this stump. Your house is on my land. What are you going to do about it?"

What indeed! I stood over the stump and squinted. "Why, Mrs. Albee," I said, "it does! It certainly does — six inches of it; six inches of the corner of my eaves. Gee, but I'm sorry. I'll tell you what let's do. We'll get a surveyor to survey the line, and mark it on the eaves. And then I'll take a saw and cut the corner off, right on the line. How about that?"

Then Mrs. Albee squinted; then she raved some more. She went on like a wound-up thing; and like a wound-up thing at last ran down. "Well, then," she said, "I guess you can let it be." And somewhat mollified she strode away.

As we then let it be, it is today.

The little house on Monhegan — yes, we bought it back; one is apt to get things that one wants a lot — the house proved to be in deplorable condition; and Sally and I, on our return there in the spring, spent virtually every hour of our month of ten or twelve hour working days pulling out nails from plaster walls and wooden trim, scraping and scrubbing, patching and painting — and, outdoors, digging, grubbing, chopping, lopping — so that at our vacation's end we not only had a place that was almost fit to live in and a view to look at, but such properly hard hands and muscles and good spirits as we had not enjoyed for ages. The house, having been added to, had now two bedrooms and an attic, a kitchen and a bathroom. And — how things on Monhegan had changed! — running water!

Things *had* changed on Monhegan. From a remote island settlement of fishermen and their families, visited in summer by occasional artists and such city folks as loved the island's rocks and headlands and its isolated, simple life, it had become a Down East Provincetown that sprouted cottages as though some careless hand had spilled their seed. But for the fortunate seclusion of the spot that I had built on, and the out-of-season times we picked to visit there, we should have found the place too alien to our tastes and habits to endure. However, in early spring and fall the cottages stood closed; and the headlands and woodland paths were as silent and deserted as I had known them in the primeval era of almost half a century ago. And, to me, as moving.

So that as the work of rehabilitation advanced I began to paint again and, it seems to me, with undiminished love for the familiar scenes. Again, though with far less agility than in earlier years, I lugged my canvases across the gulleys, up the headlands; and although to paint Monhegan cost far more in toil than I had used to pay, I'd meet the price, and gladly, to the limit of my strength. Then, as though Fate had planned it, it was at Monhegan that, a year ago, I was to write the chapters of this book about my life there. And as I wrote, those days returned to me in all their poignant beauty. Yet, it is true: the island, all the world, has changed: and it is by studied self-delusion, made possible by the remoteness of the little house — and, without a telephone, electric light and radio, its un-modernity — that I re-live my youth or, better, become young again.

MARSDEN HARTLEY
1877–1943

Marsden Hartley is best known as an artist, primarily as a painter of landscapes of his native Maine. That he also wrote essays and poems is less well known, although he gave equal time to each, setting himself a schedule of writing in the morning and painting in the afternoon.

The youngest of nine children, Hartley was born in Lewiston, the son of English immigrants. The family was not well off, and young Hartley left school to work in a shoe factory. In 1890 he went west to Cleveland, where he studied art, and then on to New York, where he continued his schooling at the Art Students' League with William Merritt Chase and became part of the contemporary art scene. He was a friend of Rockwell Kent's and a compatriot, if not a soulmate, of the social realists who made up the Ashcan School. He had his first exhibit at Alfred Stieglitz's 291 Gallery on Fifth Avenue in 1909, and in 1913 his work was included in the trend-setting Armory Show.

Europe and the revolutionary concepts of art espoused by the modernists attracted Hartley. He went to France, where he was influenced by the impressionists, and then to Germany, where he adopted some of the tenets of the strong abstractionists painting at that time. His own colorful geometric paintings of this period clearly show their influence.

Hartley's return to Maine signaled a return to realism in his painting and to the concept of a strong identification with place. John Baur, writing in *Maine and Its Role in American Art,* describes Hartley's later Maine work: "The Maine that emerges from Hartley's painting is a land of enduring, majestic strength, a rock in both the physical and spiritual sense. . . . That he truly found himself only after his return to Maine in the last decade of his life is a measure of how necessary, to Hartley at least, were roots in a place — a measure also of how strong a force regionalism . . . still can be."

Hartley's parallel career as a writer started early, and he published in such literary magazines as *Poetry* and *The Dial*. His first book, *Twenty-five Poems,* was published in 1925 by a small press in Paris when he was living among the famous generation of American expatriates that included Gertrude Stein, Ernest Hemingway, and Ezra Pound. But he had to wait until the forties to find publishers for the rest of his prodigious output. In 1987, 250 of his poems were brought together by Gail Scott in *The Collected Poetry of Marsden Hartley.*

As a poet, Hartley called himself a primitive, by which he did not mean unsophisticated but rather spontaneous, nonacademic. As he wrote, "We present ourselves in spite of ourselves. We are most original when we are most like life." His strong identification with Maine is clear, and his feelings about the importance of an artist's emotional locality in determining the nature of his work are evident in these examples of his prose and poetry.

From "Is There an American Art?" (c. 1938)

Outside of occasional excursions into the field of prevailing esthetics, I have done nothing else but prove my own specific localism which has been to paint my own native Maine and I do nothing else at the present moment and never expect to do anything else, and I am completely recognized as an authentic painter of Maine born in Maine, but this recognition comes I am happy to say from the state itself and the native spirit which recognizes the authenticity of my private and local emotion.

And for exactly this reason and no other I returned to my tall timbers and my granite cliffs — because in them rests the kind of integrity I believe in and from which source I draw my private strength both spiritually and esthetically. . . .

From "On the Subject of Nativeness — A Tribute to Maine" (1937)

The Androscoggin, the Kennebec, and the Penobscot flow down to the sea as solemnly as ever, and the numberless inland lakes harbour the loon, and give rest to the angles of geese making south or north according to season, and the black bears roam over the mountain tops as usual.

If the Zeppelin rides the sky at night, and aeroplanes set flocks of sea gulls flying, the gulls remain the same and the rocks, pines, and thrashing seas never lose their power and their native tang.

Nativeness is built of such primitive things, and whatever is one's nativeness, one holds and never loses no matter how far afield the traveling may be. . . .

And so I say to my native continent of Maine, be patient and forgiving, I will soon put my cheek to your cheek, expecting the welcome of the prodigal, and be glad of it, listening all the while to the slow, rich, solemn music of the Androscoggin, as it flows along.

If We Could

If we could do what the white birds
do,
break the brink of the wind with blade
of stiff wing,
shatter it to splinters as wave-dash

takes the rocks, shrieking loudly,
O I can take it if you can, almost smiling
and the light smoke-curves from incessant
chimneys
clinging to a cloud that is white,
can afford to be explicitly
erudite.

If we could do what the white birds
do,
measuring every width of sea so nonchalantly,
take the kick of thunder to our ribs,
politely,
or the upflare of morning with applause,
that would be something by which to
remember us,
who ponder, thus.

Lewiston Is a Pleasant Place

I admire my native city because
it is part of the secret sacred rite
of love of place.
My childhood which was hard, it is always
hard to be alone at the wrong time,
brought seizures of intensity to the years;
the harsh grinding of the mills rang in
my ears for years — and a sordid sort of music
came out of it.
I return to instances that are the basic images
of my life as it now is.

I go back to the Franklin pasture which for
us children was the Asia and Africa of
our first impressions.

Spring —
and myself walking with my father along the
edges of a cool clear stream, gathering water cresses,
trilliums, dogtooth violets, and in
the fall — at times — mushrooms;
white violets and blue, growing on little hillocks
with trailing evergreens and boxberry leaves,
and here and there, pushing up out of the snow,
the arbutus, or as we called them, Mayflowers.

Drama number one,
the image of all that was to come after:
the death of the white kitten —
wrapping it carefully in something soft —
laying it gently in a wooden saltbox —
fastening the lid down
burying it deep in a hollow, with tears,
and my sister, Lillie May, joining in the rites.

There were toboggans in winter, made of end to end
joined barrel staves, seat in the middle, gliding
dangerously into the Asiatic valleys below.
Scene-shifting a little later, the pasture a
deep, religious memory;
the Androscoggin
forever flowing solemnly through my brain,
coursing in and out of my flesh and bone,
as it still does, sacredly.

There was Dr. Alonzo Garcelon, always known to us
as Dr. "Gasselon," flying through Haymarket Square
behind his racing steed, spitting tobacco juice
as he went; and the amazing vision of his beautiful
daughter Edith, at church of a Sunday morning
Mamie Straw and Lizzie Janes, sharp images of a day
so somehow past —
Miss Janes at the organ, pumped by a boy at the
back, out of sight — with the Ascension of Christ
over us all in not too good stained glass, as we
sang magnificats and epiphanies — and

"Lead kindly light amid . . . " "Lord now lettest thy
servant depart in peace, according to thy word."

Skinny Jinny was a tall, dark-clothed woman with
her thin arms akimbo under her black shawl,
wan-white, frightened of the solitudes that
enveloped her being, we children running madly for
home when we saw her — because "she has a butcher knife
under her shawl" — as if she hated little children and
maybe she did — so many do.

The Canadians came to the city — giving it new
life, new fervors, new charms, new vivacities, lighter
touches, pleasant shades of cultivation, bringing no
harm to the city, bringing what it now has — a freshening
of city style, richer sense of plain living.
Recently I walked the streets of my native city
and there was gaiety in the air.
My thoughts returned to a white house in Howe Street,
a home with green blinds, the front ones always shut,
where a poet of distinction lived, wrote fine poetry,
cooked Savarinesque foods, writing poetry that few knew
the worth of — and almost none know the value, now.
Wallace Gould, if he is still fact, is a man of great
male beauty and gigantic proportions; he is almost a complete
legend to us now, none of us know where he is,
or if he even lives at all.
Gould was, in the careful use of the word, a genius;
he had high vision and plain habits; he was
a great cook, a superior pianist, with a frantic
worship of Byron.
He had image after image in photo of his idol,
and an impressive replica in plaster.

Gould devoted himself to Greek outline, Horatian
simplicity, with pagan notions of the
livingness of the moment.
He cared nothing for the traditions, customs, mechanical
habits — lived the quiet life of a thinking being,
worshipping also his foster mother, genial in his
behaviors,

out of which evolved
The Children of the Sun.

The mills and factories that were once gigantic
in the vision of a child, monstrous, terrifying,
prison-like, are now mere objects on the horizon,
just as the garages and the filling stations have become.
The Androscoggin flows by them all, giving them
power through the solemn canals, minding none of
them, going onward because it has business with the sea.
Lumber was once a great industry; we all saw the
log-drives and jams above the falls, tumbling down
over the waters at West Pitch, settling into
jackstraw patterns as they may now be seen in places
like Trois-Rivieres in Quebec — these logs later turning
into paper, turning into stockings, extraneous lingerie;
I myself having seen the moment when wood becomes syrup,
then silk.

On the breast of David's Mountain
many an adolescent dream was slain,
later to be snatched from early death
when manhood gave them back their breath
again.

VACATIONLAND

Vacationland

Tourism has long been an important economic and social influence on the State of Maine. In its early days, tourism took simple forms: sportsmen and mountain climbers camping out in the woods, artists and natural scientists boarding with Mainers along the coast. But by the 1850s, the word was out about the beauty of Maine, and the natives had learned about the money to be made from visitors from Boston and Philadelphia and New York. Vacationing in Maine was no longer simple.

By the 1890s "cottagers" were a fixture at Bar Harbor, and eighteen grand hotels accommodated some 2,500 guests. Bar Harbor remained "famous and crowded" well into the present century. Social clubs were organized, solidifying a commitment to the resort as the rich and famous incorporated the town into their lives.

Nevertheless, two world wars and the emergence of the automobile brought about a change in the nature of tourism in Maine, aided by the great fire of 1947, which accelerated the end of Bar Harbor's fading grandeur. Motels and campgrounds satisfied an ever-increasing transient summer population. Simpler homes replaced the elaborate "cottages," and the elegant resort became a thing of the past.

EDWIN LAWRENCE GODKIN
1831–1902

Edwin Lawrence Godkin, a journalist, editor, and author, in 1865 founded the weekly *Nation* and later became editor-in-chief of the *New York Post*. Here he describes the genesis of the affluent summer society that was exemplified by Bar Harbor during its heyday in the 1890s.

The Evolution of a Summer Resort

Nothing is more remarkable in the history of American summering than the number of new resorts which are discovered and taken possession of by "the city people" every year, the rapid increase in the means of transportation both to the mountains and the sea, and the steady encroachments of the cottager on the boarder in all the more desirable resorts. The growth of the American watering-place, indeed, now seems to be as much regulated by law as the growth of asparagus or strawberries, and is almost as easy to foretell. The place is usually first discovered by artists in search of sketches, or by a family of small means in search of pure air, and milk fresh from the cow, and liberty — not to say license — in the matter of dress. Its

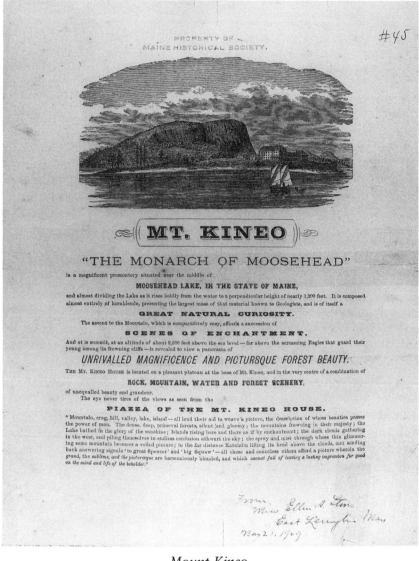

Mount Kineo

development then begins by some neighboring farmer's agreeing to take them to board — a thing he has never done before, and now does unwillingly, and he is very uncertain what to charge for it. But as a venture he fixes what seems to him an enormous sum — say $5 to $7 a week for each adult. His ideas about food for city people are, however, very vague. The only thing about their tastes of which he

Map of Bar Harbor

feels certain is that what they seek in the country is, above all things, change, and that they accordingly do not desire what they get at home. Accordingly he furnishes them with a complete set of novelties in the matter of food and drink, forgetting, however, that they might have got them at home if they pleased. The tea and coffee and bread differ from what they are used to at home simply in being worse. He is, too, at the seaside, very apt to put them on an exclusively fish diet, in the belief that it is only people who live by the sea who get fish, and that city people, weary of meat, must be longing for fish. The boarders, this first summer, having persuaded him to take them, are of course too modest to remonstrate, or even to hint, and go on to the end eating what is set before them, and pretending to be thankful, and try to keep up their failing strength by being a great deal in the open air, and admiring the scenery. After they leave, he is apt to be astonished by the amount of cash he finds himself possessed of, probably more than he ever handled before at one time, except when he mortgaged his farm, and comes to the conclusion that taking summer boarders is an excellent thing, and worth cultivating.

In the next stage he seeks them, and perhaps is emboldened by the advice of somebody to advertise the place, and try to get hold of some editors or ministers whose names he can use as references, and who will talk it up. He soon secures one or two of each, and they then tell him that his house is frequented by intellectual or "cultured" people; and he becomes more elated and more enterprising, enlarges the dining-room, adds on a wing, relieves his wife of the cooking by hiring a woman in the nearest town, and gives more meat and stronger coffee, and, little by little, grows into a hotel-keeper, with an office and a register. His neighbors, startled by his success, follow his example, it may be only *longo intervallo*, and soon the place becomes a regular "resort," with girls and boys in white flannel, lawn-tennis (which succeeds croquet), a livery-stable, stages, an ice-cream store with a soda-water fountain, a new church, and with strange names taken out of books for the neighboring hills and lanes and brooks.

This stage may last for years — in some places it has been known to last thirty or forty without any change, beyond the opening of new hotels — and it becomes marked by crowds of people, who go back every year in the character of old boarders, get the best rooms, and are on familiar terms of friendship with the proprietor and the older waiter-girls. But it may be brought to a close, and is now being brought to a close in scores of American watering-places by the appearance of the cottager, who has become to the boarder what the red squirrel is to the gray, a ruthless invader and exterminator. The first cottager is almost always a boarder, so that there is no means of discovering his approach and resisting his advances. In nine cases out of ten he is a simple guest at the farm-house or hotel, without any discoverable airs or pretensions, on whom the scenery has made such an impression that he quietly buys a lot with a fine view. The next year he builds a cottage on it, and gradually, and it may be at first imperceptibly, separates himself in feeling and in standards from his fellow-boarders. The year after he is in the cottage and the mischief is done. The change has come. Caste has been established, with all its attendant evils. The community, once so simple and homogeneous, is now divided into two classes, one of which looks down on the other. More cottages are built, with trim lawns and private lawn-tennis grounds, with "shandy-gaff" and "tennis-cup" concealed on tables in tents. Then the dog-cart with the groom in buckskin and boots, the Irish red setter, the saddle-horse with the banged tail, the phaeton with the two ponies, the young men in knickerbockers carrying imported racquets, the girls with the banged hair, the club, ostensibly for newspaper reading, but really for secret gin-fizzes and soda-cocktails, make their appearance, with numerous other monarchical excrescences. The original farmer, whose pristine board was the beginning of all this, has probably by this time sold enough land to the cottagers to enable him to give up taking boarders and keeping a hotel, and is able to stay in bed like a gentleman most of the winter, and sit on a bench in his shirt-sleeves all summer. . . .

The progress made by the cottager in driving the boarder away from some of the most attractive places, both in the hills and on the seaboard, is very steady. Among these Bar Harbor occupies a leading position. It was, for fully fifteen years after its discovery, frequented exclusively by a very high order of boarders, and probably has been the scene of more plain living and high thinking than any other summer spot on the seacoast. It was, in fact, remarkable at one time for an almost unhealthy intellectual stimulation through an exclusively fish diet. But the purity of the air and the grandeur of the scenery brought a yearly increasing tide of visitors from about 1860 onward. These visitors were, until about five years ago, almost exclusively boarders, and the development of the place as a summer resort was prodigious. The little houses of the original half farmers, half fishermen, who welcomed, or rather did not welcome, the first explorers, grew rapidly into little boarding-houses, then into big boarding-houses, then into hotels with registers. Then the hotels grew larger and larger, and the callings of the steamer more frequent, until the place became famous and crowded.

SAMUEL ADAMS DRAKE
1833–1905

Samuel Adams Drake was a historian, an antiquarian, and a prolific writer who published a series of historical surveys, books about the history of the Boston area, and several guidebooks in which he expressed his own very frank commentaries on the places he visited. His observations of Bar Harbor, written at the end of the nineteenth century, indicate his displeasure with the commercialization of the town while conveying his admiration for the spectacular beauty of the island of Mount Desert. Drake fears the encroachments of the rich on "puny" little Bar Harbor and at the same time is amused by their pretensions.

In some of his comments he was prescient. Bar Harbor was indeed ravaged by a great fire, in 1947, and the question of preserving public access to the oceanfront is as much of an issue in Maine today as it was in 1891. The following chapter is from Drake's 1891 guide to Maine, *The Pine Tree Coast*.

In and out of Bar Harbor

Accurately speaking, Bar Harbor is no harbor at all, but a roadstead only half sheltered by the Porcupine Islands, — five weird lumps of granite, protruding above water, a little way off the land, the largest of which has a submarine attachment with Mount Desert, formed of a strip of shingle that is bared at low water, all awash at high tide, and covered again at the flood. This bar and island make clear the genesis of the name of Bar Harbor.

The other islands of this group stretch off irregularly round the roadstead, a kind of broken-down barricade, with deep water between to show where the sea has breached it.

There is a farmhouse on Bar Island, and some land under cultivation there, — a strip of greensward and a shag of woods, — but we notice that the farmer-owner, who awoke one fine day to find himself a millionaire, has also fenced in the bar joining his island to Mount Desert, with a row of saplings, so getting the benefit of the crops of herring, mackerel, or porgies that are brought up by this weir, and left stranded by the tide, when one would only have to gather up his loaves and fishes, so to speak.

This simple statement will elucidate the whole philosophy of life at Bar Harbor up to the time when the golden shower began falling, and every one who owned a little land ran out to hold his hat. Some men are born rich, but here it would seem as if wealth had literally been thrust upon them.

Not a few of our best-known seashore resorts are but the natural expansion of decaying villages, — the evolution of the grub into the butterfly, so to speak, — to which the advent of summer visitors has given a new lease of life; others are so many evidences of a cold purpose to turn out a watering place to order. While there is a certain not unpleasing mellowness about the ready-made article which is

Hotel staff, Bar Harbor

wanting to the product of a day, yet it is not to be denied that a great many very worthy people look upon country life as a species of exile, and country living as but another name for actual privation. At Bar Harbor they find their Arcadia; so that odd but not uncommon feeling that one is being cheated if he happens into a place where money will not procure him luxuries finds nothing to feed its egotism upon at Bar Harbor, where money will buy everything. Indeed, Choate's famous *mot,* "Give me the luxuries, and I will do without the necessaries of life" might be taken as the accepted creed of a very large following.

The sum of the matter is that few places afford ground for a more instructive study of character than a fashionable watering-place; and now I think of it, why may not that be a primary cause for the rise of a new literature, — the literature of the summer resort, in fact, — since even one summer must furnish no end of affairs of the heart?

The study might appropriately begin with the arrival of the boat at the pier. The millionaire gets into his carriage and rolls off to his cottage, followed by admiring looks; the half-millionaire goes to the most exclusive hotel, pursued with obsequious attentions; the hundred-thousand-dollar man, to the most pretentious one, hardly

Grand Central Hotel, Mount Desert Island

noticed at all; the man with a salary, to a respectable one, whose
guests receive him much as a garrison that is already short of provisions might an unlooked-for re-enforcement; and so on, down to the
unfortunate who has to reckon on the cost of everything beforehand,
and who feels it a privilege to be allowed to slip away unobserved to
some modest corner. Everybody is subjected to the same magical
touchstone. Consequently head-waiters who can tell how much a
guest is worth, simply by noticing the way he walks into the dining-
room, are sure of being engaged for the next season. . . .

A person who had not visited Bar Harbor for fifteen years would have to turn often to the mountains, the sea, and the islands to convince himself that he was really standing on the site of the puny village of that day. Without doubt, it is the most notable example of rapid growth New England can show in this direction, and unless all signs fail, it bids fair to hold a proud preeminence as "the capital of polite life, the mustering-place of the pleasures of the world of fashion."

It is curious to observe, however, that while fashionable people came here to get away from the crowd, they have drawn the crowd after them.

But what was it that first drew these fashionable people here, — the people of cultivated taste, travelled people, refined people, who know Nice and Naples, and Monte Carlo and Venice, and are not easily carried off their feet by the noisy applause of the *claque*?

Twenty-two years ago Bar Harbor began to draw to it a little of the travel that, before that time, had centered wholly about Southwest Harbor and that shore. It came overland, by way of Somesville, at first; for there was then no wharf at Bar Harbor at which a steamer could land. Tobias Roberts, who was the pioneer landlord here, built the first public house, the "Agamont," in 1867. Roberts was also the storekeeper and general factotum of this out-of-the-way little hamlet. Daniel Rodick, the owner of Bar Island, built soon after Roberts; and so late as 1874 there were, perhaps, twenty buildings all told, strung out at intervals along the lane then leading down to the landing-place — those for the public being flimsy, hastily built structures, half furnished and half finished, kept by fishermen or farmers turned landlords for better profit; because, as one of them very honestly said, he could make more money out of one summer boarder, in a single season, than from the labor of three men on his whole farm. These worthy landlords are now represented in the second generation, as the first indifferent accommodations are by the great hotels over which they preside.

It is hardly possible to discover a trace of this petty village in the long rows of buildings now stretching far out into the country on every hand, or of the primitive hotels in the monster hostelries now occupying the same sites, or of the landlords themselves, raw products of this rough, strong soil, that they were, — in the spruced-up personages who own the same surnames. Certainly it is no discredit to the guild that men who are island born and bred should have known how to compel the wave of prosperity to carry them along with it.

Though of imposing appearance, these Bar Harbor hotels, with

their pie-crust decorations, are cheaply built, and, with few excep-
tions, cheaply furnished. They appeal strongly, however, to the national demand for the biggest of everything. If crowded, they are
insupportable; when there are only a handful of guests, they are
inexpressibly dreary. The big landlords say, "We must have a net to
make a big haul." That is true, except when the fish have struck off.

Bar Harbor is conspicuously lacking in the charm imparted to
Newport by its delightful historic associations. It is not so much as
mentioned in the standard history of the state. Hence no other resource is open but our eyes and ears. Our excursion of yesterday did
not skim off all the picturesqueness or all the poetry.

I have just returned from a stroll through the suburbs. The day's
routine was evidently just beginning. A string of carriages lined the
curb from the Rodick as far as the Grand Central. Two or three
omnibuses were already in waiting to take passengers to Green
Mountain [now Cadillac Mountain], the top of which is in full view
from the streets. For the longer drives to Schooner Head, Great Head
or Somesville, most tourists seemed to prefer the mountain buck-
board wagon, a most democratic sort of vehicle, partly suggestive of
riding on a rail, and partly of being tossed in a blanket. You are
reassured, however, on being told that if one is overturned, the
vehicle ordinarily escapes without injury.

The most striking thing I saw about the throng in the streets was
the singular medley of costumes. One gets the impression that most
of the visitors have travelled hundreds of miles in order to play at
tennis. The aquatic side of life is also well represented. I came frequently across the gilded sailor, who is always shivering his timbers
at the "hops," or smashing his tarry top-lights in the tennis-courts.
Upper-tendom rolls languidly by in elegant turnouts; sharp-set land
agents lurk in the open doorways; florists, caterers, milliners, photographers, all have spread out their most appetizing or enticing displays
for the expected customers. There goes a gun in the harbor! Another
nickel-plated yacht has come to anchor. Another floating *salon* ten-
ders its round of visits, receptions, and *petits-soupers* to break the
monotony of life.

The winding shore path leading to Cromwell's Cove is still as
charming a promenade as ever. You enjoy the open sea-view, the
bracing sea-air, the splash of the waves at your feet, the gliding sails,
the tasteful cottages, with their spaces of bright turf, their variegated
colors, their carefully tended shrubbery and flowers. You see grave-
looking men tossing pebbles into the water with boyish satisfaction,

peering into crevices, picking up shells, or attentively examining what they may never have though worth noticing in the whole course of their lives.

There is something in that, at all events.

I found it quite different, however, when walking in the street skirting this fine bit of shore. Here the inhospitable warnings, "No Thoroughfare," "No Trespassing," or "No Passage," stare one in the face as often as some inviting by-way tempts one to turn aside, Would not such of our seashore towns as have any ocean-front left, show a wise forecast by setting apart some portion of it for the use of the people, — the common people? . . .

A turn around the skirt of the village brings one up to the high ridge which overlooks it at a distance, like the seats of an amphitheatre. In this place, those builders who found the shorefront already taken up have intrenched themselves, as it were, against the advancing village, which is fast closing in upon them. Here, they are far from the madding crowd; at least, for the present. And here they may enjoy that seclusion which is no longer attainable on the shore or in the village itself. Beautiful residences of almost every known type — rare products of the most correct taste, the best skill, the most lavish expenditure — stand thick among the evergreen groves, from which a warm, resinous odor exhales, mixed with the salt breezes from the bay. This hill colony stretches a belt of mottled colors around the skirt of the village, of which it is the fashionable citadel.

Not infrequently, when deep in the woods, I came across a sort of skeleton tower, looking quite like an oil derrick; at least if it had been in the oil region of the Keystone State, I should have had no doubt about it whatever. A closer examination, however, showed them to be lookouts, run up above the surrounding woods, so that by ascending the rounds of a ladder for seventy or eighty feet, intending purchasers might get an idea of what the view would be from the roofs of imaginary houses. Is the Eiffel Tower but an adaptation of the Bar Harbor land-agents' fertile invention? . . .

I should say that the greatest drawback to the future prosperity of Bar Harbor lay in the ever-present menace of a disastrous conflagration. A city of boards, built on a bare, treeless plain, can offer little resistance to the spread of the flames.

One of the Desert Mountains, which Champlain first brought to the light of history, rises back of the village; yet as far as I have been able to discover, the name of Champlain is nowhere commemorated on this island. This is Green Mountain, and the view from its summit easily ranks first among Bar Harbor's many attractions. There is a house of entertainment there for the convenience of tourists making the ascent. It is said that the windows of this house flash out their "good morning" as far as Belfast and Montville, fifty and sixty miles away.

Visitors go to the mountain in vehicles as far as Eagle Lake, a beautiful little piece of water two miles long, lying underneath it near the Somesville road. They are then taken across in a steamboat, and finish the ascent by means of a railway sixty-three hundred feet in length. There is also a carriage road to the summit. Pedestrians who are not afraid of a little healthy exertion find little difficulty in climbing up through the ravine opening a wide gap between Green Mountain and Dry Mountain.

By whichever route he may have arrived, the visitor will hardly be able to keep back an exclamation of delighted surprise at the wonderful and memorable panorama of sea and shore which he is looking down upon, perhaps for the first time in his life. For many a year will those seas and islands float through his memory as he strives to recall the scene from the mountain top. Long will he treasure up the image of those lovely lakes set like gems in that "silent sea of pines." Never will he forget how suddenly, as if a veil had dropped from his eyes, a new, absorbing sense of the sublimity of nature came over him, or the almost tender realization that he had been lifted up in his whole being, out of the world below, almost to see as the immortals see.

The tribute may even be something bizarre withal, though sincere, like this one. Once upon a time two of my countrywomen stood here, the dumb witnesses to the glories of the sunset. All at once one broke out with, "Oh, isn't it gorgeous? Isn't it grand?" The other, who pressed closely to her companion's side in a kind of ecstasy, replied with decision, "Yes, 'Manda, it is slick!"

Although not a high mountain, this one is so commandingly placed that a very wide arc of land and sea is thrown open to the eye. You do not, however, lose the sense of proportion or perspective as you would from some higher summit. Under favorable conditions everything is clearly seen, — the swarm of islands advancing out into the vast sparkling plain of the sea from the grim bastions of the coast like a cloud of skirmishers, the far-off islands emerging like monsters rising to take a breath, the leagues on leagues of forest rolling back their billows into the north. Lonely old Katahdin stands there at the edge like a spectre whom the day has surprised. Statuesque Blue Hill guards his lovely bay. The Camden Hills send greeting from the west;

the Schoodic Hills, from the east. Then the eye drops down among the deep gorges of the island, rude cradles of the little lakes which seem to be turning their bright faces up to their shaggy guardians to be kissed.

Driving is by all odds the favorite pastime, one might almost say the favorite occupation, at Bar Harbor, and it lends an agreeable diversity to the almost numberless excursions by water. Indeed, that is where Bar Harbor, or Mount Desert rather, claims pre-eminence over all the other seashore resorts of the Union. One may drive a hundred miles without even going off the island at all, and yet never be more than twenty or thirty from his starting point. . . .

And now, after exhausting the day's round of boating, bathing, driving, exploring the shores, or roaming the woods, of tennis, bowling, or billiards, the evening brings back city life again as certainly as flood follows ebb, with its teas, visits, hops, and receptions, its concerts, readings, and private theatricals for the young people, its quiet rubber of whist, or a book — it need not be the latest novel unless one likes — in some retired nook or corner, for the elders. This double life suggests the figure of a contribution box into which every one is expected to drop his bright idea, and for which he is to get a recipe against blue-devils out of the common fund. It follows that the great man here is by no means the senator, the general, or even the millionaire; he is the man of original ideas, who can not only devise new schemes for killing time every day and hour, but put them in successful execution.

One has only to look in at some hotel parlor of an evening to see what zest the pursuit of out-door pleasures all at once imparts to all those in-door amusements which seemed so insipid when they were one's sole resource at home.

SINCLAIR LEWIS
1885–1951

The greatest American novel of its day — and its day was a long one — was *Babbitt*, written by Sinclair Lewis in 1922. Eight years later, when Lewis became the first American to win the Nobel Prize in Literature, the Swedish academy made it clear that the award recognized, not his work as a whole, but this single novel. It is the story of George F. Babbitt, a "realtor" of Zenith, U.S.A. As he moves through, first, the hours of his day and then the days of his middle years, he acts out the most complete sociological profile of an American businessman that his country and the rest of the literate world had ever seen. Lewis had brought one American forever into focus and himself into the heart of a national controversy. Was the book a true picture of America or a distortion full of lies? Both sides agreed it was a powerful novel. Babbitt as a symbol of America is destined to live as long as Daniel Boone, said one critic; Lewis is more of a public influence than a satiric novelist, said another. Newspapers in five midwestern cities claimed their city as the model for Zenith, which suggested that American readers found Lewis's satire so perfect on its surface that they could not bear to feel the horror of it.

In the middle of the novel Lewis sends Babbitt to Maine for a fishing vacation. (Lewis discovered the Maine background he used in *Babbitt* in the summer of 1920 while he was at a resort on Lake Kennebago, correcting the galley proofs of his preceding novel, *Main Street*.) With Babbitt is his closest friend, Paul Riesling, a fellow Zenith businessman, who in the end becomes the victim of the culture in which Babbitt flourishes. The two men belong to what another American sociologist has taught us to call the lonely crowd. Babbitt is the classic joiner, the least self-aware man in the business crowd that he longs to please. In sending him to Maine, Lewis made what may be the first classic use of the state as a refuge from the modern rat race: three weeks in a Rangeley fishing camp is expected to provide a temporary fix and send the rat happily back to the race. A year later, Paul is in prison for the attempted murder of his wife and Babbitt returns to the fishing resort alone. But this visit is a failure. He is beginning to learn at last that Maine has no potency against Zenith; he can't live outside the crowd.

George F. Babbitt Takes a Maine Vacation

I

They had four hours in New York between trains. The one thing Babbitt wished to see was the Pennsylvania Hotel, which had been built since his last visit. He stared up at it, muttering, "Twenty-two hundred rooms and twenty-two hundred baths! That's got everything in the world beat. Lord, their turnover must be — well, suppose the price of rooms is four to eight dollars a day, and I suppose maybe some ten and — four times twenty-two hundred, — say six times twenty-two hundred, — well, anyway with restaurants and everything, say summers between eight and fifteen thousand a day! Every day! I never thought I'd see a thing like that! Some town! Of course the average fellow in Zenith has got more Individual Initiative than the fourflushers here, but I got to hand it to New York. Yes, sir, town, you're all right — some ways. Well, old Paulski, I guest we've seen everything that's worth while. How'll we kill the rest of the time? Movie?"

But Paul desired to see a liner. "Always wanted to go to Europe — and, by thunder, I will, too, some day before I pass out," he sighed.

From a rough wharf on the North River they stared at the stern of the *Aquitania* and her stacks and wireless antennae lifted above the dock-house which shut her in.

"By golly," Babbitt droned, "wouldn't be so bad to go over to the Old Country and take a squint at all these ruins, and the place where Shakespeare was born. And think of being able to order a drink whenever you wanted one! Just range up to a bar and holler out loud, 'Gimme a cocktail, and darn the police!' Not bad at all. What juh like to see, over there, Paulibus?"

Paul did not answer. Babbitt turned. Paul was standing with clenched fist, head drooping, staring at the liner as in terror. His thin body, seen against the summer-glaring planks of the wharf, was childishly meager.

Again, "What would you hit for on the other side, Paul?"

Scowling at the steamer, his breast heaving, Paul whispered, "Oh, my God!" While Babbitt watched him anxiously, he snapped, "Come on, let's get out of this," and hastened down the wharf, not looking back.

"That's funny," considered Babbitt. "The boy didn't care for seeing the ocean boats after all. I thought he'd be interested in 'em."

II

Though he exulted, and made sage speculations about locomotive horse-power, as their train climbed the Maine mountain ridge and from the summit he looked down the shining way among the pines; though he remarked, "Well, by golly!" when he discovered that the station at Katadumcook, the end of the line, was an aged freight-car; Babbitt's moment of impassioned release came when they sat on a tiny wharf on Lake Sunasquam, awaiting the launch from the hotel. A raft had floated down the lake; between the logs and the shore, the water was transparent, thin-looking, flashing with minnows. A guide in black felt hat with trout-flies in the band, and flannel shirt of a peculiarly daring blue, sat on a log and whittled and was silent. A dog, a good country dog, black and woolly gray, a dog rich in leisure and in meditation, scratched and grunted and slept. The thick sunlight was lavish on the bright water, on the rim of gold-green balsam boughs, the silver birches and tropic ferns, and across the lake it burned on the sturdy shoulders of the mountains. Over everything was a holy peace.

Silent, they loafed on the edge of the wharf, swinging their legs above the water. The immense tenderness of the place sank into

Fisherman at Moosehead Lake

Babbitt, and he murmured, "I'd just like to sit here — the rest of my life — and whittle — and sit. And never hear a typewriter. Or Stan Graff fussing in the 'phone. Or Rone and Ted scrapping. Just sit. Gosh!"

He patted Paul's shoulder. "How does it strike you, old snoozer?"

"Oh, it's darn good, Georgie. There's something sort of eternal about it."

For once, Babbitt understood him.

III

Their launch rounded the bend; at the head of the lake, under a mountain slope, they saw the little central dining-shack of their hotel and the crescent of squat log cottages which served as bedrooms. They landed, and endured the critical examination of the habitués who had been at the hotel for a whole week. In their cottage, with its high stone fireplace, they hastened, as Babbitt expressed it, to "get into some regular he-togs." They came out; Paul in an old gray suit and soft white shirt; Babbitt in khaki shirt and vast and flapping khaki trousers. It was excessively new khaki; his rimless spectacles belonged to a city office; and his face was not tanned but a city pink. He made a discordant noise in the place. But with infinite satisfaction he slapped his legs and crowed, "Say, this is getting back home, eh?"

They stood on the wharf before the hotel. He winked at Paul and drew from his back pocket a plug of chewing tobacco, a vulgarism forbidden in the Babbitt home. He took a chew, beaming and wagging his head as he tugged at it. "Um! Um! Maybe I haven't been hungry for a wad of eating-tobacco! Have some?"

They looked at each other in a grin of understanding. Paul took the plug, gnawed at it. They stood quiet, their jaws working. They solemnly spat, one after the other, into the placid water. They stretched voluptuously, with lifted arms and arched backs. From beyond the mountains came the shuffling sound of a far-off train. A trout leaped, and fell back in a silver circle. They sighed together.

IV

They had a week before their families came. Each evening they planned to get up early and fish before breakfast. Each morning they lay abed until the breakfast-bell, pleasantly conscious that there were no efficient wives to rouse them. The mornings were cold; the fire was kindly as they dressed.

Paul was distressingly clean, but Babbitt reveled in a good sound dirtiness, in not having to shave till his spirit was moved to it. He treasured every grease spot and fish-scale on his new khaki trousers.

All morning they fished unenergetically, or tramped the dim and aqueous-lighted trails among rank ferns and moss sprinkled with crimson bells. They slept all afternoon, and till midnight played stud-poker with the guides. Poker was a serious business to the guides. They did not gossip; they shuffled the thick greasy cards with a deft ferocity menacing to the "sports"; and Joe Paradise, king of guides, was sarcastic to loiterers who halted the game even to scratch.

At midnight, as Paul and he blundered to their cottage over the pungent wet grass, and pine-roots confusing in the darkness, Babbitt rejoiced that he did not have to explain to his wife where he had been all evening.

They did not talk much. The nervous loquacity and opinionation of the Zenith Athletic Club dropped from them. But when they did talk they slipped into the naive intimacy of college days. Once they drew their canoe up to the bank of Sunasquam Water, a stream walled in by the dense green of the hardhack. The sun roared on the green jungle but in the shade was sleepy peace, and the water was golden and rippling. Babbitt drew his hand through the cool flood, and mused: "We never though we'd come to Maine together!"

"No. We've never done anything the way we thought we would. I expected to live in Germany with my granddad's people, and study the fiddle."

"That's so. And remember how I wanted to be a lawyer and go into politics? I still think I might have made a go of it. I've kind of got the gift of gab — anyway, I can think on my feet and make some kind of spiel on most anything, and of course that's the thing you need in politics. By golly, Ted's going to law-school, even if I didn't! Well — I guess it's all worked out all right. Myra's been a fine wife. And Zilla means well, Paulibus."

"Yes. Up here, I figure out all sorts of plans to keep her amused. I kind of feel life is going to be different, now that we're getting a good rest and can go back and start over again."

"I hope so, old boy." Shyly: "Say, gosh, it's been awful nice to sit around and loaf and gamble and act regular with you along, you old horse-thief!"

"Well, you know what it means to me, Georgie. Saved my life."

The shame of emotion overpowered them; they cursed a little, to prove they were good rough fellows; and in a mellow silence, Babbitt whistling while Paul hummed, they paddled back to the hotel.

V

Though it was Paul who had seemed overwrought, Babbitt who had been the protecting big brother, Paul became clear-eyed and merry, while Babbitt sank into irritability. He uncovered layer on layer of hidden weariness. At first he had played nimble jester to Paul and for him sought amusements; by the end of the week Paul was nurse, and Babbitt accepted favors with the condescension one always shows a patient nurse.

The day before their families arrived, the women guests at the hotel bubbled, "Oh, isn't it nice! You must be so excited;" and the proprieties compelled Babbitt and Paul to look excited. But they went to bed early and grumpy.

When Myra appeared she said at once, "Now, we want you boys to go on playing around just as if we weren't here."

The first evening he stayed out for poker with the guides and she said in placid merriment, "My! You're a regular bad one!" The second evening she groaned sleepily, "Good heavens, are you going to be out every single night?" The third evening, he didn't play poker.

He was tired now in every cell. "Funny! Vacation doesn't seem to have done me a bit of good," he lamented. "Paul's frisky as a colt, but I swear, I'm crankier and nervouser than when I came up here."

He had three weeks of Maine. At the end of the second week he began to feel calm and interested in life. He planned an expedition to climb Sachem Mountain, and wanted to camp overnight at Box Car Pond. He was curiously weak, yet cheerful, as though he had cleansed his veins of poisonous energy and was filling them with wholesome blood.

He ceased to be irritated by Ted's infatuation with a waitress (his seventh tragic affair this year); he played catch with Ted, and with pride taught him to cast a fly in the pine-shadowed silence of Skowtuit Pond.

At the end he sighed, "Hang it, I'm just beginning to enjoy my vacation. But, well, I feel a lot better. And it's going to be one great year. Maybe the Real Estate Board will elect me president, instead of some fuzzy old-fashioned faker like Chan Mott."

On the way home, whenever he went into the smoking-compartment he felt guilty at deserting his wife and angry at being expected to feel guilty, but each time he triumphed, "Oh, this is going to be a great year, a great old year!"

WILLIAM CARPENTER

1940–

Born in Waterville, Maine, William Carpenter graduated from Dartmouth College and received a doctorate in English from the University of Minnesota. He taught at the University of Chicago before returning to Maine in 1972 to the College of the Atlantic in Bar Harbor. Of his work as a poet he has said, "I never wrote anything until I moved from Chicago to down-east coastal Maine. The city is no place for a poet; there's too much reality there, which is a distraction. In Maine there's nothing to do, so you're forced upon yourself, and you write out of that encounter."

The Tourists

The tourists arrive in Maine. I hear their cars
stopping out on the road, then five or six
faces appear in the foliage near my house.
Soon, they occupy the lawn, some of them
pitching tents, some staring at the sea.
It is the sea they've come for, and the men
climb over the ledges to the beach.
At first, only a few go in, trousers

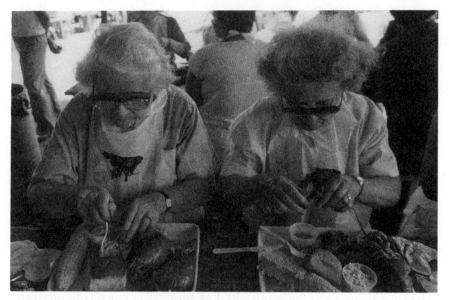

Rockland lobster festival

rolled up, stalking like egrets in the shallows,
holding their socks and shoes.
But their sons walk deeper, and one man
follows his son under the water,
his hat floating away like a white ship.
Soon, they all move over the beach, some upright,
others scuttling across the sand like crabs.
As more vanish into the surf, replacements arrive.
They stay a while in their tents, then, always
right after supper, they walk into the sea.
I am a native of this place, I grew up here, this
is my land, this is my family home, and these
are the ancestral stones, over which a beautiful
tourist bends, examining the grave of Uncle Horace.
I tell her about Horace, and, in her tent, she tells me
about Scarsdale, about her ex-husband and his dogs.
By the time we reach the shore, the tide is high,
the sea is full of hats. We are the final tourists.
Gulls pick at something on the shore:
a hermit crab. One gull flies up and drops it
on a stone. The others eat it.

She tests the water with her foot, she wades up
to her waist and waves goodbye. I wave goodbye,
wondering if what we felt was love, or just
my fascination with the transient:
women in orange tents, lost colorful tourists,
whatever blossoms on the lawn and dies.

TWENTIETH-CENTURY MAINE,
THE MIDDLE YEARS

EDNA ST. VINCENT MILLAY
1892–1950

The generation of American poets that followed Edwin Arlington Robinson included Edna St. Vincent Millay, who made a contribution of a different sort to our national literature. Unlike Robinson, who had to wait a long time for popular acceptance, Millay was awarded a Pulitzer Prize for poems written in her twenties, and she became enormously popular. During her lifetime, more than three quarters of a million copies of her books were sold. In the minds of our literary historians, Millay's poetry is closely tied to her generation, for whom she was, especially in the 1920s, a compelling literary heroine.

Millay began as a liberal idealist and a feminist and never left those faiths. She started to publish soon after World War I, an era of general revolt against contemporary conventions of morals and manners, and often took romantic subjects for her lyrics and sonnets, however wry the treatment: the nature of courtship and love, the evanescent beauties of nature, the finality of death. Maine appears as a remembered lovely background, especially the ocean itself, observed from Camden's piers or from Ragged Island, the outermost island in Casco Bay, where she and her husband lived for many summers. In a sequence of fifteen sonnets, "Sonnets from an Ungrafted Tree," she added a female portrait to that New England gallery of desperately lonely lives:

> So she came back into his house again
> And watched beside his bed until he died
> Loving him not at all. . . .

Edna Millay's own romantic revolt began in Camden when, at nineteen, her poem "Renascence" was a finalist in *The Lyric Year,* a national anthology of the hundred best poems of the year. The poem, a long lyrical meditation, began:

> All I could see from where I stood
> Was three long mountains and a wood.
> I turned and looked another way,
> And saw three islands in a bay.

The poem's subject was Keatsian, not Robinsonian, and was a remarkable assertion of a strong young personality. Her imagination reaches beyond the confining world of Camden, and she succumbs to a dark vision of an oppressive universe full of human suffering. A cleansing rain and wind storm returns her to a faith in God's presence in a beautiful natural world and in her own aspiring human spirit. It probably contained an extension of the conditions of Millay's actual life. Her father, a teacher and school superintendent, was divorced by her mother because of his compulsive gambling, and Edna, at the age of eight, and her two younger sisters shared for the next dozen years an economically sparse life with a heroic mother who, to support them, became a practical nurse. But the sisters' lives were full of their mother's ambitions for them, and, thrown back on themselves, they found ways to study literature and music and make summer excursions to the Camden hills, the seashore, and the ocean. They knew the names of mosses, flowers, and birds. All three were musical; one sister, Norma, became a singer and actress. Edna — called Vincent then — considered a career as a pianist.

During the summer of 1912, Norma worked at the Whitehall Inn on Route 1. At an entertainment arranged by the employees, she performed a song and then introduced Vincent, who recited "Renascence." A visitor from New York was struck by the young high school graduate and asked to meet her. The result was the discovery of a patron who arranged for Vincent's education at Vassar College and the beginning of the young poet's life beyond Maine.

From Vassar, where she wrote plays and poetry and first experimented with literary conventions, Edna moved to Greenwich Village, then joined the Provincetown Players as an actress and as the author of a bitter and popular antiwar play, *Aria da Capo.* Edna and Norma started their New York life in a small cold-water flat, where they were eventually joined by their youngest sister and their mother, who, to bring the whole Camden family into this new age, bobbed her hair too. So began the great years of Edna Millay's productive life. When

Potato farming, 1945

her famous quatrain about the candle that burns at both ends was published, first in *Poetry* and then in her second book, *A Few Figs from Thistles*, it was taken as her generation's answer to Longfellow's "Psalm of Life."

Sonnet

Oh, oh, you will be sorry for that word!
Give back my book and take my kiss instead.
Was it my enemy or my friend I heard,
"What a big book for such a little head!"
Come, I will show you now my newest hat,

"Fording the River"

And you may watch me purse my mouth and prink!
Oh, I shall love you still, and all of that.
I never again shall tell you what I think.
I shall be sweet and crafty, soft and sly;
You will not catch me reading anymore:
I shall be called a wife to pattern by;
And some day when you knock and push the door,
Some sane day, not too bright and not too stormy,
I shall be gone, and you may whistle for me.

Inland

People that build their houses inland,
People that buy a plot of ground
Shaped like a house, and build a house there,
Far from the sea-board, far from the sound

Of water sucking the hollow ledges,
Tons of water striking the shore, —
What do they long for, as I long for
One salt smell of the sea once more?

People the waves have not awakened,
Spanking the boats at the harbour's head,
What do they long for, as I long for, —
Starting up in my inland bed,

Beating the narrow walls, and finding
Neither a window nor a door,
Screaming to God for a death by drowning, —
One salt taste of the sea once more?

Northern April

O mind, beset by music never for a moment quiet, —
The wind at the flue, the wind strumming the shutter;

The soft, antiphonal speech of the doubled brook, never
    for a moment quiet;
The rush of the rain against the glass, his voice in the
    eaves-gutter!

Where shall I lay you to sleep, and the robins be quiet?
Lay you to sleep — and the frogs be silent in the marsh?
Crashes the sleet from the bough and the bough sighs
    upward, never for a moment quiet.
April is upon us, pitiless and young and harsh.

O April, full of blood, full of breath, have pity upon us!
Pale, where the winter like a stone has been lifted away,
    we emerge like yellow grass.
Be for a moment quiet, buffet us not, have pity upon us,
Till the green come back into the vein, till the giddiness
    pass.

Ragged Island

There, there where those black spruces crowd
To the edge of the precipitous cliff,
Above your boat, under the eastern wall of the island;
And no wave breaks; as if
All had been done, and long ago, that needed
Doing; and the cold tide, unimpeded
By shoal or shelving ledge, moves up and down,
Instead of in and out;
And there is no driftwood there, because there is no beach;
Clean cliff going down as deep as clear water can reach;

No driftwood, such as abounds on the roaring shingle,
To be hefted home, for fires in the kitchen stove;
Barrels, banged ashore about the boiling outer harbor;
Lobster-buoys, on the eel-grass of the sheltered cove:

There, thought unbraids itself, and the mind becomes single.
There you row with tranquil oars, and the ocean

Shows no scar from the cutting of your placid keel;
Care becomes senseless there; pride and promotion
Remote; you only look; you scarcely feel.

Even adventure with its vital uses,
Is aimless ardour now; and thrift is waste.

Oh, to be there, under the silent spruces,
Where the wide, quiet evening darkens without haste
Over a sea with death acquainted, yet forever chaste.

HENRY BESTON
1888–1968

Henry Beston was born in Quincy, Massachusetts, the son of a New England doctor and a French mother. He graduated from Harvard in 1909, earned a master's degree, and went to France, where he taught for several years at the University of Lyons. After serving in the U.S. Navy during World War I, Beston spent a year alone on the outer dunes of Eastham, on Cape Cod. *The Outermost House* is the classic chronicle of this reflective time. Years later, in 1964, the house itself was awarded National Literary Landmark status, which gave Beston great pleasure.

Beston spent some time in Maine, cruising along the coast and visiting friends in Damariscotta. Shortly after his marriage to the writer Elizabeth Coatsworth in 1930, they decided to buy Chimney Farm, overlooking Damariscotta Lake in Nobleboro. Here Beston lived and worked until his death.

He wrote steadily — primarily about his adopted state. Maine returned the favor when both Bowdoin College and the University of Maine awarded him honorary degrees. *Northern Farm,* from which this excerpt is taken, is a collections of columns Beston wrote for the *Progressive.* His several books about Maine are gentle observations of his world and reflect his pleasure in his friends and surroundings.

Elizabeth Coatsworth tells of his writing gifts in her collection of Beston's works, *Especially Maine:* "Perhaps Henry's greatest gift was to call attention to things that had always been there, but whose significance had gone largely unnoticed until he spoke or wrote about them. He was a great opener of windows."

The Alewife Run

I have just returned from a visit to Damariscotta Mills and the alewife run. Every year we all go over to see this great run of fish which is one of the marvels of our coast.

Some three miles away as the crow flies, the long, narrow arm of our pond flows south to a natural dam some fifty feet high, and there winds and tumbles down a stairway of cascades into the salt water of a tidal bay. The glen of the cascades is such a scene as one might find in an old Currier and Ives print or imagine for oneself out of Thoreau's America — a glen, a vale, of old rocks and tall, peaceful elms, of the incessant sound of waterfalls, and the white wings of seagulls coming and going, going and coming, far above and in the blue. Old houses have closed in to one side, their shingles forever wet with spray where they stand above the water, and the open windows of their kitchens and sheds forever full of the beautiful, incessant sound of the pouring streams.

It is to these waters that the alewives come every spring, going up to the pond to spawn from their unknown winter refuge in the outer sea. Though we call such runs here "herring runs," the fish is not a true herring, though it resembles one in size and shape. Our word "alewife" is a sort of early colonial transformation into English sound of an Indian word used by the redmen of seventeenth-century Massachusetts, and carried downeast by early settlers of our towns.

Perhaps a million or so fish crowd and swarm into the bay. They arrive in April, and their presence in the salt river is signalled to us by a simultaneous arrival of fishing birds from all our region of the coast. The gulls come, a cloud of wings and hungry cries, the fierce osprey finds himself a shelter and a watch-tower and the fiercer and piratic eagle comes to take the osprey's catch. The fish show no haste in going up into the pond. The living mass waits for good weather, and for a new warmth in the outlet stream. On some fine morning in May, with the sun shining overhead, the run begins.

Entering from the bay, the thickly-crowding, blue-backed, golden-bellied masses are confronted by a channel which branches at the dam into two wild, outrushing brooks. One stream leads to the cascades and to wooden basins from which the alewives are dipped in nets and sent to the smokehouse, for there is an ancient commerce in these fish between our villages and the West Indian isles. It is probably the last relic of the eighteenth-century economy of colonial America. The other stream leads to a winding stair of old fieldstone basins built well over a hundred years ago to help the run move up into the pond.

Built as ruggedly as our boulder walls, and mellowed now by water and the years, these basins on the slope interpose their twistings and turnings to the furious descent of one branch of the outlet stream and at the top lead out of crying foam and currents into the mild and quiet haven of the pond.

The day being warm and summerish and the tide high in the morning, there was a fine run moving upstream when I arrived. One could see the unnumbered mass moving in from the bay, and holding its own in the strong current of fresh water, a stream of life battling an opposing stream. There was a touch of lavender in the blue-black color of the massed fish as they swam under the skin of the brown and rippled water, the swarm pressing close together, each fish having just room to move its fins and no more.

Above and in the channel of the basins the stream was all a miracle of water and life, of life pressing onward, struggling fiercely to turn, climbing, climbing through the wild watery roar and the torrent whose foam was swift with the shadow and sunlight of the elms overhead, life pressing on, believing in itself, keeping the first faith, and remembering the immemorial decree.

FARM DIARY

A household catastrophe. While rummaging about on the kitchen table, I knock over my bottle of ink and spill a great, black puddle on the Mennonite tablecloth. Household remedies come quickly into play, a rinsing, a twenty-four hour soaking in sour milk, and a last treatment with salt and lemon juice. Our kind friend Mrs. Linwood Palmer tells Elizabeth to be sure to use the lemon and salt treatment

"A Day's Catch"

in full sunlight. Presto change-o! All well again, and you'd never know that anything had happened. The gasoline pump at the pond having developed a cussedness of being slow to start, my new neighbor, Freddy French, late First Sergeant USA, comes over to give me a friendly and much appreciated lift, and soon has the engine going in good style. Weather bureau warning of a cold night and a possible frost, and the whole neighborhood in a rush to cover what tomatoes have been hazarded outdoors. Temperature at one A.M., 36.

Among the many things for which I remain profoundly grateful is the fact that so much of life defies human explanation. The unimaginative and the dull may insist that they have an explanation for everything, and level at every wonder and mystery of life their popgun theories, but God be praised, their wooden guns have not yet dislodged the smallest star. It is well that this be so, for the human spirit can die of explanations, even if, like many modern formulae, they are but explanations which do not explain.

A world without wonder, and a way of mind without wonder, becomes a world without imagination, and without imagination man is a poor and stunted creature. Religion, poetry, and all the arts have their sources in this upwelling of wonder and surprise. Let us thank God that so much will forever remain out of reach, safe from our inquiry, inviolate forever from our touch.

ABBIE HUSTON EVANS
1881–1983

Abbie Huston Evans was a Maine nature poet of the finest kind. She was raised in Camden, where her father, a former Welsh coal miner, was the minister of the Congregational church. She went to Radcliffe College for her B.A. and M.A. degrees, worked in Colorado, and spent her last years in Pennsylvania. Yet her sense of identification with Maine remained at the core of her poetry, as these lines from "Hill-born" attest:

> My outline fixed forever, I was I,
> Stamped by this rocky corner like a die,
> Shaped by these five hills and this edge of sea.

When young Abbie taught Sunday school, Edna St. Vincent Millay was one of her pupils. Later, in the foreword to the first collection of Evans's poems, *Outcrop,* Millay said, "These are the poems of one more deeply and more constantly aware than most people are of the many voices and faces of lively nature." Yet Evans's natural world was less the stuff of wildflowers and fleecy clouds than of the spare hard land of the seacoast, of the barren Camden Hills, and, uniquely, of the rocks of Maine, the geological formations that tie us to our most distant past. "Pebbles from Sister Island" reminds us of this connection and leads us to look anew at the shingle beaches that grace most of Maine's convoluted coastline.

Evans, a measured and quiet poet, published only three books of verse between 1928 and 1961. Her last collection, encompassing these books and a few new poems, appeared in 1970, when she was in her nineties. She received her share of honors: several literary awards for her poetry and an honorary degree from Bowdoin College in 1961. Abbie Evans died at the age of one hundred and two.

Silhouette

The lamp flared in a quick gust. — "Yet," I said,
"You've had a full life, Sarah." — "That depends;
"If you mean busy, I suppose so. Yes.
"What with the old folks — and Aunt Jane — and Mandy."
She took her basket and got up to go,
Her hand a gaunt root wrapped about the handle.
" — Nothing ever took me off my feet.
"That's the whole story. — Well," she said, "good night."

I held the lamp to light her down the path.

From an Offshore Island
(*September Gale*)

Hear now the ocean trouncing off this island,
The under-roar of wind down unfenced sea,
And through chance flaws, like dim light down a tunnel,
The bell buoy spent with distance.

Orion's chill, washed, subterranean glitter
Wheels up from under, and great Rigel blazes
Between tossed oak boughs that the gale of autumn
Tears at, lifts, lets fall.

"Island Home"

Old ocean's hoarse and implicated roaring
Brings me up sitting at the dead of night,
Its pent-in mouthless fury calling back
The wild first of creation,

The rage, the might, the rampage.
       — How shall I
Up from this anchored island not make answer,
I with my bones of rock dust hardly knitted
And my blood still salt from the sea?

Pebbles from Sister Island

       Eight miles off shore,
Worn down to velvet by the thumb and finger
Of the sea incessant-shaping, tight-grained, polished,
Foreign to granite (these are granite's grinders),
Powdered with salt they lie up. The steep beach
Is strange with jasper and outlandish stone

Dim-colored, brown-flecked, olive, chiefly black,
Most like old pagan basalt from the depths
Bared when the moon tore free.

The night Columbus talked with Isabella
These rocks were slatting on the coast of Maine.
When Rome fell, and Atlantis, they were here.
They rode the glacier down from Canada,
Maybe, in state; and dropped in the sack of the sea.
To-fro, to-fro, interminably washing,
Hurled and haled back with screeching from the shore,
To-fro, to-fro, they carved the great pink-granite
Platform of the island into hollows
Till it stands up from the glass floor of the sea
Like something out of Dali.

On the foot rule of time scaled to the vast they are new,
But their newness is nothing to mine; I tremble before
Their hoary generation. None the less
Let me hold them in my hand a moment, sense
Duration, through delight of touch approve
The buffing of the lapidary sea,
Darkly partake of the being of first rock.

E. B. WHITE
1899–1985

E. B. White was a Mainer by choice. His career as an essayist, poet and humorist began in New York, where he and his wife, Katharine, worked at *The New Yorker* magazine — White as a staff writer, his wife as fiction editor. His ties to Maine dated from childhood summers spent in Belgrade. Subsequent visits strengthened these ties, and in 1938 the Whites bought an eighteenth-century farmhouse at Allen Cove, near Blue Hill, which they had first seen in 1933 while cruising along the Maine coast.

The decision to leave the city, her job, and his commitment to *The New Yorker* was a major one. Both Whites knew they could continue to write and to edit from this distance, and they also knew the decision was not necessarily permanent. But at this time in their lives, Maine seemed irresistible. The beauty of their part of Maine, a windfall inheritance from Katharine's father, a sense that Maine was a better place than New York to raise their young son, and a feeling of confidence about their careers (White had just signed a contract for a column, "One Man's Meat," with *Harper's Magazine*) contributed to their decision to leave the city. For E. B. White the "Home-Coming" brought him back to a place which had always been part of his life; it gave him an opportunity to live a modest farmer's life, and it enabled him to set to work writing something more solid than the material he had been contributing to *The New Yorker*. Out of these times came his classic children's novels *Stuart Little* and *Charlotte's Web*.

The move to Maine in 1938 turned out to be a temporary one. In 1943 concerns about the condition of *The New Yorker*, involvement with his country's role in World War II, and health problems took them back to the city, and it was not until 1957 that the permanent move to Maine was made. It was to be E. B. White's home until his death.

White started writing his "Letters from the East" in the winter of 1957–1958, sending back to *The New Yorker* his wry comments on Maine life in general and on his farm in particular. Responding to a letter from a reader of *Charlotte's Web*, he typically understated his philosophy: "All that I hope to say in books, all that I ever hope to say, is that I love the world. I guess you can find that in there if you dig around." The pleasure White took in his surroundings, his neighbors, his farm animals, his family, and his friends is evoked in his clean, sensitive prose, and his gentle commentaries speak eloquently of his affection for his new, and final, home.

Home-Coming

Allen Cove, December 10, 1955

On the day before Thanksgiving, toward the end of the afternoon, having motored all day, I arrived home and lit a fire in the living room. The birch logs took hold briskly. About three minutes later, not to be outdone, the chimney itself caught fire. I became aware of this development rather slowly. Rocking contentedly in my chair, enjoying the stupor that follows a day on the road, I thought I heard the dull, fluttering roar of a chimney swift, a sound we who live in this house are thoroughly accustomed to. Then I realized that there would be no bird in residence in my chimney at this season of the year, and a glance up the flue made it perfectly plain that, after twenty-two years of my tenure, the place was at last afire.

The fact that my chimney was on fire did not greatly surprise or depress me, as I have been dogged by small and large misadventures for the past ten years, the blows falling around my head day and night, and I have learned to be ready for anything at any hour. I

E. B. White

phoned the Fire Department as a matter of routine, dialing a number I had once forehandedly printed in large figures on the edge of the shelf in the telephone closet, so that I would be able to read it without my glasses. (We keep our phone in a closet here, as you might confine a puppy that isn't fully house-trained. The dial system is unpopular anyway in this small rural Maine community, and as far as I am concerned, the entire New England Telephone & Telegraph Co. deserves to be shut up in a closet for having saddled us with dials and deprived us of our beloved operators, who used to know where everybody was and just what to do about everything, including chimney fires.)

My call was answered promptly, but I had no sooner hung up than I observed that the fire appeared to be out, having exhausted itself, so I called back to cancel the run, and was told that the department would like to come anyway. In the country, one excuse is as good as another for a bit of fun, and just because a fire has grown cold is no reason for a fireman's spirits to sag. In a very short time, the loud, cheerful apparatus, its red signal light blinking rapturously, careened into the driveway, and the living room filled rapidly with my fire-fighting friends. My fire chief is also my barber, so I was naturally glad to see him. And he had with him a robust accomplice who had recently been up on my roof installing a new wooden gutter, dry and ready to receive the first sparks from a chimney fire, so I was glad to see *him*. And there was still a third fire-eater, and everyone was glad to see everyone else, as near as I could make out, and we all poked about learnedly in the chimney for a while and then the department left. I have had dozens and dozens of home-comings at the end of an all-day ride on U.S. 1, but strangely enough this was one of the pleasantest.

Shortly before he died, Bernard DeVoto gave the Maine coast a brisk going over in his *Harper's* column, using some four-letter words that raised the hackles of the inhabitants. Mr. DeVoto used the word "slum" and the word "neon." He said that the highway into Maine was a sorry mess all the way to Bucksport, and that the whole strip was overpopulated and full of drive-ins, diners, souvenir stands, purulent amusement parks, and cheap-Jack restaurants. I was thinking about this indictment at lunch the other day, trying to reconstruct my own cheap-Jack impressions of the familiar route after my recent trip over it. As I sat at table, gnawing away at a piece of pie, snow began falling. At first it was an almost imperceptible spitting from the gray sky, but it soon thickened and came driving in from the northeast. I watched it catch along the edge of the drive, powder the stone wall, dust the spruce cover on the flower borders, coat the plowed land, and whiten the surface of the dark frozen pond, and I knew that all along the coast from Kittery on, the worst mistakes of men were being quietly erased, the lines of their industrial temples, and U.S. 1

crowned with a cold, inexpensive glory that DeVoto unhappily did not live to see.

Even without the kindly erasures of the snow, the road into Maine does not seem a slum to me. Like highways everywhere, it is a mixed dish: Gulf and Shell, bay and gull, neon and sunset, cold comfort and warm, the fussy facade of a motor court right next door to the pure geometry of an early-nineteenth-century clapboard house with barn attached. You can certainly learn to spell "moccasin" while driving into Maine, and there is often little else to do, except steer and avoid death. Woods and fields encroach everywhere, creeping to within a few feet of the neon and the court, and the experienced traveler into this land is always conscious that just behind the garish roadside stand, in its thicket of birch and spruce, stands the delicate and well-proportioned deer; just beyond the overnight cabin, in the pasture of granite and juniper, trots the perfectly designed fox. This is still our triumphant architecture, and the Maine man does not have to penetrate in depth to be excited by his coastal run; its flavor steals into his consciousness with the first ragged glimpse of properly textured woodland, the first whiff of punctually drained cove.

Probably a man's destination (which is ever in the motorist's thoughts) colors the highway, enlarges or diminishes its defects. Gliding over the tar, I was on my way home. DeVoto, traveling the same route, was on his way to what he described rather warily as "professional commitments," by which he probably meant that he was on his way somewhere to make a speech or get a degree. Steering a car toward home is a very different experience from steering a car toward a rostrum, and if our findings differ, it is not that we differed greatly in powers of observation but that we were headed in different emotional directions. I sometimes suspect that when I am headed east, my critical faculties are retarded almost to the vanishing point, like a frog's heartbeat in winter.

What happens to me when I cross the Piscataqua and plunge rapidly into Maine at a cost of seventy-five cents in tolls? I cannot describe it. I do not ordinarily spy a partridge in a pear tree, or three French hens, but I do have the sensation of having received a gift from a true love. And when five hours later, I dip down across the Narramissic and look back at the tiny town of Orland, the white spire of its church against the pale-red sky stirs me in a way that Chartres could never do. It was the Narramissic that once received as fine a lyrical tribute as was ever paid to a river — a line in a poem by a schoolboy, who wrote of it, "It flows through Orland every day." I never cross that mild stream without thinking of his testimonial to the constancy, the dependability of small, familiar rivers.

Familiarity is the thing — the sense of belonging. It grants exemption from all evil, all shabbiness. A farmer pauses in the doorway of his barn and he is wearing the right boots. A sheep stands under an apple tree and it wears the right look, and the tree is hung with puckered frozen fruit of the right color. The spruce boughs that bank the foundations of the homes keep out the only true winter wind, and the light that leaves the sky at four o'clock automatically turns on the yellow lamps within, revealing to the soft-minded motorist interiors of perfect security, kitchens full of a just and lasting peace. (Or so it seems to the homing traveler.)

Even journalism in Maine has an antic quality that gives me the feeling of being home. The editorial in our weekly paper, after taking DeVoto to task for his disparaging remarks, ended on a note of delirious maladroitness. The editorialist strongly urged DeVoto to return — come back and take a second look, see the *real* Maine. Then he added, "Note: DeVoto has died since this article was written."

Benny DeVoto, a good fighter in all good causes, would enjoy that one thoroughly if he could indeed return for one more look around.

The deer season is all over for 1955. One day last week, half the hunters in town converged on the swamp south of here, between the road and shore, for a final drive. As I rode into the village that afternoon, there was a rifleman at every crossing, and the cries of the beaters could be heard from the woods, the voice of one of them much louder and clearer than the others — a buglelike sound that suggested the eagerness of a hound. During November, a deer can't move anywhere in this community without having its whereabouts flashed via the grapevine. As the season draws to a close, a sort of desperateness infects the male population. That afternoon it was almost as though the swamp contained an escaped convict. I heard two shots just before dark, but I learned later that neither of them took effect, and was secretly glad. Still, this business of favoring the deer over the hunter is a perplexing one; some of my best friends are deerslayers, and I never wish a man bad luck. As a spectator at the annual contest between deer and man, I am in the same fix as at the Harvard-Yale game — I'm not quite sure which club I'm rooting for.

In the village, I found three big trucks loading fir-balsam wreaths for Boston. They were lined up in formation, headed out, ready for the starter's gun. The loads were already built high in the air. Fir balsam is like no other cargo; even a workaday truck is exalted and wears a consecrated look when carrying these aromatic dumplings to the hungry dwellers in cities. This is the link that must not be broken. The head man in charge of wreaths was standing in front of his platoon, directing operations. He was one of those who had officiated at my chimney fire. His cheeks were red with cold. I asked him if he would be going to Boston himself with one of the trucks, and he said no, he couldn't go, because he had pneumonia.

"You really got pneumonia?" I asked as the wicked wind tugged at our shirts.

"Yes, indeed," he replied cheerfully. "Can't seem to shake it."

I report this conversation so the people of Boston will not take their Christmas greens for granted. Wreaths do not come out of our wood lots and roll up to Boston under their own steam; they must be pried out and boosted on their way by a man with pneumonia. I noted that several of the crew were fellows whom I had last seen a few weeks ago shingling the roof of my ell in Indian summer. Hereabouts a man must know every trade. First he tacks cedar shingles to a neighbor's roof, then he's off to Boston to shingle the front doors of Beacon Hill with the living green.

Maine sends about a million Christmas trees out of the state every year, according to my latest advices. It is an easy figure to remember, and an easy one to believe as you drive about the county and see the neatly tied bundles along the road, waiting to be picked up, their little yellow butts so bright and round against the darkling green. The young fir balsam is a standard cash crop, just like the middle-aged clam. The price paid for trees "at the side of the road" ranges from a dollar a bundle (four or five trees) to $3.75. A man can be launched, or catapulted, into the Christmas tree business quite by surprise. I wandered across the road the other day and up into the maple woods beyond my hayfield, and discovered that a miracle had taken place while my back was turned; the grove was alive with young firs, standing as close together as theatergoers between the acts.

The Christmas-tree harvest is hard on the woods, though. People tend to cut wastefully, hacking away wherever the going is good. And the enemy is always at our gates in the form of bugs and blights. I have just read a report on the forest-insect situation, sent me by the county agent. We have all sorts of picturesque plagues. The balsam woolly aphid. Birch dieback. Dutch elm disease. Spruce budworm. (A spruce "bud" in Maine parlance is a spruce cone — the thing a red squirrel eats the seeds of, sitting on a rock, and the thing Boston and New York celebrants like to put on their mantelpieces. The bud-worm comes into the state in the form of a moth, on the northeast wind, in summertime. I don't know whether a squirrel or a wood-lot owner has more at stake in this particular crisis.)

There are only a few small items of news to report at this season. Canada jays have been observed in the vicinity, and they managed to get into the paper, under the headline "UNUSUAL BIRD SEEN." I felt pretty good about this, because I had spotted two of these whis-key-jacks (not to be confused with cheap-Jacks) way back in October. The liquor store in the county seat was held up by a masked gunman recently and robbed of $2,672.45, which turned out to be the day's receipts and, of course, gave a much clearer picture of the amount of drinking done around here than any previous event. It would appear that the whiskey-jacks are here advisedly: they just like the sound of the place. Under the big shade trees in front of the house, the lawn is littered with dozens of half-eaten apples. I studied these, wondering what had been going on. Then I discovered that it was the work of crows. The crows pick little yellow apples from the old tree by the shed and carry them to some high perch before rifling them for seeds. In this respect they are no different from the people of San Francisco, who like to drink at the Top of the Mark, where they can really see what they are doing.

Here in New England, each season carries a hundred foreshadow-ings of the season that is to follow — which is one of the things I love about it. Winter is rough and long, but spring lies all round about. Yesterday, a small white keel feather escaped from my goose and lodged in the bank boughs near the kitchen porch, where I spied it as I came home in the cold twilight. The minute I saw the feather, I was projected into May, knowing that a barn swallow would be along to claim the prize and use it to decorate the front edge of its nest. Immediately, the December air seemed full of wings of swallows and the warmth of barns. Swallows, I have noticed, never use any feather but a white one in their nest-building, and they always leave a lot of it showing, which makes me believe that they are interested not in the feather's insulating power but in its reflecting power, so that when they skim into the dark barn from the bright outdoors they will have a beacon to steer by.

JEAN STAFFORD
1915—1979

The snow of winter did lie very long upon the ground.
— Christopher Levett

Out of the Bosom of the Air,
  Out of the cloud-folds of her garments shaken
Over the woodlands brown and bare,
  Over the harvest-fields forsaken,
  Silent, and soft, and slow
  Descends the snow.
— Henry Wadsworth Longfellow

It is commonly assumed that Maine winters are long and cold and onerous. While this is often true, it does not take into account the wide climatic swings between northeastern and southwestern Maine. In such a large state (almost as large as the five other New England states combined), with a 300-mile north-south axis, there is bound to be variety; Maine's annual snowfall can range from 90 to 110 inches in the northern mountains and from 50 to 70 inches along the coast. The ocean moderates the extremes of temperature both summer and winter and accounts for a 10-degree higher annual temperature along the coast than in the northern interior. Coastal winters are nowhere near as severe as those in northern Maine — or New York or Minnesota. What is true about all of Maine's winters is that they can be very beautiful.

Jean Stafford embraced the best qualities of her Maine winter with a novelist's perception and sensitivity. She had bought a house in Damariscotta Mills in 1945 with the proceeds of her best-selling first novel, *Boston Adventure*. Moving into it, her first house, was exciting, but her enthusiasm for it and for Maine became inextricably

"Rockport — Winter"

entwined with the unhappy nature of her relationship with her husband, the poet Robert Lowell. Their 1940 marriage had survived physical and intellectual turmoil as well as Lowell's imprisonment as a conscientious objector in 1943, but it was rapidly disintegrating. The brief time they spent in the Maine house, in 1945–1946, did, however, provide Stafford with material for the following essay on a Maine winter, so full of hope and enjoyment, and for several short stories. "Polite Conversations" is an acerbic commentary on the shallowness of two of her neighbors. "A Country Love Story" and "Influx of Poets" are personal stories of the unfolding anguish of her marriage.

Stafford continued to write, primarily novels and short stories, and her *Collected Stories* won the Pulitzer Prize for fiction in 1970. Her deep, perceptive involvement with the people and places she knew combined with her clear, crisp style to produce some of the finest fiction of her period.

New England Winter

After the summer people have gone back to town and the birds have gone south and the roadside stands with their Moxie and authentic braided rugs have been boarded up along the highways, New England confronts the most serious time of year — long, massive, magnificent, as exciting to the eye, as tonic, as any natural splendor in the land. . . .

And though the felicities of progress and sophistication have tempered the tyranny of the northern winter, it is still a challenging and heady time; it is not all a winter carnival and chic resorts. Away from the cities and away from the skiing centers, along the shores of Maine where the North Atlantic mightily declaims and in the farming lands of New Hampshire and Vermont, the winter has not lost its rigors; it is old-fashioned, it is hard, beautiful, solemn; it is a season of great character and living through it requires pride and stamina. The rewards of the struggle are bountiful: the eye is continually delighted and refreshed, the heart is eased by the imposition of simplicity upon it, the intellect admires the imperious rages of the elements and the Yankee refusal to be cowed by them.

Some years ago, my husband and I lived on a hillside at the outskirts of Damariscotta Mills, a Maine village that is unacquainted, winter and summer, with the tourist trade and relies for its support on modest marine and agrarian endeavors. Its residents have either lived there all their lives or are in retirement, and it is not concerned with the arrival and departure of station wagons but is governed only by the seasons. . . . I do not remember any places of business in Damariscotta Mills except a post office, a somnolent railroad depot, a volunteer fire station and a general store where it was possible to buy bread and beans and overshoes; the men who sat by the stove and whittled had the countenances and the clothes and the politics of cracker-barrel philosophers, but I never heard one of them utter an epigram. It seems to me that they talked factually and with no unusual similes about how cold it was; it was somehow satisfying to know that the thermometer read eighteen below zero and we therefore had the right to have the shivers. . . .

The snows of Maine are like those romantically believed to belong to history, to an enchanted and irrevocable past time, to exist now only on Christmas cards, in Currier and Ives prints and in the memories of childhood. The answer to the pensive question, "Where are the snows of yesteryear?" is, "They are still falling faithfully in Maine from November (and often earlier) until April (and sometimes later)." It is astonishing to awaken to the rising of the sun over meadows and pine woods and church spires which, during the night, have secretly been mantled and disguised by a profound and noble fall of snow; all harsh contours have been smoothed away and all eyesores hidden by this ample, luminous vesture, pink in the places where the early sun has touched, blue in the shadows. The lower branches of the evergreens drag with their handsome burden and the upper ones glint with fangs of ice; the fern brakes left by the frost on windowpanes are as subtle and elegant as the patterns of damask; immense, pellucid stalactites threateningly depend from the eaves. Each morning looks like Christmas. As early as this, the hush is boundless and breathless and chaste; an icicle shattering rings like shot. Presently the snowplow and the ditcher will restore the buried roads to their uses, but now the landscape is uninhabited except, occasionally, by deer emboldened by the quiet and the solitude to visit salt licks, and by joyful dogs that madly root and roll. These snows are not ephemeral and do not dissolve in slush; they acquire a sparkling, crackling crust on which the next billowing mass will innocently settle down; snowmen made of it enjoy an impressive longevity; snowballs made of it are businesslike. Walking through an unfamiliar field is an experience of great suspense since one never knows, from one labored step to the next, where, under that deceptive plane surface, the sudden dips and holes and rocks may be.

There must have been overcast days, but I recall only brilliant skies and blinding sun on the undulant reaches of snow and dry, inebriating alpine air, as fresh to city lungs as spring water to a thirsty throat. The sun was hot like mountain sun and the southern rooms of our house at high noon took so much warmth from it that they were like solaria. This house had plumbing and electricity but it had no central heating, and we spent a good many of our waking hours feeding voracious stoves. There were dreadful times when the banked fires went out during the night and we awoke to a cold as cruel and crippling as if no part of the house had ever been warmed; the walls and floors seemed stiff and aged like neglected bones. We were such greenhorns that the first fierce cold caught us unawares and one morning I got up to find icicles hanging from all the bathroom taps and great tumors and hideous fractures in the pipes. After the repair, we nightly swaddled the pipes like babies with sweat shirts and wool socks. During the time the plumber was making the replacements at a snail's pace, we depended on the well for all our water; each morning the well was covered with a perfect spiderweb left by the frost, so meticulous and chaste that I hated to disturb it even for a pail of the most delicious water imaginable.

When I was not working or attending to the mechanics of keeping warm, I spent most of my time contemplating the landscape; I would stand at a window for half an hour doing nothing at all but looking out at the branches of the spiraea ingeniously frozen in their tangles, or at the line of tall fir trees at the lake's edge casting their emphatic shadows on the ice, whose surface snow bore here and there the print of wagon wheels or cloven hoofs; nothing, I thought, had ever looked so totally abandoned as the beached canoes on the banks. Or, after I had done my shopping at the store, I would go down to the river where the villagers fished for smelt through the ice. From their tar-paper shelters, sometimes painted fancifully in red or blue, came the thick wood smoke of their fires; these flimsy, canting little shacks had a raffish, gypsy look in the austere countryside, but their occupants were in earnest, angling hour after hour in an ice-cold arm of the North Atlantic.

If I were inclined to be more enterprising in my idling, I would take a walk to the brow of a hill that rose from the far shore of the lake. I would go plunging down through a field where, in some clever place, a smart fox was sleeping, a creature we had sometimes seen on autumn evenings flirting his fine red bush as he raced to cover over a route so adroitly ambiguous that he could never be caught, he had harried the cats and stolen the chickens, and made fools of the dogs and now, remorseless, he was asleep. If I were in luck, I might see a stoat metamorphosed into an ermine, invisible against the snow except for the black tip of its tail and its vivid eyes. As I went through the stand of firs, something might disturb a branch above me and I would be suddenly showered with a spray so surprisingly cold that my teeth began to chatter wildly. On the lake, school children had cleared a skating rink and were wheeling round and round, bundled to their eyes, their stocking caps flying like banners, their shouts echoing metallically in the thin and painful air. Sometimes they had built an amateurish fire that burned fitfully and smokily.

There was an extensive view from the crest of the hill, down the broadening, immobilized river, and over the soft hills where, in distant farmyards, I could see huddles of cows and horses; sometimes there were families of goats and I could hear their human, unsociable voices irascibly complaining about everything. On these quiet days, the weather vanes on barns stood still, the whales and chanticleers motionless but poised for change; the smoke ascending from the stout old chimneys went straight up in dead-white plumes and loitered long. From this elevation, the pace of everything seemed stately and deliberate: the children on the lake looked to be describing their parabolas and figure eights in slow motion; an ox-drawn wagon was an eternity traversing a quarter of a mile; the mixed train moved through the valley like something tired to death. Sounds were quick and sudden but the stillness held them and they were not dissipated for a long time; the ring of an ax was doubled and tripled and quadrupled and was not entirely obliterated until the woodcutter struck again; a single church bell sounded like a carillon; one voluble gray squirrel sounded like a dozen; the whistle of the train lagged behind long after the locomotive had disappeared.

Ossified by ice though it first appeared to be, there was on this scene incessant motion and a sense, everywhere, of hidden and arrested life. Invisible beneath the thick lid of ice, the tides of the sea were constant in the river; effete hydrangeas were still alive in the greenhouses whose windows received the nutritious sunlight; the rose gardens, swathed in burlap, nestled scrawnily under the snow, sheltered from the wind by old stone walls. There were, however, a few corpses of scarecrows, twice as degraded and sad and foolish as when they had guarded the cabbages at their feet.

When the sun began to set, blood red and vast and violent, harshly showing forth the bony bareness of the beech ridges, a numbing chill came on and everyone made for the reassuring lights that began to show warmly in the hearts of the houses. Once when I alone, so far as I could judge, was still abroad at this hour, I saw two moose reconnoitering at the edge of the lake; they were there for only a moment and then, alarmed by something nearby, they went crashing noisily through a thicket and vanished in the gathering dusk. Only the ice fishermen stayed on after sunset; the catch was better when the night fell and, obstinate and warmed with rum, they would tarry on the river half the night. It was not uncommon, at this silent hour, to see quail and pheasant in one's path and in the enriching, final rays of the sun, the plumage of a cock pheasant shone like sumptuous jewels.

At night, there was a more formal kind of elegance. The land was pale and the trees and waterways were black, but the firmament was indigo and the sharp stars were furiously bright. Such was the marvelous clarity of the atmosphere that not even the galaxy was blurred and counting the stars seemed not improbable. Except that it was much too cold outside and infinitely pleasant within, beside a crackling, hissing fire in an iron stove with a profusion of decorative knobs and grilles and splayed feline feet.

We read ceaselessly and everything. There was a great deal of nocturnal industry in our house, but presently the racket did not interfere with our concentration and we seldom looked up from our books. The mice and rats (nothing smaller could have set up such a commotion) worked tirelessly and monotonously in the walls — restoring and remodeling; sometimes there was a scuffle followed by a chase, and at other times someone seemed to be pouring acorns down a tinnily reverberating chute. Now and then there was a thin, terrified scream. In the attics and in the barn, especially on moonlight nights, the ghosts of restless sea captains and swindled Indians took no pains to walk softly but thumped and fumbled loudly overhead; a team of juvenile specters played a hopscotch tournament over the kitchen that lasted from the first frost in October until the line storm in mid-April. These were not ominous haunts; they were only bored and fretful. Sometime in the dead of winter, we saw the northern lights in abrupt arcs and streamers, patinating the water and besilvering the hemlocks. Almost as strange and lovely in their effect were the fogs that occasionally came billowing in from the coast, enlarging what they did not dematerialize. The cupola of Kavanaugh Mansion, next door to us, appeared to be disengaged from the house and to hover above the roof without support. The trunks of the elm trees in our yard were hugely magnified and so were the pickets of our stubby fence. A walker's flashlight was as weird and evasive as a will-o'-the-wisp. But inland fogs are rare and brief and by sunup they have perished.

The only drawback to a traditional New England winter is that it lasts a little too long and in February there starts everywhere to be a sense of waiting and of impatience with the limitations of activity imposed by the cold. Subjects of conversation have been milked dry and it is vexatious to have to suck on desiccated rinds. Fishermen begin to mend their landing nets and gardeners to order seeds. Tired of the loyal winter birds, the snow buntings and the chickadees, we began to wish for warblers and whippoorwills; we began to imagine the rustling sounds of spring when the tree frogs never stopped their chirping and the loons nasally hallooed in the cattails and the marsh reeds. We were tantalized by balmy days when the snow came off the roofs in avalanches and the icicles fell and smashed themselves to smithereens. But likely as not, in the middle of the night that followed such a day, I would be roused out of sleep by the drone and sigh of the ditcher as it labored over the hilly road; flashing blue and red lights like evil eyes; by morning the splintered icicles would be replaced and the roofs laden with a new accumulation. Still, if our prospect tired us with its sameness, we could change our scene for a day — for the versatility of its landscape is one of Maine's excellences — and leave our pastoral village and go to look at the bleak old Light at Pemaquid and at the surf eternally pounding the rocky shores of the peninsula; beyond the point the ocean swept vast and forever.

But when the spring finally came, I missed the winter; my views were obscured by the leaves and there was something almost insipid in the ease of living. I even missed the noises in the walls at night, for the animals quit the house as soon as it was warm and went to live the life of Riley out of doors. The spring, though, was praiseworthy and had been worth waiting for just as the pleasures and the spectacles of the winter had been easily worth the discomfort and the ruined pipes and the fire tending. To people nerve-racked by the city's fidgets, there is no experience at once more calming and more stimulating than the genuine struggle with a New England winter.

RACHEL CARSON
1907–1964

Anyone who has ever been fascinated by the variety of marine life in a tidal pool or by the wonders revealed by a receding tide will delight in the works of Rachel Carson. Her essays prove her to be a most felicitous combination of writer and naturalist. Her careful observations of marine biology are recorded in a lucid, lyrical prose that makes them as accessible to the casual fisherman or beachcomber as to the serious student of biology.

She wrote of the Atlantic coast. As a summer resident of Southport Island, on the Sheepscot River, Carson was able to make detailed studies of Maine marine life and geologic history which expand our knowledge and understanding of this convoluted and infinitely varied shore.

Rachel Carson studied marine biology at Johns Hopkins University and at the Marine Biological Laboratory at Woods Hole, Massachusetts. She was on the staff of the U.S. Fish and Wildlife Service for fifteen years and was editor of their publications. *Silent Spring*, written in 1962, was a primary force in the environmental movement. It was preceded by award-winning works on the littoral, including *The Edge of the Sea*, from which this selection is taken.

The Rocky Shores

When the tide is high on a rocky shore, when its brimming fullness creeps up almost to the bayberry and the junipers where they come down from the land, one might easily suppose that nothing at all lived in or on or under these waters of the sea's edge. For nothing is visible. Nothing except here and there a little group of herring gulls, for at high tide the gulls rest on ledges of rock, dry above the surf and the spray, and they tuck their yellow bills under their feathers and doze away the hours of the rising tide. Then all the creatures of the tidal rocks are hidden from view but the gulls know what is there, and they know that in time the water will fall away again and give them entrance to the strip between the tide lines.

When the tide is rising the shore is a place of unrest, with the surge leaping high over jutting rocks and running in lacy cascades of foam over the landward side of massive boulders. But on the ebb it is more peaceful, for then the waves do not have behind them the push of the inward pressing tides. There is no particular drama about the turn of the tide, but presently a zone of wetness shows on the gray rock slopes, and offshore the incoming swells begin to swirl and break over hidden ledges. Soon the rocks that the high tide had concealed rise into view and glisten with the wetness left on them by the receding water.

Small, dingy snails move about over rocks that are slippery with the growth of infinitesimal green plants; the snails scraping, scraping, scraping to find food before the surf returns.

Like drifts of old snow no longer white, the barnacles come into view; they blanket rocks and old spars wedged into rock crevices, and their sharp cones are sprinkled over empty mussel shells and lobster-pot buoys and the hard stipes of deep-water seaweeds, all mingled in the flotsam of the tide.

Meadows of brown rockweeds appear on the gently sloping rocks of the shore as the tide imperceptibly ebbs. Smaller patches of green weed, stringy as mermaids' hair, begin to turn white and crinkly where the sun has dried them.

Now the gulls, that lately rested on the higher ledges, pace with grave intentness along the walls of rock, and they probe under the hanging curtains of weed to find crabs and sea urchins.

In the low places little pools and gutters are left where the water trickles and gurgles and cascades in miniature waterfalls, and many of the dark caverns between and under the rocks are floored with still mirrors holding the reflections of delicate creatures that shun the light and avoid the shock of waves — the cream-colored flowers of the small anemones and the pink fingers of soft coral, pendent from the rocky ceiling.

In the calm world of the deeper rock pools, now undisturbed by the tumult of incoming waves, crabs sidle along the walls, their claws busily touching, feeling, exploring for bits of food. The pools are gardens of color composed of the delicate green and ocher-yellow of encrusting sponge, the pale pink of hydroids that stand like clusters of fragile spring flowers, the bronze and electric-blue gleams of the Irish moss, the old-rose beauty of the coralline algae.

And over it all there is the smell of low tide, compounded of the faint, pervasive smell of worms and snails and jellyfish and crabs — the sulphur smell of sponge, the iodine smell of rockweed, and the salt smell of the rime that glitters on the sun-dried rocks.

One of my own favorite approaches to a rocky seacoast is by a rough path through an evergreen forest that has its own peculiar enchantment. It is usually an early morning tide that takes me along that forest path, so that the light is still pale and fog drifts in from the sea beyond. It is almost a ghost forest, for among the living spruce and balsam are many dead trees — some still erect, some sagging earthward, some lying on the floor of the forest. All the trees, the living and the dead, are clothed with green and silver crusts of lichen. Tufts of the bearded lichen or old man's beard hang from the branches like bits of sea mist tangled there. Green woodland mosses and a yielding carpet of reindeer moss cover the ground. In the quiet of that place even the voice of the surf is reduced to a whispered echo and the sounds of the forest are but the ghosts of sound — the faint sighing of evergreen needles in the moving air; the creaks and heavier groans of half-fallen trees resting against their neighbors and rubbing bark against bark; the light rattling fall of a dead branch broken under the feet of a squirrel and sent bouncing and ricocheting earthward.

But finally the path emerges from the dimness of the deeper forest and comes to a place where the sound of surf rises above the forest sounds — the hollow boom of the sea, rhythmic and insistent, striking against the rocks, falling away, rising again.

Up and down the coast the line of the forest is drawn sharp and clean on the edge of a seascape of surf and sky and rocks. The softness of sea fog blurs the contours of the rocks; gray water and gray mists merge offshore in a dim and vaporous world that might be a world of creation, stirring with new life.

The sense of newness is more than illusion born of the early morning light and the fog, for this is in very fact a young coast. It was only yesterday in the life of the earth that the sea came in as the coast subsided, filling the valleys and rising about the slopes of the hills, creating these rugged shores where rocks rise out of the sea and evergreen forests come down to the coastal rocks. Once this shore was like the ancient land to the south, where the nature of the coast has changed little during the millions of years since the sea and the wind and the rain created its sands and shaped them into dune and beach and offshore bar and shoal. The northern coast, too, had its flat coastal plain bordered by wide beaches of sand. Behind these lay a landscape of rocky hills alternating with valleys that had been worn by streams and deepened and sculptured by glaciers. The hills were formed of gneiss and other crystalline rocks resistant to erosion; the lowlands had been created in beds of weaker rocks like sandstones, shale, and marl.

Then the scene changed. From a point somewhere in the vicinity of Long Island the flexible crust of the earth tilted downward under the burden of a vast glacier. The regions we know as eastern Maine and Nova Scotia were pressed down into the earth, some areas being carried as much as 1200 feet beneath the sea. All of the northern coastal plain was drowned. Some of its more elevated parts are now offshore shoals, the fishing banks off the New England and Canadian coasts — Georges, Browns, Quereau, the Grand Bank. None of it remains above the sea except here and there a high isolated hill, like the present island of Monhegan, which in ancient times must have stood above the coastal plain as a bold monadnock.

Where the mountainous ridges and valleys lay at an angle to the coast, the sea ran far up between the hills and occupied the valleys. This was the origin of the deeply indented and exceedingly irregular coast that is characteristic of much of Maine. The long narrow estuaries of the Kennebec, the Sheepscot, the Damariscotta and many other rivers run inland a score of miles. These salt-water rivers, now arms of the sea, are the drowned valleys in which grass and trees grew in a geologic yesterday. The rocky, forested ridges between them probably looked much as they do today. Offshore, chains of islands jut out obliquely into the sea, one beyond another — half-submerged ridges of the former land mass. . . .

For the most part, the ruggedness of this coast is the ruggedness of the hills themselves. There are none of the wave-cut stacks and arches that distinguish older coasts or coasts of softer rock. In a few, exceptional places the work of the waves may be seen. The south shore of Mount Desert Island is exposed to heavy pounding by surf; there the waves have cut out Anemone Cave and are working at Thunder Hole to batter through the roof of the small cave into which the surf roars at high tide.

In places the sea washes the foot of a steep cliff produced by the shearing effect of earth pressure along fault lines. Cliffs on Mount Desert — Schooner Head, Great Head, and Otter — tower a hundred feet or more above the sea. Such imposing structures might be taken for wavecut cliffs if one did not know the geologic history of the region.

CONTEMPORARY WRITERS

⟨⟨⟨⟨⟨⟨⟨⟨⟨⟨

The Franco-Americans in Maine

Franco-Americans are the dominant minority group in Maine. They account for nearly a third of the state's population, and despite their steadfast adherence to their language, religion, and cultural identity, they have had a considerable impact on Maine and its economy.

Two distinct groups make up this people. The earliest Franco-Americans, descendants of seventeenth-century immigrants from Brittany, were from Acadia, the inclusive name for the Canadian regions of New Brunswick, Nova Scotia, Prince Edward Island, and Cape Breton as well as eastern Maine. A century later, in 1775, they were banished from their Canadian home by the British when they refused to promise to bear arms against Frenchmen. In an unusually cruel diaspora, marked by Henry Wadsworth Longfellow in his poem *Evangeline,* the Acadians were separated from their property and sometimes from their families. One group moved to Louisiana and established the Cajun culture, but most crossed the border and settled in colonial farming communities along the St. John River valley. They were later joined by more Acadians, who had been dispossessed by American Tories fleeing the Revolution. Today, these Acadians are a majority in such northern towns as Van Buren, Fort Kent, and Madawaska, and they have been successful in maintaining their ethnic heritage.

The second wave of immigration came from Quebec near the end of the nineteenth century. A declining farm economy at home and the active recruitment by textile factory representatives induced thousands of French Canadians to settle along the New England rivers that provided power for the mills. The Lewiston-Auburn, Biddeford, Waterville, and Brunswick areas today have sizable Franco-American populations.

Working in the mills was hard. The hours were long and the pay was low, but the French Canadians were proud, often leaving school to help support their families and spending their lives in the mills. The French-Canadian enclaves were tight and centered on the Catholic church and the parochial schools. For many, public high school was their first exposure to English, and because of their different language and foreign ways, they were subject to discrimination. The Brunswick newspaper, for example, ignored French-Canadian births, deaths, and social events in its coverage of the town.

In more recent times the closing of the mills dispersed the labor force, and the increasing use of English at home and in school helped accelerate the Franco-Americans' integration into the larger community. Nevertheless, these resilient people still retain great pride in their history and heritage. The following examples of Franco-American writing tell us much about the experience of growing up in the Québecois culture in Maine.

A. POULIN, JR.
1938–

A. Poulin, Jr., was born in Lisbon, Maine. He is a poet and now professor of English at the State University of New York at Brockport. He tells of his ambivalent feelings about his Franco-American heritage in an autobiographical essay from his translation of the poems of Anne Hébert and of the strength of his identification with this heritage in "To My Brother."

Poetry and the Landscape of Epiphany

I was born in a small inland town in New England into a family of French-Canadians — also known as Franco-Americans, Canucks, Frogs, and, with somewhat more recent ethnic diplomacy, Québecois-Americans. My mother's parents seem to have emigrated to the United States and to Lisbon, Maine, without much fanfare sometime before she was born; ironically, their somewhat demure arrival into the United States may have been due to the fact that her paternal grandmother was reputedly Irish (thus probably risking being Protestant, too). My father's utterly Catholic parents packed their nine kids into a rented car and headed south in a more tribal fashion when he was still a child. In either case, ours was and — even twenty some-odd years after most of us have moved away from Lisbon and though our numbers now include corporate vice-presidents and college professors — at wakes, weddings and anniversaries of one kind or another, ours still continues to be a thoroughly French-Canadian family whose essential characteristics are seeded deeply amidst the roots of our communal sensuous life.

An American by birth, I first spoke French — actually a hodge-podge *patois* of medieval French, French-Canadian "joual" (i.e. "horse language") and a fractured Frank-glish — before I began speaking a heavily French-accented Downeast Yankee English taught to me primarily by Verna Dingley, my Yankee childhood friend's mother so that her son and I could play together. Despite gestures toward assimilation by my parents (school clothes that were always just a little too new and just a little too neat), most of my childhood was steeped in the mores of my French-Canadian ancestors and in their "manners," what Lionel Trilling described as "the hum and buzz of implication . . . that part of a culture which is made up of half-uttered or unuttered or unutterable expressions of value."

And in their overt customs, too: a primary education at St. Berna-dette's, the parochial school run by the good sisters of the Presentation of Mary in St. Anne's Parish, where the curriculum included Catechism classes every day and *l'Histoire Sainte* (a mixture of ha-giography and Church history taught in French, the language of our Roman Catholic faith and inculcating in us the conviction that St. Laurence's martyrdom consisted of being barbecued to death); Father Leo J. Bourque celebrating Holy Mass at seven o'clock every morning of the year, the good sisters in the sacristy an hour ahead of time to lay out the vestments, fill the cruets with water and wine and prepare the altar; (in feverish glare I still see Sister Mary Edmond's and Sister Jean-Marie's black habits billowing in swirling clouds of ice-gray snow in March as they walk silently to Church in semi-darkness); Father Bourque coming to our classes once a month to read our report cards in public, praising the successful and reprimanding the sluggards; a closely knit family of tribal life involving literally dozens of aunts, uncles and cousins that rivaled any Gilbert and Sullivan operetta and often clustered around religious observances, holidays, family crises, and always returning to memory with the odors of wine, pure beeswax, incense, pork pies, baked beans and whiskey on the lips of the grownups.

"Neighbors Listen"

From birth to death our lives were governed by grand and sacred concentric calendars ruling virtually all measures of time, from the seemingly endless seasons to individual and all too breathless hours of worship or play. And during some of those hours Harold Dingley made fun of my Canuck accent, teased me because I had to go to Mass every morning during Lent, or tried to get me to eat hot-dogs

Cabot Mill workers

on Fridays. A few days before my First Communion, Harold threw a rock at me. A small sliver of that childhood stone is still lodged in my forehead and unleashes a sharp pain when I press it.

My aunts steamed their kitchens with preserves and pickles, with the bleach of their Monday-morning wash. My uncles' clothes reeked with the oil of wool and cotton mills where they worked; at night they sat on their front porches and drank warm beers late into the darkness, the stars of their cigarettes burning silently, ferociously in the gravel of their lungs. And they died — leaving clinging presences. . . .

Most French-Canadian-Americans or Franco-American-Canucks of my generation . . . and that's exactly what we were and were not: neither French, nor Canadian, nor genuinely American — we spent the better part of our adolescence and early childhood working feverishly hard at negating and trying to erase all traces of our Québecois heritage. First the accent, then the language, then the faith, the customs, the manners — anything that could be scraped, shaved or singed off.

Long before the phrase became popular in the Province of Québec

Brunswick mills

at the start of the Separatist Movement, we had come to know and feel viscerally that we were the "White Niggers" of New England. And we were hell-bent on becoming categorically assimilated (this time Calvin Klein and Bill Blass), on "making it" in any man's world other than the fiber factories of our French-Canadian fathers in Lewiston, Maine, in any woman's world other than the kitchens of our Franco-American mothers in Lowell, Massachusetts, where, even as in Québec, in the words of Anne Hébert, "the man smells the bread burning, and the center of the day collapses on us like water without seams."

And yet, after private school in Hyde Park, New York, college in Chicago, and the University in Iowa, after the start of a professional career, ostensibly assimilated by a WASP society as much as possible, some of us eventually realized that we also had severed ourselves from a vital source of our total selves, that source where the blood that feeds the soul is brewed. Having renounced the hum and buzz of a culture's implication, we also had precluded the possibility of any fruitful encounter with the living heart of the culture itself.

If we knew something about the culture of Germany and Japan, we knew nothing about our ancestral culture that eventually would play a central role in a people's evolution from the ennui of being nothing better than French-Canadian to a growing zealous pride in being Québecois. If we knew all we were expected to know about the literatures of England and America in order to pass Ph.D. comprehensive exams to become professors, we were ignorant of the voices and of the literature of our tribal sisters and brothers. (Indeed, some of us had been professors for years before realizing or at least admitting that even Jack Kerouac had been one of us all along and he'd helped to radicalize our entire generation.) In short, we realized that in the very process of assimilation (even in our Pierre Cardins and Yves St. Laurents) we simply had become transformed from factory-working to cultural and spiritual "White Niggers."

To My Brother

You'd think there was no end to this
tribe. They set out and multiplied
as if survival of their species

depended on the acid of their sperm.
Now, in the middle of the night,
they call us to come bury their dead.

So we make that black pilgrimage
back to Lisbon to slide one more
familiar corpse into the holy hillside.

We've buried twelve of them, a dozen
deaths survived, with still a dozen more
or so to live through. The horror

of their deaths and lives lives on
and haunts us: Mandia bent and stunted
by that monster riding her shoulder,

lied into believing she was partly angel;
Blackie drunk before his couple suns
rose every morning of his life, except

the last; and Larry loving various wives,
not one of them his own, his children
strangers to him even when he hemorrhaged;

one Émile lingering for months in
hospital beds infested with leukemia's
piranha, another dropping on the corner

during lunch-hour, gaping blindly back
at the mill hands watching our father
take him in his arms and whisper the act

of contrition to his soulless head.
Time and time again I resurrect them.
They gather in my head, eat, drink and

sing, celebrating their own wakes,
prolonging our interminable deaths.
But each time I return from burying one

of them, all the way back home from
Lisbon I can feel unremembered and
unknown parts of me vanish in the dark

and exhausted silence behind me.
They die, Normand, they die.
And, dying, they kill our only history.

LOUIS O. COXE
1918–

Louis O. Coxe has had a long and distinguished career as a teacher and writer — at Princeton University, his alma mater, and at the University of Minnesota — culminating in the position of Pierce Professor of English at Bowdoin College. He has published eight books of poetry, two books of criticism, and three plays. His stage adaptation, with Robert Chapman, of Melville's *Billy Budd* began with a successful Broadway production and has had a continuing lively history on American and foreign stages. Coxe has won many literary honors, including the Academy of American Poets Prize, the Brandeis Creative Arts Award, and a grant from the National Endowment for the Arts.

Coxe is a traditional poet, a formalist, well schooled in the art of lyric and narrative poetry. And his subjects are often the traditional choices: history and its heroes, even military men, Ulysses once more, and especially the moral histories of the men and women of New England. His narrative masterpiece is the book-length poem *The Middle Passage,* the story of a Salem slave ship and its master, a young adventurer into Conradian darkness.

Navigational Hazard

Suddenly underwater the ledge rises
Toward the delicate hull, and gray as old hide,
The rind of earth shaggy with weed and grasses,
Rock stares and whitens under the lee side.

We haul in sheets, jam the helm hard over,
And blocks slam and wrestle as we gibe
Running out between jaws of white water
No madder than we, no whiter, mind or no mind.

The sun sinks shafts in the sea's natural dark:
Whatever's down there, better left alone.
We've come clear this time out of rising rock,
Not our turn yet to stare and turn to stone.

Winter Headland

Watch before daylight die —
Ice at its center —
Old-squaw and Golden-eye
Wearing the winter.
East from this basalt slab,
Spain gazes toward you,
Nothing between but drab
Water to ward you:

"Fishing for Redfish"

Flooding beneath your feet
It calls disaster:
Salt on the stiffened cheek
Tells who is master.

Sequin the lighthouse rock
Gives vessels entry
Westward to naval dock,
Cradle and gantry.
Far to your right and left
Eastward the paths go —

Take the wind's winter heft,
Sheepscot and Casco,
Roll her Atlantic wide
And to become her,
Sluice her in southern tide,
Bringing back summer.

Cloudfall and snow have full
Arch to the welkin
Save where one lightstruck gull
Burns like a beacon
Gathering wisps of day
Once now together
Lest between here and May
Light die of weather,
Blue turn to posturing,
Green a romancer,
White, lovers' questioning
Deaf to the answer.

E. A. Robinson: Head Tide, October 1963

The road's hard black now, but the pheasant colors
Of fall, the dwindling Sheepscot, the meetinghouse hill,
And the houses have not changed in the hundred years
Since the brave season painted for your first fall.

Where absence signs To Let with a vacant air
"American Pen Women" have cornered you in a sign
With names and dates and themselves, wanting their share
Of something — loneliness? drink? — that lives in lines.

No soul stirs, no wind, the river barely runs,
But I feel you pass on your river walk and hear

Bare feet in the dust and smell the Gravensteins
You ruminate while an old man bends your ear.

I see what you saw; the hero turns to child
Jack to Giant, both gone uphill into sky
Where pine and hardwoods clash, mingle, and fold,
You and he black there — fierce on the eye
As the fire of this fall day flares into cold.

Constellation

Brimful of horizon trees the north well
tips out stars, great winter bear
skinned, nailed to the north wall,
and I watch that slide screened inside my head.
No one goes out there, ever — never will,
never the same space we drift in twice.
Feet apart upright pinned to the ground
I watch stars stream out from a well —
Dead souls of explorers racing for the pole.

PHILIP BOOTH
1925–

Philip Booth long ago chose life along the Maine coast as the preeminent subject of his poems. His town is Castine, where his mother's family has lived for generations. His return there during summers with his family made Booth realize that it was, in his words, "the territory that is sufficiently native to be mine as a poet." As he developed as a poet, his formal style turned toward the structures of Maine language and the tone of Maine speech. "I learned here how language is inherently used. It is at its best in Maine; although we are now losing it, God knows. . . . I certainly have always wanted to have the surface of my poems be clear. And, I would hope, increasingly transparent, so that one can look down into them."

Booth graduated from Dartmouth College in 1948 and has taught at Bowdoin, Dartmouth, and Wellesley colleges. Since 1965 he has been professor of English and poet-in-residence at Syracuse University. Colby College has awarded him the honorary degree of Doctor of Letters.

Offshore

The bay was anchor, sky
and island: a land's end
sail, and the world tidal,
that day of blue and boat.

The island swam in the wind
all noon, a seal until
the sun furled down. Orion
loomed, that night, from unfathomed

tides; the flooding sky
was Baltic with thick stars.
On watch for whatever catch,
we coursed that open sea

as if by stars sailed off
the chart; we crewed with Arc-
turus, Vega, Polaris,
tacking into the dark.

Durward: setting his trawl . . .

Durward: setting his trawl
for haddock, and handlining cod
a halfmile east of Seal Island,

"Mr. and Mrs. Alvah Thompson"

twelve miles offshore in fog.
Then his new engine went out.
A Rockland dragger spotted him,

two days later, drifting drunk
off Mount Desert Rock. He was
down to his last sixpack.

After they towed him back in,
Ordway kept asking him what
— those two days — he'd been thinking.

Nothin. I thought about nothin.
That was all there was to it.
Ord said, *Y'must've thought something.*

Nope, I thought about nothin.
You know what I thought,
I thought fuckit.

Eaton's Boatyard

To make do, making a living:
                              to throw away nothing,
practically nothing, nothing that may
come in handy;
                    within an inertia of caked paintcans,
frozen C-clamps, blown strips of tarp, and
pulling-boat molds,
                        to be able to find,
for whatever it's worth,
                            what has to be there:
the requisite tool
                      in this culch there's no end to:
the drawshave buried in potwarp,
chain, and manila jibsheets,
                                or, under a bench,

the piece that already may fit
                    the idea it begins
to shape up:
                    not to be put off by split rudders,
stripped outboards, half
a gasket, and nailsick garboards:
                              to forget for good
all the old year's losses,
                    save for
what needs be retrieved:
                    a life given to
how today feels:
                    to make of what's here
what has to be made
to make do.

LAURA RIDGEWELL

1940–

The Voice of Maine, by William Pohl and Abbie Sewall, combines interviews and portrait photographs of Maine people done in the early 1980s. A common thread of good-humored independence runs throughout these profiles, and a sense of the strength and resilience of these people emerges.

Laura Ridgewell, the wife of a lobster fisherman, lives in West Point, a fishing village on the easterly shores of Casco Bay; she was interviewed just after a strong storm had hit the coast.

Fisherman's Wife

"West Point is all fishermen. When I get up in the morning, the first thing I smell is low tide kelp and rotten bait. Tourists go around saying, 'Hummmm, the air is so invigorating.' Ugh. I have tears in my eyes, the bait smell is so heavy in the air.

"Each morning I hear boat engines. I know everyone by sound from my bedroom window. The diesel sound is normally a mellow, whirring sound that purrs like a cat. There aren't many boats like that in our harbor. Most boats here are converted automobile engines with crummy exhaust systems that consist of a pipe up through the roof. Old one-lungers — when you start them up, they rag and bleat, loud and piercing, like some dying animal.

"The sounds of engines are important. When I hear the engine of our boat, I know my husband is coming, and everything is all right. When I don't hear his engine, I know he's not coming — maybe for several days and nights until he can fetch a good catch. Maybe never.

"We listen for the boat engines and get to know everyone by sound. I say, 'There goes Frederick York. That's Eugene Atwood. Here comes Philip Wyman.' All from the bedroom window. This knowledge creeps up on us unawares.

"For the fishermen at sea, engine sounds are important. They can fall asleep to those sounds. The noise is a security blanket that says all is well. Engines that suddenly go quiet spell trouble.

"The sound of wind is also important, especially when we know that it's going to take away all of the things that we have worked so hard for. No fisherman that I know has ever put in for a loan to pay for storm damage. Instead, they scrounge. If they lost a pier, they'll push off to the islands to salvage the pieces. Like they've done before. Like Nort Wallace is doing now.

"When I can't understand something, I'm afraid. I don't understand politics. We don't know what the politicians want, and it seems that they don't care about our needs.

"We weren't qualified for loans after the storms of 1978. Even though West Point was a disaster area, the government said that the storm was at Wells Beach and other summer resorts. Fishermen who lack political influence 'didn't have a storm.'

"We're lucky. We 'didn't have a storm.' But I wish somebody told me we didn't have a storm when the winds here were gusting over 80 knots, and I couldn't see out the window because of all the sand, mud, and salt. The pickup trucks in front of the house were up to here in tide. At night I lay on my bed and felt the whole house shake in the gale. The sound of wind blotted out all other sounds.

"Fishermen are different. We respect the ocean. We don't run up to the surf on the beach and say, 'Get me if you can.' We don't do that. We take a boat out there and know that in one-half hour's time, the living-room-floor calm of the ocean can turn into a squall from which we might never return. We see a storm coming, and we get to the lee of an island. When I hear the sound of wind, Bob, my husband, says 'Don't worry, Laura.' Well how can I not worry when the ice starts to form on the riggin', masthead, and railing, turning the entire boat

Laura Ridgewell

white. When the ice topsides gets heavier than the keel, the boat capsizes. Last year a scallop boat went out and never returned. Bob was out then too.

"So we look out after ourselves. We can't depend on the government for help. We don't call upon the government for welfare. We call upon our neighbors. If someone is ill, we share food, take care of their kids, and help out. We're natural survivors.

"I see things differently too. Like Popham Beach up the road. Tourists love it in the summer, but to me, you can't see the sand because of all of the umbrellas and picnic wrappings. My beach is a fish wharf. When I jump off, it's just me, the eels and the pollack. The only pollution is what the gulls leave behind.

"I also like to see the loons in the fog, moose swimming out to the islands, whales spouting in the bay, and the seals in the cove. Which reminds me of the time I got my head stuck up a culvert. I was walking home from school in my Sunday best and saw some frog's eggs in a culvert. I took off my hat, my heels and gloves and left them by the side of the road. Then I waded into the mud to look for tadpoles.

"The school superintendent was driving by and came upon my stuff. He stopped the car and ran into the culvert saying, 'Mrs. Ridgewell, can I help you?'

"I was busy. Without looking up, I said 'No, not unless you've got a fish net or something. I'm trying to catch frog eggs.'

"Well, he let out a sigh of relief and said, 'Oh, I thought you were trying to commit suicide in the pond.' He was in a suit, and I was in my white dress, covered with mud. I had a circle of dirt around my eye from looking through a reed at the eggs. A real mess.

"Now people know me. I can stick my eye up a culvert, and people just drive by and wave. That's why I like living here at West Point.

"What else do I see? Everything that's important to me. I don't see cars or clothes hanging out to dry. I don't see poverty or severe winters or hardship. I don't see 'going back to nature.' I've already been there and don't notice those things.

"I also don't see women's liberation. My father was a fisherman who had the misfortune to have four daughters and no son. He may have been slightly annoyed, but never mentioned it to us.

"We'd go out fishing and bait the needles and steer the boat while he hauled the lobster pots. When he wasn't looking, we'd play with seahorses and starfish, and feed the bait to the seals and seagulls. Nothing boys would do.

"My father never got uptight about this. He just shrugged and said, 'Well, I guess we have to go in early today — the girls fed the bait to the seals.'

"Two years ago Bob broke his leg while jumping into the boat. He couldn't work, and we didn't have enough money to live on except for $100-a-week workmen's compensation. That's not enough for a husband, a wife, and an 11-year-old son.

"I thought about this, and I knew that I had to become a lobsterman 'till Bob recovered. That was a hell of a challenge for me. I had to stop being afraid that a lobster was going to attack me. I hate to pick up a lobster because when you think that they can't — they do.

"Nevertheless, I pushed off that week without my father, without Bob, and without pony-tails in my hair. I wasn't going to mess around with starfish or seals. I was going to captain my own boat out there for the money.

"I was petrified. I had to put on an oil slicker and gloves that were too big for my hands. I was scared of running somebody over in the boat. There's a lot of water between me and my small orange and black pot buoys. In getting to a buoy, the sea is moving, you're moving, and the buoy is bobbing. It took me a week before I could catch one. Then, I had to pull 50 heavy, water-soaked lobster traps by hand from the ocean floor in the cold every day into November. It was impossible.

"Meanwhile, you have to imagine what all of the old codgers were thinking as they stood on piers watching this woman out there chasing pot buoys. First of all, women are considered bad luck at sea. I was making circles counterclockwise around the traps which is also bad luck. Everytime I missed a buoy, I steamed a mile and a half around it before swinging back for another try. I spent more on gas that first week than I made from the entire catch.

"Soon I got the hang of it, but I never did get over one problem. When men measure how many fathoms it is to the ocean floor, they use a sounding line. Six feet of line is measured by holding the line out across one's chest with arms and hands extended as far as they'll go. Because of my bust, my fathoms were always bigger. The line floating above my traps was in danger of getting clogged in the propeller.

"Then, there was that bait smell again — ugh. I used to swim from boat to shore for my first bath, and then lemon my hands and soak in a tub. It never really goes away.

"Still, I was very popular with the men. They thought it was the funniest thing they'd ever seen, but they never made wisecracks. I was right up there with 'em. All they could see was another human being trying to survive. It wasn't a question of women's lib, and we kept ourselves off welfare while Bob was getting better.

"You know, there is so much air between Laura Ridgewell and the President of the United States. He doesn't know that I sit up nights, waiting for a boat to come in.

"Our government wants us all to be the same. If we can't make a living, they put us on welfare and under their power. Is this place too good for the fishermen? Should all waterfront housing be reserved for doctors and lawyers? And yet the government is taxing the fishermen off the land of their ancestors.

"Bob Ridgewell is a fisherman. He is not a lawyer. Like other fishermen, he sings his song solo. The government must realize that we can't be made into a chorus. Fishermen must remain independent."

DAVID WALKER
1942–

David Walker was born in Head Tide, Maine, the birthplace of E. A. Robinson. "The crucial fact of my life," he has said, "was to grow up on a dirt farm in an era when small farming had begun to die. I am the first in my family to 'break away' — to live differently, read voraciously, and reflect on the pattern of my heritage." He graduated from Bowdoin and then studied at New College, Oxford, where he earned a B.Litt. degree in 1967. From 1968 to 1971 he taught English and American literature at the University of Canterbury in New Zealand. After holding positions at Bowdoin and Holy Cross, he now teaches at the University of Southern Maine.

Aground
(A Settler's View, Maine, 17th C.)

Our boat strikes first on tideflats, then a waste
of boulders: round, but slippery to heft
and slime underfoot like moss — the bowling green
of Hell? The banks above grow eel grass, matted
riff raff cast by the tide — a clay-daubed stick
signing our New Found Land. . . . I trap my last

ship's louse, triumphant, while a bird screams loud
in a strange tree; our minister hacks, spits brown.
Ahead, the woods tell nothing I can sift.

Now a barge pulls toward the salt marsh, bearing the thick
hulks of our bellowing oxen: old world, sly,
they balk both hoof and muzzle at the greener shores
and pastures of our need. Though He smell the blood
where gnats have stung them, yet shall the The Lord provide:
He prods them through our sharp goads, lest we die.

Red through the black woods also now, the sun
declines. We huddle, gazing blind at guttering fires,
then bargain chill for rest while the watchers stare
all night into the river drained by stars.
After a cramped sleep, Lord, we pray You steer
our westering through this undergrowth at dawn.

Ancestral Photograph
(c. 1860)

Dark is darker, and the white
startling as snow in the face
my great-grandfather thrusts
in the sculpturing light; his bones
have the harsh planes of the Indian-
head nickel's Indian, his clothes
are stovepipes fresh from the blacking.

His gaze outfaces the camera's;
one shrewd hand cups
a blazing kneecap, the other
is stuffed in his waistcoat as over
a wound. . . . The curl of his lips
mutters, "They got me" in nervous

"*Maine Fishing Village*"

defiance: now captive, the last
aristocratic New England peasant.

Roots

OLD NIGHTMARE

And who owned the pickup found
on its back in the ditch
at midnight —

          the freed wheels
still trembling
and pinned beneath, that sudden
ragshape
of a best friend's wife?

REVENANT

The good old down-home boys
don't expect you back; they know
it's better out there, or so
everybody says.

And if you do return
to visit, with a child and wife
in tow, they will guess your life
has money to burn.

But should you come back alone
to speak with them, they will glance
at you sideways. Their eyes say *Once
you've left here — stay gone.*

Pigeons, Swallows, & Co.

Let nature take a turn at saying what love is.
— Marvin Bell

This spring, though the barn's ribs
are showing, its cage still welcomes
the usual flock:
                    all frantic
pootings and tweetings, they might
be quarreling in your head
those fluent mornings when you sit
outside, absorbing the green
stage set of after-rain:
light's dazzle on tents of dew,
the willow trailing its thousand
fingers of yellow lace,
and the insects repassing
like a distant conversation.

They might be, but they aren't;
it's you who's up with the birds
and inside their cries — so constant,
they must mean more than they sound
about the barn:
                    a skeleton
but talking back to the weather,
standing its dark ground.

WILLIAM R. HOPKINS
1924–1979

William R. Hopkins was born on North Haven Island in Penobscot Bay and during the course of his life worked as, among other things, a fisherman, a party boat operator, a licensed pilot, and an English teacher in local schools.

This selection, from Hopkins's only novel, *Freeman Cooper,* takes us to the center of town life — the village store. Here life and death are discussed, political careers are set in motion, and the rankling presence of people from away surfaces once again.

The Village Store

After I left Manetta's, I went back to the store.

The stormy day crowd was there. All of them. They had all been there, off and on, for a week. There is so little to do in such a blizzard of long standing, and you can soon get sick of sitting around your own house with nothing to do.

It is a good thing to have the store at such times.

Lucy was taking Bebe's place in the store, as clerk . . .

They did not stop talking when I went in, so I knew they had not been talking about me, which was a relief, in a way.

"Men in Village Store"

They were mostly natives; the foreigners do not hang around the store much. They know where they are not wanted — all except Buddy Swipes.

They seem to tolerate him, but then, he is not so bad, to talk to . . .

He was there, in the store, in his place, but not talking.

He spoke to me; the others nodded, but did not interrupt or change their conversations.

Well, well, mah ol' Buddy Free. How are you this morning, ol' Buddy, Free?

Hi, Buddy. Cold. Hi, Stinky!

Cold? Hell! What you talking about, Captain. Anybody'd ought to get a big barrel somewheres and make up a mint julep. Got plenty of ice . . .

I suppose so . . .

Ah 'spec we might . . .

Hi, Free. Quite a day. This would be a good morning to breed somebody, wouldn't it?

One thing that gets me about these summer people that comes here: they got all the money in the United States Treasury behind them, and yet they buy that cheap, rot-gut whiskey.

Not a great while to town meeting.

Almost on us.

Mrs. Castlewood, up there on the hill: they buy up all that cheapest kind of stuff they can lay their hands onto and swill it down like tap water, six to eight ounces to a time. She give me a water glass full, one of them tall ones, when I was working up there on the hill. I'd sit it under a bush somewhere and nip away on it 'till noon time.

They h'ain't much town meeting talk this time. You don't know what in hell's going on . . .

That old Mrs. Castlewood. She come up to my house one time. She's pleasant. She liked the looks of my place. She said she thought I had the prettiest spot in the world. I told her summers was all right but the winters was something shocking, and she says: they are? I can't believe it. I think this must be a perfectly darling place in the winter! I wish, by God, she could see it now. She'd take one look at that white devil-shit drove clear to the eaves on that no'th'east side, where the wind curls right between the house and the barn, and I bet she'd think it was quite darlin' now all right!

That Mrs. Castlewood, I remember the time Marland told her about the deer over to Isle au Haut. He said they were standing so thick on the shore, coming up under the land from outside at night, that their eyes lit up like Revere Beach when everything's going . . .

That Marland. He feeling any better?

No, sir. The goddamn fool.

H'ain't had his gall bladder cut out yet . . .

No, the damned fool. I told Ma last summer when he had that bad attack and we tried to get him to go into the hospital, I said: No, Ma. Don't urge him no more. What he's going to do is he's going to wait 'till the snow's right to the top of them windows, then he's going to have a goddamn ringer of an attack just so's we'll all bust our guts getting him out to the hospital, and I guess, by God, I was right. He's in the middle of a siege right now. I hit him on it this morning. I says: there, goddam ya! Lay right there and suffer! You had your chance last summer! He knows what I meant. He don't say nothin' to me no more. He knows better.

Too bad to let him suffer.

Well, I don't feel sorry for him, even if he is my own son . . .

Someone said you were running for First, Free, that right?

I've thought some about it.

Well, either you be or you be'nt. I should think you'd let us know one way or the other so's we'd see what we could do about getting you enough votes.

I think I will.

You think! Don't you know?

Yes, I know.

Well, there!

Well, it h'ain't only gall bladders today. They's gall bladders, yes, and they's lots of other real sickness, but most of that you don't have to worry much about because the doctors can fix it. They can snap out a gall bladder or they can whip out your appendixes, and it h'ain't no more trouble than snippin' off a wen. But the ones they can't seem to do nothin' about — not countin' the killin'-ones like cancers and that stuff — is the millions of people that is unwell but they h'ain't really sick yet . . .

What th'hell are you talkin' about, Az? You supposed to be a doctor, or something?

No. I h'ain't no doctor. But I got eyes, and I got brains, h'ain't I?

Well, your eyes h'ain't too good. You wear glasses, I notice. And I don't know what in hell you got for brains, but it don't make much sense talkin' about millions of people that is unwell but they h'ain't really sick yet . . .

It does too. They's millions of 'em.

Who, for instance?

Take somebody like yourself. You smoke a pile of cigarettes a day and you're hackin' on phlegm all day. Every morning you wake up and you feel like a shag shit in your mouth — takes you twenty-five minutes to get your feet braced every morning. But you don't stop smokin'! You could throw away your cigarettes and in ten days time you could feel human. But you don't do it. They h'ain't no doctor knows what to do about that. Same thing with my brother Bossie: He wakes up in the mornin' and starts right in drivin' the coffee to him. He drinks a dozen cups a day; he h'ain't never more than twenty minutes away from a cup of hot coffee. So he goes around peltin' the Roll-Aids to himself all day and his old guts feel like a forest fire and he's burpin' and fartin' himself to death by inches. He could leave the coffee alone for a whole week and his guts would normal out, his nerves would settle down, and he'd probably even stop pickin' his nose all the time. But he doesn't do it. No doctor can't make him do it neither. You fellers is just like better'n half the population today. You're unwell, but you h'ain't sick enough to stop doing what you're doing wrong. Someday you will be. Probably you'll strangle to death with a lung cancer, and my brother Bossie will end up havin' to have half his gut cut out and thrown away and starve to death on Malox and baby food.

Well, that's all settled, then. You going to run, Free, and you h'ain't going to back out on us.

I am going to run . . .

That's all we need to know. But, by God, you got to cut out these all night parties. You know that. Jesus Christ! It don't help none with them church people to have 'em carrying horny women out of your house feet first every morning . . .

It only happened once: it was an accident . . .

Accident be damned! She just got crocked, that's all. And from what I hear, I guess it weren't the first time. That don't go over too good around here — if you're looking for votes — and I suppose you are . . .

Ma says, well, everybody's been trying to get Marland to go to the hospital, but I guess he's part mule. I don't know who he takes after! And I says: I guess you better take a look in the looking glass to see who he takes after . . .

You talk about stubborn! When I was steamboatin', I fell in with a damn bastard that turned out to be an outlaw. I lived with him two weeks down to Virginia Beach . . .

Why h'ain't you took the time to tell us you was runnin'. . .

I have to bury Mother first.

I 'spec you must. It's going to be a bad one. They got the grave open yet?

They're still working.

They working today, in this?

They're doin all they can.

Well, we'll have to put it off. You'll have to put it off 'till the snow stops, Free.

You can wait just so long . . .

I know, another day or two. This will let up bim'by. They bringing her today?

This afternoon.

I s'pose she'll go right to the church. Proper thing.

It will be easier.

No point going to the house. She'll be all right at the church until we can have the service.

When d'you plan, Tuesday?

Tuesday afternoon. Two o'clock.

Most of us has our flowers coming tonight. We couldn't wait too long. But they'll keep for a while up there in the cellars to the church.

Susie was telling that most of us has ordered the pinks. We know what the plants will do this time of the year. But Etta told that most of the foreigners has ordered plants, the damned fools. Wouldn't you suppose they'd know by now plants freeze?

You don't give a plant no chance to set it on a grave this time a'year. But, then, most of them bastards don't know nothin' and most of them never will.

Well, you got to have good courage, Free. You lucky enough to get into town office and things are going to be tough. They's going to be somebody on your ass every day in the week.

Yessir, Free. You want to be braced to be criticized every time you turn around. They'll criticize everything you do — and some things you don't.

Just remember Aunt Eunice, though, Free. Aunt Eunice always said criticism takes from the tree caterpillars and blossoms together . . .

Well, I don't know so much about that either, Free. Old Doc, there, he's pretty smart sometimes. And he says a man can't neither protect nor defend himself against criticism, so he's just got to act in spite of it and sooner or later, by Jesus, it will gradually give in to him . . .

That may be true in some places, but around here . . .

You remember that time George Young tried to run the turnip farm?

Who?

George Young. He had something to say about getting criti-cized . . .

Broke his arm?

No, tried to run the turnip farm . . .

I remember George Young.

You remember George Wooster?

George Lewis? Yes, I remember him too . . .

For crissakes, Granpa, turn up your h'arkin' iron . . .

Turnips what?

Turn up your hearing aid!

T'won't do no good. She's been buzzin' lately. I guess she's broke.

Well, you give 'em hell, Free. You make it, you give 'em hell. We'll all stand behind you. Anything to get rid of old Bossie Gray and that goddamn wife of his. That Lizzie, she's the one. She's the one that runs the town. You couldn't shut her up if you clapped a rat trap tight over her goddamn beak . . .

My brother Bossie, he poisons minds too . . .

I guess that h'ain't all he poisons . . .

That Lizzie. I guess she got her comeuppance that time last summer when her sister that married that goddam Lunt from the east'ard sent that foolish kid of hers up here for Lizzie to take care of . . .

Oh, you mean that Wilbur? He was a dream.

Yeah. That was the kid that ate the toothpaste, wasn't it?

I guess he did. He was half starved, besides being half foolish. I guess he ate a whole tube of it between Friday afternoon and Monday morning 'fore they finally got rid of him and sent him back. Every time they'd lose track of him, they'd find him up in the bathroom driving the toothpaste to himself. He was half foolish.

You'd think so if you ever saw that old man of his. He's about one brick short of a load. You ever see him?

Don't think ever I did.

Jees. He was working down there to the shipyard that year I sailed for the Judge. We was in there one time and that kid's old man came down aboard with another feller to make a screen for the hatch. The old Judge lost one of the screens overboard in the night. Well, that other feller didn't quite have all his marbles either, and they were struggling with the measurements and that old Lunt, there, he looked up to me with those old buck teeth aimed right at me, and he says: Buh! We make an awful good team. He makes all the marks and I rub 'em out. Jees, he was a dream . . .

He must'a been a lot like that old Irishman that was visiting down to Magmadlin's mother's that summer. He thought he was quite a mechanic, and them summer kids showed up with that outboard motor they'd been foolin' around with. He looked her over and they asked him if he could fix it, and he said he didn't know, he'd have to think about it, and finally he says: Ah, Lads, this thinkin' makes the head ache; you'd better take her somewheres else . . .

That's what you're going to be up against, Free. You going to have to be thinking all the time, you get into office. But they h'ain't no sense to worry. You may not even make it . . .

I wouldn't want to run and not make it.

That's politics, Free.

I wouldn't want to do it.

Don't worry, Free. You run; we'll see to it you get in. But they h'ain't too many of us left. You better butter up some of those outlandishmen too . . .

To hell with the outlandishmen, Free. I'd just as liv see them run a candidate of their own. I'd like to see what would happen. I don't believe they got the strength they think they have. It's time we had a showdown and found out whether they goin' to take the town away from us or not. If they h'ain't, by God, they better pull their asses into the corner and shut up. If they be, then it's time for all us decent folks to move out. I say let's have a showdown and settle it . . .

You want to be careful, George. They just might take us. They's more and more of 'em every year . . .

I say they can't do it. Blood is thicker'n water, and . . .

It h'ain't blood; it's votes. I'd be a'feared they'd have 'em . . .

I h'ain't a'feared of nothin'. Them bastards h'ain't took us over yet, and by God, they h'ain't about to . . .

For myself, I do not care to think about it.

I had heard all I needed to at the store.

I had given them something to think about. They would have to talk it over. Everyone would want his say, now that it was out in the open. They would not want to talk about it with me there. It was almost time for noon meal anyway with Aunt Lena and Uncle Cy.

I came away.

AMY CLAMPITT
1920–

"It is hard to think of any poet who has written as well about the natural world as Amy Clampitt does. *The Kingfisher* opens with nine splendid poems about the New England seashore — its weather, its tidal flora and fauna, and its effect on the observer." Richard Tillinghast, writing in the *New York Times Book Review* in 1983, is talking about a poet who had at last achieved the literary acclaim and success that had eluded her for most of her life. Clampitt did not start publishing her poetry until 1978, when she was in her fifties. She had been fortunate to catch the eye of Howard Moss, the late poetry editor at *The New Yorker*. Subsequently, her poems have appeared in magazines and literary journals and have been collected in book form.

The New England seashore of Amy Clampitt is the northeast coast of Maine. Although born and raised in Iowa, Clampitt has spent many summers in Corea, east of Schoodic. Her rich vocabulary and delicate phrasing work well with this part of Maine, which she clearly knows and observes and likes so well.

These poems come from her collections *The Kingfisher* and *What the Light Was Like*.

Fog

A vagueness comes over everything,
as though proving color and contour
alike dispensable: the lighthouse
extinct, the islands' spruce-tips
drunk up like milk in the
universal emulsion; houses
reverting into the lost
and forgotten; granite
subsumed, a rumor
in a mumble of ocean.

                              Tactile
definition, however, has not been
totally banished: hanging
tassel by tassel, panicled
foxtail and needlegrass,
dropseed, furred hawkweed,
and last season's rose-hips
are vested in silenced
chimes of the finest,
clearest sea-crystal.

                              Opacity
opens up rooms, a showcase
for the hueless moonflower
corolla, as Georgia
O'Keeffe might have seen it,
of foghorns; the nodding
campanula of bell buoys;
the ticking, linear
filigree of bird voices.

"Deep Water"

The Cormorant in Its Element

That bony potbellied arrow, wing-pumping along
implacably, with a ramrod's rigid adherence,
airborne, to the horizontal, discloses talents
one would never have guessed at. Plummeting

waterward, big black feet splayed for a landing
gear, slim head turning and turning, vermilion-
strapped, this way and that, with a lightning glance
over the shoulder, the cormorant astounding-

ly, in one sleek involuted arabesque, a vertical
turn on a dime, goes into that inimitable
vanishing-and-emerging-from-under-the-briny-

deep act which, unlike the works of Homo Houdini,
is performed for reasons having nothing at all
to do with ego, guilt, ambition, or even money.

Low Tide at Schoodic

Force, just here, rolls up
pomaded into vast blue curls
fit for the Sun King, then crumples
to a stuff of ruffs and kerchiefs
over ruined doorposts, the rubble
of an overthrow no one remembers
except through cooled
extrapolation — tunnels
underneath the granite,
the simmering moat, the darkened sill
we walk on now,
prowling the planar windowpanes of tidepools
for glimpses of kelp's ribboned whips,
the dead men's fingers.

                Boulders
smothered in a fur of barnacles
become a slum, a barrio
of hardened wigwams, each
(notwithstanding a seeming armor
that invites, when added to the fate
of being many, the hobnails
of a murderous indifference)
holding an entity no less
perishably tender than any
neonate delivered, red
and squalling, in the singular.

                  Spruces,
turreted above the ledge,

lodge in the downdraft
of their precarious stairwells
a warbler who, all nerves tuned to
alarums, dapper in a yellow domino,
a noose of dark about his throat,
appends his anxious signature —
a wiry wheeze,
a blurred flute note.

FRED BONNIE

1945—

Fred Bonnie writes short stories, tales of bleak lives and hard times. Many of them are set in Maine, where Bonnie was born and raised. His ancestors crossed the border from Quebec more than a hundred years ago and settled in northern Maine. This heritage and his own jobs, which range from short order cook to housepainter to teacher to country-and-Western singer, have enabled him to portray working-class lives. Bonnie's people cope with their loss of control over their lives with strength and often humor.

"Widening the Road," from the collection *Squatter's Choice,* portrays a stubborn man caught between his sense of property and independence and the economic welfare of his neighbors. A classic conflict, it is increasingly evident throughout Maine as economic growth and development pressures affect the bond between a Maine man and his land.

Widening the Road

The first two mornings, Porter had held the fox in the sights of his rifle, but the next morning, he watched through his binoculars as the fox sat calmly, its dark form nestled like a stone into the clean November snow. The rifle stayed leaning against the dresser next to the window.

The fifth morning, the fox did not appear. Porter waited at the window from daybreak until Marion woke at eight to the alarm. He'd waited for her to ask him what he was doing but she didn't.

But it was the sixth morning and the fox was back. Porter knelt, watching the field, the air settling coldly in the sleep-moist creases of his face. He expected the fox to sit still in the same place, as it had the other mornings, then bolt back into the woods.

The bed stirred behind him.

"Porter?"

He said nothing.

"Porter, what are you doing?"

"Nothing."

"Well, could you do it with the window shut?"

A moment passed, then he heard her toss herself back down on the bed. He glanced back at the bundle she made against the dark wall.

She was always cold, he thought. Marion's mother had warned him that the girl needed to fatten up; that she should eat bananas every day to put some weight on before the wedding. Marion hadn't eaten bananas, though, nor much of anything else. She'd never been sick, either. Not since she'd had strep throat in the seventh grade. They'd begun to date in high school, then got married after Porter spent three years in the army. Marion's mother had insisted that he wear his uniform for the wedding. He agreed since it meant he would not have to spend money renting a tuxedo. Mama Finch liked Porter's attitude toward money and assured him that Marion would be easy to support.

"She doesn't eat anything," Mama Finch had said.

"What does she like best?"

Mama Finch smiled as if she were announcing a dowry. "Breakfast. The cheapest meal to fix at home and the cheapest one to eat out."

Porter knew that already, although he pretended to Mama Finch that they had never eaten breakfast together. That seemed almost too much of a confession that they'd slept together the night before.

"Porter, what's out there?"

"Nothing. Just a fox."

He looked back out the window. Behind him he heard Marion throw the covers back and pad to the window.

"I don't hear the hens," she said.

"He wasn't close enough."

He felt her in back of him although she didn't touch him. He watched her breath drift out the window after his own.

"Where?" she asked.

"He's gone."

"Where was he?"

"Over there by the end of the stone wall."

"That wasn't where you were looking just now," she said.

"He moved."

"Are you sure?"

"You calling me crazy?"

She backed away from the window and he listened to her crawl into the bed.

"Is that gun going to sit there for another week?" she asked.

Porter didn't answer. He looked for the fox again, then lowered the windows. He dressed quickly and went downstairs.

They owned an electric percolator, but Porter always made instant coffee. He poured himself a bowl of cold cereal. By the time he'd sliced an apple onto his cereal, the water for his coffee was boiling.

Before he sat back down, he turned on the radio to listen to Country Joe-Eddie who played fiddle and sang with his three daughters between portions of the news and farm reports. Eggs were going up, grain was going down. That was nothing new, Porter thought. It was usually followed by a period of grain shortages and a glutted egg market, meaning feed would be up and eggs down. And he was having to sell his entire stock to the Portland middleman since the local merchants had begun their boycott against him.

Country Joe-Eddie was back.

Now I eat alone at a table for two
And I was never lonely, until I met you. . . .

He heard Marion on the stairs. She wore a light blue parka over her terrycloth bathrobe. Her hair was blond in the summer, but nearly brown in the winter.

"I don't like that gun up there," she said.

"What's the matter with it?"

"It scares me." She started across the kitchen to the coffee pot. She refused to wear the slippers her mother bought her each Christmas and instead wore a pair of Porter's old basketball sneakers. He watched the untied laces flop as the soles slapped the cold linoleum floor.

He hoped she would make herself some instant and take it back upstairs with her, but she used the percolator instead, washing it first with soap rather than just rinsing it out.

After she'd dried it and set it up to percolate, she made herself a cup of instant and left the room. He listened to her thump back up the stairs. Then he listened to the percolator.

She was wise, Porter thought. She always got out of the room when she sensed he could get angry about something. He'd even thanked her for her good sense, once, before the problem over the road made it impossible for them to talk about anything.

"Don't you think I'm easy to live with just as long as nobody gets me mad?" he'd asked her. They'd been married about five years at the time. It was a Sunday morning when they'd stayed in bed late.

"Yes," she said. "And one of these days you may grow up." She was in her short summer robe by the sink. "We should have some babies after you grow up," she'd said.

Porter had been dismayed. He realized for the first time in his life that maybe sometimes he was annoying.

When the percolator stopped, he poured himself a cup of coffee.

He was ready for his breakfast cigarette but when he patted his breast pocket he remembered that the cigarettes were on the nightstand beside the bed.

He found Marion again knotted into a bundle under the blankets. Her cup sat on the nightstand empty. He didn't tell her the coffee downstairs was ready. He stood near the bed a moment before taking his cigarettes and started out of the room. He glanced into the field as he passed the window. There was the fox again, moving quickly toward the chicken-coop.

Porter grabbed his rifle before he remembered that he had to open the window first. Marion was sitting up in the bed, he could tell. By the time he was in position at the window, the fox had again disappeared. He knew in moments where it was; the hen house came alive with a single screech, then another, then forty, then four hundred. He kept what he assumed would be the fox's exit in his sights.

The gunshot seemed like an explosion inside the house. Marion screamed. Then the fox was dashing across the snow and Porter fired four more times before the fox disappeared into the woods.

When he looked back at Marion she was again under the covers with the quilt pulled over her head. He grabbed a jacket from the hook by the kitchen door and went out to the chicken-coop. The cold made him tuck his chin into the zippered jacket. The hens were in an uproar. Porter followed the fox's tracks a few yards. When he looked closely he noticed blood around the neatly stamped paw marks. A hit, he told himself. A definite hit. The farther Porter followed the tracks, the more blood he saw. He ran back to the house. Marion was in the kitchen.

"I hit it," he said, leaning the rifle in the corner by the door.

She didn't look at him. "That's good, I suppose."

He glanced at her but decided not to say anything. He opened the drawer in the kitchen table and filled the pockets of his jacket with ammunition, then stuffed some cookies into his shirt pockets.

"Where are you going?"

"Run down that fox."

"But I thought you killed him."

Porter noticed her glance at the gun. "Hit him."

"He won't be back, will he? Not after you hit him?"

"I want to make sure."

She looked more at the gun than at him. "Are you sure you shouldn't work around here instead?"

He didn't answer. It made him furious when she asked questions like that.

In the shed he found his snowshoes. Once again the air settled around him and the light wind sliced gently at his face. He carried the snowshoes to the edge of the woods, then put them on. The blood in the fox's tracks was pink and distinct.

Porter walked all morning. The fox stayed far enough ahead of him to remain out of sight but Porter felt he was gaining.

He spent most of the time thinking. Only when the tracks changed direction did he pay attention to the pursuit. At one point he realized that the fox was travelling in and out of his property and four times Porter climbed through the electrical barbed-wire fence that surrounded his land, knowing an alarm sounded in his cellar each time he touched the fence. Marion had nearly left him, or so she claimed, over the installation of the fence. Porter had it put up when the disagreement over the new road construction had degenerated to a three-way battle between himself and an alliance of the highway department and the Hampton Merchants Association. The government wanted to widen the road that went by his house. The Hampton Merchants' Association wanted the new road too. The proposed construction would remove all the roadside trees on Porter's property, eight old maples and one of the few healthy elms in that part of the state. Half his lawn was to be a paved shoulder on the new four-lane. The government had offered him $1200 for the trees and the property. Porter refused and proceeded to get a court order to halt construction of that portion of road that bordered his land. Assuming the matter would be settled quickly, the government had begun construction of the new road, completing the stretch from town to Porter's farm and continuing past his place to the lake and beyond. But in front of Porter's property, the four lanes bottlenecked to a narrow, pot-holed two-lane which was bordered by Porter's electrical fence. The fence extended around his entire 40 acres. Whenever anything brushed against the fence, a buzzer sounded in his basement.

Marion accused him of turning their home into a war zone. Porter said if that's what it took to protect your house, that's what you did.

The state set up a hearing and Porter suggested that they curve the road away from his place, through the woods, he said, so that he wouldn't have to see the road at all. The highway department representative stated that the whole purpose of rebuilding the road was to make it safer by eliminating the curves. Porter countered by saying that to the best of his knowledge, no-one had ever been hurt or killed on that road and if they really wanted to make it safer, they should leave the old road, lower the speed limit to 25, and then enforce it. Convenience was a factor, the government man explained, adding that the new offer of $1500 was double the value of the land.

"Don't make me laugh," Porter said. He glared at the government man's pocked face and hairy fingers. His suit only made Porter hate him more.

"How much will you take, then?" the government man asked.

"Five thousand," Porter said.

The government, the Merchants Association and the court all decided that an impasse had been reached. That was the last Porter had heard from the government. But the following week, all the local food retailers refused to take his eggs.

"You like all those out-of-towners throwing beer cans on your front lawn?" Porter had asked one store owner.

"It don't cost nothing to pick 'em up," was the answer he got.

Porter hated the traffic in town in the summertime. Mostly station wagons, he'd noted. Most of them full of bratty kids. It wasn't just the beer and soda cans on his lawn that annoyed him. In ten years he had six dogs and ten cats run over, invariably during the summer.

"Tie them up," one camper suggested when he stopped to buy eggs and Porter complained to him about losing a dog just the night before. The man wore a T-shirt that was too small and his belly stuck out under it.

"I don't live out here in the country to tie my dogs up, mister. It's you summer people that think you can come up here and drive the way you do down there in Boston."

The customer soured immediately. "Hey, what are you bellyaching about? You're making a buck off the summer people."

"I don't make enough to make it worth the aggravation."

"Then I'll make sure we don't come back and aggravate you."

"I hope not. Maybe you should take your vacation in Ohio next year."

"Hey, forget the eggs." He put his wallet back in his pocket.

"Goddam right," Porter said, "I wouldn't sell them to you now if you had a gun. . . ."

Porter shifted his rifle to the other shoulder and stopped at the crest of a hill where the fox's tracks had led back to the power-line trail that skirted his south pasture. He took off his glove and felt the fox's track with his finger. The two left tracks were distinct, but the right paw marks were obliterated by the hind leg which was clearly dragging. There was no longer blood in the tracks and Porter supposed the foot, if not the entire leg, had frozen. He thought about his own feet, and couldn't remember when the left one had begun to feel numb. He worked it inside his boot as he glanced at the sky. It was overcast but he could see the sun's position in the thin, grey cloud cover. He guessed it was afternoon; early, but afternoon.

From the crest where he stood he could see the southbound portion of the new road and the flashing lights that warned motorists that there was construction ahead.

If they'd pay him enough to build a new house way in the woods on his land, he'd call it a deal today, he thought. But the $5000 he was asking wouldn't pay for the wood and he knew they'd never pay him that much anyway.

Hiram Wainwright had stopped one Sunday afternoon and had sat at the kitchen table with Porter. Wainwright was fat in his dark pin-striped suit. "People travelling through hear the road from Portland to Norway isn't finished yet so they go around the Harrison side of the lake," Wainwright had told him. Wainwright had appointed himself spokesman for the merchants in town.

"They could be coming through here and spending their money on gas and charcoal briquets and eggs and all sorts of stuff. Hell, man, you've put up that fence. You could have cows and sell milk and ice cream and who knows what. I don't like the summer people any better than you do, but I'll put up with them for three months because then I can relax for the other nine." Wainwright cocked his head and raised his arms up from his sides whenever he thought he had brought common sense into the conversation. Then he dropped his arms loudly as if he alone held the only common sense in the room. Porter made it a point to speak as little as possible. He was determined not to get angry, not to laugh, not to taunt. Marion had begged him to just listen; just listen and ask honest, non-antagonistic questions and then think for one day and she would be a much happier woman. They had no choice as far as she was concerned. Sooner or later the state was going to make them sell the land, at the state's price, and that even if they got the outlandish amount Porter was asking, half of it would go to the lawyer Porter had insisted on hiring. Porter listened and eventually Wainwright left.

"All they have to do is put a bend in the road," Porter said to Marion after Wainwright had gone. She went to bed at five o'clock and Porter was unable to wake her when he went to bed at midnight.

He got up from the rock where he sat and continued down the power-line trail. It was too cold to sit in one place too long.

He remembered films from army basic training that showed troops in the Korean War who had been frostbitten. He remembered the way they limped. He began to walk faster to generate some heat in his boots and almost walked by where the tracks had cut into the woods that bordered the lake. Porter had planted Christmas trees in one section but then couldn't bear to harvest them.

In the woods it was much darker. The snow lay so thickly in the pine branches above that very little light got through, even on a bright day. Porter could see well enough. It was a lot warmer in the woods and he undid his scarf and scratched his neck. He wished he'd brought more to eat. The cookies were gone after the first few miles.

Suddenly hearing the brook in the distance, Porter realized how thirsty he was. He came to his fence again and manoeuvered between the wires. He wondered what Marion did each time the buzzer went off. She claimed that since the installation of the fence, people avoided her and that some people thought that Porter was having a nervous breakdown. Good, he'd told her. That way they'd be sure to stay away.

As he walked he grew warmer and unzipped his jacket. His hands felt sweaty in the fur-lined gloves and he took them off and stuck them in his pocket. The scarf went in the other pocket.

The clatter of the brook grew louder. The branches dripped onto the nearly snowless pine-needle floor. What snow had accumulated on the ground lay in patches with rounded, melting edges. By the time he reached the brook, its sound had become a roar in the silent forest. The banks were thick with ice, but the water rattled freely among the snow-capped rocks. Kneeling on a rock near the edge, Porter scooped the icy water to his mouth, then sat against a tree. He smoked two cigarettes and decided there was no point in the chase but that there was no point in going back to the house, either. The lake was just a little farther and he wanted to see if it had frozen yet. The lake usually didn't freeze until December, but it had been cold this fall. As he neared the end of the woods, he zipped up his jacket and put his gloves back on. After the darkness of the woods, the white mass of the lake made his eyes water. When he was able to focus again, he saw the crouched fox out on the ice not twenty yards away.

"Hey there, big fella," Porter said.

The wind played in the fox's mane, making him puff out.

Porter noticed the wounded leg. "Sorry about that," he said. "Looks like you've about run out of steam." Porter watched the fox and the fleeting funnels of wind that swirled the snow up into ghosts and twisted them away. His eyes came back to the fox and Porter raised his rifle to his shoulder and held the fox in his sights.

The fox stayed crouched, studying Porter. When Porter lowered the rifle to his side, the fox's mouth drooped open and its tongue hung out.

"I'm listening, fox. I know you've been coming all these mornings to tell me something. Am I supposed to sell or not?"

The fox was panting in hard wisps. Porter thought the fox looked young. He imagined the fox crippled for life because of its wounded leg.

"Look, I really am sorry about that, but if I'd been messing with your chickens, you would have done the same." As an afterthought Porter said, "I didn't really expect to hit you."

He remembered the way Marion had screamed when he shot at the fox. It seemed odd to him, her uneasiness about the gun. She was not a hunter but she always went with Porter when he hunted. She'd walk along in back of him, sometimes so quietly that he'd turn around to make sure she was still there. She carried a rifle, like him, but without ammunition.

"Are you married, fox?" Porter smiled. "No, huh? Just living together? Yeah, that's probably the way to do it."

The fox stood, then hopped two steps away. The hind leg looked stiff. When Porter made a small move, the fox snarled.

"I don't blame you. I know it hurts like hell. I should probably do you a favour and blow your brains out. What do you think?"

The fox still curled his lip but didn't snarl again.

"Just say the word. I'll put you in that big hen-house in the sky." He raised the rifle to his shoulder. He could hit the fox anywhere from this range, he thought. A quicker death than any suffering creature could ask for.

Once more the fox wobbled to its feet and hopped a few steps. Porter lowered the rifle. "All right. There's an answer. Don't shoot. You'll get over the damaged leg and survive, right? Just like I should hold out on the land and make them curve the road away from the house." He watched the fox pick its way among the drifts of snow. Soon Porter walked back into the woods. Any fox who can go as far as he has with a wound that bad has what it takes, he thought.

By the time he got home it was nearly dusk. The lights were on in the kitchen and the coffee pot was still plugged in. He poured himself a cup as soon as he hung up his jacket. When he sat down at the table, he found her note.

Dear Porter,

I've decided to let you stay by yourself until this whole thing about the road is over and you get back to normal. Everyone is worried about you, myself included. I waited for you until two o'clock, but I guess chasing the fox was more important than feeding the hens. I wanted to talk to you one last time before I did this, but I just couldn't wait any longer. Call me at my mother's if you have anything you want to talk about. If you don't call in a few days, I'll just figure you don't want me to come back. Sorry this had to happen, but I can't take the fences and the alarms and the guns anymore.

Love always,

Marion

Porter threw the letter on the floor. He thought about calling her to tell her that she'd been more trouble than she was worth. Instead, he went out to feed the hens. The fox had unsettled the hens so there weren't many eggs to collect.

By the time he finished the chores, it was after six o'clock. The night cold had coated the storm windows with an opaque glaze. When the phone rang, he answered abruptly.

"Hiram Wainwright here, Porter. How are you?"

"What's up?"

"We've decided to pay you the $5000 for the land, Porter."

Porter didn't hesitate. "The price went to ten early this evening."

"We'll pay that, if you want."

"The government will never go along with it."

"*I'm* buying it. The Merchants Association is buying it. And we're going to *give* it to the government."

Porter laughed. "You want that road in the worst way, don't you?"

"It will be good for all of us, Porter. I've heard you talking about dairy cattle before. Here's the money to get started."

"I've got my hands full with my hens."

"Then take the money and go on a vacation in Hawaii," Wainwright said.

"Can't stand humidity."

"It would do you some good."

"Don't worry about my health, Hiram."

"We all need to worry about each other's health. Economic and physical too."

"Why? I'm happy to keep my nose out of your business."

"It ain't a question of having your nose where it doesn't belong, Porter. It's a question of helping each other."

"That road doesn't help me a damned bit. I don't pay that much attention to the summer business. And none of your friends in town want to buy my eggs lately. What do I need a road for?"

There was a long silence. Porter paced as far as the short telephone cord would allow him.

"Just think about it, will you, Porter. $10,000. $5000 down. To-night. The rest in the morning."

Porter wanted to laugh but didn't. "Okay, Hiram. I'm going to sit right down and start thinking."

Wainwright said nothing for a moment, then said goodnight.

Porter thought about the money for only a few minutes, then thought about the fox, trying to remember every move the fox had made. Where was the fox right now? Hadn't he, in fact, fled? As he paced, he recalled Marion's accusation that he read too much into the things that went on around him. He always retorted by telling her she was oblivious to what was going on around her.

He made a pot of fresh coffee, then sat to wait for it to brew. He couldn't sit on his front porch without having everybody who drove by stare at him. And now they thought they were going to run the cars right by his porch railing and raise the speed limit to 55, which meant they'd go 80. Twenty feet away from his hammock.

The night wore slowly. When he opened the kitchen door for a moment to check the thermometer, the night chill stole in and made him shiver long after he had closed the door. He turned on two burners of the electric range and stood with his back to the stove a few minutes. He used to laugh at Marion when she did that. After he had gotten rid of the chill, he absently poured new coffee and milk into his cup but the sight of the coffee made his stomach roll.

The fox had just limped off, he remembered. He didn't need the lake. He didn't go swimming more than half a dozen times a year and went skating even less.

He couldn't take the $10,000. The town would always hold it against him. He looked for his reflection in the window, but the grey frosted glass returned nothing. He thought about going to bed, but sleep was nowhere in his body. He tried to remember when he'd last spent a night alone. Not in the army; there'd been nine other guys in his bay in the barracks. And not since he'd been married. Had he been hunting alone? He couldn't remember. All he could recall was Marion there in the tent with him, the two of them in his sleeping bag. She was so light when she laid her head on his chest. . . .

He jumped when the phone rang. It was Wainwright.

"Drove by your house a while ago, Porter. Looked like a lot of lights on for after midnight. I can't get to sleep and I figured maybe you were having the same problem."

"No problem, Hiram. Just things to do."

"Listen, if you're afraid we're going to hold the money against you, forget it. We consider it an investment. You'll use the money well, probably start a dairy and expand your operation. Hire a few people. That's good for all of us, you know. We realize that."

"Yeah, especially when you raise my taxes after the new road is finished."

Wainwright came back quickly. "Once this road is built, Porter, we'll never have to raise taxes again. Not local taxes, anyway."

Porter waited for him to continue. He didn't. "Try and get some sleep," was all Wainwright said after that.

After he hung up, Porter stood by the phone for several minutes, then slipped his jacket on. He looked for a second scarf and put on a second pair of socks. He looked for his flashlight in the closet adjoining the kitchen.

*   *   *

Porter's snowshoes creaked in the cold night snow. Halfway across the field he began to wonder if he should have brought his rifle. He didn't want to go back for it and walked faster toward the lake. He was nearly warm everywhere but on his face.

It was cold in the woods too. The night had frozen the water that had drained down the trunks all afternoon and now the trees were ablaze with the reflection of Porter's flashlight. He felt pursued and tucked himself far back into his hood and tried to look straight ahead and follow his afternoon tracks.

Ice had silenced the brook for the night and he came upon it sooner than he expected. He stumbled once, but managed to hold up the powerful flashlight. His fence snagged him as he went through and he heard his jacket tear.

He was not ready for the wind of the lake. He felt as if he were being sliced down the middle and his face was instantly numb. He turned his back to the wind and crouched, trying to figure out where he was in relation to where he'd been that afternoon. The snow ghosts that the wind carried pelted his face and twisted across the white sheet of the lake, whipping themselves to powder. As he began to amble out onto the lake, the ice cracked far up the lake and echoed across the whiteness until it was swallowed by the wind. He wandered from drift to drift, poking expectantly with his foot.

Still, he was surprised when he came upon the dead animal, stiff on its side. He watched only a moment as the wind still made tiny furrows in its fur. The idea of carrying the fox back to the house and burying it in his yard passed through his mind, but he decided against it.

Porter started back into the woods. Passing through the fence once more, he felt the barbs tear at his jacket again, then the rush of the cold night through the new hole.

He stopped at the edge of his meadow. Marion had always wanted cows. Her father had had 90 head.

He followed the fence to the road, then turned at the corner and followed it to his front yard. Several times he reached over to touch the fence and said "Bzzzzz," aloud. When he pricked his glove on a barb, he said, "Moooooo."

It was late, but he knew he could call her. He'd make hot chocolate before she got home. The hot chocolate would give them something to do so that he wouldn't have to say much. Or they could talk about how they'd move the hammock.

He looked at the fence one last time before he went in. He pictured the back yard in the summer with one of the cows swatting at flies with her tail.

JOHN GOULD
1908–

Maine humor is traditionally laconic. It is the understatement, the measured, minimal response that serves to put the outsider or the braggart in his place neatly and decisively. Oral humor is especially effective because of its ability to convey the well-known Maine accent and timing. But there is also a tradition of written Maine humor that exhibits what the dictionary calls "that quality in . . . a situation or an expression of ideas . . . which appeals to a sense of the ludicrous or absurdly incongruous."

John Gould has been mining this lode for some time. He has the requisite "droll imagination," and his books of reminiscences and humorous tales have displayed his sympathetic understanding of the Maine point of view and its sometimes quirky, often self-deprecating, always gentle, sense of humor. In the first selection here from *Stitch in Time,* Gould's little man is pitted against the big corporation and wins — well, almost — and in the second piece he illustrates typical Maine understatement.

Born in Boston, Gould was brought up in Freeport, Maine. He attended Bowdoin College, which later awarded him an honorary degree, and eventually settled on family land in Lisbon Falls. He now lives in Friendship, on Muscongus Bay. Gould, who was the co-owner and editor of the *Lisbon Enterprise,* has been a columnist for the *Christian Science Monitor* and has written some twenty books of Maine humor and reminiscences.

Around the World

When Mother Bell advertised that operators would announce their names — "Good morning, this is Nancy. May I help you?" — I resurrected a truism that I'd uttered years ago: That the telephone company is run by a bunch of people who don't know how to run a telephone company. The new way, the advertising said, will make telephone service more personal. Gracious! Back when Myrt and Gladys sat at the switchboard, telephone service *was* personal, and friendly, and in many ways more reliable and useful. But Mother Bell's minions scrapped all that and forced the impersonal upon us until the telephone service needed just one thing to bring it back to sense — personalities. Permit me to relate about the time I wanted to telephone around the world.

Mother Bell scheduled a series of advertisements that said, "Now you can talk around the world!" Thinking of Magellan and the good press he got for the small time he put in, I decided I'd like to be the first person to talk around the world, so when the first advertisement appeared, I dialed the operator at once. We had toll centers then; I don't know where mine was, but the girl offered to help, except that her tone of voice was neither Myrt nor Gladys. She was impersonal as a sheet of plywood. "Yes," I said, "now, let's take this slowly. I'm on an unusual tack, and I anticipate resistance. I beg your indulgence, and hope you'll bear with me."

"Is this an emergency call?" she asked.

"Not yet."

So I told her I saw in the magazine that I could now talk around the world and the idea intrigued me. I said, "I can't very well talk around the world to myself, so I'd like you to ring my neighbor across the way, Jim Tucker — he's home now and I can see him through his window." Fact is, I could see his telephone on the wall right by his

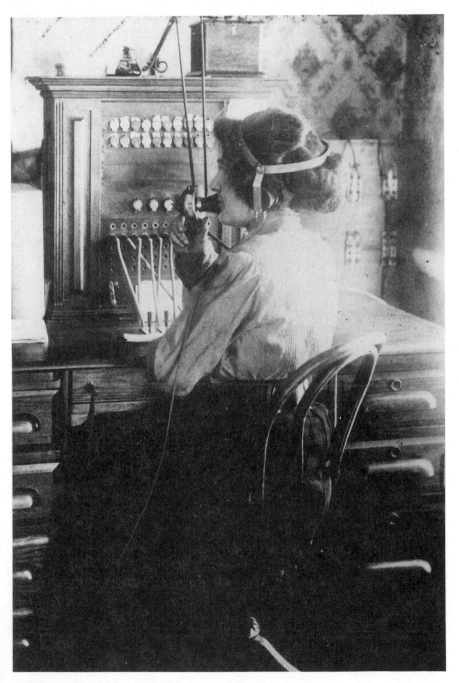

Telephone operator, Norridgewock

elbow. Be amusing, I thought, to see him jump when the bell rang, and reach for the thing, and then see his reaction when I told him we were talking around the world. So I gave the toll operator his number.

She said, "But that's a local call! You can dial that yourself."

"You haven't been paying attention," I told her. "I want this call to go around the world."

The silence was total, and extensive. "Hello, Hello!" I said. She said, "I'll let you talk to the supervisor."

The supervisor indulged me, and seemed to grasp what I had in mind, but she was baffled. She did say, "Oh, I understand . . . " with a rising inflection that meant, "Boy, oh boy! Have I ever got a ding-dong now!" But she honestly gave me the right answer. She said, "I'm frank to tell you, I wouldn't know how to set that call up."

"Well, Frank," I said, "somebody somewhere must know how to set it up, or this advertisement wouldn't be in the magazine. Why don't you go to work on the idea and call me back?"

"That's not my name," she said, and when I asked her what her name was she wouldn't tell me. "It's against regulations," she said. And the next afternoon I had a call from a manperson who said he was the traffic superintendent, and could he be of any service? I told him of my burning desire, again looking across the way at my neighbor's telephone. "Yes," he said, "that's the way I heard it." I got the idea my burning desire had been well discussed in telephone management circles, and he had been instructed to talk me out of whatever it was I wanted. This he began to do.

Well, I never did make that call. The man from traffic ran out of prepared remarks shortly, and reverted to a manner that I must admit was personal. He told me right out that some countries that would be relaying such a call were not technically ready to do so, and that fear of failure made him leery. He certainly conveyed his own belief that the call would not come off, and then he said, "Besides, those ads mean you can now talk anywhere in the world — we never meant 'around' the world."

So I said, and I thought with some reason, that maybe Mother Bell should change the wording of her advertising.

And, do you know, in a couple of weeks the wording in those advertisements was changed, and I read, "Now you can call anyplace in the world!"

And a personalized voice will say, "Hello, this is Barbara . . ."

No Haulin' Day

A couple of old-time schools of "communications" recently gave up, pleading lack of funds, and I thought at the time that communication comes in different sizes. With new electronic opportunities, ordinary schools of "journalism" became schools of "communications," and the ability to enunciate a one-minute commercial for brass polish took on academic stature. All to the good, but when a school of communications can't communicate its need for money, a small doubt about something or other should be permitted. Not too many have been privileged to see some Maine lobstermen communicating without saying a word, partly for want of an invitation to attend, and partly because lobstermen get up about 2 A.M. to do their communicating. I think a school of communications is unlikely to work this into a seminar.

There are esoterics. The Maine lobsterman is a loner by nature and rather much by trade. Even when he "goes two," which means he has a stern man, or assistant, the arrangement goes "snacks" and neither is the boss. The Internal Revenue Service, back along, tried to tell the Maine lobsterman that going snacks, share and share alike, had to be handled taxwise as employer and employed, causing a tidal hilarity that bounced along the Maine coast all one summer. Much of the satisfaction of being a lobster catcher, I'm sure, derives from being out there in your boat, man against the sea, having every bit of the beauty and the challenge for your very own. Few lobstermen admire to have a rider, a visitor, and while almost every summercator would like to "go to haul" to see what it's like, invitations to do so are seldom. As a retired highlander coming to live by the tide, I was much touched when Harold asked me if I'd care to go haul "some mornin'." Some foolish people might prefer a seat on the Supreme Court bench — I went to haul.

But at his independent best, the Maine lobsterman stays close to all other lobstermen. While hauling, his eyes keep attention over the water to see who's around. If a motor fails, and some boat isn't back in harbor on schedule, community uneasiness settles over the waterfront, and you could cut it with a knife. Those who have "come in" recollect where they last sighted the boat — off Mosquito Rock, down east'ard of Rack Island — and there is a kinship framed in anxiety. Then, when the overdue boat returns to harbor the tension eases, nobody admits to being concerned, and all go home to supper. The communion is reserved for members only. That first morning, when I arrived in the pitch dark of 2 A.M., Harold spoke a casual greeting and wanted to know if I was "down for the summer." Just to remind me that I was a guest; that I was different. Harold was standing shoulder to shoulder with Tom and John, and some others were there I didn't know or didn't recognize in the dark. "Mornin'," I said, and got silence. Everybody was communicating, and I joined the witan to face the harbor and wait for light enough to see the lobster boats on mooring. Fueled and with bait aboard, the boats would not cast off and go down the bay until the big decision had been arrived at as to whether or not this was a "haulin' day."

To haul, or not to haul?

Was this a day to run five, six, seven miles to sea, to be there at sunup when the law permits traps to be lifted, and would the sunrise be propitious? Nobody spoke, and the silence was communication.

After a time, Harold said, "Well — I dunno."

Some minutes later, Tom said, "Well — I dunno."

There began to be some light, and the shapes of the fishing boats appeared. Another few minutes, and John pushed his skiff off the wharf into the water, stepped in, and quietly skulled off toward his mooring. So, too, did Tom, and the others, and so did Harold and I — Harold taking the thwart to row his overloaded skiff. A decision had been made and agreement arrived at, and the day was a haulin' day. We were well down to Magee Island, when the sun burst from the ocean and dripped great red blobs back into the tide. John, when he pushed off his skiff, had said it would be like that, but not in words. He just communicated.

On the other hand . . . A year or so later Harold stopped by and I gave him some Brussels sprouts from my garden, and I asked, "They crawlin'?"

"Eyah," said Harold. "Some."

"I haven't been to haul this year," I said.

Harold smiled. "You can go anytime you want, you know that."

"Eyah."

He looked at the Brussels sprouts and said, "That's enough. I'm good for just about that many once a year. They don't taste so good second time."

"You haulin' tomorrow?"

"Plan to."

" 'Bout four?"

"Prolly. Four-thirty, more likely."

I said, "If I'm not there by four-thirty, I'm not coming."

I was there at four-thirty.

On a haulin' day, Friendship harbor comes to life all over. Each engine, some three hundred of them, is started and idled long enough to listen to the rhythm. It must sound right. Pumps empty the bilges. Each lobsterman gets his waterproof clothes, because no matter how calm the weather, water flies when the pot warps are brought in over the snatch blocks. The cumulative roar of all the engines keeps up until the fleet disperses "down below." Radios are turned on, and talk will continue among boats until the business of hauling warps interrupts. Friendship is a working harbor, and the fishermen have little use for the summer mahogany. Even if they did, one can't start up a motorboat and head for sea without making a noise, and once the fleet is outside Garrison Island the cottagers and the yachtsmen can go back to sleep.

Again I found Harold, with Tom and John and the others, standing in the dark facing the harbor — communicatively silent. I got the usual small hello, and I got the foolishness about being down for the summer. I had my breakfast and lunch in a clam hod, weather gear under my arm, and as a touch of light developed in the east I could see that Harold's skiff (incidentally, one I made for him) was on the wharf and hadn't been bailed after last evening's shower. There was no surge of engines off on the harbor. I didn't hear the squawk of a boat radio, turning to the Coast Guard weather. Nobody said, "I dunno." Nobody had gone off to mooring. They knew. A decision had been reached and it was unanimous. John went first, shuffling up the ramp in his rubber boots, and then one by one they all went home.

It was not to be a haulin' day.

REED WHITTEMORE
1919—

Summer visitors to Maine naturally include poets as well as those artists who come with sketchbooks and watercolor pads. Here is a meditative poem by a poet watching his small son digging at a clam hole on an ebb tide at Reid State Park in Georgetown.

Reed Whittemore has published eight volumes of poetry and criticism, including a biography of the poet William Carlos Williams, and from 1969 to 1973 he served as literary editor of the *New Republic*. He has taught at Carleton College and recently retired as a professor of English at the University of Maryland after twenty years there. Among his literary awards have been a Guggenheim Fellowship and the Award of Merit of the American Academy of Arts and Letters.

Clamming

I go digging for clams once every two or three years
Just to keep my hand in (I usually cut it),
And whenever I do so I tell the same story
Of how at the age of four I was trapped by the tide
As I clammed a sandbar. It's no story at all
But I tell it and tell it; it serves my small lust

"The Clamdiggers"

To be thought of as someone who's lived.
I've a war to fall back on, and some years of flying,
As well as a high quota of drunken parties,
A wife and children; but somehow the clamming thing
Gives me an image of me that soothes my psyche
Like none of the louder events: me helpless,
Alone with my sandpail,
As fate in the form of soupy Long Island sound
Comes stalking me.

I've a son now at that age.
He's spoiled, he's been sickly.
He's handsome and bright, affectionate and demanding.
I think of the tides when I look at him.
I'd have him alone and sea-girt, poor little boy.

The self, what a brute it is. It wants, wants,
It will not let go of its even most fictional grandeur

But must grope, grope down in the muck of its past
For some little squirting life and bring it up tenderly
To the lo and behold of death, that it may weep
And pass on the weeping, keep the thing going.

                         Son, when you clam,
Watch out for the tides and take care of yourself,
Yet no great care,
Lest you care too much and brag of the caring
And bore your best friends and inhibit your children and sicken
At last into opera on somebody's sandbar. Son, when you clam,
Clam.

JOHN N. COLE
1923–

John Cole is perhaps best known in Maine as co-founder, with Peter Cox, of the weekly newspaper *Maine Times*. Since its inception in 1968, *Maine Times* has served to unify Maine — it was then the only statewide publication — and to urge readers to look more closely and critically at some of Maine's troubling problems. As editor, Cole emphasized environmental concerns, political responsibility, and institutional accountability. His influence is still being felt.

He is now a freelance writer, the author of several books, and lives in Brunswick, Maine, and Key West, Florida. The following selections from his collection of *Maine Times* columns, *In Maine*, illustrate his close relationship with the natural world around him.

Ice Out

The ice went out of the bay last week; and I was there one afternoon to watch some of it leave with the falling tide. Afterwards I decided there can be few other natural events, if any, which are such dramatic witness to spring's arrival. Any Maine person who lives within sight of any water — stream, river, pond, bay or lake — has something of a seasonal edge on the land-bound; for without the ice-out to prove it, winter's end can too easily be prolonged.

I watched the ice move in last November. In the early mornings when I woke and looked out, I could see a slick on the still surface of the sheltered waters of the cove. I thought at first it was merely a place unruffled by the morning's light winds; then, as the sun warmed the night's frost, the slick patches would drift out into the bay like oil. I learned then that the rounded slicks were circles of early ice, too thin to survive the sun and the tides, but working each night for more of a hold.

One morning the cove ice held fast against the tide and was still there in the late afternoon. By December, the cove was immobile, and the outer edges of the ice probed the open bay. Late in that short, dark month, the wind howled for two days and nights from the northwest, bringing with it an Arctic cold. When the wind let go and the night sky cleared, the ice leapt across the entire bay and locked in the surging waters. What had been wind-tossed blue water the day before was now lifeless, little more than a flat extension of the land, without trees.

Everywhere the eye could see, the bay was white. Even with binoculars, the far horizon of the open ocean was nothing more than a blue line between sky and ice. The gulls and seabirds that had defied winter with their life at our water's edge had gone, all of them, leaving the house with nothing but the chickadees and jays — land birds. The ice completed the silence of winter; it muffled every sea sound and subdued all movement.

As the snows gathered, the frozen bay became a white desert where the wind cut dunes from the drifts and blew the snow like sand across the hard dry ice. Then, in January, came a short thaw. The snow swept away and the ice surface was cleaned. It froze clear again, and we could skate for miles across the glistening skin. Still, skating is a winter sport; there was no sense out there that underneath the bay moved with the moon.

The ice stayed so long that we almost forgot the bay had been there. Winter had become too real. Putting on the big coat every morning became habit, and the acceptance of the cold beyond the door became routine. We began to think of life as always being congealed, indoors, snow dusted and sharp.

But in February's last days, all that changed. The thin blue line on the horizon grew wide. The circling gulls that watched over the ice edge could be seen without the glasses. And in the first week of March, overnight, a ribbon of water ran through the ice from our shore across the cove. At first it was more a string than a ribbon — a thin line of gray against the white ice. It widened to a ribbon after one warm morning, became a sliver of open water just too wide to jump, although no one could tell how it had grown, so slowly did the widening take place.

That afternoon last week, as I was watching, the water ribbon became a breaking place. The acres of ice on the bay side of the gap began to move away, to slip down the bay with the first nudges of the falling tide. One field of ice — and it could have held a farmhouse, a barn, and a potato lot — moved enough to be seen. I could line up an edge with a tree on the point and then watch that edge slip out of sight behind the trunk. The great gray ice mass moved quietly, and behind it was the sudden softness of open water, tickled by the wind, capped here and there with smaller floes and ice cakes, each one drifting away on a final solo voyage to the distant sea.

Even as the ice moved, the birds returned. When the ice-out tide had finished falling and the flats came out for their first day since November, the gulls and ducks swirled over them in a feathered rain. Their cries and callings broke the long winter's silence with a surge of sound that could be heard a mile away. It was as if spring had arrived in a few afternoon hours, and that sort of seasonal turning is not like Maine, who holds her winters tightly, letting go ever so slowly, from March to May.

At least that's what I had learned to live with until that afternoon last week. Now, after watching the ice leave the bay, and knowing that it is gone for good, I can take whatever March has left to give. That's what I mean when I say that Maine people who live by water have an edge.

Captain's Log

Captain's Log of a Short Sail Around Middle Bay: distance, less than five nautical miles, mostly in a circle; time, about two hours, weather, stiff sou'west breeze.

Several flocks of white-winged scoters in the bay; probably driven in by the onshore breeze which has been blowing now for at least three days. The young scoters are comical and awkward, obviously not yet sophisticated in the ways of men or boats. I remember them as "coots," as all three species of scoters were called during my gunning days in Gardiners Bay. But those ended a while ago, and here in Maine, the young whitewings are my unwitting playmates. Sailing downwind, directly at the flocks of the large sea ducks, I discover the young birds have little or no fear of the boat. Because they cannot take off, except directly into the wind, the birds are in a bit of a quandary when they comprehend how fast my Hobie Cat is closing on them. Too late they realize that if they try to take wing, they will have to fly directly into the boat. One or two try this, their wings beating the water frantically as they run — slapslapslap slap slapslap — with their crazy webbed feet pushing at the water. They are airborne within inches of the bow; I can see the whites of their eyes, their startled looks, their total discomfort and embarrassment at being caught in such a predicament. I could almost reach up and pluck one out of the air, but I laugh as they go by and spend the next half-hour or so tacking upwind of the flocks and replaying the silly game. The birds learn after a time or two, and instead of flying, they dive.

A bit weary of the breeze in the open bay and the unending demands it makes on me and the boat, I ease into a favorite small cove on the lee side of one of the half-dozen islands in my home bay. I have always loved this cove. The island is not lived on, yet some natural whim has put what amounts to a mini-meadow at the water's edge. The open green is ringed with high pines, it shelves easily to the water and is one of the most inviting spots for a small boat sailor I have ever seen. It is almost too perfect, rather like a movie set, or picture postcard. This day, I do not go ashore, but ease the boat along the shore's edge, just looking things over, enjoying the quiet and the calm of the lee.

As I glide (and this boat is a great glider) a pair of mergansers (sheldrake) slip off the shore and start paddling in front of the boat. I know these are normally open water ducks, and believe they must have a nest in the cove if they are staying here, alone, as a pair. My nesting theory seems to be upheld when the male sheldrake goes into his crippled wing act and flutters and splashes in evident distress right in front of my boat. He manages to stay a safe distance away, though, and his flutters consistently take him (and hopefully me) in a direction away from the cove. The bird is so obviously alarmed and so distinctly courageous that I do not test him any further. I sail away from the cove, and out in the open bay I come across the female sheldrake, nonchalantly paddling about, quite confident, I guess, that her male companion is doing right by the children. The fem lib movement, I decide, will never get very far with the mergansers. Their hens seem to have already won the battle, because in most other species it is the female bird that pretends to be crippled.

On the point of the island just across the channel from the sheldrake cove is a large rock that belongs to the seals. There are many other rocks in the bay, but the seals have chosen this one. They can be found there almost every day, sunning and surfing, chasing herring, mackerel and whatever. This day, there are about a dozen taking the sun. They have been out of the water for a spell, because their fur is dry and they are sleepy. They too have some young, and they don't notice my boat until it is quite near. Then there is a shuffling surge, many heads in the air, flippers pushing, big bodies sliding and slipping and splashing all about and the rock is quite empty. By then, I am almost on top of the seals and the water is shoal. Too shoal for them to deep dive, and I can look down all around me and see the seal bodies flashing underneath. They are curious creatures, you know, and one big fellow surfaces just next to the bow, snorting and somewhat cross at having his nap upset.

The strong breeze puffs into my sail, and I'm away before the others can surface. I sail home, imagining that someone seeing the boat from shore might think it a lonely sport to be the only boat on the bay. They couldn't have seen all my company.

JOHN MCPHEE
1931–

John McPhee writes of the unusual, the independent, the more remote of America's regions and people. His journalistic essays, which
appear in *The New Yorker* and in book form, explore such diverse
subjects as the Alaskan wilderness and a greenmarket in New York
City. Of Maine, he has written about bark canoes and a man who
builds them, the life of doctors in remote rural towns, and, in the
piece excerpted here, the Great North Woods as experienced by a
game warden pilot.

McPhee spent many hours over a period of months, primarily in
the air, with his pilot, coincidentally also named John McPhee. (They
met when McPhee the pilot wrote to McPhee the journalist complaining that the *New Yorker* articles on development in the Great North
Woods were jeopardizing his job as a state employee.) The journalist
tells us in his straightforward fashion about the man from Eagle
Lake, Maine, his courage, and his commitment to his part of the
state. The warden spends most of his time flying low over the vast
wilderness that is Maine north of the Canadian Pacific Railway line.
"The C. P. line is where the Canadian Pacific Railway, encountering
the obstacle of northern Maine, overcomes the inconvenience by
crossing the state — in one side (Jackman) and out the other (Vance-
boro)." The warden's ultimate concern is for the fish, birds, and
animals that inhabit this world. His job is to ensure that hunters and
fishermen observe the state's conservation laws and to protect the
hunters from themselves. Search and rescue missions occupy a considerable amount of the pilot's time.

The landlords of this great forest area are the few big paper
companies that own most of it. The goals of the State of Maine and
of the paper companies are not always in accord. Logging methods

"Lumberjack, Great Northern Paper Co."

can be at odds with the life patterns of the animals in the woods, with conservation practices, and with the recreational habits of those who visit this largely unspoiled wilderness. McPhee describes the recent changes in the nature of lumbering operations and the sometimes devastating effect they have on the woods.

McPhee is on the staff of *The New Yorker* and teaches journalism at Princeton University. This selection comes from his article "North of the C. P. Line," from *Table of Contents*. Maine's Great North Woods are well served by both McPhees.

From "North of the C. P. Line"

My other self — as he might have been called in a brief, ambiguous novel — was in this instance a bush pilot, several hundred feet above Third Matagamon Lake, face to face with a strong winter wind. The plane was a Super Cub, scarcely large enough for the two of us. We sat in tandem and talked through an intercom. There is a lot of identification, even transformation, in the work I do — moving along from place to place, person to person, as a reporter, a writer, repeatedly trying to sense another existence and in some ways to share it. Never had that been more true than now, in part because he was sitting there with my life in his hands while placing (in another way) his life in mine. He spoke with affection about the plane, calling it a sophisticated kite and admitting his amazement that it could take such a frontal battering when all it was made of, essentially, was cotton.

I said that was amazing, right enough — and how fast did he imagine the wind was blowing?

He said he could guess, with some help from the airspeed indicator, but one way to tell for sure was to stop the plane. Flying level, holding course, he slowed down, and slowed down more, and told me to watch the ground until the spruce did not move. A steady progression over the trees became a stately progression over the trees, and ultimately — like a frame of motion picture frozen on a screen — came to a dead stop. With respect to the earth, we were stock-still. Against the deep snow, the spruce made chevrons with their shadows. Nothing in the pattern moved. Mt. Katahdin, on our flank — sparkling white above its ruff of dark trees — did not move. The black forest reached to the horizon around the white paisley shapes of the Allagash Lakes — a scene preserved before us as if it were on canvas, while we hung there at ground speed zero.

"We're indicating forty-five miles per hour," he said. "There's your answer. That's how fast the wind is blowing."

There were snowshoes on the wing struts — two pairs. He said, "You never know when the airplane is going to refuse to go." He had skis and poles and an M-1 rifle. ("The sound of a revolver doesn't carry.") A five-foot steel ice chisel was mounted on the fuselage. There was some kero dust ("kerosene and sawdust, it burns for quite a while") and strike-anywhere matches in a waterproof steel case. There was some trail mix, but no regular stores of food. ("If I carry a lot of food in the airplane, I just eat it. I carry trail mix the way some people carry chewing tobacco.") There were goose-down warmup pants and extra down parkas that were supposedly good to seventy below zero. (They reminded me of a friend who, one Alaskan winter, took a mail-order parka to Anaktuvuk Pass and came back complaining that it didn't work.) By now, I had seen about all I wanted to of the underlying landscape without apparent motion, and I listened for the sound of an advancing throttle.

This pilot, as it happened, was an author as well, and he had written magazine pieces about the North Maine Woods — its terrain, its wildlife, and related subjects — as had I. In the spring of 1976, he wrote to *The New Yorker* and complained that I was using his name. He said, "For all practical purposes he is using my name (and I his)," and he went on to explain that the signature at the bottom of my pieces had from time to time embarrassed him in his principal occupation, as an employee of the State of Maine. He said he tended to agree with some of my thoughts — for example, about the Army Corps of Engineers and its plans to dam the St. John River — but he was not at liberty to do so in open print, because he was under oath to be neutral on public issues. And now his oath seemed to be hanging out like a wet necktie, because right there in *The New Yorker* was a tirade worthy of Rumpelstiltskin, ranting against the people who wished to flood the North Maine Woods by building the twelfth-largest dam on earth — in a piece of writing that many people he knew assumed he had written, as well they might, for it was signed with his exact name.

At that time, Maine had four game-warden pilots. This one was the northernmost, with seven thousand square miles of forest as his home range. In what was by then a decade of service there, he had become known as the Flying Warden of the North Maine Woods. Nonetheless, I had never heard of him. If we are cousins, we are much removed. We are related only to the extent that we descend from a clan that immemorially occupied one small island in the Hebrides, where our surname developed. Yet for all practical purposes we are indeed using each other's names, and while I had been making my own professional journeys on lakes and streams through the woods of Maine I had in my ignorance felt no twinge of encroachment and could not have imagined being over myself in the air.

I had been to the Hebrides once, to live for a time on the clan island and gather material for a piece of writing. Now *The New Yorker,* at my request, sent that piece of writing to Maine. It was not just a matter of the postage. I was in Alaska, far from home, and a copy of his letter had been sent to me up there. In a cabin near the Yukon River, I wrote a sympathetic response — a condensed autobiography, an *apologia pro nomine suo,* always endeavoring to match his graceful good humor — and soon thereafter mailed it to Maine. The warden was not there to receive it. Taking some time off, he had got into his own airplane with his father, Malcolm, and headed northwest through Quebec in foul weather, flying low up the Saguenay River, dodging wires. ("You have to be alert. You have to watch out.") Conditions soon changed to what he calls "severe clear," and remained almost cloudless from Lac St. Jean to Moose Factory (on James Bay) to Churchill (on Hudson Bay) to Yellowknife to Great Bear Lake. Landing on floats, they were fishing all the way. They followed the Yukon River through interior Alaska, and — more or less while I was writing my letter — passed above my head on their way to the Bering Sea.

When he returned to Maine, he found my letter regretting the inconvenience I had caused him, and the story of the Scottish island, which established for him our remote kinship and common history. For a year or two, there was more correspondence, but we remained strangers. His mother told him that she could not distinguish my handwriting from his.

Then, just after breakup — or ice out, as they call it in Maine — a friend and I were on Allagash Lake when a blue-and-white floatplane came over the trees, went into a tight turn, and circled the canoe. Allagash Lake is one beautiful lake, Allagash Mountain stands beside it. There are forty-two hundred acres of water and a fleet of wooded islands. There are brook trout, lake trout. Allagash Lake has never been stocked. In its elevation, and among its circumvallate hills, it is the high coronet of the wilderness waterway, of the Allagash River system. Floatplanes are strictly forbidden to set down on Allagash Lake, but there is an official exception. I had mentioned in a letter the plans for that trip, and had described as well my dark-chocolate canoe. The airplane gave up its altitude, flared, and sent spray off the lake. It taxied toward the canoe. Then the propeller stopped and the airplane drifted. We moved alongside and took hold of a pontoon. I was ninety-nine per cent certain that I knew who was inside. Even so, there was room for surprise. The door opened. The pilot stepped down and stood on the pontoon. About forty, weathered and slim, he looked like a North-West Mounted Policeman. His uniform jacket was bright red, trimmed with black flaps over the breast pockets, black epaulets. A badge above one pocket said "STATE OF MAINE WARDEN PILOT." Above the other pocket was a brass plate incised in block letters with his name: JOHN MCPHEE. I almost fell into the lake.

He was an appealing, friendly man, and he did not ask for my fishing license. We talked for at least an hour there, canoe and airplane about a mile offshore, on the calm surface of early evening. He had a quick smile, a pilot's alert, responsive eyes. He looked a lot like my cousin John and not a little like John's father, John. We talked of the backcountry — the Allagash and St. John lake-and-river country — and the creatures that live in its woods and waters. From anecdote to anecdote, unself-consciously he poured forth his knowledge — of natural disasters and human intrusions, of isolated phenomena and recurrent events, of who was doing what to whom. I remember a wistful feeling — it has not diminished — imagining the life that had produced that knowledge. We asked if he would stay for dinner. He said he was always ready to eat. We pushed away from the pontoon and headed toward the stand of white pines below which we had pitched our tents. The warden followed, taxiing dead slow — the canoe leading the airplane, tandem, cutting three wakes across a mile of water. He tied it to one of the pines.

Several seasons later, I went down the Allagash River in October in a party of four. They were days of intermittent snowstorms — fast-moving squalls that would come blowing through, tearing up the water, obscuring the air. Time after time, as one of those storms was departing we would hear a drone from beyond the trees. An airplane would emerge from the receding clouds, a blue-and-white floatplane with a pair of canoe paddles wedged in its pontoon cross braces. After leaning over for a look, he would vanish with a waggle of the wings.

Since then, I have come to know him well, and in various seasons have spent some days with him in the air — with the state's permission, going along on his patrols. Thus, with me sitting behind him, we have been paired — one name, two people — five hundred feet in the air, scanning the country from Moosehead Lake to Estcourt Station, the north extreme of Maine. He calls me John: I call him Jack, as people do more often than not. Flying half the year with floats, the other half with skis, he has spent so much time in the air above the woods that — despite the exercise he gets snowshoeing, skiing, paddling, and splitting wood — he has "turnpike back," from (as he puts it) "sitting all day with my knees in my mouth." His home, which is also his flying base, is in Plaisted, on Eagle Lake, a few miles south of Fort Kent. To fly from the base to the most distant corner of his district takes an hour and fifteen minutes. The entire flight is over forest and never crosses a paved or public road. Looking down, he picks through the trees with his eyes. In concentration, he has learned to ignore the interference of canopies, assembling in his mind glimpses of whatever may lie below. He could spot a tent in a tropical rain forest. To hide from his surveillance seems impossible in Maine. ("You can tell about people by the way they camp. If they go to a lot of trouble to be out of the way, they're Sneaky Petes. They have something to hide.") In his district are seventeen ground wardens, their names reflective of the region where they live: Gary Pelletier, John Caron, Rodney Sirois, Phil Dumond. For them, Jack is another pair of eyes, with long perspective.

"Two Two Five Two. Two Two Six Seven. I'm over the St. John near the Big Black rapid, eastbound. Is there anything we can do for you while we're here?"

The voices of the wardens come up from the woods. A hunter near Seven Islands has lost his bearings, has no idea where he set up his camp. Jack has a look and finds the camp. A party at Nine Mile is missing one hunter. Jack hunts the hunter and finds him walking in a brook.

"We've been in the air five hours," he said one afternoon. "This is when you've really got to buckle down if you want to do this work. After five hours, your eyes might begin to skim the tops of the trees. You've got to look between the trees and see what's on the ground, or you'll miss something. I think that is why I'm sort of addicted to coffee. It helps me in the afternoon."

In winter, as he cants the airplane and studies the sign in snow, he is careful to breathe in the middle of the cabin — or the Plexiglas fogs up, the vapor freezes, and the rime obscures his view. When he lands and goes off on some mission on skis or snowshoes, he first gets out three blankets and drapes them over the engine, as if he were wrapping a horse. He tucks them up snugly, and crosses one blanket over the air intake like a scarf protecting a skater's mouth. In warm weather, he drops into tiny ponds, landing in space that a loon could not get out of, space that would make a duck think twice. Some of these ponds are in the high intervals of small connected mountains and are extremely remote. Jack keeps canoes up there, hidden in the brush. In this place and that, for purposes both professional and private, he has thirteen canoes. "I'm addicted to the backcountry," he remarked one day on the edge of an isolated pond. "I definitely am just an outdoors person." After stashing a canoe, he gave the plane a shove toward the center of the pond, leaped after it, landed on the end of a pontoon, and walked on it like a river driver walking on a log. Swinging into the cockpit, he made a downwind takeoff within a hundred yards. On the ground as well as in the air, he does indeed seem most in his element when he is out in the big woods, where he spends nearly all his working time, and a good bit of whatever remains — "out in the williwags," as he refers to the back-country. A williwag, apparently, is a place so remote that it can be reached only by first going through a boondock.

In certain lakes and ponds — McKeen Lake, Fourth Pelletier Pond — there were large dark patches, roseate bruises in the water. He said they were "boiling" springs. Trout hung around them in crowds. And the springs were not discernible except from the air. Deer in the woods looked like Dobermans, and he would be counting ten, eleven, twelve before I could separate even one from its background. Cow moose, up to their knees in water, stood motionless, like equestrian statues with missing riders. Bears were everywhere — bears in the understory, bears on the gravel bars of the St. John River, bears on the timber companies' tote roads, bears on the lawns of Jack's neighbors near the base. Flying into the sun above one shallow lake, we followed a plume of mud that something had stirred up in the water. In the caroming glare, we could not see anything at the head of the plume. "Watch," he said through the intercom. "Watch as the light flips over." We passed the plumehead and glanced back. A bull moose was walking through the water, trailing mud. There were blue herons in white pines, male mergansers in the Currier Ponds, a beaver busy in a pond of his own. "There's a beaver working. He's going to splash." With a mighty slap on the water, the beaver disappeared. Jack knew the pH of the Hudson Ponds, and the geology that had caused the high number. The geology was very evident, sticking up in the air. "That's a nice little chunk of rock," he said, swinging past it on a day when the woods were brushed with mist.

"We call these scuddy conditions," he went on. "Like that over there where the cloud is on the ridge. Flying it is called scud running — right on the deck. When some people talk about scud running, they mean thousand-foot ceilings. When I talk about it, I mean fifty-foot ceilings. That's what we often have here." All over the undulating forest, clouds lay on the ridges, and we flew in the valleys of rivers, streams, and brooks. A cold rain was falling. The outside air temperature was forty-two degrees. "This is a condition for carburetor icing," he commented. "Sometimes the old carburetor looks just like you were hand-cranking ice cream."

On the radio we heard Jimmy Dumond, a ground warden, calling the state-police barracks in Houlton. Off in the woods by one of the logging roads he had found a small car with the license plate Y WORK. He asked the police to tell him whose it was — names and addresses being useful clues to what may be happening in the woods. The car belonged to Fred Callahan of Auburn, Maine, and his apparent purpose was unspecific recreation. Dumond, somewhere near the outlet of First Musquacook Lake, then called Two Two Five Two, asking for reconnaissance of a nearby ridge.

"I'll have a look if I can stay under the scud," Jack replied, and we went up the ridge with the pontoons close to the trees. Over the intercom he said to me, "In these same conditions, if the temperature drops, the visibility is considerably less."

"Why is that?"

"Because the air is full of snowflakes."

He remarked that in scuddy conditions he always feels comfortable if he can see ahead, because he knows every valley and where it will lead — he knows "the way the land lays," he even knows "most of the trees" — but in snow he cannot see ahead. He said it was important to know the country three ways. To the unaccustomed eye, severe clarity could be just as misleading as low scud; and then, of course, there were certain emergencies requiring that he fly at night. At night, he said, he flies "like the old-timers, on instruments" — the instruments being his compass, his wristwatch, and the altimeter. Sometimes he flies that way in daytime. "I do it quite often," he said. "It's not recommended policy, but sometimes it's the best way to get around. It's actually safer than being right down on the trees and catching a wing on a dead branch you don't see — which is the sort of thing that has happened to an awful lot of bush pilots."

He also said that he had no desire whatever to tickle the dragon's tail — his expression for flying in extremely marginal conditions. He never wants to tickle the dragon unless he feels he has to. On a day of heavy gusts, when he could lose control of the plane on takeoff or landing, he does not fly unless something happens that makes a flight compelling ("unless there's an emergency, or I'm out here when the gusts come up").

One afternoon, I noticed that both fuel gauges, which were above his head and somewhat behind him on either side of the cabin, were registering empty. Trying my best to sound unconcerned, I said slowly, "How's the fuel supply? Have you got a lot of fuel?"

He did not need eyes in the back of his head to see me noticing the gauges or to read the anxiety in my face. He said he would never trust either one of those gauges — especially if they said the tanks were full. On the back of his hand he had written in ink the number 15.2 — the last digits on the tachometer's engine-hour meter when we took off from the base. The meter now said 18.4. He put 5.5 hours of fuel in the airplane before we left, and we had used 3.2. Also on his hand were three small hash marks, one for each elapsed hour. He was drawing on the wing tanks an hour at a time.

Spring, summer, deep into the fall — if the Allagash is not frozen, there are canoes on the river. People were standing in them, poling. They sometimes missed the wildlife we could see from above. We saw moose in a slough close by the river, where eight canoes were passing, screened from the moose by a narrow hummock and a fringe of trees. "More people use the Allagash each year than in the year before," Jack remarked through the intercom. "What's here is some of the last of what can be found on the East Coast. People are really flockin' to it, despite the fact that some of us who live here might say that it ain't what it used to be."

The North Maine Woods have been advertised as "the Last Eastern Frontier," and, indeed, almost nowhere in the United States below Alaska is there such a large forest with virtually no structures except a few cabins and some logging camps — this lacustrine, riverine world, independent of paved roads. A couple of centuries ago, when Maine belonged to Massachusetts, surveyors began making a checkerboard of the map of Maine, dividing uninhabited land into square "townships," normally six miles on a side. The townships were num-

bered, and (in various tracts at different latitudes) renumbered —
always from south to north. A column of townships was called a
range. Township 1, Range 12. Township 2, Range 12. Township 3,
Range 12. Through time, as populations grew, townships incorporated and took on names. Maine is half of New England, and to this
day nearly half of Maine consists of nameless unorganized townships,
so extensive are the north woods. Township 14, Range 12. Township
15, Range 12. People who work in the woods think in numbered
townships. When one warden asks another what "town" something
is happening in, he is referring almost always to twenty-three thousand acres of unpopulated forest. Township 16, Range 12. Township
17, Range 12. The ranges reach aggressively far into Canada — as
far north, for example, as latitudes of Newfoundland. Township 18,
Range 12. Township 19, Range 12. Big Twenty Township is the top
of Maine.

The remarkable preservation of so much land does not owe itself
to the environmental movement. The lakes that Henry David Thoreau paddled through in 1853 and 1857 look today much the same
as they did when he was there. Among the rare artifacts are small
dams that were built before Thoreau's time to raise the levels of lakes,
the better to float logs to sawmills downcountry. The surrounding
forests are owned, as they were in the eighteen-fifties, by companies
that harvest trees. As ever, the people who own the trees are saving
the forest: the people who own the forest are cutting down the trees.

Until fifty or sixty years ago, horses twitched logs from their
stumps to the waterways, and red-shirted river drivers moved them
southeastward through the otherwise detentive forests. In modern
times, logs are assembled by diesel-powered machines, and river
drivers have been replaced by truck drivers. Logging roads began
penetrating the woods many years ago, and the principal ones, like
the American Realty Tote Road, have checkpoints where public users
pay a modest fee. A new feature of the Maine woods, however, is that
the tote roads have much increased in number and extent. Areas
remote and previously inaccessible are now in the network. Moreover, the new roads have been built with enough sophistication to
enable even a low-slung Presidential limousine to glide over gravel to
the corners of the woods. Demand is high for pulpwood and lumber.
There have been technical advances in tree-harvesting equipment.
There is urgency in salvaging trees that have been attacked in recent
years by spruce budworm. As such factors have coalesced, there has
been an acceleration of the rate of timber cutting. The result is a
variety of perspectives. They depend on who you are and where you

sit. If you rest against the thwarts of a canoe, the woods are much the same as ever. If you climb Allagash Mountain, you look across a broadloom of hundreds of square miles of trees — and if you have come from the megalopolis you cannot help being impressed. If you sit in a Super Cub, however, and criss-cross the forest, you may suffer recurrent attacks of myocardial ambivalence. As you look to the horizons, the vastness of the evergreen forest — the great volume of unpopulated space — has lost none of its effect. Small wonder that canoes appear in navies, and tents come up like mushrooms in spring. To look down, though, at the patchwork landscape is to see and to sense something else. While the warden pilot has the most comprehensive view of his beloved backcountry, it is also in some respects the least encouraging. In many places, from the air, the terrain now looks like an old and badly tanned pelt. The hair is coming out in tufts. The new logging roads reach to amoeboid apertures in the woods, big clear-cuts on their way to become as numerous as the obsolescent lakes. Jack said on the intercom one day, with studied equanimity, "It's not a woods so much as a crop that is also used for recreation. Where the companies cut selectively, they cut a lot. They go for the big spruce and fir." The results lay below us — swaths of largely denuded ground, with the spruce and fir gone, cedars and birches standing. "The companies don't want the cedar and the birch," he went on. "We're not at a point in this country where we efficiently harvest the timber." Birches, left on their own, were fragile, and in many places had been blown down by windstorms. They looked like stubbed cigarettes after a teen-age party. There is some tension between the timber companies and the Department of Inland Fisheries and Wildlife, employer of game wardens and wildlife biologists. The state is empowered to protect its animals and words can become brittle when, for instance, deer have yarded up under ripe timber. "That's a new road down there, by the Little Black River," he said. "They'll come in here and cut heavily. The last time these woods were cut, the logs were twitched out by horse. With the equipment they have now, they'll take it out in a hurry. These people have to make a dollar, though. You've got to be reasonable, be willing to compromise. The land *does* belong to them." The American Realty Tote Road makes its way across the woods from one side to the other, and Jack, like everyone else in the region, calls it the Reality Road.

Like the long cry of the loon, the presence of moose authenticates the northern forest. Early in this century, their number was in steady decline, and by 1936 so few were left in Maine that moose hunting was declared illegal. The state animal was leaving the state. Recently, though, as clear-cut acreages have increased in the wild woods, the number of moose has increased, too. Moose seem to prosper where people knock down trees. "Moose and deer do not do well in a mature forest," Jack said one autumn day as the Super Cub crossed an area where moose and deer would do well. Generally, after a cutting, seedlings have not been planted. Natural succession functions on its own, and among the first plants to spring up are red and striped maples and birch and raspberries. Not even Ralston Purina could come up with anything more acceptable to moose and deer. "The amount of cutting has made more food, and thus more deer and moose," he continued. "Deer, in fact, are sometimes so impatient that they go to active cuts. The loggers like to say that while a chain saw is working on one end of a tree deer are browsing on the other."

I will believe anything about deer. Deer, in my opinion, are rats with antlers, roaches with split hooves, denizens of the dark primeval suburbs. Deer intensely suggest New Jersey. One of the densest concentrations of wild deer in the United States inhabits the part of New Jersey that, as it happens, I inhabit, too. Deer like people. They like to be near people. They like beanfields, head lettuce, and anybody's apples. They like hibiscus, begonias, impatiens, azaleas, rhododendrons, boxwood, and wandering Jews. I once saw a buck with a big eight-point rocking-chair rack looking magnificent as he stood between two tractor-trailers in the Frito-Lay parking lot in New Brunswick, New Jersey. Deer use the sidewalks in the heart of Princeton.

I was not prepared to receive, however, the message that was coming through to me on the Super Cub's intercom; to wit, that moose also thrive on the presence of man, that the moose of Maine have returned in great numbers in direct proportion to the felling of the forest, that the mighty symbol of the Great North Woods apparently salivates at the sound of a chain saw. Jack repeated, as we looked down into a timbered cut, "Moose eat striped maple; they eat red-maple sprouts off stumps; they eat the beech saplings, the young birch — the broadleaf hardwoods that spring up after the cutting. The bigger the cut — the more open the cut — the more it favors moose over deer."

Moose are better off where deer are scarce. Deer carry a brain worm that is almost harmless to them but fatal to moose (just as spruce budworm, ironically, is fatal to balsam fir but not to black spruce). Moose pick up the worm by inadvertently eating snails that have eaten deer feces. The worms go to the brain and destroy the moose.

"Moose have long legs," Jack went on. "They get around easier in deep snow. They can reach the canopies of the saplings. They are hardier, generally, than deer. Often, they can get to the food and the deer can't." The inference seems inescapable that when chain saws open up a landscape for high saplings and deep snow they are working for the Sierra Club. They are contributing to the survival of a vaguely endangered species.

"Beaver eat the same stuff," he said. "They eat the vegetation that appears when the forest has been cut. So beavers have been thriving, too; and they dam brooks, and that produces ponds, and the ponds produce aquatic plants — reed, cow lilies, bullhead lilies — and moose love aquatic plants." The consensus guess is that Maine in 1936 was down to two thousand moose. Now, about fifty years later, biologists are guessing anywhere from twenty thousand to sixty thousand moose. Suddenly — or so it seems — it is about as difficult to find a moose in Maine as it would be to find a dairy cow in Wisconsin. "Look at that baby!" Jack said, hanging the airplane up on its side for a good look at a dark enormous bull — thirteen hundred pounds at least, and with a five-foot rack — in slow, stately motion on a tote road. Township 13, Range 11. A few miles up the road, a yellow Jeep Wagoneer was slowly cruising. In Maine for six days in early fall, moose are hunted by a thousand permittees, who have won the opportunity by lottery. Since 1980, when moose hunting resumed, more than three thousand moose have been killed, tagged, and taken out of the woods to official weighing stations. Thus, a cycle that was set in motion by the chain saw is controlled by the rifle.

In the annual lottery, some fifty-five thousand hunters pay three hundred thousand dollars merely to throw their names in the hat. An alien or out-of-stater — in Maine the terms are synonymous — has to put up twice as much as a citizen of Maine. Aliens and out-of-staters receive a tenth of the permits. Permits and licenses cost sixty thousand dollars more. All other hunting is suspended for the six days, so that no one entering the woods without a moose-hunting permit can legitimately claim to have mistaken a moose for a bear, grouse, or porcupine.

The woods below us were full of Jeep Wagoneers, Ford pickups, Mazdas, Toyotas, and Hondas. Y WORK. A great many of them cruised the tote roads. To be sure, there were hunters walking the woods, doing it the old-fashioned way, but my impression was that of the thousand permittees nine hundred and seventy-five were trolling on the roads. The law forbids hunting from a motor vehicle. It forbids hunters to carry loaded rifles in a vehicle. But the law can hardly forbid hunters to ride from one place to another — or to get there faster than at ten miles an hour. The expanded network of tote roads has made rolling reconnaissance all the more comprehensive for a new generation of Orions. No longer do they need the Maine Hunting Shoe, invented in Freeport by Leon Leonwood Bean. A calfskin wing tip will do.

When the hunters see a moose, they are legal if they get out of their cars before they shoot. Over Township 12, Range 9, we saw a hunter standing in the back of a pickup, leaning on the cab roof, with his rifle in his hands. The vehicle, advancing, looked like a unit of the Fifth Army entering the streets of Salerno. Over Township 12, Range 13, we saw a man with a rifle in his hands leaning out a window of a van. In Township 14, Range 10, two vehicles were cruising together. "It's obvious as hell what they're doing," Jack said as he observed from above; but there was not much he could do. He could describe the vehicles to ground wardens, which he did. But each ground warden was covering about four hundred square miles. Moreover, the hunters in the vehicles were legal unless bullets were found in their guns.

Jack had a great many more things to spot than rifle barrels bristling from Toyota wagons and Oldsmobile sedans. The brooks-and-streams trout season had long since ended, but now that wardens could be presumed to be preoccupied with moose, trout fishermen were fanning out into the woods. A moose permit, of course, was only a permit, and not a guarantee. Among the frustrated hunters would be some who were tempted to steal another hunter's moose. Flying down the long straight southwest-trending United States–Canadian border — over Township 19, Range 12 — we came to the Little Black River. It comes into Maine out of Quebec, and the boundary there is unmistakable, because trees have been cut and all other vegetation has been mowed in a swath that separates the nations. Close by the Little Black River in Canada was a moose stand sixty feet high — as Jack described it on the intercom, "a Hilton up on stilts." He said it could sleep twelve. Canadian hunters who know the art of calling moose call moose out of the United States and bag them in Canada as they walk below the stand. Sometimes the calling fails to attract the animals, in which case the Canadian riflemen have not historically been shy about invading the United States. "You can put down ninety-eight per cent of that sort of thing by making a flight a day with this airplane," Jack said, adding that his border flights sometimes turned up more than poachers. Certain Canadians enter the United States to grow marijuana in old beaver ponds where the sun is good and the silt is rich. They carry the leaves home and cure them in microwave ovens.

Poaching, of course, has no season. Poachers are wont to choose, say, a stormy night at Christmastime or, if they are Canadians, the eve of an American holiday. Poachers tend to run in families, as do game wardens like the Pelletiers and the Dumonds: and in successive generations for more than a century the warden families and the poaching families have gone into the woods on the two sides of the law. They are friends. Some may be Americans, some Canadians, but all are people of the Valley — the St. John Valley — whose inhabitants have more in common with one another than they do with the people elsewhere in their own countries. Nonetheless, they hunt, and are hunted, in their perennial and various ways.

(In the Valley, the first language of many people born and raised in American towns — St. Francis, Fort Kent, Madawaska, Ouellette — is French. But the Valley's language is essentially its own. The name Pelletier is sometimes pronounced "Pelsey" and at other times "Pelkey." Sirois is pronounced "Searaway." The late Henry Taylor, celebrated hermit of the lower Allagash, was born Henri Couturier, but he translated himself many years ago.)

A large percentage of the timber cut in northern Maine goes to Canada to be sawed. Canadian loggers working in Maine and Canadian truck drivers who haul the logs have at times cooperated in the simultaneous removal of moose. The meat is packed in fifty-five-gallon drums. The drums go into the beds of trucks and are covered with fifty tons of logs. If a game warden suspects that a barrel of moose meat is under such a load, the warden has to take the logs off and put them back as well.

There is a practice known as hunting moose with a motor vehicle, which is a far more serious crime than hunting moose from a motor vehicle. The hunter — invariably a poacher — is behind the wheel, and he kills the moose by running it down. Technique is required, or the vehicle can be totalled, not to mention the driver. People who hunt this way have referred to their methodology as an art. The fine is five hundred dollars. The driver spends three days in jail. A second offense costs a thousand dollars and ten days in jail.

*   *   *

One evening, on the ground, we went into a small pond near the Allagash River and tried to call a moose. For all his deep and varied woodcraft, Jack is a novice at calling moose. We had even gone together for a lesson — into a township of Range 6 where moose were said to be as concentrated as anywhere in Maine. The person who said so was Perley Eastman, who has spent many hours in the air with Jack making population studies of wildlife. He is employed as a "wildlife technician," but he can be more accurately described as a trapper, a woodsman, an indigene of the unincorporated townships. Thirty years ago, when logs were still being driven down the Aroostook River in spring, Perley worked the drive. A man of considerable strength and endurance, he is now well along in middle age, and he has a list of medical problems ranging from hiatus hernia to hypertension and a pulse of a hundred and thirteen. Nonetheless, he participates in an annual long-distance canoe race on the river and to this date has never lost. He has his dreams. He senses that the country he prefers in Maine multiplied by a hundred is Alaska, and he has obtained an enormous photograph — eight feet high and thirteen feet long — of the Tanana terrain somewhere east of Fairbanks. The picture completely covers one of his bedroom walls. The day he put it up, he piled campfire ashes on the floor and slept that night in a down bag beside the ashes and the picture. Outside his bedroom window, the view is sweeping — across a meadow framed by the evergreen woods. The black things in motion in the meadow are bears.

With a rolled megaphone of birch bark, Perley calls moose. The call is a bovino-ungulate psychosexual grunt. Moose have pursued Perley and tried to get into his car. The call is scrapingly nasal, and is presented in metric components: two long, two short — which in American Morse code is the number seven, as any moose can tell you. On the night of our lesson, Perley had moose in cavalries circling the periphery of a bog. The rutting season was still some days away, and they lacked the lust to come get him.

And now, at sunset on the pond in the Allagash woods, moose were being called by two people who themselves were accustomed to answering to identical sounds. The horizon was orange and was broken by black jagged spruce. We stood side by side. His grunts and my grunts seemed to me to be indistinguishable and therefore equally inept. Not one moose responded. It seemed to me, as we called and called again, that a bagpiper was more likely to answer.

Hunting for moose, or for anything else, is forbidden on Sundays in Maine — a law that is frequently ignored. To deal with such violations, wardens have procedures that are known in their vernacular as "working Sunday hunters." Working Sunday hunters is how the Federal Bureau of Investigation might describe its approach to the United States Senate and the House of Representatives. The warden pilot spots a hunters' camp, picks up a ground warden, and drops him off about a mile from the camp. The ground warden advances through the forest with a sixty-power spotting scope and sets it up where he can observe the hunters. The warden pilot, who has returned to the air, now lands at the campsite, checks licenses, talks weather, drinks coffee, and flies away to look for other hunters while the ground warden, through the spotting scope, watches what happens next. The hunters go into their tents. They come out loading their guns. They head into the woods. The ground warden follows and makes arrests.

The symbiosis is complex between hunter and warden. Even with the tote roads, and the topographically guiding presence of lakes and streams, the Maine woods are so vast, the trackless areas so broad and numerous, that various people — hikers, campers, fishermen, and particularly hunters — frequently become lost. Even timber cruisers employed by the proprietary land companies sometimes get lost. An International Paper Company cruiser failed to return on the night of November 11, 1976. A skeleton discovered a few years later was thought to be his. In the autumn hunting seasons, Jack seeks and finds a lost hunter almost every day. Search-and-rescue is the most rewarding — and often, of course, the grimmest — aspect of his work. He seeks the corpses of people who drown in lakes and rivers — more than thirty in the past year. He has learned how to read a body under rapids. He is so accustomed to lost hunters — so used to their patterns of gradual disorientation — that he sometimes knows just where to go to find them. For example, there is some very good moose, beaver, trout, deer, and lost-hunter country in Township 16, Range 6. He often gets calls informing him that a Ten-Sixty — a lost hunter — is somewhere in that terrain. "It's a tangle down there," he said one day, flying over it. "There are so many beaver flowages and no landmarks. Hunters get lost, and they head the wrong way. They almost always end up in the same place, though. The configuration of the woods gradually funnels them into it." He has found more than a dozen hunters there. "One purpose of the airplane is hardcore search-and-rescue," he went on. "If you save one life a year, it's worth it. If someone is lost, optimism rises when the airplane comes. We are ninety-nine per cent successful. If a lost person is out more than three nights, the success ratio goes down markedly."

CAROLYN CHUTE
1947–

When in 1985 Carolyn Chute's novel *The Beans of Egypt, Maine* appeared, local readers rushed to buy it. The reviewers said that Maine had seen nothing like it before. The only comparisons they could turn to were earlier novels about the southern poor, such as Erskine Caldwell's *Tobacco Road* and Faulkner's stories about poor whites and long-enduring blacks. They might more appropriately have added Richard Wright's *Native Son,* for Chute's epigraph is: "In memory of real Reuben. Who spared him this occasion? Who spared him rage?" Her novel centers on Rubie Bean, a member of the dispossessed and estranged class of native sons and daughters, and is written with a controlled rage and a deep compassion for him and his kind, Maine's rural poor.

Like other good novels of protest, *The Beans of Egypt, Maine* is as far from a case history as a born storyteller can take it. Chute explains nothing, presents everything. She says that she has been writing since she was eight and that she has found she is fitted for nothing else. She discovered this as she tried working in a shoe factory and a poultry factory, for she has lived much of her life among her novel's working poor. The child writer is still in evidence in her prose. A child's imaginative power charges her images. Responses to color, smell, and feel crowd her pages. The novel is full of children reporting vividly on what they see and instinctively understand as they in their turn become the victims of the culture of poverty and the recipients of some of its blessings.

The novel covers a span of fifteen years, but since the outside world seldom intrudes on the poor, or the poor on it, calendar dates are of no importance. The place is any small crossroads settlement in Maine where logging trucks roll by and a child playing with a dog in front of a mobile home tugs on one side of an old fan belt and the dog on

Carolyn and Michael Chute

the other. Chute reports that when a movie crew arrived to go on location and asked her to take them to the story's church and general store, she said she couldn't, they were only in her head. But Chute's Egypt has taken a sure place on the map of Maine and will be there for years to come. Scenes like the following open the novel.

Earlene

LIZZIE, ANNIE, AND ROSIE'S RESCUE OF ME WITH BLUE CAKE

We've got a ranch house. Daddy built it. Daddy says it's called RANCH 'cause it's like the houses out West which cowboys sleep in. There's a picture window in all ranch houses and if you're in one of 'em out West, you can look out and see the cattle eatin' grass on the plains and the cowboys ridin' around with lassos and tall hats. But we ain't got nuthin' like that here in Egypt, Maine. All Daddy and I got to look out at is the Beans. Daddy says the Beans are uncivilized animals. PREDATORS, he calls them.

"If it runs, a Bean will shoot it! If it falls, a Bean will eat it," Daddy says, and his lip curls. A million times Daddy says, "Earlene, don't go over on the Beans' side of the right-of-way. Not ever!"

Daddy's bedroom is pine-paneled . . . the real kind. Daddy done it all. He filled the nail holes with MIRACLE WOOD. One weekend after we was all settled in, Daddy gets up on a chair and opens a can of MIRACLE WOOD. He works it into the nail holes with a putty knife. He needs the chair 'cause he's probably the littlest man in Egypt, Maine.

Daddy gets a pain in his back after dinnah so we take a nap. We get under the covers and I scratch his back. Daddy says to take off my socks and shoes and overalls to keep the bed from gettin' full of dirt.

After I'm asleep the bed starts to tremble. I clutch the side of the bed and look around. Then I realize it's only Rubie Bean comin' in his loggin' truck to eat his dinnah with other Beans. Daddy's bare back is khaki-color like his carpenter's shirts. I give his shoulder blades a couple more rakes, then dribble off to sleep once more. . . .

It's Saturday morning. All clouds. Very cold.

When Daddy's downcellah busy with his lathe, I go to the edge of our grass to get a good look at the Beans. The Beans' mobile home is one of them old ones, looks like a turquoise-blue submarine. It's got blackberry bushes growin' over the windows.

I scream, "HELLO BEANS!"

About four huge heads come out of the hole. It's a hole the Bean kids and the Bean babies have been workin' on for almost a year. Every day they go down the hole and they use coffee cans and a spade to make the hole bigger. The babies use spoons. Beside the hole is a pile of gingerbread-color dirt as tall as a house.

I say, "Need any help with the hole?"

They don't answer. One of them wipes its nose on its sleeve. They blink their fox-color eyes.

I mutter, "Must be the STUPIDEST hole."

The heads draw back into the hole.

A white car with one Bondo-color fender is turnin' off the paved road into the right-of-way. It musta lost its muffler. It rumbles along, and the exhaust exploding from all sides is doughy and enormous from the cold.

The blackberry bushes quiver, scrape at the tin walls of the mobile home like claws.

The white car slowly backs into Daddy's crushed-rock driveway and a guy with yellow hair and a short cigarette looks out at me and winks. His window's rolled down and he's got his arm hangin' out in the cold air.

I scream, "NO TURNIN' IN DADDY'S DRIVEWAY!"

There's another guy in there with him. He has a sweatshirt with a pointed hood so that all that shows is his huge pink cheeks and a smile. The car pulls ahead onto the right-of-way and the two guys get out.

I scream, "Daddy says KEEP OUT! You ain't ALLOWED!"

The men look at each other and chuckle. The yellow-hair guy is still smokin' his cigarette even though it's only a tiny stump.

My eyes water from the cold. My hair, very white, blows into my mouth.

The sweatshirt guy opens the back door and I see there's feet in there on the seat. The sweatshirt guy pulls on the feet.

The other guy helps. They both tug on the feet.

Out comes a big Bean loose, very loose, like a dead cat. His arms and legs just go all over the ground. His green felt hat plops out in the dirt. About five beer bottles skid out, too, roll and clink together. The guy with the yellow hair snatches a whiskey bottle off the seat and puts it in the Bean's hand, curls his fingers around it. Both the guys laugh. "There's your baby!" one says.

They get in the car and drive away.

My heart feels like runnin'-hard shoes. I look around. No Beans come out of the mobile home. No Beans come out of the hole.

I take a step. I'm wicked glad Daddy's in the cellah with his lathe. I can picture him down there in the bluish light in his little boy-sized clothes, pickin' over his big tools with his boy-sized hand.

I take another step.

Now I'm standin' right over the Bean. He looks to me like prob'ly the biggest Bean of all. He's got one puckered-up eye, bright purple . . . a mustache big as a black hen. I cover my nose. I think he musta messed hisself. His green workshirt has yellow stitching on one pocket. I read out loud, "R-E-U-B-E-N." I squint, trying to sound out the letters.

The whiskey bottle rolls off his hand.

I says, "Wake up, Bean!"

Then some heads come out of the hole.

A noise comes from the big Bean on the ground: GLOINK! And I say, "Wowzer!" It's blood spreadin' as big as a hand in the dirt.

The kid Beans are comin' as fast as they can. They bring their spade and spoons, cans and a pail.

I look into the Bean man's face. I say, "YOU! Hey you! Wake up!" I scooch down and inspect the pores of his skin. His wide-open mouth. Big Bean nose. My quick hand goes out . . . touches the nose. I say, "Stop bleedin', Bean."

His good eye opens.

I jump away.

Fox-color eye.

Out of the open mouth comes a hiss. The chest heaves up. Somethin' horrible leaks out of the corner of his mouth, catches in the hairs of the big mustache.

The kid Beans stand around starin' down at the green workshirt with the blood movin' out around their shoes.

I say, "Some guys brought him." I point up the road. I look among their faces for signs of panic. I say, "R-E-U-B-E-N. What's that spell?"

They look at me, breathin' through their mouths. One of 'em giggles and says, "That spells coo coo."

Another one pokes at the big Bean's shoulder with its green rubber boot. The big Bean goes, "AAAARRRRR!" And his lips peel back over clenched yellow teeth.

A kid Bean with a spade says to a kid Bean with a pail, "Go get Ma off the bed. Rubie's been stabbed again."

"Go tell'er yourself," says the kid Bean with the pail.

"No . . . you!" says the one with the spade.

"No-suh. I ain't gonna miss gettin' to see Rubie die."

I look down at the big Bean and his hand slowly drags across the dirt to his side to the torn fabric, a black place in the body, like an open mouth. And blood fills the cup of his hand.

Daddy opens the front door and hollers, "EARLENE!"

The big Bean's eye is lookin' right at me.

I says to the eye, "In heaven they got streets of gold."

Daddy screams my name again.

The big fox-color eye closes.

I say, "Oh no! He's dead!"

The kid with the spade say, "Nah! He's still breathin'."

Daddy comes off the step. "Earlene! Get away! NOW!!"

I say, "Bean wake up! Don't die!"

Rubie Bean don't move. His mouth is wide open like he's died right in the middle of a big laugh. I see the blood has surrounded my left sneaker, has splashed on my white sock. I can hear the Bean kids shift in their rubber boots.

I drop down on all fours and put my ear right there on the shirt pocket where it says R-E-U-B-E-N.

"Get away from there!" Daddy almost whimpers. He's comin' fast across the grass.

The heart. A huge BOOM-BANG! almost punches at my temple through the Bean's shirt.

"Hear anything?" a Bean with a coffee can asks.

The fox-color big Bean eye opens, the teeth come together, make a deep rude raspy grunt. He say, "You kids . . . get the hell away from me, you goddam cock-suckin' little sons-a-whores!!"

'Bout then Daddy's boy-sized hands close around me. . . .

Across the right-of-way the Beans' black dog stands by an old rug, looking at me. "Yoo hoo!" I call through cupped hands.

Daddy's gone to Oxford to work on a bank . . . He's late gettin' home. They say the roads are greasy.

I take a step onto the Beans' side of the right-of-way. The black dog watches me, the hair on its back raised. But it don't bark.

I step over a spinach can with water froze in it, a clothespin, an Easter basket, the steerin' wheel of a car.

Out of the dog's nose its frozen breath pumps. I draw nearer to the hole with the spoons and coffee cans ringed around it. The dog charges. It gallops sideways with stiff rocking-horse legs.

I says, "You bite me and you'll regret it!!"

I look up at the closed metal door. No Beans.

The dog's eyes glow a bluish white. Its bluish tongue flutters. I say, "Beat it!" and kick a beer bottle at it.

It noses the beer bottle, picks it up in its teeth, and drops it at my feet.

"Go away! I ain't playin'." I look at the Bean windows. No faces. The dog smells my small moving feet. "You ugly grimy Bean dog. You're gointa BURN IN HELL!"

There's a scalloped serving spoon at the edge of the hole. "So this is the hole," I says to myself. The dog watches me pick up a trowel. I point it at the dog. "ZEEP!" I scream. "You are instantly DEAD!" The dog blinks.

The corridor of the hole is curved. I slide down on my bottom, workin' my legs, the entrance behind me dwindling to a woolly little far-off cloud in the distance. I feel soda bottles along the way. A measuring cup. A rock drops from the ceiling and thwonks my shoulder. A spray of dirt lets go and fills my hair. I enter a big warm room. In apple crates are what feels like Barbie clothes and Barbie accessories. There's a full-sized easy chair.

"Jeezum!" I gasp. I sit in the chair. "This is real cozy."

I lean forward and feel of the dirt walls, dirt floor. My hand closes around a naked Barbie.

All of a sudden there's a thunder up there.

The warm earth lets go, feels like hundreds of butterflies on my face.

"It's GOD," I says in a choking whisper. My heart flutters.

It's Rubie Bean. The tires of his old logging rig hiss over Daddy's crushed-rock driveway. There's the ernk! of the gears.

"Uh oh!" I says to myself. "I'm trapped in this hole. I can't go up there now."

A rock from the ceiling punches my outstretched legs.

More Beans come. Three or four carloads. The mobile home door opens, closes, opens, closes. Out in their yard Bean kids big as men run over the earth's crust above me. THUMP THUMP THUMP THUMP. The soft slap of sand is on my neck. The Bean kids throw something for the black dog to catch. It sounds like a piece of tail pipe.

I hear Daddy's car.

After a while there's Daddy's voice: "Earlene! Supper!"

It's very very dark. The Beans have gone indoors.

The dog is up there at the top of the hole, sniffin' for me.

Hours and hours and hours pass. Hours of pitch black.

I says to myself in a squeak, "I am gointa get the strap." I turn naked Barbie over and over in my nervous fingers. I mutter, "Well . . . I just ain't *ever* gonna leave THIS HOLE."

There is light again at the top. The light flutters. Boots tromp. They come down waving a flashlight — Annie Bean, Lizzie Bean, Rosie Bean. They put the light in my face. "What're you doin' in here?" one of them asks.

"Nuthin'," I says. My stomach growls.

They make wet thick sniffin' sounds. Their open mouths are echoey. They fill this dirt room with their broad shoulders, broad heads. Dirt sifts down from the ceiling through the enormous light.

"You runnin' away from the law?" one of them asks.

"NO WAY!" I scream. My scream makes more of the ceiling fall. I think I'm gonna gag from this light in my face. Now and then I can make out a Bean nose, a sharp tooth. Then it fades into the glare.

"You runnin' away from home?" asks one of them.

I bristle. "No! I ain't!"

"Well, how come your father's up there cryin'?"

One of them pushed a saucer with cake on it into the light. There is only the cake, the saucer, the hand. The cake is sky-blue. "Here!" a voice says.

Their clothes rustle.

"What's that?" I scrunch up my nose.

"We was goin' ta eat it, but you can have it. Ain't you starved?"

I look at the cake, squinting up one eye.

"I didn't run away," I says softly.

"You prob'ly fell in here," one says.

"No-suh!" I holler.

I make out a fox-color eye which is round and hard and caked with sleepin' sand.

I take the saucer and arrange it on my knee next to Barbie. I says, "I ain't never leavin' this hole. I'm stayin' here forever . . . as long as I live."

"You like it here pretty well, huh?" one of 'em says.

I am alone. Between me and them is this wall of light. I hold the saucer with both hands, careful not to touch the cake. A bit of sand spills from the ceiling onto the cake.

The three of them giggle.

The cake is the blue of a birdless airplaneless sunless cloudless leafless sky . . . warm steaming blue. "Prob'ly POISON!" I gasp.

"No way!" one of 'em says. "It ain't. It's Betty Crocker."

Additional Reading

ANTHOLOGIES, COLLECTIONS

Beck, Horace. *The Folklore of Maine*. Philadelphia: Lippincott, 1957.

Beston, Henry, ed. *White Pine and Blue Water, A State of Maine Reader*. Camden: Down East Books, 1950.

Eckstorm, Fannie Hardy, and Mary Winslow Smith, eds. *Minstrelsy of Maine Songs and Ballads of the Woods and Coast*. Cambridge: Houghton Mifflin, 1927.

Fischer, Jeff. *Maine Speaks: An Anthology of Maine Literature*. Brunswick: Maine Writers and Publishers Alliance, 1989.

Lecker, Robert, and Kathleen R. Brown, eds. *An Anthology of Maine Literature*. Orono: University of Maine Press, 1982.

Lee, W. Storrs, ed. *Maine, A Literary Chronicle*. New York: Funk and Wagnalls, 1968.

Melnicove, Mark, ed. *Inside Vacationland*. South Harpswell: Dog Ear Press, 1985.

Phippen, Sanford, Charles Waugh, and Martin Greenberg, eds. *The Best Maine Stories*. Augusta: Lance Tapley, 1986.

Putz, Georg, ed. *A Collection of Maine Island Writing*. Rockland: Island Institute, 1987.

Shain, Charles and Samuella. *Growing Up in Maine*. Camden: Down East Books, 1991.

Simpson, Dorothy. *The Maine Islands*. The Maine Writers Research Club. New York: Harper & Row, 1960.

Smith, David C., and Edward O. Schriver. *Maine, A History through Selected Readings*. Dubuque, Iowa: Kendall/Hunt, 1985.

ART

Abbott, Berenice. *A Portrait of Maine*. Text by Chenoweth Hall. New York: Macmillan, 1968.

Dibner, Martin. *Seacoast Maine. People and Places*. Photographs by George A. Tice. New York: Doubleday, 1973.

Gray, Cleve, ed. *John Marin*. New York: Holt, Rinehart and Winston, 1970.

Mellon, Gertrude A., coordinate ed., Elizabeth F. Wilder, ed. (Under the auspices of Colby College, Waterville, Maine.) *Maine and Its Role in American Art*. New York: Viking, 1963.

Moore, Jim. *Maine Coastal Portrait by Three Maine Photographers: Jim Moore, Kosti Ruohamaa, Carroll Thayer Berry*. Rockland: Seth Low Press, 1959.

Peladeau, Marius B. *Chansonetta: The Life and Photographs of Chansonetta Stanley Emmons*. Waldoboro: Maine Antiques Digest, Dobbs Ferry, N.Y., 1977.

Scott, Gail R. *Marsden Hartley*. New York: Abbeville Press, 1988.

Sewall, Abbie. *Message Through Time: The Photographs of Emma D. Sewall, 1836–1919*. Gardiner: Harpswell Press, 1989.

ESSAYS, LETTERS

Barringer, Richard. *A Maine Manifest*. Bath: Allagash Group, 1972.

Browne, Charles Farrar. *The Complete Works of Artemus Ward*. New York: Dillingham, 1898.

Chamberlain, Joshua L. *Maine: Her Place in History*. Augusta: Sprague, Owen and Nash, 1877.

Chase, Virginia. *Speaking of Maine*. Camden: Down East Books, 1983.

Eckstorm, Fannie Hardy. *The Penobscot Man*. Somersworth, N.H.: New Hampshire Publishing, 1972.

Jewett, Sarah Orne. *Letters*, ed. Annie Fields. Boston: Houghton Mifflin, 1911.

Smith, Seba. *The Life and Writings of Major Jack Downing of Downingsville*. Boston: Lilly, Wait, Colman and Holden, 1834.

FICTION

Brace, Gerald W. *The World of Carrick's Cove*. New York: Norton, 1957.

Chute, Carolyn. *Letourneau's Used Auto Parts*. New York: Harper & Row (Perennial Library), 1989.

Cummings, Rebecca. *Turnip Pie, and Other Stories*. Orono: Puckerbrush Press, 1986.

Johnson, Willis. *The Girl Who Would Be Russian and Other Stories*. New York: Harcourt Brace Jovanovich, 1986.

Kellogg, Elijah. *Good Old Times*. Boston: Lothrop, Lee and Shepard, 1905.

MacDougall, Arthur R., Jr. *Dud Dean Yarns*. Bingham, Me.: Bingham Press, 1934.

Moore, Ruth. *Spoonhandle*. New York: Morrow, 1946.

Pelletier, Cathie. *The Funeral Makers*. New York: Macmillan, 1986.

Robichaud, Gerard. *The Apple of His Eye*. New York: Doubleday, 1965.

Stowe, Harriet Beecher. *The Pearl of Orr's Island*. Boston: Houghton Mifflin, 1896.

Tarkington, Booth. *Mirthful Haven*. Garden City, N.Y.: Doubleday Doran, 1930.

Thorndike, John. *The Potato Baron*. New York: Villard Books, 1989.
Williams, Ben Ames. *Fraternity Village*. Boston: Houghton Mifflin, 1949.

HISTORY, MEMOIRS, BIOGRAPHIES

Averill, Gerald. *Ridge Runner*. Thorndike, Me.: North Country Press, 1976.
Barbour, Philip L. *The Three Worlds of Captain John Smith*. Boston: Houghton Mifflin, 1964.
Baxter, James P. *The Trelawney Papers,* Collections of the Maine Historical Society, Second Series, Vol. III, Portland, 1884.
Burrage, Henry S. *The Beginnings of Colonial Maine,* 1601–1658. Portland: Marks Printing House, 1914.
Butler, Joyce. *Wildfire Loose: The Week Maine Burned*. Kennebunkport, Me.: Durrell Publications, 1978.
Caldwell, Bill. *Islands of Maine, Where America Really Began*. Portland: Guy Gannett, 1981.
Chamberlain, Joshua L. *The Passing of the Armies*. Dayton, Ohio: Morningside Bookshop, 1974.
Clark, Charles E. *Maine: A Bicentennial History*. New York: Norton, 1977.
———. *The Eastern Frontier*. New York: Knopf, 1970.
Conkling, Philip W. *Islands in Time*. Camden: Down East Books, 1981.
Day, Clarence A. *A History of Maine Agriculture,* 1604–1860. University of Maine Studies, Second Series. No. 68. Orono, 1954.
———. *Farming in Maine,* 1860–1940. University of Maine Studies, Second Series. No. 78. Orono, 1963.
Downs, Jacques. *The Cities on the Saco*. Norfolk, Va.: Donning, 1985.
Duncan, John E. *The Sea Chain*. Scotia, N.Y.: Americana Review, 1986.
Eliot, Charles W. *John Gilley, Maine Farmer and Fisherman*. Boston: Boston Unitarian Association, 1905.
Elledge, Scott B. *E. B. White: A Biography*. New York: Norton, 1984.
Field, Rachel. *In God's Pocket*. New York: Macmillan, 1934.
Godfrey, John E. *The Journals of John Edwards Godfrey, Bangor, Maine,* 1863–1869. Rockland: Courier-Gazette, 1985.
Griffin, Carl R., III, and Faulkner, Alaric. *Coming of Age on Damariscove Island, Maine*. Old Town: Northeast Folklore Society, Penobscot Times, 1981.
Hatch, Louis Clinton. *Maine: A History*. A facsimile of the 1919 edition, with a new introduction and bibliography by William B. Jordan, Jr. Somersworth, N.H.: New Hampshire Publishing, 1974.
Hendrickson, Dyke. *Quiet Presence*. Portland: Guy Gannet, 1980.
Irland, Lloyd C. *Maine's Economic Heritage*. Augusta: Irland Group, 1989.
Isaacson, Dorris, ed. *Maine, A Guide "Down East."* Rockland: Courier-Gazette, 1970.
Jackson, Annette. *My Life in the Maine Woods*. New York: Norton, 1954.
Jones, Rufus M. *A Small Town Boy*. New York: Macmillan, 1941.

Ledoux, Denis. *What Became of Them and Other Stories from Franco-America.* Lisbon Falls, Me.: Soleil Press, 1988.

Mitchell, Wilmot B. *Elijah Kellogg, The Man and His Work.* Boston: Lee and Shepard, 1903.

Montgomery, M. R. *In Search of L. L. Bean.* Boston: Little, Brown, 1984.

Morison, Samuel E. *The European Discovery of America, The Northern Voyages.* New York: Oxford University Press, 1971–1974.

Pullen, John J. *The Twentieth Maine.* Philadelphia: Lippincott, 1957.

Rich, Louise D. *State O' Maine.* New York: Harper & Row, 1964.

Rosier, James. *Rosier's Relation of Waymouth's Voyage to the Coast of Maine.* ed. Henry S. Burrage. Portland: Printed for the Gorges Society, 1887.

Rowe, William H. *The Maritime History of Maine.* New York: Norton, 1946.

Saltonstall, Richard. *Maine Pilgrimage: The Search for an American Way of Life.* Boston: Little, Brown, 1974.

Smith, David C. *A History of Lumbering in Maine, 1861–1960.* Orono: University of Maine, 1972.

Stowe, Charles E. *Life of Harriet Beecher Stowe.* Boston: Houghton Mifflin, 1889.

Sullivan, James. *A History of the District of Maine.* (Reprint of the 1795 edition.) Augusta: Maine State Museum, 1970.

Thaxter, Celia. *Among the Isles of Shoals.* Boston: Houghton Mifflin, 1915.

Tufts, Henry. *The Autobiography of a Criminal,* ed. Edmund Pearson. New York: Duffield, 1930.

Violette, Maurice. *The Franco-Americans.* New York: Vantage Press, 1976.

Wallace, Willard M. *Soul of the Lion: A Biography of General Joshua L. Chamberlain.* New York: T. Nelson, 1910; Gettysburg, Pa.: Stan Clark Military Books, 1991.

Wasson, George S. *Sailing Days on the Penobscot.* Salem, Mass.: Marine Research Society, 1932.

Wiggin, Kate Douglas. *My Garden of Memory.* Boston: Houghton Mifflin, 1923.

Williamson, William D. *The History of the State of Maine.* Hallowell, Me.: Glazier, Masters, 1832.

Winthrop, Theodore. *Life in the Open Air.* Boston: Ticknor & Fields, 1863.

POETRY

Coffin, R. P. T. *Collected Poems.* New York: Macmillan, 1948.

Snow, Wilbert. *The Collected Poems of Wilbert Snow.* Middletown, Conn.: Wesleyan University Press, 1963.

Credits and Sources

TEXT

"Verrazzano's Letter to the French King" from *The Voyages of Giovanni da Verrazzano,* edited by Lawrence C. Wroth. New Haven: Yale University Press, 1970. From the CELERE CODEX of Verrazzano's diaries, translated by Susan Tarrow. Reprinted by permission of the translator.

"A Description of New-England" from *The Complete Works of Captain John Smith,* vol. 1, edited by Philip Barbour. © 1986 by the University of North Carolina Press. Published for the Institute of Early American History and Culture, Williamsburg. Reprinted by permission.

"A Voyage into New England" from *Captain Levett of York, The Pioneer Colonist in Casco Bay,* edited by James Phinney Baxter. Portland: Gorges Society, 1893.

"Letter to the Governor of Massachusetts" to Governor John Leverett from Henry Jocelyn and Joshua Scotto, 1676. From the Collections of the Maine Historical Society.

"Memoirs of Odd Adventures, Strange Deliverances, etc." from *Memoirs of Odd Adventures, Strange Deliverances, etc.* by John Giles. Cincinnati: Spiller & Gates, 1869.

"The Accusation of a Witch." Deposition by Thomas Burnam, Jr., April 22, 1692, naming Rachel Senton as a witch. From the Collections of the Maine Historical Society.

"Arnold's March to Quebec: The Journal of Abner Stocking" from *Journals of the Members of Arnold's Expedition,* edited by Kenneth Roberts. New York: Doubleday Doran, 1938.

"Thoughts on the Settling of Maine" from *Travels: In New-England and New-York 1821–1822,* by Timothy Dwight. New Haven: Timothy Dwight, 1821.

"Our State Christening" from *Our State Christening, Its Name* by George F. Emery. From the Collections of the Maine Historical Society.

"Hawthorne Visits Two Friends in Maine" from *The American Notebooks* by

Nathaniel Hawthorne, edited by Claude M. Simpson. Columbus: Ohio State University Press, copyright 1932, 1960, 1972.

"The Death of Cilley," reprinted courtesy of Bowdoin College.

"My Lost Youth," "A Psalm of Life," "The Building of the Ship," from *The Complete Works of Henry Wadsworth Longfellow,* edited by Horace E. Scudder. Boston: Houghton Mifflin, 1893.

"A Few Days in the Life of Ben Foster," from *Benjamin Browne Foster, Down East Diary,* edited by Charles H. Foster. Orono: University of Maine Press, 1975. Reprinted by permission of the publisher.

"Autobiography," from an unpublished manuscript by Captain Charles C. Duncan. Reprinted by permission of John E. Duncan, Scotia, N.Y.

"Letters from Maine" by Harriet Beecher Stowe. Reprinted from the *National Era,* August 5, September 9, 1852.

"A Moosehead Journal," from *Fireside Travels* by James Russell Lowell. Boston: Ticknor & Fields, 1864.

"A Moose Hunt," from *The Maine Woods* by Henry David Thoreau. New York: Thomas Y. Crowell, 1961.

"The Slaver," from *True Tales of the Sea* by Edward Clarence Plummer. Portland: Marks Printing House, 1930.

"A Volunteer from Biddeford," from *The Rebel Yell and the Yankee Hurrah: The Civil War Journal of a Maine Volunteer,* edited by Ruth Silliker. Camden: Down East Books, 1985. Reprinted by permission of the publisher.

"Appomattox and the Surrender," from "Not a Sound of Trumpet" by General Joshua L. Chamberlain. Reprinted courtesy of Bowdoin College.

"The River Drive," from *Forest Life and Forest Trees* by John S. Springer. New York: Harper & Bros., 1851.

"A Taste of Maine Birch" by John Burroughs, from *The Atlantic Monthly,* June 1881.

"The McCormick Brothers' Logging Camp," from *My Life in the North Woods* by Robert Smith. Copyright © 1986 by Robert Smith. Boston: Atlantic Monthly Press, 1986. Reprinted by permission of the author.

"Casco Bay, The Power of Melody, The Haddock, Jewell's Island," "A Storm off Cape Seguin, Boothbay, The Coast Survey Schooner," from *A Summer Cruise on the Coast of New England,* by Robert Carter. Boston: Crosby & Nash, 1864.

"Mackerel Fishing off Monhegan," from "Fish and Men in the Maine Islands" by William Henry Bishop. *Harper's New Monthly Magazine,* September 1880.

"Life Aboard the *R. W. Hopkins,*" from *The Log of the Skipper's Wife* edited by James W. Balano. Camden: Down East Books, 1979. Reprinted courtesy of Elsie K. Balano.

"Seamen and Sea Serpents," from *Trending into Maine* by Kenneth Roberts. Boston: Little, Brown, 1938. Reprinted by permission of the estate of Kenneth Roberts.

"The Town Poor," from *The Country of the Pointed Firs* by Sarah Orne Jewett. Boston: Houghton Mifflin, 1925. Reprinted courtesy of Houghton Mifflin.

"The Lord's Day in the Nineties," from *A Goodly Heritage* by Mary Ellen Chase. New York: Henry Holt, 1932. Copyright 1932 and renewed © 1960 by Mary Ellen Chase. Reprinted by permission of Henry Holt and Company, Inc.

"Man and Woman," from *A Maine Hamlet* by Lura Beam. Published by Wilfred Funk Inc. Copyright © 1957 by Lura Beam, renewed © 1985 by Eileen Hayes. Reprinted by permission of Lance Tapley, Publisher.

"Mr. Flood's Party" by Edwin Arlington Robinson. Reprinted with permission of Macmillan Publishing Company from *Collected Poems by Edwin Arlington Robinson*. Copyright 1921 by Edwin Arlington Robinson, renewed 1949 by Ruth Nivison.

"Cliff Klingenhagen," "The Clerks," from *The Children of the Night* by Edwin Arlington Robinson, 1910. Courtesy Charles Scribner's Sons.

"New England" by Edwin Arlington Robinson. Reprinted with permission of Macmillan Publishing Company from *Collected Poems by Edwin Arlington Robinson*. Copyright 1925 by Edwin Arlington Robinson, renewed 1953 by Ruth Nivison and Barbara Holt.

"The Harvest of Diamonds," from *Maine Doings* by Robert P. Tristram Coffin. New York: Bobbs-Merrill, 1950. Reprinted by permission of June M. Coffin.

"Life and Art on Monhegan," from *It's Me O Lord, The Autobiography of Rockwell Kent* by Rockwell Kent. New York: Dodd, Mead, 1955.

"Is There an American Art?" and "On the Subject of Nativeness — A Tribute to Maine," from *On Art* by Gail Scott. New York: Horizon Press, 1982. Reprinted by permission of the author.

"If We Could," "Lewiston Is a Pleasant Place," from *The Collected Poems of Marsden Hartley* 1904–1943 edited by Gail Scott. Santa Rosa, Calif.: Black Sparrow Press, 1987. Reprinted by permission of Black Sparrow Press.

"The Evolution of a Summer Resort," from *Reflections and Comments, 1865–1895* by Edwin Lawrence Godkin. New York: Charles Scribner's Sons, 1895.

"In and Out of Bar Harbor," from *The Pine Tree Coast* by Samuel Adams Drake. Boston: Estes & Lauriat, 1891.

"George F. Babbitt Takes a Maine Vacation," from *Babbitt* by Sinclair Lewis, copyright 1922 by Harcourt Brace Jovanovich, Inc.; renewed 1950 by Sinclair Lewis. Reprinted by permission of the publisher.

"The Tourists," from *Rain* by William Carpenter. Copyright © 1985 by William Carpenter. Reprinted with the permission of Northeastern University Press.

"Sonnet" "Inland," "Northern April," "Ragged Island," by Edna St. Vincent Millay from *Collected Poems*, Harper & Row. Copyright © 1921, 1928, 1934, 1948, 1954, 1955, 1962, 1982 by Edna St. Vincent Millay and Norma Millay Ellis. Reprinted by permission.

"The Alewife Run," from *Northern Farm: A Chronicle of Maine* by Henry

"The Village Store," from *Freeman Cooper* by William Hopkins. New York: Vantage Press, 1971. Reprinted by permission of June Hopkins.

"Fog," "The Cormorant in Its Element," from *The Kingfisher* by Amy Clampitt. Copyright © 1983 by Amy Clampitt. Reprinted by permission of Alfred A. Knopf, Inc.

"Low Tide at Schoodic," from *What the Light Was Like* by Amy Clampitt. Copyright © 1985 by Amy Clampitt. Reprinted by permission of Alfred A. Knopf, Inc.

"Widening the Road" from *Squatter's Rights* by Fred Bonnie. Ottawa: Oberon Press, 1979. Reprinted by permission of the author.

"Around the World," "No Haulin' Day," reprinted from *Stitch in Time* by John Gould by permission of the author and the publisher, W. W. Norton & Company, Inc. Copyright © 1985 by John Gould.

"Clamming," from *The Feel of Rock* by Reed Whittemore. Tacoma Park, Md.: Dryad Press, 1982. Reprinted by permission of the author.

"Ice Out," "Captain's Log," from *In Maine* by John N. Cole. New York: Dutton, 1974. Reprinted courtesy of the author.

"From 'North of the C. P. Line,' " from *Table of Contents* by John McPhee. Copyright © 1985 by John McPhee. Originally appeared in *The New Yorker*. Reprinted by permission of Farrar, Straus and Giroux, Inc.

"Earlene," from *The Beans of Egypt, Maine* by Carolyn Chute. Copyright © 1985 by Carolyn Chute. Reprinted by permission of Ticknor & Fields, a Houghton Mifflin Company.

ILLUSTRATIONS

Maine State Seal, 1837, courtesy of the Library of Congress.

"Monhegan," by Stow Wengenroth, from the collection of the William A. Farnsworth Library and Art Museum.

Captain John Smith, 1615, from the collections of the Maine Historical Society.

Land sales broadside, 1818, from the collections of the Maine Historical Society.

"Mount Katahdin from Ripogenous Gorge," by Carroll Thayer Berry, from the collection of the William A. Farnsworth Library and Art Museum.

The Reverend Timothy Dwight, courtesy of the Library of Congress.

Mail stage broadside, 1826, from the collections of the Maine Historical Society.

"Oaklands," courtesy of the Maine Historic Preservation Commission.

The Honorable Jonathan Cilley, courtesy of the Library of Congress.

"Cilley of Maine, Murdered by Graves of Kentucky," 1838, courtesy of the Bowdoin College Library. Photograph by David Etnier.

The *Charles Crooker,* courtesy of the Maine Maritime Museum.

"Spinning," by Chansonetta Stanley Emmons, courtesy of the Colby College Museum of Art.

"Rogers House, Phippsburg," by Emma D. Sewall, from Abbie Sewall, *Message Through Time: The Photographs of Emma D. Sewall 1836–1919,* courtesy of the Harpswell Press.

A Maine moose, from John S. Springer, *Forest Life and Forest Trees,* Harper & Bros., 1851.

The 31st Regiment Maine Volunteers, courtesy of the Maine Historic Preservation Commission.

Letter from W. Coombs, 1865, courtesy of the Pejepscot Historical Society.

General Joshua Chamberlain, courtesy of the Library of Congress.

Camp at Russell Pond, from the collections of the Maine Historical Society.

Logjam, from the Northeast Archives of Folklore and Oral History, no. 345.

John Burroughs, courtesy of the Library of Congress.

"Saw-mills on the Penobscot River, at Oldtown, Maine," 1854, courtesy of the Library of Congress.

Lumber camp crew, from the Northeast Archives of Folklore and Oral History, no. 314.

Schooner under tow on the Saco River, 1911, courtesy of the McArthur Library.

"Harpooning swordfish," from *Harper's New Monthly,* September 1880.

Dorothea Moulton Balano, courtesy of Elsie Balano.

Kenneth Roberts, from the collections of the Maine Historical Society.

"Off duty, at Monhegan," from *Harper's New Monthly,* September 1880.

"East Machias Post Office," by Berenice Abbott, from the collection of the William A. Farnsworth Library and Art Museum.

"Noonday Meal, West New Portland, Maine," by Chansonetta Stanley Emmons, from the collection of the William A. Farnsworth Library and Art Museum.

Mary Ellen Chase, courtesy of the Maine Women Writers Collection, Westbrook College.

"Parlor Music (Melodeon and Fiddle)," by Chansonetta Stanley Emmons, courtesy of the Colby College Museum of Art.

Robert P. Tristram Coffin, courtesy of the Pejepscot Historical Society.

Ice harvest on the Kennebec, 1888, courtesy of the Maine Historical Preservation Commission.

Visitors landing on Monhegan Island, 1911, courtesy of Charles I. Rice/Library of Congress.

"The Boatman," by Rockwell Kent, from the collection of the William A. Farnsworth Library and Art Museum.

Mount Kineo, from the collections of the Maine Historical Society.

"Bar Harbor, Mt. Desert Island," courtesy of the Library of Congress.

Hotel staff, Bar Harbor, courtesy of the Maine Historic Preservation Commission.

Grand Central Hotel, Mount Desert Island, courtesy of the Maine Historic Preservation Commission.

Rockland lobster festival, 1987, photograph by Maryellen Sullivan, courtesy of the Portland Newspapers.

Fisherman at Moosehead Lake, from the collections of the Maine Historical Society.

Potato farming, 1945, from the Maine State Archives.

"Fording the River," by Emma D. Sewall, from Abbie Sewall, *Message Through*